Advanced Computational Methods for Fluid Dynamics and Applications

Advanced Computational Methods for Fluid Dynamics and Applications

Guest Editor

Zhenquan Li

MDPI

Basel • Beijing • Wuhan • Barcelona • Belgrade • Novi Sad • Cluj • Manchester

Guest Editor
Zhenquan Li
School of Computing,
Mathematics and Engineering
Charles Sturt University
Thurgoona
Australia

Editorial Office
MDPI AG
Grosspeteranlage 5
4052 Basel, Switzerland

This is a reprint of the Special Issue, published open access by the journal *Mathematics* (ISSN 2227-7390), freely accessible at: https://www.mdpi.com/journal/mathematics/special_issues/KT06TDHFGF.

For citation purposes, cite each article independently as indicated on the article page online and as indicated below:

Lastname, A.A.; Lastname, B.B. Article Title. *Journal Name* **Year**, *Volume Number*, Page Range.

ISBN 978-3-7258-8063-8 (Hbk)
ISBN 978-3-7258-8064-5 (PDF)
https://doi.org/10.3390/books978-3-7258-8064-5

Contents

About the Editor

Zhenquan Li

Zhenquan Li holds a PhD in Applied Mathematics. He has held academic positions ranging from Lecturer to Professor at universities in China, Japan, New Zealand, Fiji, and Australia. His research interests include computational fluid dynamics, fuzzy neural networks, and mathematical modelling.

mathematics

Editorial

Preface to the Special Issue on "Advanced Computational Methods for Fluid Dynamics and Applications"

Zhenquan Li

School of Computing, Mathematics and Engineering, Charles Sturt University, Thurgoona, NSW 2640, Australia; jali@csu.edu.au

Fluid flows are typically described by governing equations that are too complex to be solved analytically. Consequently, numerical solutions of these equations are widely used to analyze and predict flow behavior in complex systems. The quality of numerical results depends critically on the performance of the computational/numerical methods employed. Although significant progress has been made in the development of computational methods for fluid flow, further research is still required to improve accuracy, reliability, and other related aspects. This Special Issue presents recent advances and achievements in this field.

The paper by Contribution 1 presents a comprehensive comparison of the computational efficiency and accuracy of bi-directional evolutionary structural optimization (BESO) and proportional topology optimization (PTO) for stress minimization problems. The results are problem-dependent, and the conclusions clearly outline the respective advantages and disadvantages of each method across different stress-related optimization scenarios.

The paper by Contribution 2 investigates the linear stability of bedform evolution using a one-dimensional, vertically averaged moment approach. A small-amplitude perturbation analysis is applied to an initially flat bed, ensuring that the results are relevant to conditions observed in natural systems. The limitations of the analysis, along with possible extensions, are discussed in Section 6.

The paper by Contribution 3 investigates fluid flow through an inclined channel under isothermal boundary conditions. The governing equations for velocity, temperature, and entropy generation are derived using the Casson constitutive model in conjunction with the first and second laws of thermodynamics. The effects of various fluid parameters on the flow behavior, heat transfer, and entropy production rate are examined and reported.

The paper by Contribution 4 presents a mathematical analysis of the combined effects of chemical reactions, variable fluid properties, and thermal stability on a hydromagnetic couple-stress fluid flowing through a microchannel driven by both electro-osmosis and a pressure gradient. Numerical solutions are obtained using the spectral Chebyshev collocation method and validated via the shooting Runge–Kutta method. The contributions and limitations of the study are discussed in Section 6.

The paper by Contribution 5 examines the isothermal process of incompressible viscous fluid filtration in an oil-saturated, fractured-porous reservoir. A mathematical model for two-phase fluid mass transfer is developed based on the classical laws of continuum mechanics and Darcy's law, incorporating fluid exchange between low-permeability pores and high-permeability natural fractures within the framework of the Warren–Root model. The numerical solution is obtained using the finite-difference method combined with a splitting scheme for physical processes and spatial coordinates. The accuracy of the numerical results is validated against existing real data, with errors not exceeding 8%.

Contribution 6 verifies the accuracy of a two-dimensional adaptive mesh refinement method with an arbitrary finite number of refinements using lid-driven cavity flow. The refinement criterion is derived from the qualitative theory of differential equations. The algorithm of the adaptive mesh refinement method is developed by combining this qualitative refinement criterion with existing quantitative/numerical schemes. The authors conduct extensive validation of their proposed two- and three-dimensional adaptive mesh refinement methods, evaluating accuracy, computational complexity, and performance across different numerical schemes. These methods are applicable to incompressible and steady fluid flow problems.

The Ericksen–Leslie model is widely used to study the dynamics of liquid crystal materials. Contribution 7 investigates two fully discrete finite element schemes with second-order accuracy in time for a modified Ericksen–Leslie model. The numerical solutions are obtained using a convex splitting method to handle the nonlinear potentials, combined with the second-order backward differentiation formula and the leapfrog method for temporal discretization, and the finite element method for spatial discretization. Numerical results demonstrate that both schemes achieve second-order convergence in time and space. The experiments also indicate that the leapfrog scheme is more computationally efficient than the backward differentiation formula.

The paper by Contribution 8 proposes an entropy-stable finite difference scheme for nonlinear hyperbolic systems of conservation laws. The scheme not only preserves discrete entropy inequality but also achieves high-order accuracy. The results demonstrate that it captures steep discontinuous transitions while maintaining high-order accuracy. However, its application is limited to uniform meshes or smoothly transformed curved meshes in two-dimensional cases.

Contribution 9 investigates the unconditional superconvergence error analysis of a semi-implicit Euler scheme combined with a low-order conforming mixed finite element discretization for the time-dependent Navier–Stokes equations. The numerical solution in the $L\infty$-norm is obtained using an error-splitting technique together with high-accuracy error estimates for the element pair on rectangular meshes, without imposing any time-step restrictions. Unconditional superclose error estimates are derived through a rigorous treatment of the trilinear term. Global superconvergence results are then achieved via an interpolation post-processing approach.

As Guest Editor of this Special Issue, I sincerely thank all authors for their valuable contributions. I also extend my appreciation to the reviewers for their insightful and constructive comments, which greatly enhanced the quality of the submitted manuscripts. The objective of this Special Issue was to attract quality and novel research in the field of Advanced Computational Methods for Fluid Dynamics and Applications. We hope that the selected papers will have a meaningful impact on the international scientific community and will stimulate further research into computational methods for addressing complex problems across a wide range of disciplines and application areas.

Conflicts of Interest: The author declares no conflicts of interest.

List of Contributions:

1. Zheng, Y.; Qiu, J.; Chen, Z. Numerical Comparisons of Heuristic Stress Topology Optimization Methods. *Mathematics* **2025**, *13*, 2353. https://doi.org/10.3390/math13152353.
2. Elgamal, M.H.; Mumtaz, M.A. Stability Diagrams of Bed Evolution for Vertically Averaged and Moment (VAM) Models. *Mathematics* **2025**, *13*, 1997. https://doi.org/10.3390/math13121997.
3. Njor, B.E; Lebelo, R.S; Adesanya, S.O. Irreversibility Analysis of Hydromagnetic Casson Fluid Flow Through an Inclined Channel with Isothermal Boundary Conditions. *Mathematics* **2025**, *13*, 1208. https://doi.org/10.3390/math13071208.

https://doi.org/10.3390/math14030391

4. Banjo, P.O.; Lebelo, R.S.; Adesanya, S.O.; Unuabonah, E.I. Energy Efficacy Enhancement in a Reactive Couple-Stress Fluid Induced by Electrokinetics and Pressure Gradient with Variable Fluid Properties. *Mathematics* **2025**, *13*, 615. https://doi.org/10.3390/math13040615.
5. Uzyanbaev, R.M.; Bobremeva, Y.O.; Poveshchenko, Y.A.; Podryga, V.O.; Polyakov, S.V.; Rahimly, P.I.; Gubaydullin, I. Numerical Modeling of Two-Phase Fluid Filtration for Carbonate Reservoir in Two-Dimensional Formulation. *Mathematics* **2024**, *12*, 3412. https://doi.org/10.3390/math12213412.
6. Lal, R.; Li, Z.; Li, M. Accuracy Verification of a 2D Adaptive Mesh Refinement Method by the Benchmarks of Lid-Driven Cavity Flows with an Arbitrary Number of Refinements. *Mathematics* **2024**, *12*, 2831. https://doi.org/10.3390/math12182831.
7. Liao, C.; Wang, D.; Zhang, H. The Second-Order Numerical Approximation for a Modified Ericksen–Leslie Model. *Mathematics* **2024**, *12*, 672. https://doi.org/10.3390/math12050672.
8. Zhang, Z.; Zhou, X.; Li, G.; Qian, S.; Niu Q. A New Entropy Stable Finite Difference Scheme for Hyperbolic Systems of Conservation Laws. *Mathematics* **2023**, *11*, 2604. https://doi.org/10.3390/math11122604.
9. Meng, X.; Yang, H. Unconditional Superconvergence Error Estimates of Semi-Implicit Low-Order Conforming Mixed Finite Element Method for Time-Dependent Navier–Stokes Equations. *Mathematics* **2023**, *11*, 1945. https://doi.org/10.3390/math11081945.

https://doi.org/10.3390/math14030391

mathematics

MDPI

Article

Unconditional Superconvergence Error Estimates of Semi-Implicit Low-Order Conforming Mixed Finite Element Method for Time-Dependent Navier–Stokes Equations

Xiaoling Meng and Huaijun Yang *

School of Mathematics, Zhengzhou University of Aeronautics, Zhengzhou 450046, China; mengxiaol@126.com
* Correspondence: huaijunyang@zua.edu.cn

Abstract: In this paper, the unconditional superconvergence error analysis of the semi-implicit Euler scheme with low-order conforming mixed finite element discretization is investigated for time-dependent Navier–Stokes equations. In terms of the high-accuracy error estimates of the low-order finite element pair on the rectangular mesh and the unconditional boundedness of the numerical solution in L^∞-norm, the superclose error estimates for velocity in H^1-norm and pressure in L^2-norm are derived firstly by dealing with the trilinear term carefully and skillfully. Then, the global superconvergence results are obtained with the aid of the interpolation post-processing technique. Finally, some numerical experiments are carried out to support the theoretical findings.

Keywords: Navier–Stokes equations; linearized Euler scheme; low-order conforming MFEM; superconvergence error estimates

MSC: 65N06; 65N55

1. Introduction

In this paper, we consider the following two-dimensional time-dependent incompressible Navier–Stokes equations:

$$u_t - \Delta u + (u \cdot \nabla)u + \nabla p = f, (x,t) \in \Omega \times (0,T], \tag{1}$$

$$\nabla \cdot u = 0, (x,t) \in \Omega \times (0,T], \tag{2}$$

$$u(x,t) = 0, \quad (x,t) \in \partial\Omega \times (0,T], \tag{3}$$

$$u(x,0) = u_0(x), \quad x \in \Omega,\ t = 0, \tag{4}$$

where $\Omega \subset \mathbb{R}^2$ is a rectangular domain with boundary $\partial\Omega$, $u = (u_1, u_2) = (u_1(x), u_2(x))$ represents the velocity vector, $p = p(x)$ denotes the pressure, and $f = (f_1(x), f_2(x))$ is the prescribed body force, $x = (x, y)$. Moreover, u_0 is the initial velocity and $T > 0$ is the final time.

Navier–Stokes equations are a classical incompressible fluid model and have been widely applied in the mathematical physics and the computational fluid dynamics fields [1–3]. It is an unrealistic thing to find the the exact solutions of the Navier–Stokes equations due to their nonlinear and incompressible properties. Therefore, numerous works have been devoted to the development of efficient numerical approximations for Navier–Stokes Equations (1)–(4), including finite difference methods [4–7], Galerkin finite element methods [8–21] and other methods [22–26]. In particular, a new second-order accurate finite difference scheme for the incompressible Navier–Stokes equations was discussed in [4] by the primitive variable formulation. Based on the vorticity stream-function formulation and a fast Poisson solver defined on a general domain using the immersed interface method, a fast finite difference method was proposed and studied in [5] for the incompressible Navier–Stokes equations. A new fully discrete finite element nonlinear Galerkin method was established in [8] for the Navier–Stokes equations with two-grid finite element discretization in the spatial direction and Euler explicit scheme with variable time step size in the temporal direction. The boundedness, convergence and stability condition of the presented method were discussed under certain time-step constraints dependent on the coarse grid parameter. A Lagrange–Galerkin mixed finite element approximation was presented for the Navier–Stokes equations in [13], and optimal error estimates were obtained with the mesh restriction $\tau = O(h^{\sigma})$, where $\sigma > (d-1)/2$, and τ, h and d denote the time step size, the mesh size and the dimension of the domain, respectively. In [14], in terms of the special properties of a low-order nonconforming mixed finite element pair on the rectangular mesh, the superconvergence error estimates were derived for Navier–Stokes equations with the time-step constraints $\tau = O(h^{1+\alpha})$, $\alpha > 0$ due to the inverse inequality used in the error analysis. In [18], in terms of the error splitting technique developed in [27,28], the unconditional stability and convergence of a typical modified characteristics finite element method were studied for the time-dependent Navier–Stokes equations by introducing an iterated characteristic time-discrete system. Optimal error estimates were obtained under the boundedness of the numerical solution in $W^{1,\infty}$-norm. Subsequently, the unconditionally optimal error estimates were derived in [20] under the boundedness of the numerical solution in L^{∞}-norm, which is weaker than that in [18].

It should be pointed out that optimal error estimates were obtained in [20] due to roughly handling trilinear terms. Moreover, the superconvergence error estimates were derived in [14] with a certain time-step restriction. To the best of our knowledge, there are few contributions on the unconditionally superclose and superconvergence error estimates for problems (1)–(4). The purpose of this paper is to consider the unconditionally superclose and superconvergence error estimates for incompressible time-dependent Navier–Stokes Equations (1)–(4). It should be pointed out that the difficulties come from the trilinear term (i.e., the convection term) $(\boldsymbol{u} \cdot \nabla)\boldsymbol{u}$ in the superclose and superconvergence error analysis. Therefore, we should deal with them carefully and skillfully.

In the present work, we focus on a low-order conforming finite element approximation, which is called the bilinear-constant scheme [4,29,30], for problems (1)–(4). The key to our analysis is to employ the special properties (high-accuracy error estimation; see Lemmas 1–2 below) on the rectangular mesh and to treat the convection term $(\boldsymbol{u} \cdot \nabla)\boldsymbol{u}$ rigorously and skillfully. The superclose error estimates are obtained firstly for the velocity in H^1-norm and for the pressure in L^2-norm. Then, in terms of an efficient interpolation post-processing approach, the global superconvergence results are derived for the velocity in the H^1-norm and for the pressure in the L^2-norm. In addition, some numerical experiments are presented and tested.

The remainder of this paper is organized as follows. In Section 2, some preliminaries and lemmas are introduced, and the semi-implicit Euler fully discrete finite element approximation of the problem (1)–(4) is presented. In Section 3, the detailed superclose error estimates are studied with the help of the special properties of the bilinear-constant finite element pair combined with skillfully dealing with the trilinear term. Then, the global superconvergence error estimates are established by the interpolation post-processing technique. In Section 4, some numerical results are provided to verify the theoretical findings.

2. Preliminaries

We denote by $W^{m,p}(\Omega)$ the Sobolev spaces with the norm $\|\cdot\|_{m,p}$ and semi-norm $|\cdot|_{m,p}$ defined by

$$\|u\|_{m,p} = \begin{cases} \left(\sum_{|\beta|\leq k} \int_{\Omega} |D^{\beta}u|^p dxdy\right)^{\frac{1}{p}}, & 1 \leq p < \infty, \\ \sum_{|\beta|\leq k} \text{ess sup}_{\Omega} |D^{\beta}u|, & p = \infty, \end{cases}$$

where $D^\beta = \frac{\partial^{|\beta|}}{\partial x^{\beta_1}\partial y^{\beta_2}}$ for the multi-index $\beta = (\beta_1, \beta_2)$, $\beta_1 \geq 0$, $\beta_2 \geq 0$ and $|\beta| = \beta_1 + \beta_2$. For $p = 2$, we let $H^m(\Omega)$ denote $W^{m,2}(\Omega)$. We omit the subscript when $p = 2$ and write $\|\cdot\|_{0,2}$ and $|\cdot|_{0,2}$ as $\|\cdot\|_0$ and $|\cdot|_0$ for simplicity. Moreover, we use $(\cdot,\cdot)$ to represent the L^2 inner product, i.e.,

$$(u,v) = \int_\Omega uv dxdy.$$

For the mathematical setting of the problem (1)–(4), we introduce the following Sobolev spaces V and M [31], i.e.,

$$V = (H_0^1(\Omega))^2, \quad P = L_0^2(\Omega) = \{q \in L^2(\Omega) : \int_\Omega q\, dxdy = 0\}.$$

Moreover, for any Banach space X and $I = [0,T]$, let $L^p(I;X)$ be the space of all measurable function $f : I \to X$ with the norm

$$\|f\|_{L^p(I;X)} = \begin{cases} (\int_0^T \|f\|_X^p dt)^{\frac{1}{p}}, & 1 \leq p \leq \infty, \\ \text{ess sup}_{t\in I}\|f\|_X, & p = \infty. \end{cases}$$

Let $\mathcal{T}_h = \{e\}$ be a uniform rectangular mesh over Ω with mesh size h. For a given element $e \in \mathcal{T}_h$, its four vertices are denoted by $a_i(x_i, y_i)$, $i = 1,2,3,4$ in the counterclockwise order (see Figure 1 left). For the velocity, we choose V_h as the general bilinear finite element space. For the pressure, we assume that the subdivision $\mathcal{T}_h$ is obtained from $\mathcal{T}_{2h} = \{\tau\}$ by dividing each element of $\mathcal{T}_{2h}$ into four small congruent rectangles. Let P_h' consist of piecewise constant functions with respect to $\mathcal{T}_h$ such that the local basis functions for P_h' on a 2×2-patch of τ (see Figure 1 right) are indicated in Figure 2. Then, the finite element space for pressure is defined by $P_h' \cap L_0^2(\Omega)$. In the following discussion, we always assume that $\tau = \cup_{i=1}^4 e_i \in \mathcal{T}_{2h}$ with $e_i \in \mathcal{T}_h$ $(1 \leq i \leq 4)$ (see Figure 1 right). Thus, the finite element approximation spaces V_h and M_h for the bilinear-constant scheme are described by ([1,29,30])

$$V_h = \{v \in (C(\overline{\Omega}))^2 : v|_e \in (Q_{11}(e))^2, v|_{\partial\Omega} = 0, e \in \mathcal{T}_h\},$$
$$M_h = \{p \in L_0^2(\Omega) : p|_\tau = \sum_{i=1}^3 \lambda_i^\tau \varphi_i^\tau, \sum_{\tau\in\mathcal{T}_{2h}} \lambda_1^\tau = 0, \tau \in \mathcal{T}_{2h}\},$$

where Q_{11} denotes the space of all polynomials of degree ≤ 1 with respect to each of the two variables, x and y. It is shown in [1,29,30] that the bilinear-constant scheme satisfies the Babuška–Brezzi condition, i.e.,

$$\sup_{0\neq v_h\in X_h} \frac{(q_h, \nabla\cdot v_h)}{\|v_h\|_1} \geq \beta\|q_h\|_0, \quad \forall q_h \in M_h, \tag{5}$$

where $\beta > 0$ is a constant, independent of h.

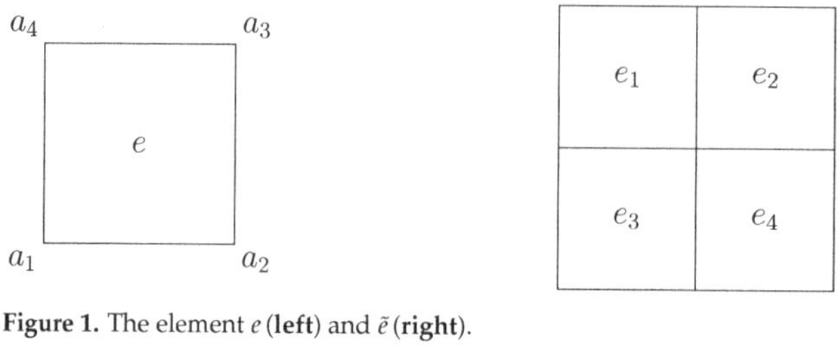

Figure 1. The element e (**left**) and $\tilde{e}$ (**right**).

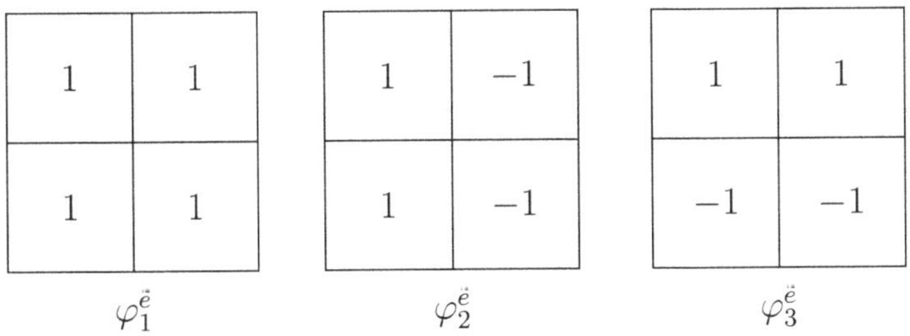

Figure 2. Local basis functions of $P_h^{'}$.

For the velocity, we use the Lagrange nodal interpolation operator $I_h : (C(\overline{\Omega}))^2 \mapsto \boldsymbol{V}_h$ as the corresponding interpolation operator. For the pressure, we first introduce the local L^2-projection $J_h^{'}p$ of p by

$$J_h^{'}p = \frac{1}{|e|}\int_e p\, dx_1 dx_2, \quad \forall e \in \mathcal{T}_h, \tag{6}$$

and then define the operator J_h with respect to $\tilde{e}$ by

$$J_h p = \begin{cases} J_h^{'}p - \frac{1}{4}\alpha_{\tilde{e}}, & i = 1,4, \\ J_h^{'}p + \frac{1}{4}\alpha_{\tilde{e}}, & i = 2,3, \end{cases} \tag{7}$$

where $\alpha_{\tilde{e}} = p_1^{\tilde{e}} - p_2^{\tilde{e}} - p_3^{\tilde{e}} + p_4^{\tilde{e}}$ with the notations of $p_i^{\tilde{e}} = \frac{1}{|e_i|}\int_{e_i} p\, dx_1\, dx_2$, $(i = 1,2,3,4)$. We can check that

$$J_h p|_{\tilde{e}} = \frac{1}{4}\left[\left(\sum_{i=1}^{4} p_i^{\tilde{e}}\right)\varphi_1^{\tilde{e}} + (p_1^{\tilde{e}} - p_2^{\tilde{e}} + p_3^{\tilde{e}} - p_4^{\tilde{e}})\varphi_2^{\tilde{e}} + (p_1^{\tilde{e}} + p_2^{\tilde{e}} - p_3^{\tilde{e}} - p_4^{\tilde{e}})\varphi_3^{\tilde{e}}\right],$$

which implies that $J_h p \in M_h$ for $p \in L_0^2(\Omega)$.

Lemma 1 ([29]). *Suppose that $\boldsymbol{u} \in (H^3(\Omega))^2$ and $p \in H^2(\Omega)$, then there hold*

$$(\nabla(\boldsymbol{u} - I_h\boldsymbol{u}), \nabla \boldsymbol{v}_h) \le Ch^2\|\boldsymbol{u}\|_3\|\nabla \boldsymbol{v}_h\|_0, \quad \forall \boldsymbol{v}_h \in \boldsymbol{V}_h, \tag{8}$$

$$(p - J_h p, \nabla \cdot \boldsymbol{v}_h) \le Ch^2\|p\|_2\|\nabla \boldsymbol{v}_h\|_0, \quad \forall \boldsymbol{v}_h \in \boldsymbol{V}_h, \tag{9}$$

$$(\nabla \cdot (\boldsymbol{u} - I_h\boldsymbol{u}_h), q_h) \le Ch^2\|\boldsymbol{u}\|_3\|q_h\|_0, \quad \forall q_h \in P_h. \tag{10}$$

Lemma 2. *Supposing that $u \in H^3(K)$ on element e, we have*

$$((u - I_h u)_x, v)_e + ((u - I_h u)_y, v)_e \le Ch_e^2\|u\|_{3,e}\|v\|_{0,e}, \quad \forall v \in P_h^{'}. \tag{11}$$

Furthermore, there holds for $u \in H^3(\Omega)$

$$((u - I_h u)_x, v) + ((u - I_h u)_y, v) \le Ch^2\|u\|_3\|v\|_0 \quad \forall v \in P_h^{'}. \tag{12}$$

Proof. In order to obtain a second-order accuracy estimate, we adopt the high-accuracy integral technique developed in [32]. We introduce the following error function on an element e (see Figure 3):

$$F(y) = \frac{1}{2}[(y - y_e)^2 - h_y^2], \tag{13}$$

where (x_e, y_e) denotes the barycentric coordinate of element e. One can check that $F^{''}(y) = 1$, $F(y)|_{l_1,l_3} = 0$. Note that v is constant on an element e, and we have

$$((u-I_hu)_x,v)_e=\int_e(u-I_hu)_xvdxdy=v\int_e(u-I_hu)_xdxdy=v\int_e(u-I_hu)_xF''(y)dxdy$$
$$=v\left[\left(\int_{l_3}-\int_{l_1}\right)(u-I_hu)_xF'(y)dx-\int_e(u-I_hu)_{xy}F'(y)dxdy\right]$$
$$=-\left[\left(\int_{l_3}-\int_{l_1}\right)(u-I_hu)_{xy}F(y)dx-\int_e(u-I_hu)_{xyy}F(y)dxdy\right]$$
$$=\int_e F(y)u_{xyy}vdxdy\le Ch_e^2\|u\|_{3,e}\|v\|_{0,e},\tag{14}$$

where we have that $(u-I_hu)(a_i)=0$, $(i=1,\ldots,4)$ and $F'(y)|_{l_1,l_3}$ are constants in the above estimate.

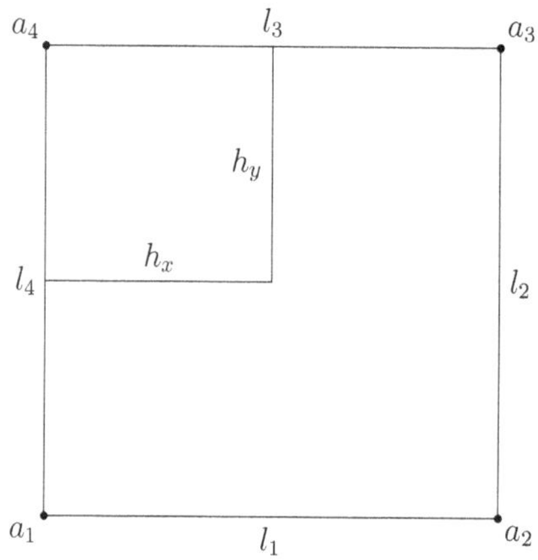

Figure 3. The element $\tilde{e}$.

In the same way, we also have

$$((u-I_hu)_x,v)_e\le Ch_e^2\|u\|_{3,e}\|v\|_{0,e}.\tag{15}$$

Therefore, by adding (14) and (15), the desired result (11) is derived. Furthermore, summing up (11) with respect to $e\in\mathcal{T}_h$ gives the result (12). □

We present the discrete Gronwall's inequality, which is useful in the following error analysis.

Lemma 3 ([33,34]). *Let τ, B and a_k, b_k, c_k, γ_k, for integers $k\ge 0$, be non-negative numbers such that*

$$a_n+\tau\sum_{k=0}^n b_k\le\tau\sum_{k=0}^n\gamma_k a_k+\tau\sum_{k=0}^n c_k+B,\quad\text{for } n\ge 0,$$

suppose that $\tau\gamma_k<1$, for all k, and set $\sigma_k=(1-\tau\gamma_k)^{-1}$. Then

$$a_n+\tau\sum_{k=0}^n b_k\le\exp\left(\tau\sum_{k=0}^n\gamma_k\sigma_k\right)\left(\tau\sum_{k=0}^n c_k+B\right),\quad\text{for } n\ge 0.$$

The Young inequality will be frequently used in the following analysis, and we present it here.

$$ab \leq \frac{a^2}{2\epsilon} + \frac{\epsilon b^2}{2}, \quad \text{for } \epsilon > 0.$$

The weak formulation of (1)–(4) is as follows: find $(\boldsymbol{u}, p) : [0, T] \to (H_0^1(\Omega))^2 \times L_0^2(\Omega)$, such that

$$(\boldsymbol{u}_t, \boldsymbol{v}) + (\nabla \boldsymbol{u}, \nabla \boldsymbol{v}) + ((\boldsymbol{u} \cdot \nabla)\boldsymbol{u}, \boldsymbol{v}) - (p, \nabla \cdot \boldsymbol{v}) = (\boldsymbol{f}, \boldsymbol{v}), \quad \forall \boldsymbol{v} \in (H_0^1(\Omega))^2, \tag{16}$$

$$(\nabla \cdot \boldsymbol{u}, q) = 0, \quad \forall q \in L_0^2(\Omega). \tag{17}$$

Moreover, in order to give the fully discrete scheme, let $0 = t_0 < t_1 < \cdots < t_N = T$ be a given uniform partition of the time interval with time step $\tau = T/N$ and $t_n = n\tau$, $n = 0, 1, \ldots, N$. For a smooth function w defined on $[0, T]$, denote

$$w^n = w(t_n), \qquad D_\tau w^n = \frac{(w^n - w^{n-1})}{\tau}.$$

Then, the semi-implicit backward Euler low-order conforming mixed finite element scheme (bilinear-constant scheme) is as follows: for given $(\boldsymbol{u}_h^{n-1}, p_h^{n-1}) \in \boldsymbol{V}_h \times M_h$, find $(\boldsymbol{u}_h^n, p_h^n) \in \boldsymbol{V}_h \times M_h$ such that

$$(D_\tau \boldsymbol{u}_h^n, \boldsymbol{v}_h) + (\nabla \boldsymbol{u}_h^n, \nabla \boldsymbol{v}_h) + ((\boldsymbol{u}_h^{n-1} \cdot \nabla)\boldsymbol{u}_h^n, \boldsymbol{v}_h) - (p_h^n, \nabla \cdot \boldsymbol{v}_h) = (\boldsymbol{f}^n, \boldsymbol{v}_h), \quad \forall \boldsymbol{v}_h \in \boldsymbol{V}_h, \tag{18}$$

$$(\nabla \cdot \boldsymbol{u}_h^n, q_h) = 0, \quad \forall q_h \in M_h, \tag{19}$$

with the initial approximation $\boldsymbol{u}_h^0 = I_h \boldsymbol{u}_0 = I_h \boldsymbol{u}(0)$.

The unconditionally optimal error estimate for scheme (18)–(19) is shown in [20] by using the error splitting technique with the low-order conforming mixed finite element method, specifically, by introducing the following time-discrete system [18,20]:

$$D_\tau \boldsymbol{U}^n - \Delta \boldsymbol{U}^n + (\boldsymbol{U}^{n-1} \cdot \nabla)\boldsymbol{U}^n + \nabla P^n = \boldsymbol{f}^n, \tag{20}$$

$$\nabla \cdot \boldsymbol{U}^n = 0, \tag{21}$$

$$\boldsymbol{U}^n = 0, \tag{22}$$

$$\boldsymbol{U}^0 = \boldsymbol{u}_0. \tag{23}$$

Then, the error between the exact solution and the numerical solution comprises two parts, where one is the temporal error and the other is the spatial error. Therefore, the numerical solution in the L^∞-norm can be bounded without any time-step restrictions. Here, we present a lemma to state the τ-independent boundedness of the numerical solution.

Lemma 4 ([20]). *Suppose that $(\boldsymbol{u}^n, p^n)$ is the solution of (1)–(4) with suitable regularity and $(\boldsymbol{U}^n, P^n)$ and $(\boldsymbol{u}_h^n, p^n)$ are the solutions of (20)–(23) and (18)–(19). Then, there exist positive constants τ_0 and h_0 such that when $\tau \leq \tau_0$ and $h \leq h_0$, we have the τ-independent boundedness of numerical solutions*

$$\|\boldsymbol{u}_h^n\|_{0,\infty} \leq K, \quad n = 0, 1, \ldots, N, \tag{24}$$

where K is a constant, which is not dependent on h, τ and n.

3. Superclose and Superconvergence Error Estimates

In this section, we firstly present the superclose error estimates for the velocity and pressure variables. Then, we give the superconvergence result in terms of the superclose error estimates as well as the interpolation technique.

Theorem 1. *Suppose that* $(\boldsymbol{u}, p)$ *and* $(\boldsymbol{u}_h^n, p_h^n)$ *are the solutions of* (16)–(19) *and* $\boldsymbol{u} \in L^\infty((H^3(\Omega))^2 \cap (H_0^1(\Omega))^2)$, $\boldsymbol{u}_t \in L^\infty((H^3(\Omega))^2)$, $\boldsymbol{u}_{tt} \in L^2((L^2(\Omega))^2)$ *and* $p \in L^\infty(H^2(\Omega))$. *Then, we have the following superclose estimates*

$$\|\nabla(I_h\boldsymbol{u}^n - \boldsymbol{u}_h^n)\|_0 \le C(h^2+\tau), \qquad \tau\sum_{k=1}^{n}\|J_hp^n - p_h^n\|_0 \le C(h^2+\tau). \tag{25}$$

Furthermore, we have the following optimal error estimates:

$$\|\boldsymbol{u}^n - \boldsymbol{u}_h^n\|_0 \le C(h^2+\tau), \quad \|\nabla(\boldsymbol{u}^n - \boldsymbol{u}_h^n)\|_0 \le C(h+\tau), \quad \tau\sum_{k=1}^{n}\|p^n - p_h^n\|_0 \le C(h+\tau). \tag{26}$$

Proof. For simplicity, we split the errors $\boldsymbol{u} - \boldsymbol{u}_h$ and $p - p_h$ as follows:

$$\begin{aligned}\boldsymbol{u}^n - \boldsymbol{u}_h^n &= \boldsymbol{u}^n - I_h\boldsymbol{u}^n + I_h\boldsymbol{u}^n - \boldsymbol{u}_h^n := \boldsymbol{\rho}^n + \boldsymbol{\theta}^n,\\ p^n - p_h^n &= p^n - J_hp^n + J_hp^n - p_h^n := \xi^n + \eta^n.\end{aligned}$$

At $t = t_n$, from (16)–(17), we have

$$\begin{aligned}(D_\tau\boldsymbol{u}^n, \boldsymbol{v}_h) + (\nabla\boldsymbol{u}^n, \nabla\boldsymbol{v}_h) + ((\boldsymbol{u}^{n-1}\cdot\nabla)\boldsymbol{u}^n, \boldsymbol{v}_h) - (\nabla\cdot\boldsymbol{v}_h, p^n) &= (\boldsymbol{f}^n, \boldsymbol{v}_h) + (D_\tau\boldsymbol{u}^n - \boldsymbol{u}_t^n, \boldsymbol{v}_h)\\ &\quad + (((\boldsymbol{u}^{n-1} - \boldsymbol{u}^n)\cdot\nabla)\boldsymbol{u}^n, \boldsymbol{v}_h), \quad \forall \boldsymbol{v}_h \in \boldsymbol{V}_h, \end{aligned} \tag{27}$$

$$(\nabla\cdot\boldsymbol{u}^n, q_h) = 0, \quad \forall q_h \in M_h. \tag{28}$$

Subtracting (18)–(19) from (27)–(28) gives the following error equations:

$$\begin{aligned}(D_\tau\boldsymbol{\theta}^n, \boldsymbol{v}_h) + (\nabla\boldsymbol{\theta}^n, \nabla\boldsymbol{v}_h) - (\nabla\cdot\boldsymbol{v}_h, \eta^n) &= -(D_\tau\boldsymbol{\rho}^n, \boldsymbol{v}_h) - (\nabla\boldsymbol{\rho}^n, \nabla\boldsymbol{v}_h) + (\nabla\cdot\boldsymbol{v}_h, \xi^n)\\ &\quad - ((\boldsymbol{u}^{n-1}\cdot\nabla)\boldsymbol{u}^n - (\boldsymbol{u}_h^{n-1}\cdot\nabla)\boldsymbol{u}_h^n, \boldsymbol{v}_h) + (D_\tau\boldsymbol{u}^n - \boldsymbol{u}_t^n, \boldsymbol{v}_h)\\ &\quad + (((\boldsymbol{u}^{n-1} - \boldsymbol{u}^n)\cdot\nabla)\boldsymbol{u}^n, \boldsymbol{v}_h), \quad \forall \boldsymbol{v}_h \in \boldsymbol{V}_h,\end{aligned} \tag{29}$$

$$(\nabla\cdot\boldsymbol{\theta}^n, q_h) = -(\nabla\cdot\boldsymbol{\rho}^n, q_h), \quad \forall q_h \in M_h. \tag{30}$$

Alternatively, we have

$$(\nabla\cdot D_\tau\boldsymbol{\theta}^n, q_h) = -(\nabla\cdot D_\tau\boldsymbol{\rho}^n, q_h), \quad \forall q_h \in M_h. \tag{31}$$

Taking $\boldsymbol{v}_h = D_\tau\boldsymbol{\theta}^n$ in (29) and $q_h = \eta^n$ in (31) yields that

$$\begin{aligned}\|D_\tau\boldsymbol{\theta}^n\|_0^2 &+ \frac{1}{2\tau}(\|\nabla\boldsymbol{\theta}^n\|_0^2 - \|\nabla\boldsymbol{\theta}^{n-1}\|_0^2 + \|\nabla(\boldsymbol{\theta}^n - \boldsymbol{\theta}^{n-1})\|_0^2) = -(D_\tau\boldsymbol{\rho}^n, D_\tau\boldsymbol{\theta}^n)\\ &- (\nabla\boldsymbol{\rho}^n, \nabla D_\tau\boldsymbol{\theta}^n) + (\xi^n, \nabla\cdot D_\tau\boldsymbol{\theta}^n) - (\nabla\cdot D_\tau\boldsymbol{\rho}^n, \eta^n)\\ &- ((\boldsymbol{u}^{n-1}\cdot\nabla)\boldsymbol{u}^n - (\boldsymbol{u}_h^{n-1}\cdot\nabla)\boldsymbol{u}_h^n, D_\tau\boldsymbol{\theta}^n)\\ &+ (D_\tau\boldsymbol{u}^n - \boldsymbol{u}_t^n, D_\tau\boldsymbol{\theta}^n) + (((\boldsymbol{u}^{n-1} - \boldsymbol{u}^n)\cdot\nabla)\boldsymbol{u}^n, D_\tau\boldsymbol{\theta}^n) := \sum_{k=1}^{7}E_k.\end{aligned} \tag{32}$$

Now, we start to estimate E_k, $(k = 1, \cdots, 7)$ term by term. By the Cauchy–Schwarz inequality and interpolation theory, we have

$$\begin{aligned}E_1 = -(D_\tau\boldsymbol{\rho}^n, D_\tau\boldsymbol{\theta}^n) &\le Ch^2\|\boldsymbol{u}_t\|_{L^\infty((H^2(\Omega))^2)}\|D_\tau\boldsymbol{\theta}^n\|_0\\ &\le Ch^2\|D_\tau\boldsymbol{\theta}^n\|_0 \le Ch^4 + \epsilon\|D_\tau\boldsymbol{\theta}^n\|_0^2.\end{aligned} \tag{33}$$

Applying the following equality

$$(a^n, D_\tau b^n) = D_\tau(a^n, b^n) - (D_\tau a^n, b^{n-1}), \tag{34}$$

we have

$$\begin{aligned} E_2 &= -(\nabla \boldsymbol{\rho}^n, \nabla D_\tau \boldsymbol{\theta}^n) = -D_\tau(\nabla \boldsymbol{\rho}^n, \nabla \boldsymbol{\theta}^n) + (\nabla D_\tau \boldsymbol{\rho}^n, \nabla \boldsymbol{\theta}^{n-1}) \\ &\le -D_\tau(\nabla \boldsymbol{\rho}^n, \nabla \boldsymbol{\theta}^n) + Ch^2 \|\boldsymbol{u}_t\|_{L^\infty(H^3(\Omega))^2} \|\nabla \boldsymbol{\theta}^{n-1}\|_0 \\ &\le -D_\tau(\nabla \boldsymbol{\rho}^n, \nabla \boldsymbol{\theta}^n) + Ch^4 + C\|\nabla \boldsymbol{\theta}^{n-1}\|_0^2, \end{aligned} \tag{35}$$

where we used (8) of Lemma 1 in the above estimate.

With an application of (34) again, it follows that

$$\begin{aligned} E_3 &= (\xi^n, \nabla \cdot D_\tau \boldsymbol{\theta}^n) = D_\tau(\xi^n, \nabla \cdot \boldsymbol{\theta}^n) - (D_\tau \xi^n, \nabla \cdot \boldsymbol{\theta}^{n-1}) \\ &\le D_\tau(\xi^n, \nabla \cdot \boldsymbol{\theta}^n) + Ch^2 \|p_t\|_{L^\infty(H^2(\Omega))} \|\nabla \boldsymbol{\theta}^{n-1}\|_0 \\ &\le D_\tau(\xi^n, \nabla \cdot \boldsymbol{\theta}^n) + Ch^4 + C\|\nabla \boldsymbol{\theta}^{n-1}\|_0^2, \end{aligned} \tag{36}$$

where we used (9) of Lemma 1 in the above estimate.

According to (10) of Lemma 1, E_4 can be bounded by

$$E_4 = -(\nabla \cdot D_\tau \boldsymbol{\rho}^n, \eta^n) \le Ch^2 \|\boldsymbol{u}_t\|_{L^\infty(H^3(\Omega))^2} \|\eta^n\|_0 \le Ch^2 \|\eta^n\|_0. \tag{37}$$

To bound E_5, we split $(\boldsymbol{u}^{n-1} \cdot \nabla)\boldsymbol{u}^n - (\boldsymbol{u}_h^{n-1} \cdot \nabla)\boldsymbol{u}_h^n$ as follows:

$$\begin{aligned} (\boldsymbol{u}^{n-1} \cdot \nabla)\boldsymbol{u}^n - (\boldsymbol{u}_h^{n-1} \cdot \nabla)\boldsymbol{u}_h^n &= ((\boldsymbol{u}^{n-1} - \boldsymbol{u}_h^{n-1}) \cdot \nabla)\boldsymbol{u}^n + (\boldsymbol{u}_h^{n-1} \cdot \nabla)(\boldsymbol{u}^n - \boldsymbol{u}_h^n) \\ &= ((\boldsymbol{u}^{n-1} - I_h \boldsymbol{u}^{n-1}) \cdot \nabla)\boldsymbol{u}^n + ((I_h \boldsymbol{u}^{n-1} - \boldsymbol{u}_h^{n-1}) \cdot \nabla)\boldsymbol{u}^n \\ &+ (\boldsymbol{u}_h^{n-1} \cdot \nabla)(\boldsymbol{u}^n - I_h \boldsymbol{u}^n) + (\boldsymbol{u}_h^{n-1} \cdot \nabla)(I_h \boldsymbol{u}^n - \boldsymbol{u}_h^n) \\ &= ((\boldsymbol{u}^{n-1} - I_h \boldsymbol{u}^{n-1}) \cdot \nabla)\boldsymbol{u}^n + ((I_h \boldsymbol{u}^{n-1} - \boldsymbol{u}_h^{n-1}) \cdot \nabla)\boldsymbol{u}^n \\ &+ ((\boldsymbol{u}_h^{n-1} - I_h \boldsymbol{u}^{n-1}) \cdot \nabla)(\boldsymbol{u}^n - I_h \boldsymbol{u}^n) + ((I_h \boldsymbol{u}^{n-1} - \boldsymbol{u}^{n-1}) \cdot \nabla)(\boldsymbol{u}^n - I_h \boldsymbol{u}^n) \\ &+ (\boldsymbol{u}^{n-1} \cdot \nabla)(\boldsymbol{u}^n - I_h \boldsymbol{u}^n) + (\boldsymbol{u}_h^{n-1} \cdot \nabla)(I_h \boldsymbol{u}^n - \boldsymbol{u}_h^n) := \sum_{k=1}^{6} F_k. \end{aligned} \tag{38}$$

In terms of the Cauchy–Schwarz inequality and interpolation theory, we have

$$\begin{aligned} -(F_1, D_\tau \boldsymbol{\theta}^n) - (F_2, D_\tau \boldsymbol{\theta}^n) &\le (\|\boldsymbol{\rho}^{n-1}\|_0 + \|\boldsymbol{\theta}^{n-1}\|_0) \|\nabla \boldsymbol{u}^n\|_{0,\infty} \|D_\tau \boldsymbol{\theta}^n\|_0 \\ &\le C(h^2 + \|\nabla \boldsymbol{\theta}^{n-1}\|_0) \|D_\tau \boldsymbol{\theta}^n\|_0 \\ &\le Ch^4 + C\|\nabla \boldsymbol{\theta}^{n-1}\|_0^2 + 2\epsilon \|D_\tau \boldsymbol{\theta}^n\|_0^2. \end{aligned} \tag{39}$$

Using inverse inequality and interpolation theory, we have

$$\begin{aligned} -(F_3, D_\tau \boldsymbol{\theta}^n) - (F_4, D_\tau \boldsymbol{\theta}^n) &\le (\|\boldsymbol{\theta}^{n-1}\|_0 + \|\boldsymbol{\rho}^{n-1}\|_0) \|\nabla \boldsymbol{\rho}^n\|_0 \|D_\tau \boldsymbol{\theta}^n\|_{0,\infty} \\ &\le C(\|\nabla \boldsymbol{\theta}^{n-1}\|_0 + h^2 \|\boldsymbol{u}^{n-1}\|_2)(Ch\|\boldsymbol{u}^n\|_2)(Ch^{-1}\|D_\tau \boldsymbol{\theta}^n\|_0) \\ &\le C(h^2 + \|\nabla \boldsymbol{\theta}^{n-1}\|_0) \|D_\tau \boldsymbol{\theta}^n\|_0 \\ &\le Ch^4 + C\|\nabla \boldsymbol{\theta}^{n-1}\|_0^2 + 2\epsilon \|D_\tau \boldsymbol{\theta}^n\|_0^2. \end{aligned} \tag{40}$$

With the aid of (34), one can check that

$$\begin{aligned} -(F_5, D_\tau \boldsymbol{\theta}^n) &= -((\boldsymbol{u}^{n-1} \cdot \nabla)\boldsymbol{\rho}^n, D_\tau \boldsymbol{\theta}^n) = -D_\tau((\boldsymbol{u}^{n-1} \cdot \nabla)\boldsymbol{\rho}^n, \boldsymbol{\theta}^n) + (D_\tau((\boldsymbol{u}^{n-1} \cdot \nabla)\boldsymbol{\rho}^n), \boldsymbol{\theta}^{n-1}) \\ &= -D_\tau((\boldsymbol{u}^{n-1} \cdot \nabla)\boldsymbol{\rho}^n, \boldsymbol{\theta}^n) + ((D_\tau \boldsymbol{u}^{n-1} \cdot \nabla)\boldsymbol{\rho}^n, \boldsymbol{\theta}^{n-1}) + ((\boldsymbol{u}^{n-2} \cdot \nabla)D_\tau \boldsymbol{\rho}^n, \boldsymbol{\theta}^{n-1}). \end{aligned} \tag{41}$$

In order to obtain a high-accuracy error estimate, i.e., second-order accuracy, we introduce the local L^2-projection defined as follows:

$$\mathcal{P}_e u = \frac{1}{|e|} \int_e u dx dy, \quad (42)$$

where e is an element of the partition of $\mathcal{T}_h$ and $|e|$ is the measure of e. Then, we have

$$\|\mathcal{P}_e u\|_{0,e} \leq \|u\|_{0,e}, \quad \|u - \mathcal{P}_e u\|_{0,e} \leq Ch_e \|u\|_{1,e}, \quad \|u - \mathcal{P}_e u\|_{0,\infty,e} \leq Ch_e \|u\|_{1,\infty,e}. \quad (43)$$

Therefore, we have

$$\begin{aligned}
((D_\tau \boldsymbol{u}^{n-1} \cdot \nabla)\boldsymbol{\rho}^n, \boldsymbol{\theta}^{n-1}) &= \sum_{e \in \mathcal{T}_h} ((D_\tau \boldsymbol{u}^{n-1} \cdot \nabla)\boldsymbol{\rho}^n, \boldsymbol{\theta}^{n-1})_e \\
&= \sum_{e \in \mathcal{T}_h} (((D_\tau \boldsymbol{u}^{n-1} - \mathcal{P}_e D_\tau \boldsymbol{u}^{n-1}) \cdot \nabla))\boldsymbol{\rho}^n, \boldsymbol{\theta}^{n-1})_e \\
&+ \sum_{e \in \mathcal{T}_h} ((\mathcal{P}_e D_\tau \boldsymbol{u}^{n-1} \cdot \nabla))\boldsymbol{\rho}^n, \boldsymbol{\theta}^{n-1} - \mathcal{P}_e \boldsymbol{\theta}^{n-1})_e \\
&+ \sum_{e \in \mathcal{T}_h} ((\mathcal{P}_e D_\tau \boldsymbol{u}^{n-1} \cdot \nabla))\boldsymbol{\rho}^n, \mathcal{P}_e \boldsymbol{\theta}^{n-1})_e \\
&\leq \sum_{e \in \mathcal{T}_h} \|D_\tau \boldsymbol{u}^{n-1} - \mathcal{P}_e D_\tau \boldsymbol{u}^{n-1}\|_{0,\infty,e} \|\nabla \boldsymbol{\rho}^n\|_{0,e} \|\boldsymbol{\theta}^{n-1}\|_{0,e} \\
&+ C \sum_{e \in \mathcal{T}_h} \|\nabla \boldsymbol{\rho}^n\|_{0,e} \|\boldsymbol{\theta}^{n-1} - \mathcal{P}_e \boldsymbol{\theta}^{n-1}\|_{0,e} + Ch^2 \sum_{e \in \mathcal{T}_h} \|\boldsymbol{u}^n\|_{3,e} \|\mathcal{P}_e \boldsymbol{\theta}^{n-1}\|_{0,e} \\
&\leq Ch^2 \sum_{e \in \mathcal{T}_h} \|\boldsymbol{u}^n\|_{2,e} \|\boldsymbol{\theta}^{n-1}\|_{0,e} + Ch^2 \sum_{e \in \mathcal{T}_h} \|\boldsymbol{u}^n\|_{2,e} \|\boldsymbol{\theta}^{n-1}\|_{1,e} \\
&+ Ch^2 \sum_{e \in \mathcal{T}_h} \|\boldsymbol{u}^n\|_{3,e} \|\boldsymbol{\theta}^{n-1}\|_{0,e} \leq Ch^2 \|\boldsymbol{u}^n\|_3 \|\boldsymbol{\theta}^{n-1}\|_1 \leq Ch^2 \|\boldsymbol{u}^n\|_3 \|\nabla \boldsymbol{\theta}^{n-1}\|_0 \\
&\leq Ch^4 + C\|\nabla \boldsymbol{\theta}^{n-1}\|_0^2,
\end{aligned} \quad (44)$$

where we used Lemma 2 in the above estimate.

In the same way, we also have

$$((\boldsymbol{u}^{n-2} \cdot \nabla) D_\tau \boldsymbol{\rho}^n, \boldsymbol{\theta}^{n-1}) \leq Ch^2 \|\nabla \boldsymbol{\theta}^{n-1}\|_0 \leq Ch^4 + C\|\nabla \boldsymbol{\theta}^{n-1}\|_0^2. \quad (45)$$

Hence, there holds

$$-(F_5, D_\tau \boldsymbol{\theta}^n) = -D_\tau((\boldsymbol{u}^{n-1} \cdot \nabla)\boldsymbol{\rho}^n, \boldsymbol{\theta}^n) + Ch^4 + C\|\nabla \boldsymbol{\theta}^{n-1}\|_0^2. \quad (46)$$

By (24) of Lemma 4, the numerical solution $\boldsymbol{u}_h^n$ is bounded unconditionally in L^∞-norm, and we have

$$\begin{aligned}
-(F_6, D_\tau \boldsymbol{\theta}^n) &\leq \|\boldsymbol{u}_h^n\|_{0,\infty} \|\nabla \boldsymbol{\theta}^n\|_0 \|D_\tau \boldsymbol{\theta}^n\|_0 \leq C\|\nabla \boldsymbol{\theta}^n\|_0 \|D_\tau \boldsymbol{\theta}^n\|_0 \\
&\leq C\|\nabla \boldsymbol{\theta}^n\|_0^2 + \epsilon \|D_\tau \boldsymbol{\theta}^n\|_0^2.
\end{aligned} \quad (47)$$

Based on the above estimates $(F_k, D_\tau \boldsymbol{\theta}^n)$, $(k = 1, \ldots, 6)$, E_5 reduces to

$$E_5 \leq Ch^4 + C(\|\nabla \boldsymbol{\theta}^n\|_0^2 + \|\nabla \boldsymbol{\theta}^{n-1}\|_0^2) + 5\epsilon \|D_\tau \boldsymbol{\theta}^n\|_0^2 - D_\tau((\boldsymbol{u}^{n-1} \cdot \nabla)\boldsymbol{\rho}^n, \boldsymbol{\theta}^n). \quad (48)$$

Moreover, by Taylor expansion, we have

$$\begin{aligned}
E_6 + E_7 &\leq C\tau \|\boldsymbol{u}_{tt}\|_{L^\infty(L^2(\Omega))} \|D_\tau \boldsymbol{\theta}^n\|_0 + C\tau \|\boldsymbol{u}_t\|_{L^\infty(L^2(\Omega))} \|\nabla \boldsymbol{u}\|_{L^\infty(L^\infty(\Omega))} \|D_\tau \boldsymbol{\theta}^n\|_0 \\
&\leq C\tau \|D_\tau \boldsymbol{\theta}^n\|_0 \leq C\tau^2 + \epsilon \|D_\tau \boldsymbol{\theta}^n\|_0^2.
\end{aligned} \quad (49)$$

With the estimates E_k, $(k = 1, \ldots, 6)$, we obtain

$$\|D_\tau \theta^n\|_0^2 + \frac{1}{2\tau}(\|\nabla\theta^n\|_0^2 - \|\nabla\theta^{n-1}\|_0^2) \leq C(h^4 + \tau^2) + C(\|\nabla\theta^n\|_0^2 + \|\nabla\theta^{n-1}\|_0^2) + 7\epsilon\|D_\tau\theta^n\|_0^2 + Ch^2\|\eta^n\|_0 - D_\tau(\nabla\rho^n, \nabla\theta^n) + D_\tau(\xi^n, \nabla\cdot\theta^n) - D_\tau((u^{n-1}\cdot\nabla)\rho^n, \theta^n). \tag{50}$$

On the other hand, from (29), it follows that

$$(\nabla\cdot v_h, \eta^n) = (D_\tau\theta^n, v_h) + (D_\tau\rho^n, v_h) + (\nabla\theta^n, \nabla v_h) + (\nabla\rho^n, \nabla v_h) - (\nabla\cdot v_h, \xi^n) + ((u^{n-1}\cdot\nabla)u^n - (u_h^{n-1}\cdot\nabla)u_h^n, v_h) - (D_\tau u^n - u_t^n, v_h) - (((u^{n-1} - u^n)\cdot\nabla)u^n, v_h), \quad \forall v_h \in V_h. \tag{51}$$

Then, one can check that by the Cauchy–Schwarz inequality and interpolation theory,

$$(D_\tau\theta^n, v_h) + (D_\tau\rho^n, v_h) \leq (\|D_\tau\theta^n\|_0 + \|D_\tau\rho^n\|_0)\|v_h\|_0 \leq C(h^2 + \|D_\tau\theta^n\|_0)\|\nabla v_h\|_0 \tag{52}$$

and

$$(\nabla\theta^n, \nabla v_h) \leq \|\nabla\theta^n\|_0\|\nabla v_h\|_0. \tag{53}$$

By Lemma 1, we have

$$(\nabla\rho^n, \nabla v_h) - (\nabla\cdot v_h, \xi^n) \leq Ch^2\|\nabla v_h\|_0. \tag{54}$$

Using a similar estimate process as E_5, there holds

$$((u^{n-1}\cdot\nabla)u^n - (u_h^{n-1}\cdot\nabla)u_h^n, v_h) \leq C(h^2 + \|\nabla\theta^n\|_0 + \|\nabla\theta^{n-1}\|_0)\|\nabla v_h\|_0. \tag{55}$$

As an application of the Taylor expansion, we have

$$-(D_\tau u^n - u_t^n, v_h) - (((u^{n-1} - u^n)\cdot\nabla)u^n, v_h) \leq C\tau\|\nabla v_h\|_0. \tag{56}$$

Therefore, we conclude that

$$(\nabla\cdot v_h, \eta^n) \leq C(h^2 + \tau + \|\nabla\theta^n\|_0 + \|\nabla\theta^{n-1}\|_0 + \|D_\tau\theta^n\|_0)\|\nabla v_h\|_0. \tag{57}$$

Then, thanks to the discrete LBB condition (β is a positive constant independent of mesh-size h), we have

$$\beta\|\eta^n\|_0 \leq \sup_{0\neq v_h\in V_h}\frac{(\nabla\cdot v_h, \eta^n)}{\|\nabla v_h\|_0} \leq C(h^2 + \tau + \|\nabla\theta^n\|_0 + \|\nabla\theta^{n-1}\|_0 + \|D_\tau\theta^n\|_0). \tag{58}$$

Substituting (58) into (50) and using the Young inequality, (50) reduces to

$$\|D_\tau \theta^n\|_0^2 + \frac{1}{2\tau}(\|\nabla\theta^n\|_0^2 - \|\nabla\theta^{n-1}\|_0^2) \leq C(h^4 + \tau^2) + C(\|\nabla\theta^n\|_0^2 + \|\nabla\theta^{n-1}\|_0^2) + 8\epsilon\|D_\tau\theta^n\|_0^2 - D_\tau(\nabla\rho^n, \nabla\theta^n) + D_\tau(\xi^n, \nabla\cdot\theta^n) - D_\tau((u^{n-1}\cdot\nabla)\rho^n, \theta^n). \tag{59}$$

Choosing $\epsilon = \frac{1}{16}$ in (59) and summing up the resulting inequality, we have

$$\frac{\tau}{2}\sum_{k=1}^{n}\|D_\tau\theta^k\|_0^2+\frac{1}{2}\|\nabla\theta^n\|_0^2\le C(h^4+\tau^2)+C\tau\sum_{k=1}^{n}\|\nabla\theta^k\|_0^2-(\nabla\rho^n,\nabla\theta^n)$$
$$+(\xi^n,\nabla\cdot\theta^n)-((u^{n-1}\cdot\nabla)\rho^n,\theta^n),$$
$$\le C(h^4+\tau^2)+C\tau\sum_{k=1}^{n}\|\nabla\theta^k\|_0^2+Ch^2\|u^n\|_3\|\nabla\theta^n\|_0$$
$$+Ch^2\|p^n\|_3\|\nabla\theta^n\|_0+Ch^2\|u^n\|_3\|\nabla\theta^n\|_0$$
$$\le C(h^4+\tau^2)+C\tau\sum_{k=1}^{n}\|\nabla\theta^k\|_0^2+\frac{1}{4}\|\nabla\theta^n\|_0^2, \tag{60}$$

where we used $\theta^0=0$, Lemma 1 and the same estimate process (44) for $-((u^{n-1}\cdot\nabla)\rho^n,\theta^n)$.

Hence, from (60), there holds

$$\tau\sum_{k=1}^{n}\|D_\tau\theta^k\|_0^2+\|\nabla\theta^n\|_0^2\le C(h^4+\tau^2)+C\tau\sum_{k=1}^{n}\|\nabla\theta^k\|_0^2. \tag{61}$$

Then, an application of the Gronwall lemma (see Lemma 3) yields

$$\tau\sum_{k=1}^{n}\|D_\tau\theta^k\|_0^2+\|\nabla\theta^n\|_0^2\le C(h^4+\tau^2). \tag{62}$$

Putting (62) into (58) gives that

$$\tau\sum_{k=1}^{n}\|\eta\|_0\le C(h^2+\tau)+\tau\sum_{k=1}^{n}\|D_\tau\theta^n\|_0$$
$$\le C(h^2+\tau)+C\left(\tau\sum_{k=1}^{n}\|D_\tau\theta^k\|_0^2\right)^{\frac{1}{2}}$$
$$\le C(h^2+\tau). \tag{63}$$

The desired results are obtained, and the proof is complete. □

With the aid of the superclose error estimate in Theorem 1, we adopt the interpolation post-processing approach to improve the accuracy of the numerical solution (u_h^n,p_h^n) on the whole domain. Let I_{2h} be the piecewise biquadratic nodal interpolation operator for the velocity associated with $\mathcal{T}_{2h}$. Moreover, for the pressure, the postprocessing operator J_{2h} is defined as

$$\begin{cases} J_{2h}p\in Q_{11}(\tilde{e}),\\ \frac{1}{|e_i|}\int_{e_i}(J_{2h}p-p)dx_1x_2=0, \quad i=1,2,3,4.\end{cases}$$

The following properties are shown in [29]:

$$\begin{cases} I_{2h}I_h=I_{2h},\\ \|I_{2h}v\|_1\le C\|v\|_1, \quad \forall v\in V_h,\\ \|I_{2h}u-u\|_1\le Ch^2\|u\|_3,\end{cases}\qquad \begin{cases} J_{2h}J_h'=J_{2h},\\ \|J_{2h}q\|_0\le C\|q\|_0,\forall q\in P_h,\\ \|J_{2h}p-p\|_0\le Ch^2\|p\|_2.\end{cases} \tag{64}$$

Moreover, we also have from [29] that for $p\in H^2(\Omega)$,

$$\|p - J_{2h}J_h p\|_0 \leq Ch^2 \|p\|_2. \tag{65}$$

Now, we state the global superonvergence result in the following theorem:

Theorem 2. *Under the condition of Theorem 1, there holds*

$$\|\boldsymbol{u}^n - I_{2h}\boldsymbol{u}_h^n\|_1 + \|p^n - J_{2h}p_h^n\|_0 \leq C(h^2 + \tau). \tag{66}$$

Proof. By (64) and (65), we have

$$\begin{aligned}
\|\boldsymbol{u}^n - I_{2h}\boldsymbol{u}_h^n\|_1 + \|p^n - J_{2h}p_h^n\|_0 &\leq \|\boldsymbol{u}^n - I_{2h}I_h\boldsymbol{u}^n\|_1 + \|I_{2h}I_h\boldsymbol{u}^n - I_{2h}\boldsymbol{u}_h^n\|_1 \\
&\quad + \|p^n - J_{2h}J_hp^n\|_0 + \|J_{2h}J_hp^n - J_{2h}p_h^n\|_0 \\
&\leq Ch^2\|\boldsymbol{u}^n\|_3 + C\|I_h\boldsymbol{u}^n - \boldsymbol{u}_h^n\|_1 + Ch^2\|p^n\|_2 + C\|J_hp^n - p_h^n\|_0 \\
&\leq C(h^2 + \tau).
\end{aligned}$$

The proof is complete. □

4. Numerical Experiment

In this section, we present some numerical results to confirm the correctness of the theoretical analysis. The software we used is MATLAB 2018a with a 3.20 GHz Intel Core i5-6500 CPU processor and 8 GB memory.

Example 1. Let $\Omega = (0,1)^2$, and divide Ω into $m \times n$ uniform rectangles. Moreover, the function f and the initial and boundary conditions are chosen corresponding to the exact solution [35]:

$$\begin{aligned}
u_1 &= e^{-t}(x_1^4 - 2x_1^3 + x_1^2)(4x_2^3 - 6x_2^2 + 2x_2), \\
u_2 &= -e^{-t}(x_2^4 - 2x_2^3 + x_2^2)(4x_1^3 - 6x_1^2 + 2x_1), \\
p &= 10e^{-t}(2x_1 - 1)(2x_2 - 1).
\end{aligned}$$

We set the final time $T = 1.0$ in the computation. In order to confirm the error estimates in Theorems 1 and 2, we present the numerical errors in Tables 1–6 at $t = 0.1$, 0.6, 1.0, respectively. Obviously, it can be seen that the numerical results are in agreement with the theoretical analysis, i.e., the errors $\|\boldsymbol{u}^n - \boldsymbol{u}_h^n\|_0$, $\|\boldsymbol{u}^n - \boldsymbol{u}_h^n\|_1$, $\|I_h\boldsymbol{u}^n - \boldsymbol{u}_h^n\|_1$ and $\|\boldsymbol{u}^n - I_{2h}\boldsymbol{u}_h^n\|_1$ for the velocity $\boldsymbol{u}$ are of order $O(h^2)$, $O(h)$, $O(h^2)$ and $O(h^2)$, respectively. In addition, the errors $\|p^n - p_h^n\|_0$, $\|J_hp^n - p_h^n\|_0$ and $\|p^n - J_{2h}p_h^n\|_0$ for the pressure p are of orders $O(h)$, $O(h^2)$ and $O(h^2)$, respectively. At the same time, we also give the graphics of the exact solutions ($\boldsymbol{u}$, p) and finite element solutions ($\boldsymbol{u}_h$, p_h) at $t = 1.0$ on mesh 32×32 (see Figures 4–7), respectively. It can be seen that the numerical results are also in good agreement with the theoretical analysis.

Table 1. The numerical errors and convergence orders at $t = 0.1$ of $\boldsymbol{u}$.

$m \times n$	4×4	8×8	16×16	32×32
$\|\boldsymbol{u}^n - \boldsymbol{u}_h^n\|_0$	6.9832×10^{-4}	1.7443×10^{-4}	4.0642×10^{-5}	1.0779×10^{-5}
Order	/	2.0012	2.1016	1.9147
$\|\boldsymbol{u}^n - \boldsymbol{u}_h^n\|_1$	2.7565×10^{-2}	1.3929×10^{-2}	6.9778×10^{-3}	3.4900×10^{-3}
Order	/	0.98469	0.99730	0.99953
$\|I_h\boldsymbol{u}^n - \boldsymbol{u}_h^n\|_1$	5.1545×10^{-3}	1.7229×10^{-3}	4.9365×10^{-4}	1.1691×10^{-4}
Order	/	1.5810	1.8033	2.0780
$\|\boldsymbol{u}^n - I_{2h}\boldsymbol{u}_h^n\|_1$	1.6546×10^{-2}	4.4691×10^{-3}	1.1290×10^{-3}	2.7815×10^{-4}
Order	/	1.8884	1.9849	2.0211

Table 2. The numerical errors and convergence orders at $t = 0.1$ of p.

$m \times n$	**8 × 8**	**16 × 16**	**32 × 32**	**64 × 64**
$\|p - p_h\|_0$	$1.1969\times10^{+0}$	5.4990×10^{-1}	2.6876×10^{-1}	1.3356×10^{-1}
Order	/	1.1221	1.0329	1.0088
$\|J_h p - p_h\|_0$	5.7535×10^{-1}	1.4260×10^{-1}	3.6042×10^{-2}	8.9144×10^{-3}
Order	/	2.0125	1.9842	2.0154
$\|p - J_{2h} p_h\|_0$	7.6225×10^{-1}	1.8945×10^{-1}	4.7655×10^{-2}	1.1841×10^{-2}
Order	/	2.0084	1.9911	2.0089

Table 3. The numerical errors and convergence orders at $t = 0.6$ of $\boldsymbol{u}$.

$m \times n$	**4 × 4**	**8 × 8**	**16 × 16**	**32 × 32**
$\|\boldsymbol{u}^n - \boldsymbol{u}_h^n\|_0$	2.4270×10^{-4}	6.3566×10^{-5}	1.4898×10^{-5}	3.9554×10^{-6}
Order	/	1.9329	2.0931	1.9132
$\|\boldsymbol{u}^n - \boldsymbol{u}_h^n\|_1$	$1.6737\times10^{-}$	8.4489×10^{-3}	4.2323×10^{-3}	2.1168×10^{-3}
Order	/	0.98623	0.99734	0.99953
$\|I_h \boldsymbol{u}^n - \boldsymbol{u}_h^n\|_1$	$3.5044\text{e}\times10^{-3}$	1.0579×10^{-3}	3.0068×10^{-4}	7.1119×10^{-5}
Order	/	1.7279	1.8149	2.0799
$\|\boldsymbol{u}^n - I_{2h} \boldsymbol{u}_h^n\|_1$	1.0152×10^{-2}	2.7162×10^{-3}	6.8536×10^{-4}	1.6879×10^{-4}
Order	/	1.9022	1.9867	2.0216

Table 4. The numerical errors and convergence orders at $t = 0.6$ of p.

$m \times n$	**8 × 8**	**16 × 16**	**32 × 32**	**64 × 64**
$\|p - p_h\|_0$	7.2597×10^{-1}	3.3353×10^{-1}	1.6301×10^{-1}	8.1008×10^{-2}
Order	/	1.1221	1.0329	1.0088
$\|J_h p - p_h\|_0$	3.4897×10^{-1}	8.6491×10^{-2}	2.1860×10^{-2}	5.4069×10^{-3}
Order	/	2.0125	1.9842	2.0154
$\|p - J_{2h} p_h\|_0$	4.6233×10^{-1}	1.1491×10^{-1}	2.8905×10^{-2}	7.1817×10^{-3}
Order	/	2.0084	1.9911	2.0089

Table 5. The numerical errors and convergence orders at $t = 1.0$ of $\boldsymbol{u}$.

$m \times n$	**4 × 4**	**8 × 8**	**16 × 16**	**32 × 32**
$\|\boldsymbol{u}^n - \boldsymbol{u}_h^n\|_0$	1.2510×10^{-4}	3.2199×10^{-5}	8.0816×10^{-6}	2.0220×10^{-6}
Order	/	1.9580	1.9943	1.9989
$\|\boldsymbol{u}^n - \boldsymbol{u}_h^n\|_1$	1.1202×10^{-2}	5.6624×10^{-3}	2.8366×10^{-3}	1.4189×10^{-3}
Order	/	0.98430	0.99724	0.99938
$\|I_h \boldsymbol{u}^n - \boldsymbol{u}_h^n\|_1$	1.7780×10^{-3}	6.0911×10^{-4}	1.6246×10^{-4}	4.1252×10^{-5}
Order	/	1.5455	1.9066	1.9775
$\|\boldsymbol{u}^n - I_{2h} \boldsymbol{u}_h^n\|_1$	6.6492×10^{-3}	1.7801×10^{-3}	4.4318×10^{-4}	1.1058×10^{-4}
Order	/	1.9012	2.0060	2.0029

Table 6. The numerical errors and convergence orders at $t = 1.0$ of p.

$m \times n$	**8 × 8**	**16 × 16**	**32 × 32**	**64 × 64**
$\|p - p_h\|_0$	4.8472×10^{-1}	2.2345×10^{-1}	1.0923×10^{-1}	5.4300×10^{-2}
Order	/	1.1172	1.0325	1.0084
$\|J_h p - p_h\|_0$	2.2993×10^{-1}	5.7482×10^{-2}	1.4370×10^{-2}	3.5926×10^{-3}
Order	/	2.0000	2.0000	2.0000
$\|p - J_{2h} p_h\|_0$	3.0657×10^{-1}	7.6642×10^{-2}	1.9160×10^{-3}	4.7901×10^{-3}
Order	/	2.0000	2.0000	2.0000

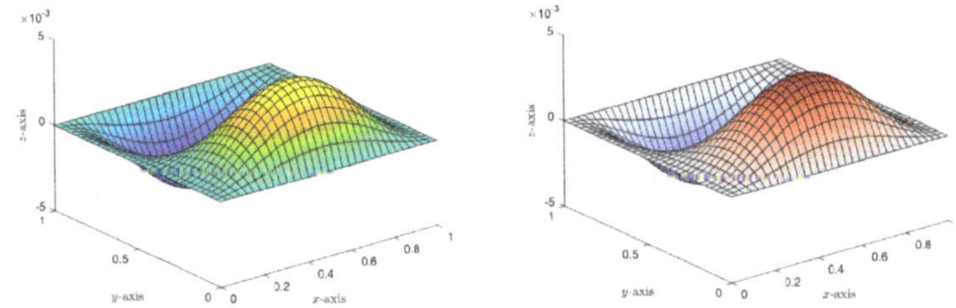

(**a**) Exact solution u_1^n.

(**b**) Numerical solution u_{1h}^n.

Figure 4. The graphics of u_1^n and u_{1h}^n on mesh 32×32.

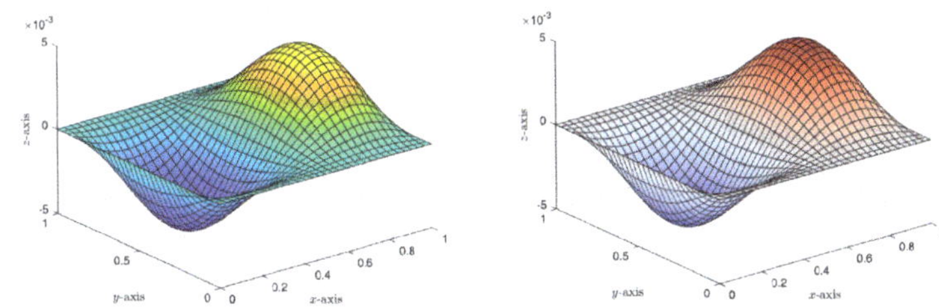

(**a**) Exact solution u_2^n.

(**b**) Numerical solution u_{2h}^n.

Figure 5. The graphics of u_2^n and u_{2h}^n on mesh 32×32.

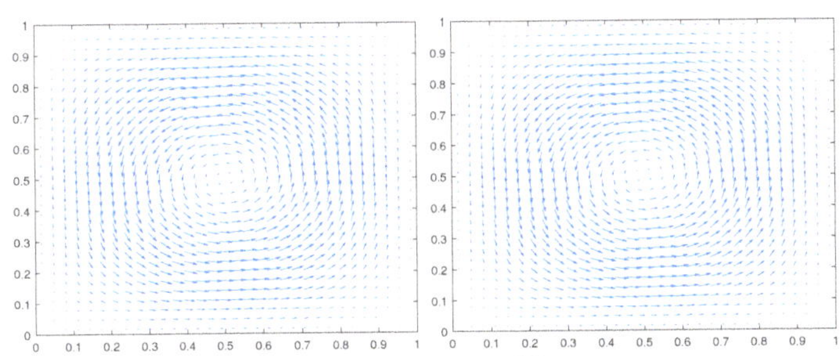

(**a**) The vector field of $\boldsymbol{u}^n$.

(**b**) The vector field of $\boldsymbol{u}_h^n$.

Figure 6. The graphics of the vector fields on mesh 32×32.

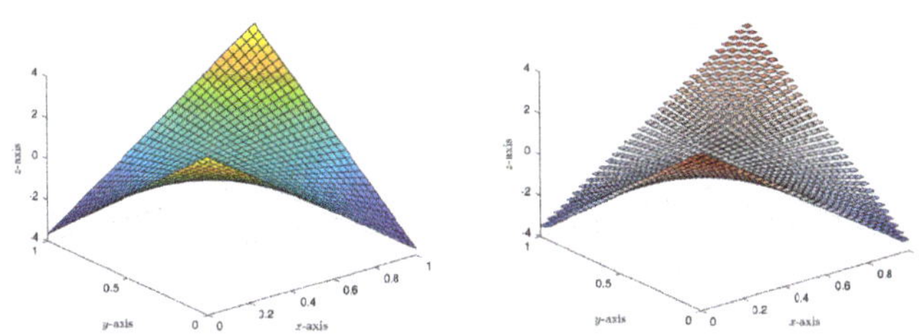

(**a**) Exact solution p^n.

(**b**) Numerical solution p_h^n.

Figure 7. The graphics of p^n and p_h^n on mesh 32×32.

Example 2. Let $\Omega = (0,1)^2$ and divide Ω into $m \times n$ uniform rectangles. Moreover, the function f and the initial and boundary conditions are chosen corresponding to the exact solution [14]:

$$\begin{aligned} u_1 &= -e^{-2t}\sin^2(\pi x)\sin(\pi y)\cos(\pi y), \\ u_2 &= e^{-2t}\sin(\pi x)\cos(\pi x)\sin^2(\pi y), \\ p &= e^{-4t}\sin(\pi x)\sin(\pi y). \end{aligned}$$

We set the final time $T = 10$ in the computation. In order to confirm the error estimates in Theorems 1 and 2, we present the numerical errors in Tables 7 and 8 at $t = 10$. Obviously, it can be seen that numerical results are in agreement with the theoretical analysis.

Table 7. The numerical errors and convergence orders at $t = 10$ of $\boldsymbol{u}$.

$m \times n$	4×4	8×8	16×16	32×32
$\Vert \boldsymbol{u}^n - \boldsymbol{u}_h^n \Vert_0$	3.9072×10^{-18}	9.6945×10^{-19}	2.4129×10^{-19}	6.0248×10^{-20}
Order	/	2.0109	2.0064	2.0018
$\Vert \boldsymbol{u}^n - \boldsymbol{u}_h^n \Vert_1$	2.0623×10^{-9}	1.0366×10^{-9}	5.1886×10^{-10}	2.5950×10^{-10}
Order	/	0.99241	0.99839	0.99959
$\Vert I_h\boldsymbol{u}^n - \boldsymbol{u}_h^n \Vert_1$	3.0875×10^{-10}	1.0500×10^{-10}	2.8119×10^{-11}	7.1483×10^{-12}
Order	/	1.5560	1.9008	1.9759
$\Vert \boldsymbol{u}^n - I_{2h}\boldsymbol{u}_h^n \Vert_1$	1.2562×10^{-9}	4.2567×10^{-10}	1.0848×10^{-10}	2.7240×10^{-11}
Order	/	1.5612	1.9723	1.9937

Table 8. The numerical errors and convergence orders at $t = 10$ of p.

$m \times n$	8×8	16×16	32×32	64×64
$\Vert p - p_h \Vert_0$	2.4684×10^{-10}	7.9753×10^{-11}	2.0617×10^{-11}	5.1913×10^{-12}
Order	/	1.6300	1.9517	1.9896
$\Vert J_h p - p_h \Vert_0$	2.4684×10^{-10}	7.9753×10^{-11}	2.0617×10^{-11}	5.1913×10^{-12}
Order	/	1.6300	1.9517	1.9896
$\Vert p - J_{2h} p_h \Vert_0$	2.8503×10^{-10}	8.7022×10^{-11}	2.1086×10^{-11}	5.2215×10^{-12}
Order	/	1.7117	2.0451	2.0138

5. Conclusions

In this paper, a low-order conforming mixed finite element method is investigated for time-dependent Navier–Stokes equations with the semi-implicit Euler scheme. With the help of the error splitting technique and the high-accuracy error estimates of the element pair on the rectangular mesh, the numerical solution in L^{infty}-norm is obtained without any time-step restrictions. Furthermore, the unconditionally superclose error estimates are derived by treating the trilinear term rigorously and skillfully. Moreover, the global superconvergence results are acquired in terms of the interpolation post-processing approach. It should be pointed out there are many interesting topics to study in future works, such as high-order time (e.g., Crank–Nicolson scheme and BDF2 scheme), low-order nonconforming mixed finite element methods, and fast computing for discretized linear system. We will study these topics in the future.

Author Contributions: X.M.; writing—original draft preparation; H.Y.; writing—review and editing, methodology, software. All authors have read and agreed to the published version of the manuscript.

Funding: H.Y. is supported by the National Natural Science Foundation of China (No. 12101568).

Data Availability Statement: The authors will supply the relevant data in response to reasonable requests.

Conflicts of Interest: The authors declare no conflict of interest.

References

1. Girault, V.; Raviart, P.A. *Finite Element Methods for Navier-Stokes Equations*; Theory and Algorithms; Springer: Berlin/Heidelberg, Germany, 1986.
2. Temam, R. *Navier-Stokes Equations, Theory and Numerical Analysis*; American Mathematical Society: North-Holland, The Netherlands; Amsterdam, The Netherlands; New York, NY, USA; Oxford, UK , 1984.
3. Giraldo, F.X.; Restelli, M.; Laeuter, M. Semi-implicit formulations of the Navier-Stokes equations: Application to nonhydrostatic atmospheric modeling. *SIAM J. Sci. Comput.* **2010**, *32*, 3394–3425. [CrossRef]
4. Strikwerda, J.C. Finite difference methods for the Stokes and Navier-Stokes equations. *SIAM J. Sci. Stat. Comput.* **1984**, *50*, 56–68. [CrossRef]
5. Wang, C.; Liu, J.G. Analysis of finite difference schemes for unsteady Navier-Stokes equations in vorticity formulation. *Numer. Math.* **2002**, *91*, 543–576. [CrossRef]
6. Li, Z.L.; Wang, C. A fast finite difference method for solving Navier-Stokes equations on irregular domains. *Commun. Math. Sci.* **2003**, *1*, 181–197. [CrossRef]
7. Hou, T.Y.; Wetton, B.T.R. Convergence of a finite difference scheme for the Navier-Stokes equations using vorticity boundary conditions. *SIAM J. Numer. Anal.* **1992**, *29*, 615–639. [CrossRef]
8. He, Y.N., Li, K.T. Convergence and stability of finite element nonlinear Galerkin method for the Navier-Stokes equations. *Numer. Math.* **1998**, *79*, 77–106. [CrossRef]
9. He, Y.N.; Sun, W. Sability and convergence of the Crank-Nicolson/Adams-Bashforth scheme for the time-dependent Navier-Stokes equations. *SIAM J. Numer. Anal.* **2007**, *45*, 837–869. [CrossRef]
10. Li, J.; He, Y.N.; Chen, Z.X. A new stabilized finite element method for the transient Navier-Stokes equations. *Comput. Methods Appl. Mech. Eng.* **2007**, *197*, 22–35. [CrossRef]
11. He, Y.N.; Li, J. A stabilized finite element method based on local polynomial pressure projection for the stationary Navier-Stokes equation. *Appl. Numer. Math.* **2008**, *58*, 1503–1514. [CrossRef]
12. He, Y.N. A fully discrete stablized finite element method for the time-dependent Navier- Stokes problem. *IMA J. Numer. Anal.* **2003**, *23*, 665–691. [CrossRef]
13. Suli, E. Convergence and nonlinear stability of the Lagrange-Galerkin method for the Navier-Stokes equations. *Numer. Math.* **1988**, *53*, 459–483. [CrossRef]
14. Yang, H.J.; Shi, D.Y.; Liu, Q. Superconvergence analysis of low order nonconforming mixed finite element methods for time-dependent Navier-Stokes equations. *J. Comput. Math.* **2021**, *39*, 63–80. [CrossRef]
15. Han, H.D. A finite element approximation of Navier-Stokes equations using nonconforming elements. *J. Comput. Math.* **1984**, *2*, 77–88.
16. Xu, X.J. On the accuracy of nonconforming quadrilateral Q_1 element approximation for the Navier-Stokes problem. *SIAMJ. Numer. Anal.* **2000**, *38*, 17–39. [CrossRef]
17. Shi, D.Y.; Ren, J.C.; Hao, X.B. A new second order nonconforming mixed finite element scheme for the stationary Stokes and Navier-Stokes equations. *Appl. Math. Comput.* **2009**, *207*, 462–477. [CrossRef]
18. Si, Z.Y.; Wang, J.L.; Sun, W.W. Unconditional stability and error estimates of modified characteristics FEMs for the Navier-Stokes equations. *Numer. Math.* **2016**, *134*, 139–161. [CrossRef]
19. Li, M.H.; Shi, D.Y.; Li, Z.Z.; Chen, H.R. Two-level mixed finite element methods for the Navier-Stokes equations with damping. *J. Math. Anal. Appl.* **2019**, *470*, 292–307. [CrossRef]
20. Yang, H.J.; Shi, D.Y. Unconditionally optimal error estimates of the bilinear-constant scheme for time-dependent Navier-Stokes equations. *J. Comput. Math.* **2022**, *40*, 127–146.
21. Li, M.H.; Xiao, L.C.; Li, Z.Z. The supercloseness property of the Stoke projection for the transient Navier-Stokes equations and global superconvergence analysis. *J. Appl. Math. Comput.* **2023**, *69*, 2041–2057. [CrossRef]
22. Shen, J. On error estimates of projection methods for Navier-Stokes equations: First-order schemes. *SIAM J. Numer. Anal.* **1992**, *29*, 57–77. [CrossRef]
23. Shen, J. On error estimates of the projection, methods for the Navier-Stokes equations: Second-order schemes. *Math. Comput.* **1996**, *65*, 1039–1066. [CrossRef]
24. Huang, P.Z.; Zhang, T.; Ma, X.L. Superconvergence by L^2-projection for a stabilized finite volume method for the stationary Navier-Stokes equations. *Comput. Math. Appl.* **2011**, *62*, 4249–4257. [CrossRef]
25. Huang, P.Z.; Feng, X.L. Error estimates for two-level penalty finite volume method for the stationary Navier-Stokes equations. *Math. Methods Appli. Sci.* **2013**, *36*, 1918–1928. [CrossRef]
26. Liu, X.; Li, J.; Chen, Z.X. A weak Galerkin finite element method for the Navier–Stokes equations. *J. Comput. Appl. Math.* **2018**, *333*, 442–457. [CrossRef]
27. Li, B.Y.; Sun, W.W. Error analysis of linearized semi-implicit Galerkin finite element methods for nonlinear parabolic equations. *Int. J. Numer. Anal. Model.* **2013**, *10*, 622–633.
28. Li, B.Y.; Sun, W.W. Unconditional convergence and optimal error estimates of a Galerkin-mixed FEM for incompressible miscible flow in porous media. *SIAM J. Numer. Anal.* **2013**, *51*, 1959–1977. [CrossRef]
29. Pan, J. Global superconvergence for the bilinear-constant scheme for the Stokes problem. *SIAM J. Numer. Anal.* **1997**, *36*, 2424–2430. [CrossRef]

30. Liu, H.P.; Yan, N.N. Global superconvergence for optimal control problems governed by Stokes equations. *Int. J. Numer. Anal. Model.* **2006**,*3*, 283–302.
31. Adams, R.A.; Fournier, J.J.F. *Sobolev Spaces*; Academic Press: Cambridge, MA, USA, 2003.
32. Lin, Q.; Lin, J.F. *Finite Element Methods: Accuracy and Improvement*; Science Press: Beijing, China, 2006.
33. Heywood, J.G.; Rannacher, R. Finite element approximation of the nonstationary Navier-Stokes problem IV: Error analysis of second-order time-discretization. *SIAM J. Numer. Anal.* **1990**, *27*, 353–384. [CrossRef]
34. Gao, H.D. Optimal error analysis of Galerkin FEMs for nonlinear Joule heating equations. *J. Sci. Comput.* **2014**, *58*, 627–647. [CrossRef]
35. Xu, C.; Shi, D.Y.; Liao, X. Low order nonconforming mixed finite element method for nonstationary incompressible Navier-Stokes equations. *Appl. Math. Mech. Engl. Ed.* **2016**, *37*, 1095–1112. [CrossRef]

mathematics

MDPI

Article

A New Entropy Stable Finite Difference Scheme for Hyperbolic Systems of Conservation Laws

Zhizhuang Zhang [1], Xiangyu Zhou [1], Gang Li [1,*], Shouguo Qian [1] and Qiang Niu [2]

[1] School of Mathematics and Statistics, Qingdao University, Qingdao 266071, China; 2021020250@qdu.edu.cn (Z.Z.); 2021020245@qdu.edu.cn (X.Z.); shouguoqian@qdu.edu.cn (S.Q.)

[2] Department of Applied Mathematics, Xi'an Jiaotong-Liverpool University, Suzhou 215123, China; qiang.niu@xjtlu.edu.cn

* Correspondence: gangli1978@163.com

Abstract: The hyperbolic problem has a unique entropy solution, which maintains the entropy inequality. As such, people hope that the numerical results should maintain the discrete entropy inequalities accordingly. In view of this, people tend to construct entropy stable (ES) schemes. However, traditional numerical schemes cannot directly maintain discrete entropy inequalities. To address this, we here construct an ES finite difference scheme for the nonlinear hyperbolic systems of conservation laws. The proposed scheme can not only maintain the discrete entropy inequality, but also enjoy high-order accuracy. Firstly, we construct the second-order accurate semi-discrete entropy conservative (EC) schemes and ensure that the schemes meet the entropy identity when an entropy pair is given. Then, the second-order EC schemes are used as a building block to achieve the high-order accurate semi-discrete EC schemes. Thirdly, we add a dissipation term to the above schemes to obtain the high-order ES schemes. The term is based on the Weighted Essentially Non-Oscillatory (WENO) reconstruction. Finally, we integrate the scheme using the third-order Runge–Kutta (RK) approach in time. In the end, plentiful one- and two-dimensional examples are implemented to validate the capability of the scheme. In summary, the current scheme has sharp discontinuity transitions and keeps the genuine high-order accuracy for smooth solutions. Compared to the standard WENO schemes, the current scheme can achieve higher resolution.

Keywords: hyperbolic conservation laws; finite difference scheme; entropy stable scheme; high-order accuracy

MSC: 35L50; 65L12

1. Introduction

In this article, we concentrate on constructing high-order numerical schemes. Because of the high nonlinearity of the governing equations, theoretical analysis is very difficult. Numerical solving by high-order schemes is an effective approach and has attracted extensive attention in the field of scientific computing [1–3]. The nonlinear systems in one-dimensional (1D) space read as

$$\mathbf{U}_t + \mathbf{F}(\mathbf{U})_x = 0. \tag{1}$$

Representative research of high-order schemes for the nonlinear systems (1) mainly include: the kinetic scheme [4], gas-kinetic scheme [5], central-upwind scheme [6], weighted essentially non-oscillatory (WENO) schemes [7–16], Hermite WENO scheme [17], central schemes [18,19], the Runge–Kutta discontinuous Galerkin (RKDG) methods [20–22], ADER (Arbitrary DERivatives in space and time) schemes [23,24], spectral element method [25], Godunov-type method [26], element-free Galerkin method [27], and ADER-DG method [28]. For other high-order schemes, we refer to [29–33].

However, there may not be exact solutions when calculating the nonlinear systems of hyperbolic conservation laws (1). Therefore, we need to define the weak solutions in a distributional sense. However, these weak solutions may lack uniqueness. In fact, the entropy condition is significant in screening entropy solutions (physically relevant solutions) [34].

Definition 1 (Entropy function [35])**.** *A strictly convex function $\eta(\mathbf{U})$ can be an entropy function of the system* (1)*, if there exists associated entropy fluxes $q(\mathbf{U})$ such that*

$$q'(\mathbf{U}) = \mathbf{V}^\top \mathbf{F}'(\mathbf{U}), \tag{2}$$

where $\mathbf{V} = \eta'(\mathbf{U})^\top$ is an entropy variable and (η, q) is known as an entropy pair.

With respect to the given entropy pair (η, q), multiplying both sides of (1) by $\mathbf{V}^\top$, the solutions which are smooth of (1) meet the following identity

$$\frac{\partial \eta(\mathbf{U})}{\partial t} + \frac{\partial q(\mathbf{U})}{\partial x} = 0. \tag{3}$$

However, the above identity (3) no longer holds in the case of the emergence of discontinuous solutions. In particular, the entropy solution $\mathbf{U}$ meets the following inequality

$$\frac{\partial \eta(\mathbf{U})}{\partial t} + \frac{\partial q(\mathbf{U})}{\partial x} \leq 0. \tag{4}$$

Generally, both the entropy identity (3) and the entropy inequality (4) are called as the entropy conditions. Theoretically, entropy conditions play a crucial role with respect to the well-posedness of the systems such as (1). Numerically, high-order schemes which meet the above inequality according to (4) can improve its own robustness. Therefore, it is significant to construct schemes meeting entropy inequality with regard to a given entropy pair. The schemes satisfying discrete entropy inequality are also called entropy stable (ES) schemes. In recent years, the research on ES schemes has attracted wide attention, such as in: the discontinuous Galerkin (DG) spectral element method [36] nodal DG method [37], DG methods [38,39], and finite difference schemes [40].

The main aim of this article is to present a high-order ES scheme for the systems. Firstly, we establish a two-point EC flux to construct a second-order EC scheme, which satisfies the entropy identity. Next, we achieve a high-order EC scheme based on the above scheme. However, there might be numerical oscillations around discontinuity. To overcome this shortcoming, some suitable dissipation terms using the WENO reconstruction are performed to realize a high-order ES scheme, which satisfies the entropy inequality. Finally, the ES scheme is integrated with high-order RK approach and achieves the fully discrete high-order accurate scheme.

The structure of this paper is as follows: Firstly, we propose high-order EC and ES schemes for 1D nonlinear hyperbolic systems in Section 2. In Section 3, we expand the schemes to two dimensions (2D). In Section 4, we implement plentiful numerical examples to illustrate the performance of the proposed scheme. Finally, the conclusions are presented in Section 5.

2. Construction of One-Dimensional High-Order ES Scheme

2.1. The EC Schemes

Firstly, we divide the spatial domain by a uniform mesh with $x_0 < x_1 < x_2 < \cdots < x_N$ as the nodes together with the spatial step size $\Delta x = x_i - x_{i-1}$. The semi-discrete finite difference scheme for (1) has the following form

$$\frac{d}{dt}\mathbf{U}_i = -\frac{1}{\Delta x}\left(\widehat{\mathbf{F}}_{i+\frac{1}{2}} - \widehat{\mathbf{F}}_{i-\frac{1}{2}}\right). \tag{5}$$

Here , $\widehat{\mathbf{F}}_{i+\frac{1}{2}}$ is called the numerical flux approximating $\mathbf{F}$ at $x_{i+\frac{1}{2}} = x_i + \Delta x/2$. For example, $\widehat{\mathbf{F}}_{i+\frac{1}{2}} = \widehat{\mathbf{F}}_{i+\frac{1}{2}}(u_i, u_{i+1})$ is a two-point flux.

In particular, scheme (5) is known as ES if the solution of (5) satisfies the following semi-discrete entropy identity

$$\frac{d}{dt}\eta(\mathbf{U}_i) + \frac{1}{\Delta x}\left(\widetilde{q}_{i+\frac{1}{2}} - \widetilde{q}_{i-\frac{1}{2}}\right) = 0, \tag{6}$$

for the numerical entropy flux $\widetilde{q}_{i+\frac{1}{2}}$, which is consistent with the entropy flux q. Thus, the numerical flux $\widehat{\mathbf{F}}_{i+\frac{1}{2}}$ is called the EC flux correspondingly.

The following lemma presents a sufficient condition for the semi-discrete scheme (5) to be EC.

Lemma 1. *The semi-discrete scheme* (5) *is EC and second-order accurate, provided that a symmetric consistent two-point numerical flux* $\widehat{\mathbf{F}}_{i+\frac{1}{2}} := \widehat{\mathbf{F}}(\mathbf{U}_i, \mathbf{U}_{i+1})$ *used in* (5) *satisfies*

$$[[\mathbf{V}]]^{\top}\widehat{\mathbf{F}} = [[\Psi]], \tag{7}$$

where $[[a]] = a_{i+1} - a_i$. *The numerical entropy flux in* (6) *enjoys the form*

$$\widetilde{q}_{i+\frac{1}{2}} = \{\{\mathbf{V}\}\}^{\top}_{i+\frac{1}{2}}\widehat{\mathbf{F}}_{i+\frac{1}{2}} - \{\{\Psi\}\}_{i+\frac{1}{2}}, \tag{8}$$

with the following notation $\{\{a\}\}_{i+\frac{1}{2}} = \frac{1}{2}(a_i + a_{i+1})$.

Proof. Multiplying both sides of (5) by $\mathbf{V}_i^{\top}$ gives

$$\frac{d\eta_i}{dt} = -\frac{1}{\Delta x}\left[\mathbf{V}_i^{\top}\left(\widehat{\mathbf{F}}_{i+\frac{1}{2}} - \widehat{\mathbf{F}}_{i-\frac{1}{2}}\right)\right].$$

We can rearrange the items on the right side:

$$\begin{aligned}
&\mathbf{V}_i^{\top}\left(\widehat{\mathbf{F}}_{i+\frac{1}{2}} - \widehat{\mathbf{F}}_{i-\frac{1}{2}}\right)\\
=&\left(\{\{\mathbf{V}\}\}_{i+\frac{1}{2}} - \frac{1}{2}[[\mathbf{V}]]_{i+\frac{1}{2}}\right)^{\top}\widehat{\mathbf{F}}_{i+\frac{1}{2}} - \left(\{\{\mathbf{V}\}\}_{i-\frac{1}{2}} + \frac{1}{2}[[\mathbf{V}]]_{i-\frac{1}{2}}\right)^{\top}\widehat{\mathbf{F}}_{i-\frac{1}{2}}\\
=&\{\{\mathbf{V}\}\}^{\top}_{i+\frac{1}{2}}\widehat{\mathbf{F}}_{i+\frac{1}{2}} - \frac{1}{2}[[\Psi]]_{i+\frac{1}{2}} - \{\{\mathbf{V}\}\}^{\top}_{i-\frac{1}{2}}\widehat{\mathbf{F}}_{i-\frac{1}{2}} - \frac{1}{2}[[\Psi]]_{i-\frac{1}{2}}\\
=&\left(\{\{\mathbf{V}\}\}^{\top}_{i+\frac{1}{2}}\widehat{\mathbf{F}}_{i+\frac{1}{2}} - \{\{\Psi\}\}_{i+\frac{1}{2}}\right) - \left(\{\{\mathbf{V}\}\}^{\top}_{i-\frac{1}{2}}\widehat{\mathbf{F}}_{i-\frac{1}{2}} - \{\{\Psi\}\}_{i-\frac{1}{2}}\right)\\
=&\widetilde{q}_{i+\frac{1}{2}} - \widetilde{q}_{i-\frac{1}{2}}.
\end{aligned}$$

In the above derivation process, we use the notations $a_i = \{\{a\}\}_{i+\frac{1}{2}} - \frac{1}{2}[[a]]_{i+\frac{1}{2}}$ and $a_i = \{\{a\}\}_{i-\frac{1}{2}} + \frac{1}{2}[[a]]_{i-\frac{1}{2}}$ in the first equality; we employ condition (7) in the second one. In addition, we apply the equality $\frac{1}{2}[[a]]_{i+\frac{1}{2}} + \frac{1}{2}[[a]]_{i-\frac{1}{2}} = \{\{a\}\}_{i+\frac{1}{2}} - \{\{a\}\}_{i-\frac{1}{2}}$ in the third one. Therefore, scheme (5) is EC with the form

$$\frac{d\eta_i}{dt} + \frac{1}{\Delta x}\left(\widetilde{q}_{i+\frac{1}{2}} - \widetilde{q}_{i-\frac{1}{2}}\right) = 0,$$

together with the numerical flux $\widehat{\mathbf{F}}_{i+\frac{1}{2}} = \widehat{\mathbf{F}}_{i+\frac{1}{2}}(\mathbf{U}_i, \mathbf{U}_{i+1})$. Moreover, the results in [34] illustrate that the discretization of the flux gradient is also second-order accurate. Consequently, scheme (5) along with $\widehat{\mathbf{F}}_{i+\frac{1}{2}} = \widehat{\mathbf{F}}_{i+\frac{1}{2}}(\mathbf{U}_i, \mathbf{U}_{i+1})$ is second-order accurate. □

Then, we construct EC schemes for shallow water equations and Euler equations, respectively.

2.1.1. The EC Schemes for Shallow Water Equations

Next, we construct the EC schemes for the shallow water equations (SWEs), which describe a wave that affects the movement of water quality points when the ratio of water depth to wavelength is small. In one-dimensional space, the SWEs read as

$$\begin{pmatrix} h \\ hu \end{pmatrix}_t + \begin{pmatrix} hu \\ hu^2 + \frac{1}{2}gh^2 \end{pmatrix}_x = 0,$$

where h denotes the fluid height, u denotes the fluid velocity, and g is the gravitational constant.

For the one-dimensional SWEs, we find an entropy pair as

$$\eta = \eta(\mathbf{U}) = \frac{1}{2}(hu^2 + gh^2), \quad q = q(\mathbf{U}) = \frac{1}{2}hu^3 + gh^2u.$$

In fact, according to the general form of entropy condition,

$$\begin{aligned} \nabla q(\mathbf{U})^\top &= \nabla \eta(\mathbf{U})^\top \frac{\partial f(\mathbf{U})}{\partial \mathbf{U}} \\ &= \left(gh - \frac{1}{2}u^2, u\right)\begin{pmatrix} 0 & 1 \\ gh - u^2 & 2u \end{pmatrix} \\ &= \left(ghu - u^3, gh + \frac{3}{2}u^2\right). \end{aligned}$$

Then, we can obtain $q(\mathbf{U})$ by the integral computation of $\nabla q(\mathbf{U})$. Furthermore, the entropy variables and potential can be calculated as follows:

$$\mathbf{V} = \frac{\partial \eta(\mathbf{U})}{\partial \mathbf{U}} = \left(gh - \frac{1}{2}u^2, u\right)^\top, \quad \Psi = \mathbf{V}^\top \mathbf{F}(\mathbf{U}) - q(\mathbf{U}) = \frac{1}{2}gh^2u.$$

Accordingly, the second order EC numerical flux is

$$\widehat{\mathbf{F}} = \widehat{\mathbf{F}}(\mathbf{U}_i, \mathbf{U}_{i+1}) = \begin{pmatrix} \{\{h\}\}_{i+\frac{1}{2}}\{\{u\}\}_{i+\frac{1}{2}} \\ \{\{h\}\}_{i+\frac{1}{2}}(\{\{u\}\}_{i+\frac{1}{2}})^2 + \frac{g}{2}\{\{h^2\}\}_{i+\frac{1}{2}} \end{pmatrix}. \tag{9}$$

In particular, it is easy to demonstrate that the EC flux (9) is consistent with the physical flux $\mathbf{F}(\mathbf{U})$. Actually, letting $(h_L, u_L) = (h_R, u_R) = (h, u)$ in (9) leads to

$$\widehat{\mathbf{F}}^1 = hu \quad \text{and} \quad \widehat{\mathbf{F}}^2 = hu^2 + \frac{1}{2}gh^2.$$

2.1.2. Entropy Conservative Schemes for Euler Equations

The Euler equations are the most important fundamental equations in non-viscous fluid dynamics and these refer to the differential equation of motion obtained by applying Newton's second law to non-viscous fluid micromasses. For an ideal gas in one-dimensional space, the governing equations are as follows

$$\begin{pmatrix} \rho \\ \rho u \\ E \end{pmatrix}_t + \begin{pmatrix} \rho u \\ \rho u^2 + P \\ u(E+P) \end{pmatrix}_x = 0, \tag{10}$$

where ρ, u, and P denote the density, velocity, and pressure, respectively. The total energy is defined as $E = \frac{P}{\gamma-1} + \frac{1}{2}\rho u^2$, where γ is the gas constant. Moreover, let $s = log(p) - \gamma log(\rho)$

be the thermodynamic entropy. In this article, we take $\eta(\mathbf{U}) = \frac{-\rho s}{\gamma-1}$ as the entropy function. According to the general form of entropy condition, we have

$$\nabla q^{\top} = \nabla\eta(\mathbf{U})^{\top}\frac{\partial \mathbf{F}(\mathbf{U})}{\partial \mathbf{U}} = \left(u\frac{\gamma}{\gamma-1} - \frac{1}{2}\frac{\rho u^3}{P}, \frac{s}{1-\gamma} + \frac{\rho u^2}{P}, -\frac{\rho u}{P}\right),$$

where

$$\nabla\eta(\mathbf{U})^{\top} = \left(\frac{\partial\eta}{\partial\rho}, \frac{\partial\eta}{\partial(\rho u)}, \frac{\partial\eta}{\partial E}\right) = \left(\frac{\gamma-s}{\gamma-1} - \frac{\rho u^2}{2P}, \frac{\rho u}{P}, \frac{-\rho}{P}\right),$$

$$\frac{\partial \mathbf{F}(\mathbf{U})}{\partial \mathbf{U}} = \begin{pmatrix} \frac{\partial \rho u}{\partial \rho} & \frac{\partial \rho u}{\partial \rho u} & \frac{\partial \rho u}{E} \\ \frac{\partial(\rho u^2+\rho)}{\partial\rho} & \frac{\partial(\rho u^2+\rho)}{\partial\rho u} & \frac{\partial(\rho u^2+\rho)}{\partial E} \\ \frac{\partial(u(E+\rho))}{\partial\rho} & \frac{\partial(u(E+\rho))}{\partial\rho u} & \frac{\partial(u(E+\rho))}{\partial E} \end{pmatrix}$$

$$= \begin{pmatrix} 0 & 1 & 0 \\ \frac{\gamma-3}{2}u^2 & (3-\gamma)u & (\gamma-1) \\ -u(\frac{E+P}{\rho} - \frac{\gamma-1}{2}u^2) & \frac{E+P}{\rho} + (1-\gamma)u^2 & \gamma u \end{pmatrix}.$$

Obviously, we can obtain the entropy flux $q(\mathbf{U}) = \frac{-\rho u s}{\gamma-1}$, the entropy variable $\mathbf{V} = \nabla\eta = \left(\frac{\gamma-s}{\gamma-1} - \frac{\rho u^2}{2P}, \frac{\rho u}{P}, \frac{-\rho}{P}\right)^{\top}$, the entropy potential $\phi = \mathbf{V}\mathbf{U} - \eta(\mathbf{U}) = \rho$, and the entropy flux potential $\psi = \mathbf{V}^{\top}\mathbf{F}(\mathbf{U}) - q(\mathbf{U}) = \rho u$.

In a recent paper, Roe and Ismail [41] structured an EC flux to calculate the Euler equations. They defined a parameter vectors Z as

$$Z = (z_1, z_2, z_3) = \left(\sqrt{\frac{\rho}{P}}, \sqrt{\frac{\rho}{P}}u, \sqrt{\rho P}\right),$$

with which we then know that entropy conservation numerical flux

$$\mathbf{F}^{EC}_{i+\frac{1}{2}} = (\ \hat{\rho}\hat{u}, \hat{\rho}\hat{u}^2 + \hat{P}_1, \hat{\rho}\hat{u}\hat{H}\ )^{\top}.$$

Here, $\hat{}$ represents the average values of the following relations at the unit interface

$$\hat{\rho} = \overline{z_1} z_3^{ln}, \quad \hat{u} = \frac{\overline{z_2}}{\overline{z_1}}, \quad \hat{P}_1 = \frac{\hat{z_3}}{\hat{z_1}}, \quad \hat{P}_2 = \frac{\gamma+1}{2\gamma}\frac{z_3^{ln}}{z_1^{ln}} + \frac{\gamma-1}{2\gamma}\frac{z_3^{ln}}{z_1^{ln}}, \quad \hat{H} = \frac{1}{2}\hat{u}^2 + \frac{\gamma}{\gamma-1}\frac{\hat{P}_2}{\hat{\rho}},$$

where $a^{ln}_{i+\frac{1}{2}} = \frac{a_{i+1}-a_i}{ln(a_{i+1})-ln(a_i)}$.

2.2. The High-Order EC Scheme

Based on the existing second-order EC scheme, our next task is to construct high-order EC schemes.

Following the means from [42], we construct the EC flux of the $2p$th-order accurate scheme by means of the linear convex combinations of the existing second-order accurate EC flux (9), namely,

$$\widetilde{\mathbf{F}}^{2pth}_{i+\frac{1}{2}} = \sum_{r=1}^{p}\alpha_r^p \sum_{s=0}^{p}\widetilde{\mathbf{F}}(\mathbf{U}_{i-s}, \mathbf{U}_{i-s+r}), \tag{11}$$

which satisfies

$$\frac{1}{\Delta x}\left(\widetilde{\mathbf{F}}^{2pth}_{i+\frac{1}{2}} - \widetilde{\mathbf{F}}^{2pth}_{i-\frac{1}{2}}\right) = \left.\frac{\partial \mathbf{F}}{\partial x}\right|_{x_i} + \mathcal{O}(\Delta x^{2p}),$$

for more details, we refer to [42].

In summary, we acquire the following $2p$th-order semi-discrete EC scheme

$$\frac{d}{dt}\mathbf{U}_i = -\frac{1}{\Delta x}\left(\widetilde{\mathbf{F}}^{2pth}_{i+\frac{1}{2}} - \widetilde{\mathbf{F}}^{2pth}_{i-\frac{1}{2}}\right) \tag{12}$$

to approximate (5). Accordingly, the high-order numerical entropy flux reads as follows

$$\widetilde{q}^{2pth}_{i+\frac{1}{2}} = \sum_{r=1}^{p}\alpha_r^p\sum_{s=0}^{p}\widetilde{q}(\mathbf{U}_{i-s},\mathbf{U}_{i-s+r}),$$

which is actually a linear combination of the two-point numerical entropy flux in (8).

In this study, we take $p = 3$ and obtain the following 6th-order accurate EC flux

$$\begin{aligned}\widetilde{\mathbf{F}}^{6th}_{i+\frac{1}{2}} = &\frac{3}{2}\widetilde{\mathbf{F}}(\mathbf{U}_i,\mathbf{U}_{i+1}) - \frac{3}{10}\left(\widetilde{\mathbf{F}}(\mathbf{U}_{i-1},\mathbf{U}_{i+1}) + \widetilde{\mathbf{F}}(\mathbf{U}_i,\mathbf{U}_{i+2})\right)\\ &+\frac{1}{30}\left(\widetilde{\mathbf{F}}(\mathbf{U}_{i-2},\mathbf{U}_{i+1}) + \widetilde{\mathbf{F}}(\mathbf{U}_{i-1},\mathbf{U}_{i+2}) + \widetilde{\mathbf{F}}(\mathbf{U}_i,\mathbf{U}_{i+3})\right).\end{aligned} \tag{13}$$

2.3. High-Order ES Scheme

It is well known that, for the nonlinear hyperbolic system of conservation laws, the entropy identity is only available when the solutions are smooth. In other words, the entropy is not conserved due to the presence of discontinuities such as the shock waves. Moreover, the EC scheme may produce non-physical oscillations near the strong discontinuities. These phenomena motivate us to develop the ES scheme by adding a suitable dissipation term to the EC scheme. The main purpose is to make the resulting ES scheme meet the inequality according to (4) for the given entropy pair. Furthermore, the ES scheme can avoid the non-physical oscillations. Following the idea from [34], we append a dissipation term to the EC flux $\widetilde{\mathbf{F}}_{i+\frac{1}{2}}$ and obtain the ES flux with the form

$$\widehat{\mathbf{F}}_{i+\frac{1}{2}} = \widetilde{\mathbf{F}}_{i+\frac{1}{2}} - \frac{1}{2}\mathbf{D}_{i+\frac{1}{2}}[[\mathbf{V}]]_{i+\frac{1}{2}}, \tag{14}$$

which satisfies

$$[[\mathbf{V}]]^{\top}\widehat{\mathbf{F}}_{i+\frac{1}{2}} - [[\Psi]] \leq 0, \tag{15}$$

where $\mathbf{D}$ is a positive semidefinite matrix. Herein, we adopt

$$\mathbf{D} = \mathbf{R}|\Lambda|\mathbf{R}^{\top}, \tag{16}$$

where $\mathbf{R}$ denotes the matrix of right eigenvectors of the Jocabian matrix $\frac{\partial \mathbf{F}}{\partial \mathbf{U}}$, and $|\Lambda| = \mathrm{diag}(|\lambda_1|,|\lambda_2|,\cdots,|\lambda_m|)$ with $\lambda_1 < \lambda_2 < \cdots < \lambda_m$ as the eigenvalues of $\frac{\partial \mathbf{F}}{\partial \mathbf{U}}$.

In addition, we also need to improve the dissipation term in (14) to obtain the high-order ES scheme ultimately. For instance, Fjordholm et al. [43] have constructed high-order ES scheme using the Essentially Non-Oscillatory (ENO) reconstruction with respect to the scaled entropy variables $\mathbf{w} = \mathbf{R}^{\top}\mathbf{V}$. More specifically, Fjordholm et al. [43] apply the kth order accurate ENO reconstruction of $\mathbf{w}$ to obtain $\mathbf{w}^-_{i+\frac{1}{2}}$ and $\mathbf{w}^+_{i+\frac{1}{2}}$, then define

$$\langle\langle \mathbf{w}\rangle\rangle_{i+\frac{1}{2}} = \mathbf{w}^+_{i+\frac{1}{2}} - \mathbf{w}^-_{i+\frac{1}{2}},$$

and construct the numerical flux as follows,

$$\widehat{\mathbf{F}}^{kth}_{i+\frac{1}{2}} = \widetilde{\mathbf{F}}^{2pth}_{i+\frac{1}{2}} - \frac{1}{2}\alpha_{i+\frac{1}{2}}\mathbf{R}_{i+\frac{1}{2}}\langle\langle \mathbf{w}\rangle\rangle_{i+\frac{1}{2}}, \tag{17}$$

where $p = (k+1)/2$ for odd k and $p = k/2$ for even k.

Combining the ES flux with the reconstructed jump in $\widetilde{\mathbf{F}}^{2pth}$ (17) leads to the following kth-order ES scheme

$$\frac{d}{dt}\mathbf{U}_i = -\frac{1}{\Delta x}\left(\widehat{\mathbf{F}}^{kth}_{i+\frac{1}{2}} - \widehat{\mathbf{F}}^{kth}_{i-\frac{1}{2}}\right). \tag{18}$$

Actually, the above scheme (18) is ES provided that the reconstruction satisfies the following "sign property" from [43]

$$sign\left(\langle\langle \mathbf{w}\rangle\rangle_{i+\frac{1}{2}}\right) = sign\left([[\mathbf{w}]]_{i+\frac{1}{2}}\right). \tag{19}$$

Especially, the ENO reconstruction holds the property (19); see [44] for more details.

Moreover, one can also obtain a higher-order accurate ES scheme with the WENO reconstruction instead of the ENO reconstruction if the same number of candidate points values are used. For example, it is possible to perform the fifth-order WENO reconstruction based on

$$\begin{aligned} \mathbf{w}_j &= \mathbf{R}^{\top}_{i+\frac{1}{2}}\mathbf{V}_j, \quad j = i-2, i-1, i, i+1, i+2, \\ \mathbf{w}_j &= \mathbf{R}^{\top}_{i+\frac{1}{2}}\mathbf{V}_j, \quad j = i-1, i, i+1, i+2, i+3, \end{aligned}$$

to obtain $\mathbf{w}^{-,\text{WENO}}_{i+\frac{1}{2}}$ and $\mathbf{w}^{+,\text{WENO}}_{i+\frac{1}{2}}$ respectively, so that the high-order WENO dissipation term is given by $-\frac{1}{2}\alpha_{i+\frac{1}{2}}\mathbf{R}_{i+\frac{1}{2}}\langle\langle \mathbf{w}\rangle\rangle_{i+\frac{1}{2}}$ with $\langle\langle \mathbf{w}\rangle\rangle_{i+\frac{1}{2}} := \mathbf{w}^{+,\text{WENO}}_{i+\frac{1}{2}} - \mathbf{w}^{-,\text{WENO}}_{i+\frac{1}{2}}$. Here, we take $\alpha_{i+\frac{1}{2}} = \max_i\{|u| + c\}$, with $c = \sqrt{gh}$ for the SWEs and $c = \sqrt{\frac{\gamma p}{\rho}}$ for the Euler equations, respectively. However, the standard WENO reconstruction may not satisfy the "sign property" (19). To meet the "sign property", following the procedure from [45], the dissipation term may be altered

$$\widehat{\mathbf{F}}^{kth}_{i+\frac{1}{2}} = \widetilde{\mathbf{F}}^{2pth}_{i+\frac{1}{2}} - \frac{1}{2}\alpha_{i+\frac{1}{2}}\mathbf{S}_{i+\frac{1}{2}}\mathbf{R}_{i+\frac{1}{2}}\langle\langle \mathbf{w}\rangle\rangle_{i+\frac{1}{2}}, \tag{20}$$

where $\mathbf{S}^l_{i+\frac{1}{2}}$ is a switch function defined by

$$\mathbf{S}^l_{i+\frac{1}{2}} = \begin{cases} 1, & \text{if sign}\left(\langle\langle \mathbf{w}\rangle\rangle^l_{i+\frac{1}{2}}\right) = \text{sign}\left([[\mathbf{w}]]^l_{i+\frac{1}{2}}\right), \\ 0, & \text{otherwise}, \end{cases} \tag{21}$$

as in [45] for the sign preserving property. Here, the superscript l denotes the lth component of the jump of $\mathbf{w}$ or the lth entry of the diagonal matrix $\mathbf{S}_{i+\frac{1}{2}}$. Then, the final ES flux is given as

$$\widehat{\mathbf{F}}^{kth}_{i+\frac{1}{2}} = \widetilde{\mathbf{F}}^{2pth}_{i+\frac{1}{2}} - \frac{1}{2}\alpha_{i+\frac{1}{2}}\mathbf{S}_{i+\frac{1}{2}}\mathbf{R}_{i+\frac{1}{2}}\langle\langle \mathbf{w}\rangle\rangle_{i+\frac{1}{2}}, \tag{22}$$

following [35].

The new scheme (18) is ES and the demonstration is as follows. This treatment has been used in [35] to construct the high-order ES scheme for the shallow water Magneto-hydrodynamics.

2.4. The Temporal Discretization

Scheme (18) reads as the following ordinary differential equations (ODE)

$$\frac{d}{dt}\mathbf{U}_i = \mathcal{F}(\mathbf{U}_i) := -\frac{1}{\Delta x}\left(\widehat{\mathbf{F}}^{kth}_{i+\frac{1}{2}} - \widehat{\mathbf{F}}^{kth}_{i-\frac{1}{2}}\right). \tag{23}$$

Then, we use the third-order RK approach

$$\begin{aligned} \mathbf{U}^{(1)} &= \mathbf{U}^n + \Delta t \mathcal{F}(\mathbf{U}^n), \\ \mathbf{U}^{(2)} &= \frac{3}{4}\mathbf{U}^n + \frac{1}{4}(\mathbf{U}^{(1)} + \Delta t \mathcal{F}(\mathbf{U}^{(1)})), \\ \mathbf{U}^{n+1} &= \frac{1}{3}\mathbf{U}^n + \frac{2}{3}(\mathbf{U}^{(2)} + \Delta t \mathcal{F}(\mathbf{U}^{(2)})), \end{aligned} \tag{24}$$

for the temporal discretization to the above ODE (23).

2.5. Summary of the Proposed Scheme

The concrete procedures of scheme (18) for the 1D system (1) are summarized as follows:

(1) First, obtain point values $\{\mathbf{U}_i\}_{i=1}^N$.
(2) Construct the high-order EC flux as in (11).
(3) Calculate the dissipation term, add it to the original EC flux (11), and build the high-order ES flux (20).
(4) Obtain the semi-discrete scheme (23).
(5) Apply the RK approach (24).
(6) Repeat steps (2)–(5).

3. Extension to a Two-Dimensional System

We extend the one-dimensional scheme to the following two-dimensional problems

$$\frac{\partial \mathbf{U}}{\partial t} + \frac{\partial \mathbf{F}(\mathbf{U})}{\partial x} + \frac{\partial \mathbf{G}(\mathbf{U})}{\partial y} = 0. \tag{25}$$

Firstly, we deal with a rectangle computational domain $\Omega = [a, b] \times [c, d]$ discretized uniformly by N_x and N_y cells in the x- and y-direction, respectively. The cells are labeled by $I_{i,j} = \left[x_{i-\frac{1}{2}}, x_{i+\frac{1}{2}}\right], \left[y_{j-\frac{1}{2}}, y_{j+\frac{1}{2}}\right]$ with $\Delta x = x_{i+\frac{1}{2}} - x_{i-\frac{1}{2}}$ and $\Delta y = y_{j+\frac{1}{2}} - y_{j-\frac{1}{2}}$ as the cell sizes.

A semi-discrete finite difference scheme for (25) enjoys the following form

$$\frac{\mathrm{d}}{\mathrm{d}t}\mathbf{U}_{i,j} + \frac{1}{\Delta x}\left(\widehat{\mathbf{F}}_{i+\frac{1}{2},j} - \widehat{\mathbf{F}}_{i-\frac{1}{2},j}\right) + \frac{1}{\Delta y}\left(\widehat{\mathbf{G}}_{i,j+\frac{1}{2}} - \widehat{\mathbf{G}}_{i,j-\frac{1}{2}}\right) = 0. \tag{26}$$

Here, $\widehat{\mathbf{F}}_{i+\frac{1}{2},j}$ and $\widehat{\mathbf{G}}_{i,j+\frac{1}{2}}$ denote numerical fluxes at inter-cells in the x- and y-direction, respectively.

3.1. The Two-Dimensional SWEs

With respect to the two-dimensional space, the SWEs from (25) are accompanied by

$$\mathbf{U} = \begin{pmatrix} h \\ hu \\ hv \end{pmatrix}, \ \mathbf{F}(\mathbf{U}) = \begin{pmatrix} hu \\ hu^2 + \frac{1}{2}gh^2 \\ huv \end{pmatrix}, \ \mathbf{G}(\mathbf{U}) = \begin{pmatrix} hv \\ huv \\ hv^2 + \frac{1}{2}gh^2 \end{pmatrix}.$$

In analogy to the 1D space, we take the following entropy function

$$\eta(\mathbf{U}) = \frac{1}{2}(hu^2 + hv^2 + gh^2),$$

along with the entropy variables

$$\mathbf{V} = \eta'(\mathbf{U})^\top = \left(gh - \frac{1}{2}u^2 - \frac{1}{2}v^2, u, v\right)^\top.$$

The entropy fluxes in the x- and y-directions are defined by

$$q^x = \frac{1}{2}hu^3 + gh^2u + \frac{1}{2}(hu)v^2,$$
$$q^y = \frac{1}{2}hv^3 + gh^2v + \frac{1}{2}(hv)u^2.$$

The EC fluxes are defined by

$$\widetilde{\mathbf{F}}_{i+\frac{1}{2},j} = \widetilde{\mathbf{F}}(\mathbf{U}_{i,j}, \mathbf{U}_{i+1,j}) = \begin{pmatrix} \{\{h\}\}_{i+\frac{1}{2},j}\{\{u\}\}_{i+\frac{1}{2},j} \\ \{\{h\}\}_{i+\frac{1}{2},j}\{\{u\}\}^2_{i+\frac{1}{2},j} + \frac{g}{2}\{\{h^2\}\}_{i+\frac{1}{2},j} \\ \{\{h\}\}_{i+\frac{1}{2},j}\{\{u\}\}_{i+\frac{1}{2},j}\{\{v\}\}_{i+\frac{1}{2},j} \end{pmatrix},$$

$$\widetilde{\mathbf{G}}_{i,j+\frac{1}{2}} = \widetilde{\mathbf{G}}(\mathbf{U}_{i,j}, \mathbf{U}_{i,j+1}) = \begin{pmatrix} \{\{h\}\}_{i,j+\frac{1}{2}}\{\{v\}\}_{i,j+\frac{1}{2}} \\ \{\{h\}\}_{i,j+\frac{1}{2}}\{\{u\}\}_{i,j+\frac{1}{2}}\{\{v\}\}_{i,j+\frac{1}{2}} \\ \{\{h\}\}_{i,j+\frac{1}{2}}\{\{v\}\}^2_{i,j+\frac{1}{2}} + \frac{g}{2}\{\{h^2\}\}_{i,j+\frac{1}{2}} \end{pmatrix}.$$

3.2. The Two-Dimensional Euler Equations

In addition, the 2D Euler equations from (25) have

$$\mathbf{U} = \begin{pmatrix} \rho \\ \rho u \\ \rho v \\ E \end{pmatrix}, \ \mathbf{F}(\mathbf{U}) = \begin{pmatrix} \rho u \\ \rho u^2 + P \\ \rho uv \\ (E+P)u \end{pmatrix}, \ \mathbf{G}(\mathbf{U}) = \begin{pmatrix} \rho v \\ \rho uv \\ \rho v^2 + P \\ (E+P)v \end{pmatrix}.$$

Here, the density ρ, the velocity field (u, v), the pressure P, and the total energy P are related by the equation of state

$$E = \frac{P}{\gamma - 1} + \frac{1}{2}\rho(u^2 + v^2).$$

The entropy function, fluxes, variables, and potentials are given by $\eta(\mathbf{U}) = \frac{-\rho s}{\gamma-1}$, $q^x(\mathbf{U}) = \frac{-\rho us}{\gamma-1}$, $q^y(\mathbf{U}) = \frac{-\rho vs}{\gamma-1}$, $\mathbf{V} = \nabla\eta = \left(\frac{\gamma-s}{\gamma-1} - \frac{\rho(u^2+v^2)}{2P}, \frac{\rho u}{P}, \frac{\rho v}{P}, \frac{-\rho}{P}\right)^\top$, $\psi^x = \rho u$, $\psi^y = \rho v$, with s being the thermodynamic entropy.

Defining the parameter vectors Z as

$$Z = \left(\sqrt{\frac{\rho}{P}}, \sqrt{\frac{\rho}{P}}u, \sqrt{\frac{\rho}{P}}v, \sqrt{\rho P}\right).$$

Then, EC fluxes are given by $\widetilde{\mathbf{F}}_{i+\frac{1}{2}} = \left(\widetilde{\mathbf{F}}^1_{i+\frac{1}{2}}, \widetilde{\mathbf{F}}^2_{i+\frac{1}{2}}, \widetilde{\mathbf{F}}^3_{i+\frac{1}{2}}, \widetilde{\mathbf{F}}^4_{i+\frac{1}{2}}\right)^\top$ and $\widetilde{\mathbf{G}}_{i+\frac{1}{2}} = (\widetilde{\mathbf{G}}^1_{i+\frac{1}{2}}, \widetilde{\mathbf{G}}^2_{i+\frac{1}{2}}, \widetilde{\mathbf{G}}^3_{i+\frac{1}{2}}, \widetilde{\mathbf{G}}^4_{i+\frac{1}{2}})^\top$ with

$$\widetilde{\mathbf{F}}^1_{i+\frac{1}{2},j} = \overline{z_2} z_4^{ln},$$
$$\widetilde{\mathbf{F}}^2_{i+\frac{1}{2},j} = \frac{\overline{z_4}}{\overline{z_1}} + \frac{\overline{z_2}}{\overline{z_1}}\widetilde{\mathbf{F}}^1_{i+\frac{1}{2},j},$$
$$\widetilde{\mathbf{F}}^3_{i+\frac{1}{2},j} = \frac{\overline{z_3}}{\overline{z_1}}\widetilde{\mathbf{F}}^1_{i+\frac{1}{2},j},$$
$$\widetilde{\mathbf{F}}^4_{i+\frac{1}{2},j} = \frac{1}{2\overline{z_1}}\left(\frac{\gamma+1}{\gamma-1}\frac{\widetilde{\mathbf{F}}^1_{i+\frac{1}{2},j}}{z_1^{ln}} + \overline{z_2}\widetilde{\mathbf{F}}^2_{i+\frac{1}{2},j} + \overline{z_3}\widetilde{\mathbf{F}}^3_{i+\frac{1}{2},j}\right),$$

and

$$\widetilde{\mathbf{G}}^1_{i,j+\frac{1}{2}} = \overline{z_3} z_4^{ln},$$
$$\widetilde{\mathbf{G}}^2_{i,j+\frac{1}{2}} = \frac{\overline{z_2}}{\overline{z_1}} \widetilde{\mathbf{G}}^1_{i,j+\frac{1}{2}},$$
$$\widetilde{\mathbf{G}}^3_{i,j+\frac{1}{2}} = \frac{\overline{z_4}}{\overline{z_1}} + \frac{\overline{z_3}}{\overline{z_1}} \widetilde{\mathbf{G}}^1_{i,j+\frac{1}{2}},$$
$$\widetilde{\mathbf{G}}^4_{i,j+\frac{1}{2}} = \frac{1}{2\overline{z_1}} \left(\frac{\gamma+1}{\gamma-1} \frac{\widetilde{\mathbf{G}}^1_{i,j+\frac{1}{2}}}{z_1^{ln}} + \overline{z_2} \widetilde{\mathbf{G}}^2_{i,j+\frac{1}{2}} + \overline{z_3} \widetilde{\mathbf{G}}^3_{i,j+\frac{1}{2}} \right).$$

Similarly, we can construct high-order ES schemes for the 2D SWEs and Euler equations.

4. Numerical Results

In this section, extensive examples are presented to show that the scheme performs well. First, we take the time step meeting the following condition $\Delta t = CFL\frac{\Delta x}{\alpha}$ for the numerical stability. Here, α denotes the estimation of the maximum wave propagation velocity. In addition, the CFL (Courant, Friedrichs, Lewy) number is taken as 0.18 in all the computations. In addition, we present the numerical results by the fifth-order finite difference WENO schemes to make a comparison.

4.1. The SWEs

4.1.1. Example 1

The initial data of the first example is as follows

$$(h,u)(x,0) = \begin{cases} (1,2.5), & \text{if } 0 \le x \le 10, \\ (0.1,0), & \text{otherwise,} \end{cases}$$

on a domain $[0,50]$. Figure 1 shows the solutions at $t = 7$ on a mesh with 200 cells.

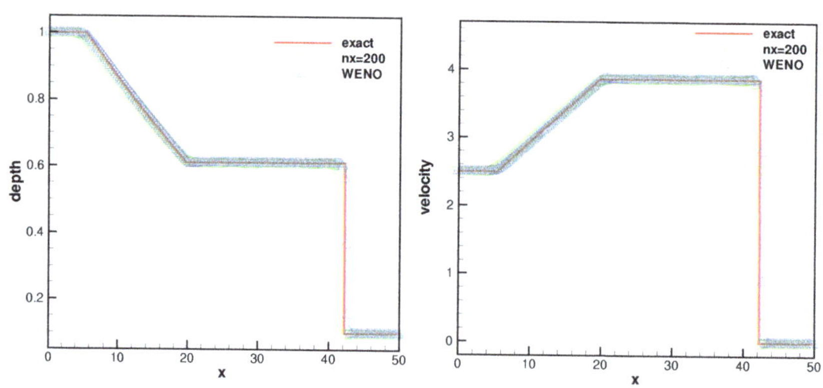

Figure 1. The depth h (**left**) and the velocity u (**right**) of the water in Example 1.

The numerical solutions are all well resolved and fit well with the exact results. In addition, the results fit well with the results by the WENO schemes.

4.1.2. Example 2

For the second example, we apply the following data

$$(h,u)(x,0) = \begin{cases} (1,0), & \text{if } 0 \le x \le 1000, \\ (0.5,0), & \text{otherwise,} \end{cases}$$

on a domain $[0,2000]$. Figure 2 presents the numerical solutions at $t = 240$.

Clearly, the current scheme produces well resolved solutions, which fit well with the exact solutions.

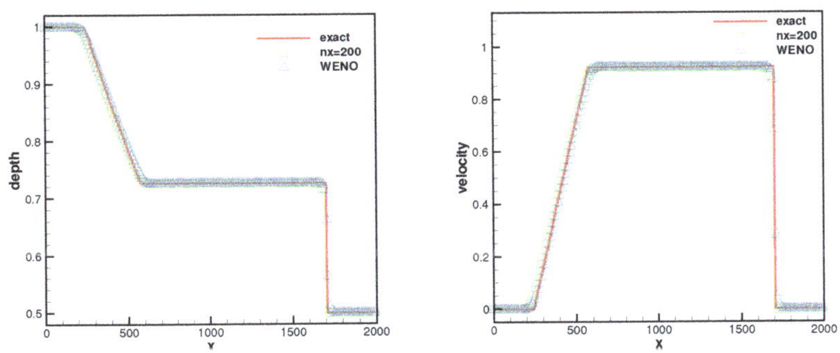

Figure 2. The depth h (**left**) and the velocity u (**right**) of the water in Example 2.

4.1.3. Example 3

Further, we adopt the following data

$$(h,u)(x,0) = \begin{cases} (1,-5), & \text{if } 0 \le x \le 25, \\ (1,5), & \text{otherwise,} \end{cases}$$

on a domain $[0,50]$. We implement it on a grid with 200 cells and compute this example until $t = 2.5$. Figure 3 presents the numerical solutions and indicates that the results fit well with the exact ones.

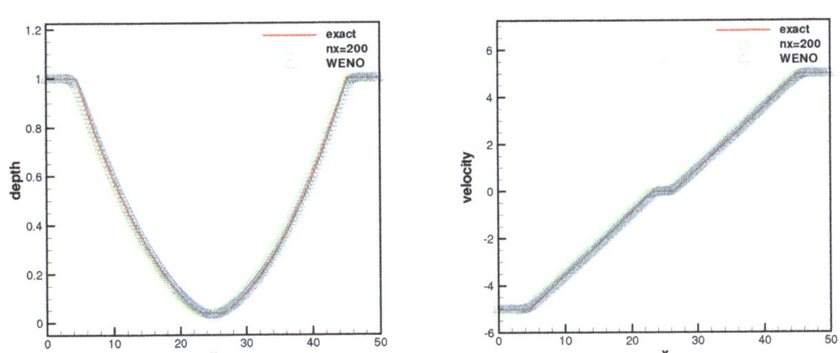

Figure 3. The depth h (**left**) and the velocity u (**right**) of the water in Example 3.

4.1.4. Example 4

Subsequently, we deal with a dam break example using the following data

$$(h,u)(x,0) = \begin{cases} (1,0), & \text{if } -1000 \le x \le 0, \\ (0.5,0), & \text{otherwise,} \end{cases}$$

on a domain $[-1000, 2000]$. Then, we solve it up to $t = 240$ on a grid with 200 cells.

Figure 4 shows the numerical solutions and indicates that the results are clearly consistent with the exact ones.

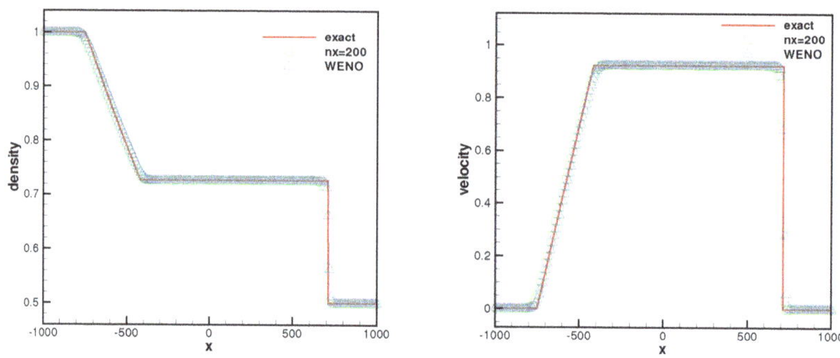

Figure 4. The depth h (**left**) and the velocity u (**right**) of the water in Example 4.

4.1.5. Example 5: Circular Dam Break Problem

Here, we simulate a circular dam break problem [46] for the 2D SWEs. We use this problem to testify the ability of the current scheme to maintain cylindrical symmetry. The following data are used for calculation.

$$h = \begin{cases} 10, & \text{if } \sqrt{(x-25)^2 + (y-25)^2} \leq 11, \\ 1, & \text{otherwise.} \end{cases}$$
$$u = v = 0.$$

The domain is $[0, 50] \times [0, 50]$ with the outflow boundary conditions.

Figure 5 presents the results $t = 0, 0.2, 0.4, 0.6, 0.8, 1.0$ obtained on a mesh with 200×200 cells, which shows that our ES scheme can well capture the wave structures.

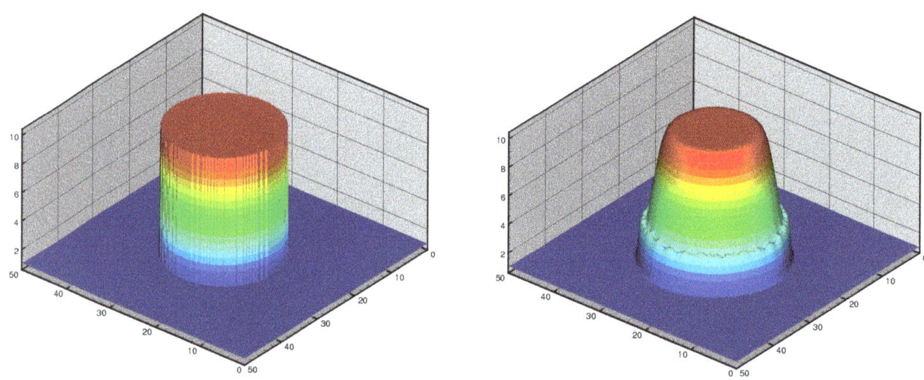

$t = 0$ $\qquad$ $t = 0.2$

Figure 5. *Cont.*

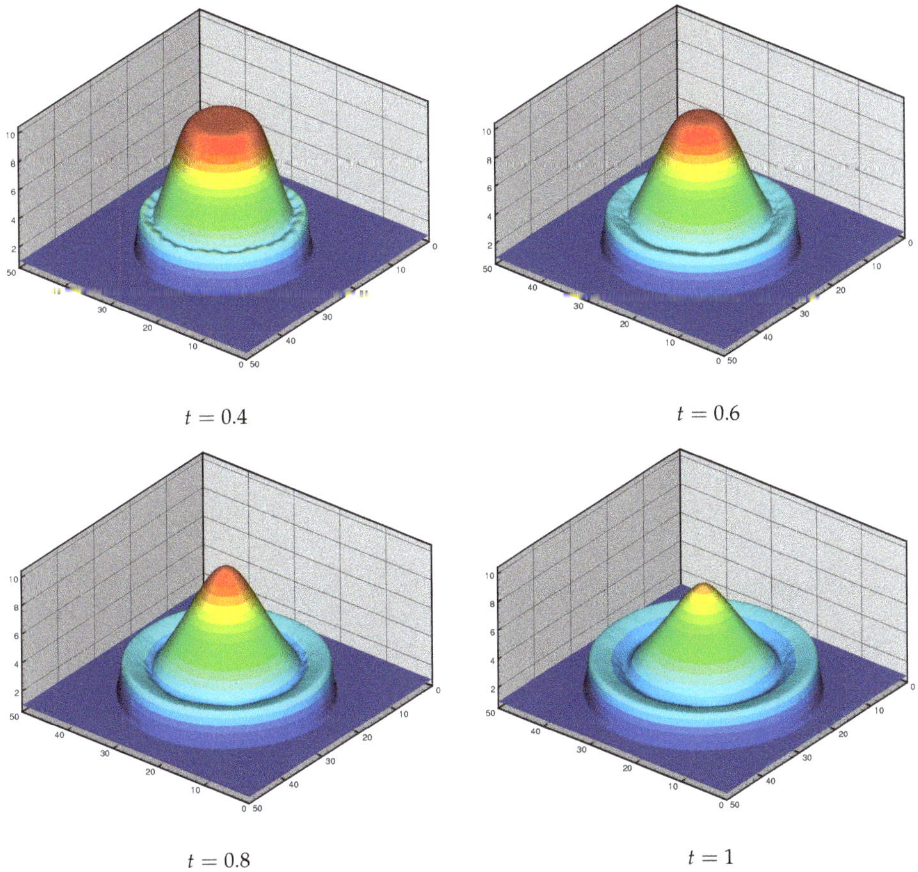

Figure 5. The contours of the height h on a mesh with 200×200 cells.

4.2. The Euler Equations of Gas Dynamics

4.2.1. Testing the Order of Accuracy

In order to demonstrate the order of accuracy, we take an example from [47].

$$\rho(x,t) = 1 + 0.2\sin(\pi(x-t)), \quad u(x,t) = 1, \quad p(x,t) = 1, \quad x \in [0,2].$$

We apply periodic boundary conditions on both ends of the domain. Table 1 shows the errors at time $t = 2$ and the orders of accuracy. It should be pointed out that we here take the step size of time as $\Delta t = CFL\dfrac{(\Delta x)^{\frac{5}{3}}}{\alpha}$ to keep the spatial errors dominant.

Table 1. The errors and orders of accuracy.

Cells	L^∞ Error	Order	L^1 Error	Order	L^2 Error	Order
25	7.1557×10^{-9}		5.4250×10^{-9}		4.6434×10^{-9}	
50	1.4620×10^{-9}	2.29	5.0198×10^{-10}	3.43	5.4977×10^{-10}	3.08
100	3.2688×10^{-11}	5.48	1.1626×10^{-11}	5.43	1.2667×10^{-11}	5.44
200	1.2699×10^{-12}	4.69	5.8475×10^{-13}	4.31	5.2894×10^{-13}	4.58

4.2.2. Sod Problem

The initial data are as in [48]

$$(\rho, u, p)(x, 0) = \begin{cases} (1, 0, 1) & \text{if } x \le 0, \\ (0.125, 0, 0.1) & \text{if } x > 0, \end{cases}$$

on $[-5, 5]$. Figure 6 shows the density at time $t = 2$. Clearly, the contact discontinuities are well decomposed and the results maintain a steep discontinuity transition.

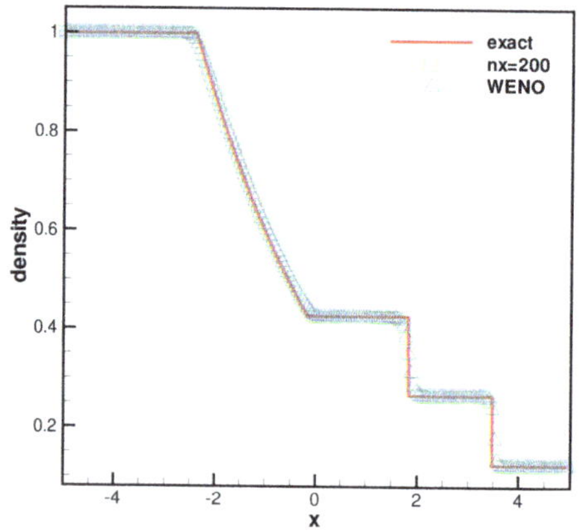

Figure 6. The density of the Sod problem at $t = 2$.

4.2.3. Lax Problem

We use the following data

$$(\rho, u, p)(x, 0) = \begin{cases} (0.445, 0.698, 3.528) & \text{if } x \le 0, \\ (0.5, 0, 0.571) & \text{if } x > 0, \end{cases}$$

on $[-5, 5]$. We can find a contact discontinuity that is hard to solve. Figure 7 shows the density at $t = 1.3$ and makes a comparison with the exact one.

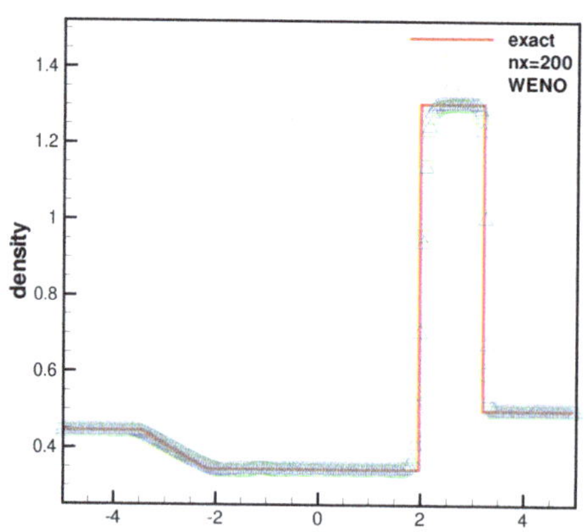

Figure 7. The density of the Lax problem at $t = 1.3$.

4.2.4. Shu–Osher Problem

We adopt the initial data from [49]

$$(\rho, u, p)(x, 0) = \begin{cases} (3.857143, 2.629369, 10.333333) & \text{if } x < -4, \\ (1 + 0.2\sin(5x), 0, 1) & \text{if } x \geq -4, \end{cases}$$

on a domain $[-5, 5]$. A shock is produced and it interacts with the smooth regions. Figure 8 presents the density at time $t = 1.8$.

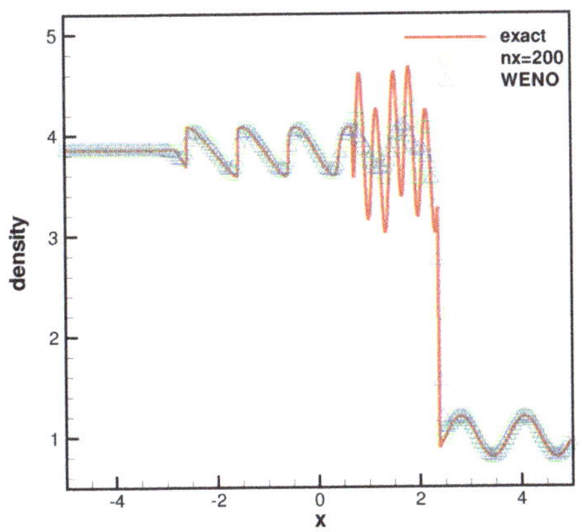

Figure 8. The density of the Shu-Osher problem at $t = 1.8$.

4.2.5. 123 Problem

The data are given by [50]

$$(\rho, u, p)(x, 0) = \begin{cases} (1, -2, 0.4) & \text{if } x < 0.5, \\ (1, 2, 0.4) & \text{if } x > 0.5, \end{cases}$$

on $[0, 1]$. Figure 9 shows the density at time $t = 0.15$. It is clear that the new scheme can adequately resolve the central expansion regions.

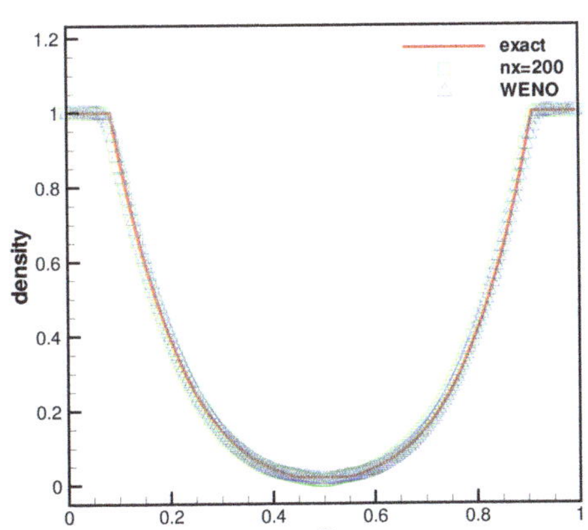

Figure 9. The density of the 123 problem at $t = 0.15$.

4.2.6. Modified Shock/Turbulence Interaction

We conduct an example [51] that is actually a modification of the shock/turbulence problem developed in [52,53]. The initial conditions are as follows

$$(\rho, u, p)(x, 0) = \begin{cases} (1.515695, 0.523346, 1.805) & \text{if } x \leq -4.5, \\ (1 + 0.1\sin(20\pi x), 0, 1) & \text{if } x > -4.5, \end{cases}$$

on a domain $[-5, 5]$. Using a mesh with 1000 cells, Figure 10 shows the density at time $t = 5$. Both schemes provide exceptional resolution for oscillations.

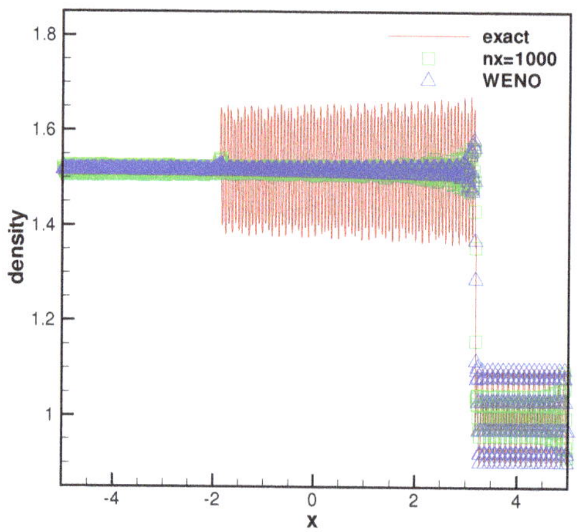

Figure 10. The density of the modified shock/turbulence interaction problem at $t = 5$.

5. Conclusions

This article proposes a high-order accurate ES finite difference scheme for nonlinear hyperbolic systems of conservation laws. This article mainly contains two innovative points: on one hand, a high-order accurate EC scheme is achieved by building the second-order EC schemes; on the other hand, the WENO reconstruction is employed based on the scaled entropy variables to obtain the high-order dissipation term. Furthermore, extensive results illustrate that the proposed scheme enjoys steep discontinuous transitions and keeps high-order accuracy. The current scheme can only be applied to uniform meshes or smooth transformed curve meshes for two-dimensional cases. In future research, we aim to expand the proposed scheme to uniform meshes.

Author Contributions: Conceptualization, G.L.; methodology, G.L.; software, Z.Z.; validation, X.Z.; Formal analysis, S.Q.; investigation, S.Q.; resources, Q.N.; data curation, X.Z.; writing—original draft preparation, Z.Z.; writing—review and editing, Z.Z.; visualization, Z.Z. All authors have read and agreed to the published version of the manuscript.

Funding: The author Shouguo Qian is supported by the Natural Science Foundation of Shandong Province (Grant No. ZR2021MA072).

Data Availability Statement: Not applicable.

Conflicts of Interest: The authors declare no conflict of interest.

References

1. Bradford, S.F.; Sanders, B.F. Finite volume model for shallow water flooding of arbitrary topography. *J. Hydraul. Eng.* **2002**, *128*, 289–298. [CrossRef]
2. Gottardi, G.; Venutelli, M. Central scheme for the two-dimensional dam-break flow simulation. *Adv. Water Resour.* **2004**, *27*, 259–268. [CrossRef]
3. Vreugdenhil, C.B. *Numerical Methods for Shallow-Water Flow*; Springer: Dordrecht, The Netherlands, 1995; pp. 15–25.

4. Perthame, B.; Simeoni, C. A kinetic scheme for the Saint-Venant system with a source term. *Calcolo* **2001**, *38*, 201–231. [CrossRef]
5. Xu, K. A well-balanced gas-kinetic scheme for the shallow-water equations with source terms. *J. Comput. Phys.* **2002**, *178*, 533–562. [CrossRef]
6. Kurganov, A.; Levy, D. Central-upwind schemes for the Saint-Venant system. *Math. Model. Numer. Anal.* **2002**, *36*, 397–425. [CrossRef]
7. Vukovic, S.; Sopta, L. ENO and WENO schemes with the exact conservation property for one-dimensional shallow water equations. *J. Comput. Phys.* **2002**, *179*, 593–621. [CrossRef]
8. Vukovic, S.; Crnjaric-Zic, N.; Sopta, L. WENO schemes for balance laws with spatially varying flux. *J. Comput. Phys.* **2004**, *199*, 87–109. [CrossRef]
9. Xing, Y.L.; Shu, C.-W. High order finite difference WENO schemes with the exact conservation property for the shallow water equations. *J. Comput. Phys.* **2005**, *208*, 206–227. [CrossRef]
10. Noelle, S.; Pankratz, N.; Puppo, G.; Natvig, J. Well-balanced finite volume schemes of arbitrary order of accuracy for shallow water flows. *J. Comput. Phys.* **2006**, *213*, 474–499. [CrossRef]
11. Xing, Y.L.; Shu, C.-W. High order well-balanced finite volume WENO schemes and discontinuous Galerkin methods for a class of hyperbolic systems with source terms. *J. Comput. Phys.* **2006**, *214*, 567–598. [CrossRef]
12. Noelle, S.; Xing, Y.; Shu, C.-W. High-order well-balanced finite volume WENO schemes for shallow water equation with moving water. *J. Comput. Phys.* **2007**, *226*, 29–58. [CrossRef]
13. Li, G.; Lu, C.; Qiu, J. Hybrid well-balanced WENO schemes with different indicators for shallow water equations. *J. Sci. Comput.* **2012**, *51*, 527–559. [CrossRef]
14. Li, G.; Caleffi, V.; Qi, Z.K. A well-balanced finite difference WENO scheme for shallow water flow model. *Appl. Math. Comput.* **2015**, *265*, 1–16. [CrossRef]
15. Zhu, Q.; Gao, Z.; Don, W.S.; Lv, X. Well-balanced hybrid compact-WENO scheme for shallow water equations. *Appl. Numer. Math.* **2017**, *112*, 65–78. [CrossRef]
16. Li, J.J.; Li, G.; Qian, S.G.; Gao, J.M. High-order well-balanced finite volume WENO schemes with conservative variables decomposition for shallow water equations. *Adv. Appl. Math. Mech.* **2021**, *13*, 827–849.
17. Caleffi, V. A new well-balanced Hermite weighted essentially non-oscillatory scheme for shallow water equations. *Int. J. Numer. Methods Fluids* **2011**, *67*, 1135–1159. [CrossRef]
18. Russo, G. Central schemes for balance laws. In Proceedings of the VIII International Conference on Nonlinear Hyperbolic Problems, Magdeburg, Germany, 28 February–3 March 2000.
19. Touma, R.; Khankan, S. Well-balanced unstaggered central schemes for one and two-dimensional shallow water equation systems. *Appl. Math. Comput.* **2012**, *218*, 5948–5960. [CrossRef]
20. Ern, A.; Piperno, S.; Djadel, K. A well-balanced Runge-Kutta discontinuous Galerkin method for the shallow-water equations with flooding and drying. *Int. J. Numer. Methods Fluids* **2008**, *58*, 1–25. [CrossRef]
21. Xing, Y. Exactly well-balanced discontinuous Galerkin methods for the shallow water equations with moving water equilibrium. *J. Comput. Phys.* **2014**, *257*, 536–553. [CrossRef]
22. Li, G.; Song, L.N.; Gao, J.M. High order well-balanced discontinuous Galerkin methods based on hydrostatic reconstruction for shallow water equations. *J. Comput. Appl. Math.* **2018**, *340*, 546–560. [CrossRef]
23. Vignoli, G.; Titarev, V.A.; Toro, E.F. ADER schemes for the shallow water equations in channel with irregular bottom elevation. *J. Comput.* **2008**, *227*, 2463–2480. [CrossRef]
24. Navas-Montilla, A.; Murillo, J. Energy balanced numerical schemes with very high order. The Augmented Roe Flux ADER scheme. Application to the shallow water equations. *J. Comput. Phys.* **2015**, *290*, 188–218. [CrossRef]
25. Gassner, G.J.; Winters, A.R.; Kopriva, D.A. A well balanced and entropy conservative discontinuous Galerkin spectral element method for the shallow water equations. *Appl. Math. Comput.* **2016**, *272*, 291–308. [CrossRef]
26. Berthon, C.; Chalons, C. A fully well-balanced, positive and entropy-satisfying Godunov-type method for the shallow-water equations. *Math. Comput.* **2016**, *85*, 1281–1307. [CrossRef]
27. Yuan, X.H. A well-balanced element-free Galerkin method for the nonlinear shallow water equations. *Appl. Math. Comput.* **2018**, *331*, 46–53. [CrossRef]
28. Li, G.; Li, J.J.; Qian, S.G.; Gao, J.M. A well-balanced ADER discontinuous Galerkin method based on differential transformation procedure for shallow water equations. *Appl. Math. Comput.* **2021**, *395*, 125848. [CrossRef]
29. Liu, Y.Y.; Yang, L.M.; Shu, C.; Zhang, H.W. Three-dimensional high-order least square-based finite difference-finite volume method on unstructured grids. *Phys. Fluids* **2020**, *32*, 123604. [CrossRef]
30. Liu, Y.Y.; Shu, C.; Yang, L.M.; Liu, Y.G.; Liu, W.; Zhang, Z.L. High-order implicit RBF-based differential quadrature-finite volume method on unstructured grids: Application to inviscid and viscous compressible flows. *J. Comput. Phys.* **2023**, *478*, 111962. [CrossRef]
31. Jitendra; Chaurasiya, V.; Rai, K.N.; Singh, J. Legendre wavelet residual approach for moving boundary problem with variable thermal physical properties. *Int. J. Nonlinear Sci. Numer. Simul.* **2022**, *23*, 947–956.
32. Chaurasiya, V.; Jain, A.; Singh, J. Numerical study of a non-linear porous sublimation problem with temperature-dependent thermal conductivity and Concentration-Dependent Mass Diffusivity. *ASME J. Heat Mass Transf.* **2023**, *145*, 072701. [CrossRef]

33. Chaudhary, R.K.; Chaurasiya, V.; Singh, J. Numerical estimation of temperature response with step heating of a multi-layer skin under the generalized boundary condition. *J. Therm. Biol.* **2022**, *108*, 103278. [CrossRef]
34. Fjordholm, U.S.; Mishra, S.; Tadmor, E. The numerical viscosity of entropy stable schemes for systems of conservation laws. I. *Math. Comput.* **1987**, *49*, 91–103.
35. Duan, J.M.; Tang, H.Z. High-order accurate entropy stable finite difference schemes for the shallow water magneto-hydrodynamics. *J. Comput. Phys.* **2021**, *431*, 110136. [CrossRef]
36. Winters, A.R.; Gassner, G.J. A comparison of two entropy stable discontinuous Galerkin spectral element approximations for the shallow water equations with non-constant topography Author links open overlay panel. *J. Comput. Phys.* **2015**, *301*, 357–376. [CrossRef]
37. Wintermeyer, N.; Winters, A.R.; Gassner, G.J.; Kopriva, D.A. An entropy stable nodal discontinuous Galerkin method for the two dimensional shallow water equations on unstructured curvilinear meshes with discontinuous bathymetry. *J. Comput. Phys.* **2017**, *340*, 200–242. [CrossRef]
38. Wintermeyer, N.; Winters, A.R.; Gassner, G.J.; Warburton, T. An entropy stable discontinuous Galerkin method for the shallow water equations on curvilinear meshes with wet/dry fronts accelerated by GPUs. *J. Comput. Phys.* **2018**, *375*, 447–480. [CrossRef]
39. Wen, X.; Don, W.S.; Gao, Z.; Xing, Y.L. Entropy stable and well-balanced discontinuous Galerkin methods for the nonlinear shallow water equations. *J. Sci. Comput.* **2020**, *83*, 66. [CrossRef]
40. Liu, Q.S.; Liu, Y.Q.; Feng, J.H. The scaled entropy variables reconstruction for entropy stable schemes with application to shallow water equations. *Comput. Fluids* **2019**, *192*, 104266. [CrossRef]
41. Ismail, F.; Roe, P.L. Affordable, entropy-consistent Euler flux functions II: Entropy production at shocks. *J. Comput. Phys.* **2009**, *228*, 5410–5436. [CrossRef]
42. Lefloch, P.G.; Mercier, J.M.; Rohde, C. Fully discrete entropy conservative schemes of arbitrary order. *SIAM J. Numer. Anal.* **2002**, *40*, 1968–1992. [CrossRef]
43. Fjordholm, U.S.; Mishra, S.; Tadmor, E. Arbitrarily high-order accurate entropy stable essentially non-oscillatory schemes for systems of conservation laws. *SIAM J. Numer. Anal.* **2012**, *50*, 544–573. [CrossRef]
44. Fjordholm, U.S.; Mishra, S.; Tadmor, E. ENO reconstruction and ENO interpolation are stable. *Found. Comput. Math.* **2013**, *13*, 139–159. [CrossRef]
45. Biswas, B.; Dubey, R.K. Low dissipative entropy stable schemes using third order WENO and TVD reconstructions. *Adv. Comput. Math.* **2018**, *44*, 1153–1181. [CrossRef]
46. Alcrudo, F.; Garcia-Navarro, P. A high-resolution Godunov-type scheme in finite volumes for the 2D shallow-water equations. *Int. J. Numer. Methods Fluids* **1993**, *16*, 489–505. [CrossRef]
47. Qiu, J.; Shu, C.-W. Hermite WENO schemes and their application as limiters for Runge–Kutta discontinuous Galerkin method: One-dimensional case. *J. Comput. Phys.* **2003**, *193*, 115–135. [CrossRef]
48. Sod, G. A survey of several finite difference methods for systems of nonlinear hyperbolic conservation laws. *J. Comput. Phys.* **1978**, *27*, 1–31. [CrossRef]
49. Shu, C.-W.; Osher, S. Efficient implementation of essentially non-oscillatory shock capturing schemes. *J. Comput. Phys.* **1988**, *77*, 439–471. [CrossRef]
50. Toro, E.F. *Riemann Solvers and Numerical Methods for Fluid Dynamics: A Practical Introduction*; Springer: Berlin/Heidelberg, Germany, 1999.
51. Toro, E.F.; Titarev, V.A. TVD fluxes for the high-order ADER schemes. *J. Sci. Comput.* **2005**, *24*, 285–309. [CrossRef]
52. Jiang, G.S.; Shu, C.-W. Efficient Implementation of weighted ENO Schemes. *J. Comput. Phys.* **1996**, *126*, 202–228. [CrossRef]
53. Balsara, D.S.; Shu, C.-W. Monotonicity preserving weighted essentially non-oscillatory schemes with increasingly high order of accuracy. *J. Comput. Phys.* **2000**, *160*, 405–452. [CrossRef]

mathematics

MDPI

Article

The Second-Order Numerical Approximation for a Modified Ericksen–Leslie Model

Cheng Liao [1,†], Danxia Wang [1,2,*,†] and Haifeng Zhang [1,†]

1 School of Mathematics, Taiyuan University of Technology, Jinzhong 030600, China; liaocheng@tyut.edu.cn (C.L.); zhanghaifeng@tyut.edu.cn (H.Z.)
2 Shanxi Key Laboratory for Intelligent Optimization Computing and Blockchain Technology, Taiyuan 030024, China
* Correspondence: wangdanxia@tyut.edu.cn
† These authors contributed equally to this work.

Abstract: In this study, two numerical schemes with second-order accuracy in time for a modified Ericksen–Leslie model are constructed. The highlight is based on a novel convex splitting method for dealing with the nonlinear potentials, which is integrated with the second-order backward differentiation formula (BDF2) and leap frog method for temporal discretization and the finite element method for spatial discretization. The unconditional energy stability of both schemes is further demonstrated. Finally, several numerical examples are presented to demonstrate the efficiency and accuracy of the proposed schemes.

Keywords: Ericksen–Leslie model; convex splitting method; backward differentiation formula; leap frog method; unconditional energy stability

MSC: 65M12; 65M60; 65N30; 35Q35

1. Introduction

Liquid crystal is typically viewed as a state of matter that is distinct from the solid, liquid, and gaseous states. This is due to the fact that liquid crystal is an intermediate phase between a liquid and a solid. It can flow like a liquid, but it also exhibits a partial order in the mesoscopic scale of the solid phase, which is normally due to its anisotropic microstructures. According to the degree of positional or orientational ordering shown by the molecules, different degrees of ordering can be achieved, which depends on the temperature and the concentration of the solute in the solvent. The nematic phase is considered the simplest liquid crystal phase; it is composed of elongated rod-like molecules with similar sizes. Its centers of mass have no positional order in an isotropic liquid, but they tend to align along certain locally preferred directions and confer an anisotropic structure. In recent years, the hydrodynamic systems that describe the motion of nematic liquid crystals have become more important in technology. Readers are referred to [1] for a review of dynamic phenomena in liquid crystal materials.

To the best of our knowledge, the famous continuum theory for flows of liquid crystal was first initiated by Oseen and then developed mainly by Eriksen and Leslie [2–5]. As far as liquid crystal is concerned, there are a large number of works in the literature dedicated to diverse features of a system modeling the dynamics of the nematic liquid crystal flows—the so called Ericksen–Leslie model. The Ericksen–Leslie model describes the fluid dynamics of nematic liquid crystals, and it is a coupling between the Navier–Stokes system and the Ginzburg–Landau equations. This system has been investigated widely from various perspectives [6–10].

The Ericksen–Leslie model is a strongly nonlinear coupled system. Due to its complexity, exact solutions of this system are extremely rare. Numerical methods are an important tool for solving these highly nonlinear systems. Consequently, our interest is in constructing numerical approximations for the Ericksen–Leslie model. Lin and Liu [11] developed an extremely significant discovery, which is the existence of energy estimates for the simplified Ericksen–Leslie equations. Liu and Walkington [8] demonstrated implicit Euler time stepping and the finite element approximation in the spatial domain. Lin and Liu [12] discussed a splitting scheme combined with a fixed-point iterative method, which largely reduced the computational time. F.M. Guillen-Gonzalez and J.V. Gutierrez-Santacreu [13] introduced a linear semi-implicit scheme for the Ericksen–Leslie system. V. Girault and F. Guillen-Gonzalez [14] presented a decoupling algorithm. The above papers were all first-order accurate in time for the Ericksen–Leslie system. Then, Santiago, B. et al. [15] proposed a Crank–Nicolson time integration scheme that was unconditionally stable, preserving the energy law. Bao et al. [16] considered a time discretization scheme of a simplified system that preserved spherical constraints at each node, had a discrete energy law, and led to a linear and decoupled elliptic equation solution at each time step. Wang et al. [17] considered a numerical scheme with a second-order backward differentiation formula (BDF) by combining the Lagrange multiplier method and the pressure correction strategy. Cheng et al. [18] proposed and analyzed a first-order exact time difference scheme for the Ericksen–Leslie system. Recently, Wang et al. [19] constructed a first-order sphere-constraint-preserving numerical scheme for the variable-density Ericksen–Leslie equation, and they derived the unconditional energy stability and strict time error estimates. Miao et al. [20] proposed a numerical scheme of the second-order backward differential formula (BDF) for the Ericksen–Leslie model of nematic liquid crystal by combining the convex splitting method and the pressure correction strategy, and this was unconditionally stable in terms of energy. Zhang et al. [10] constructed a second-order numerical scheme with the advantages of complete decoupling, linearization, and unconditional stability of energy in order to numerically approximate the penalized Ericksen–Leslie equations. As far as we know, the second-order numerical method is more accurate than the first-order one in time. So, we developed two second-order time-accurate schemes for the Ericksen–Leslie model in this study. For the backward differentiation formula scheme, this study applied the pressure-correction [21,22] strategy to decouple the pressure from the velocity in order to reduce the computational cost. Then, the leap frog scheme is proposed for the coupling system. It is worth noting that algorithm development is a significant point for the highly complex coupled and nonlinear characteristics.

It is obvious that one of the difficulties in numerically resolving the nonlinear-phase field model is expediently dealing with the nonlinear term in the model. We review some methods for dealing with the potential function, such as the invariant energy quadratization (IEQ) method, the scalar auxiliary variable (SAV) method, the Lagrange multiplier method, and the convex splitting method. Yang [23] mentioned the invariant energy quadratization (IEQ) method, which can be applied to a large number of free energies for phase field models. Shen et al. [24,25] introduced the scalar auxiliary variable method (SAV) for gradient flows, and it is an insufficient case that a scalar auxiliary variable only depends on the time variable. F. Guillen-Gonzalez and G. Tierra [26] presented a linear unconditionally stable scheme for the Cahn–Hilliard equation based on the Lagrange multiplier method. There is the convex splitting method [27,28], which treats the convex part of the potential function implicitly and the concave part explicitly. It was first proposed by Elliott and Stuart [29] and developed by Eyre [30] to solve phase flow equations and nematic liquid crystal flows. However, the IEQ method and SAV method involve more complicated variable coefficients in comparison with the Lagrange multiplier method of linearizing nonlinear potential. The introduction of the Lagrange multiplier and the convex splitting method are extremely common methods, and they are usually used to solve the Cahn–Hilliard equations with double-well potential. For the Ericksen–Leslie model, this study shows a novel convex splitting method for dealing with the penalty term. There has been no recent theoretical or numerical analysis.

The rest of this paper is organized as follows. In Section 2, we briefly discuss the modified Ericksen–Leslie model and the energy dissipation law of the model. In Section 3, fully discrete numerical schemes are constructed, and we prove that the second-order backward differentiation formula and the leap frog scheme satisfy unconditional energy stability. In Section 4, several numerical experiments are carried out to confirm the numerical accuracy and defect dynamics of liquid crystals. We give some concluding remarks in the last section.

2. The Model and Its Energy Law

Some notations are given here. We assume that $\Omega \in \mathbb{R}^d$ (dimension d = 2, 3) is an open and bounded domain with a smooth boundary $\partial\Omega$. For scalar functions u and v and vector functions $\mathbf{u} = (u_1, u_2)$ and $\mathbf{v} = (v_1, v_2)$, we can define the L^2 inner product and norm as follows:

$$(u,v) = \int_\Omega uv dx\,, \qquad \|u\|^2 = (u,u),$$
$$(\mathbf{u},\mathbf{v}) = \int_\Omega \mathbf{u}\mathbf{v}^T d\mathbf{x} = \sum_{i=1}^{n}\int_\Omega u_i v_i d\mathbf{x}\,, \quad \|\mathbf{u}\|^2 = (\mathbf{u},\mathbf{u}).$$

We provide a brief introduction to the modified Ericksen–Leslie model [31]. We define $Q = (0,T) \times \Omega$; $\mathbf{u} : \Omega \to R^2$ is the unknown velocity field, and $\mathbf{d} : \Omega \to R^2$ is the preferential orientation vector of molecules. The total energy E reads as follows:

$$E = E_{kin} + E_{ela}, \tag{1}$$

where E_{kin} is the kinetic energy and E_{ela} is the elastic energy, and they are, respectively, given in the following:

$$E_{kin} = \frac{1}{2}\int_\Omega |\, \mathbf{u}\,|^2\, dx, \quad E_{ela} = \int_\Omega \frac{\lambda}{2} \,|\, \nabla \mathbf{d}\,|^2 + \lambda F(\mathbf{d}) dx. \tag{2}$$

Here, $F(\mathbf{d}) = \frac{1}{4\epsilon^2}(|\,\mathbf{d}\,|^2 - 1)^2$ is the Ginzburg–Landau potential [32], and ϵ is a model parameter measuring the size of the defect core.

The modified Ericksen–Leslie model reads as follows:

$$\begin{aligned} &\partial_t \mathbf{d} + \mathbf{u}\cdot\nabla\mathbf{d} = \gamma\mathbf{h}, && in\ Q,\\ &\mathbf{h} = \Delta\mathbf{d} - f(\mathbf{d}) && in\ Q,\\ &\partial_t \mathbf{u} + \mathbf{u}\cdot\nabla\mathbf{u} = \eta\Delta\mathbf{u} - \nabla p - \lambda\mathbf{h}\nabla\mathbf{d}, && in\ Q,\\ &\nabla\cdot\mathbf{u} = 0, && in\ Q. \end{aligned} \tag{3}$$

Here, $\mathbf{h} = -\frac{\delta E}{\delta \mathbf{d}}$ is the molecular field, p is the pressure, $f(\mathbf{d}) = F'(\mathbf{d}) = \frac{1}{\epsilon^2}(\mathbf{d}^3 - \mathbf{d})$, η is dimensionless and is for the viscosity, γ is the relaxation time parameter, and λ is the elastic parameter. We consider the following boundary conditions:

$$\mathbf{u}\,|_{\partial\Omega} = 0, \qquad \mathbf{n}\cdot\nabla\mathbf{d} = 0, \tag{4}$$

where $\mathbf{n}$ is the unit outward normal of the domain Ω. The initial conditions are

$$\mathbf{d}(\mathbf{x},0) = \mathbf{d}_0\,, \quad \mathbf{u}(\mathbf{x},0) = \mathbf{u}_0\,, \quad \phi(\mathbf{x},0) = \phi_0\,, \quad \mathbf{x}\in\Omega. \tag{5}$$

Remark 1. *This study uses the convex splitting strategy to develop new schemes for the modified Ericksen–Leslie model. The traditional convex splitting strategy refers to treating the convex part of the potential function implicitly and the concave part explicitly, that is,* $g(\mathbf{d}) = g_1(\mathbf{d}) + g_2(\mathbf{d}) =$

$\frac{1}{\epsilon^2}\mathbf{d}^3 - \frac{1}{\epsilon^2}\mathbf{d}$. *However, the potential function* $F(\mathbf{d})$ *in this study can be split into the following convex function and concave function, respectively:*

$$F_1(\mathbf{d}) = \frac{1}{\epsilon^2}(\mathbf{d}^2 + \frac{1}{4}), \qquad F_2(\mathbf{d}) = \frac{1}{\epsilon^2}(\frac{1}{4}\mathbf{d}^4 - \frac{3}{2}\mathbf{d}^2).$$

Correspondingly,

$$f_1(\mathbf{d}) = \frac{2}{\epsilon^2}\mathbf{d}, \qquad f_2(\mathbf{d}) = \frac{1}{\epsilon^2}(\mathbf{d}^3 - 3\mathbf{d}).$$

3. Numerical Schemes

3.1. The Backward Differentiation Formula Scheme

Let S_h be a set of triangulations of Ω with $\overline{\Omega} = \cup_{k\in S_h} k$, where $h \to 0$ is assumed to be uniformly regular. Here, $h = \sup_{k\in S_h} diam(k)$. We denote the finite element spaces $X_h \in X, Y_h \in Y$. Then, the discrete divergence-free space V_h is given by $V_h = \{v_h \in X_h : (\nabla \cdot v_h, r_h) = 0,\ \forall r_h \in R_h\}$. The pressure stability relies on the inf-sup condition. There exists $\beta > 0$ with no restriction of the mesh grid size h such that $\inf_{r_h\in R_h} \sup_{v_h\in V_h} \frac{(r_h, \nabla \cdot v_h)}{\|r_h\|_0\|v_h\|_1} \geq \beta$. The strategy of pressure correction is the time-marching method, which is composed of two steps. In the first step, the pressure is treated explicitly or ignored. In the second step, the pressure is projected by the former velocity onto the space V_h. A pressure-correction scheme is used to decouple the computation of the pressure from that of the velocity. Let N be a positive integer, let the time interval $[0, T]$ be uniformly dissected with $0 = t_0 < t_1 < \cdots < t_N = T$, and let the time nodes satisfy $t_i = i\tau (i = 0, 1, \cdots, N)$; τ is the time step. For $n \geq 1$, the numerical scheme reads as follows:

Scheme I Step 1. Given $(\mathbf{d}_h^{n-1}, \mathbf{d}_h^n, \mathbf{u}_h^{n-1}, \mathbf{u}_h^n, p_h^n) \in V_h \times V_h \times V_h \times V_h \times Y_h$, find $(\mathbf{d}_h^{n+1}, \tilde{\mathbf{u}}_h^{n+1}) \in (V_h \times V_h)$ as the solution of

$$D_\tau \mathbf{d}_h^{n+1} + \tilde{\mathbf{u}}_h^{n+1} \cdot \nabla \hat{\mathbf{d}}_h^{n+1} = \gamma \mathbf{h}_h^{n+1}, \tag{6}$$

$$\mathbf{h}_h^{n+1} - \Delta \mathbf{d}_h^{n+1} + f_1(\mathbf{d}_h^{n+1}) + f_2(\mathbf{d}_h^{n+1}, \hat{\mathbf{d}}_h^{n+1}) = 0, \tag{7}$$

$$D_\tau \tilde{\mathbf{u}}_h^{n+1} + \hat{\mathbf{u}}_h^{n+1} \cdot \nabla \tilde{\mathbf{u}}_h^{n+1} = -\nabla p_h^n + \eta \Delta \tilde{\mathbf{u}}_h^{n+1} - \lambda \mathbf{h}_h^{n+1} \nabla \hat{\mathbf{d}}_h^{n+1}, \tag{8}$$

$$\tilde{\mathbf{u}}_h^{n+1} \mid_{\partial\Omega} = 0, \qquad \frac{\partial \mathbf{d}_h^{n+1}}{\partial \mathbf{n}} \mid_{\partial\Omega} = 0. \tag{9}$$

Step 2. Given $(\tilde{\mathbf{u}}_h^{n+1}, p_h^n) \in V_h \times Y_h$, find $(\mathbf{u}_h^{n+1}, p_h^{n+1}) \in (V_h \times Y_h)$ as the solution of

$$3\frac{\mathbf{u}_h^{n+1} - \tilde{\mathbf{u}}_h^{n+1}}{2\tau} + \nabla(p_h^{n+1} - p_h^n) = 0, \tag{10}$$

$$\nabla \cdot \mathbf{u}_h^{n+1} = 0, \tag{11}$$

where $D_\tau \mathbf{d}_h^{n+1} = \frac{3\mathbf{d}_h^{n+1} - 4\mathbf{d}_h^n + \mathbf{d}_h^{n-1}}{2\tau}$, $D_\tau \tilde{\mathbf{u}}_h^{n+1} = \frac{3\tilde{\mathbf{u}}_h^{n+1} - 4\mathbf{u}_h^n + \mathbf{u}_h^{n-1}}{2\tau}$,

$D_\tau \mathbf{u}_h^{n+1} = \frac{3\mathbf{u}_h^{n+1} - 4\mathbf{u}_h^n + \mathbf{u}_h^{n-1}}{2\tau}$, $\hat{\mathbf{d}}_h^{n+1} = 2\mathbf{d}_h^n - \mathbf{d}_h^{n-1}$, $\hat{\mathbf{u}}_h^{n+1} = 2\mathbf{u}_h^n - \mathbf{u}_h^{n-1}$,

$f_1(\mathbf{d}_h^{n+1}) = \frac{2}{\epsilon^2}\mathbf{d}_h^{n+1}$, $f_2(\mathbf{d}_h^{n+1}, \hat{\mathbf{d}}_h^{n+1}) = \frac{1}{\epsilon^2}((\hat{\mathbf{d}}_h^{n+1})^2 \mathbf{d}_h^{n+1} - 3\hat{\mathbf{d}}_h^{n+1})$.

For n = 1, given $\mathbf{u}_h^0, p_h^0, \mathbf{d}_h^0$, find $\mathbf{u}_h^1, \mathbf{d}_h^1, p_h^1$ as the solution of

$$\begin{aligned}
&\frac{\mathbf{d}_h^1 - \mathbf{d}_h^0}{\tau} + \mathbf{u}_h^1 \cdot \nabla \mathbf{d}_h^0 = \gamma \mathbf{h}_h^1, \\
&\mathbf{h}_h^1 = \Delta \mathbf{d}_h^1 - (f_1(\mathbf{d}_h^1) + f_2(\mathbf{d}_h^1, \mathbf{d}_h^0)), \\
&\frac{\mathbf{u}_h^1 - \mathbf{u}_h^0}{\tau} + \mathbf{u}_h^0 \cdot \nabla \mathbf{u}_h^1 = -\nabla p_h^1 + \eta \Delta \mathbf{u}_h^1 - \lambda \mathbf{h}_h^1 \nabla \mathbf{d}_h^0,
\end{aligned} \tag{12}$$

$$\mathbf{u}_h^1 \mid_{\partial\Omega} = 0, \qquad \frac{\partial \mathbf{d}_h^1}{\partial \mathbf{n}} \mid_{\partial\Omega} = 0,$$
$$\nabla \cdot \mathbf{u}_h^1 = 0.$$

Now, we prove that Scheme I is unconditionally stable in terms of energy.

Theorem 1 (Energy Stability). *Scheme I satisfies the discrete energy dissipation law as follows:*

$$\frac{1}{\tau}(\Xi^{n+1} - \Xi^n) \leq -2\eta\|\nabla \tilde{\mathbf{u}}_h^{n+1}\|^2 - 2\lambda\gamma\|\mathbf{h}_h^{n+1}\|^2 \leq 0, \tag{13}$$

where

$$\begin{aligned} \Xi^{n+1} =& E^{n+1} + \frac{1}{2}\|2\mathbf{u}_h^{n+1} - \mathbf{u}_h^n\|^2 + \frac{\lambda}{2}\|2\nabla \mathbf{d}_h^{n+1} - \nabla \mathbf{d}_h^n\|^2 \\ &+ \frac{\lambda}{\epsilon^2}\|2\mathbf{d}_h^{n+1} - \mathbf{d}_h^n\|^2 + \frac{\lambda}{2\epsilon^2}\|\hat{\mathbf{d}}_h^{n+1}(2\mathbf{d}_h^{n+1} - \mathbf{d}_h^n)\|^2 \\ &+ \frac{9\lambda}{2\epsilon^2}(1 - \|\mathbf{d}_h^{n+1}\|^2) + \frac{2\tau^2}{3}\|\nabla p_h^{n+1}\|^2, \\ E^{n+1} =& \frac{1}{2}\|\mathbf{u}_h^{n+1}\|^2 + \frac{\lambda}{2}\|\nabla \mathbf{d}_h^{n+1}\|^2 + \frac{\lambda}{4\epsilon^2}(\|\mathbf{d}_h^{n+1}\|^2 - 1)^2. \end{aligned} \tag{14}$$

Proof. For (8), we take the inner product with $\tilde{\mathbf{u}}_h^{n+1}$ in L^2 to obtain

$$\begin{aligned} &(D_\tau \tilde{\mathbf{u}}_h^{n+1}, \tilde{\mathbf{u}}_h^{n+1}) + (\hat{\mathbf{u}}_h^{n+1} \cdot \nabla \tilde{\mathbf{u}}_h^{n+1}, \tilde{\mathbf{u}}_h^{n+1}) - (p_h^n, \nabla \cdot \tilde{\mathbf{u}}_h^{n+1}) \\ &+ \eta(\nabla \tilde{\mathbf{u}}_h^{n+1}, \nabla \tilde{\mathbf{u}}_h^{n+1}) = -\lambda(\mathbf{h}_h^{n+1}\nabla \hat{\mathbf{d}}_h^{n+1}, \tilde{\mathbf{u}}_h^{n+1}). \end{aligned} \tag{15}$$

Then, we put (6) into the right part of (15) to get

$$\begin{aligned} \lambda(\mathbf{h}_h^{n+1}, \tilde{\mathbf{u}}_h^{n+1} \cdot \nabla \hat{\mathbf{d}}_h^{n+1}) &= \lambda(\mathbf{h}_h^{n+1}, \gamma(\mathbf{h}_h^{n+1} - D_\tau \mathbf{d}_h^{n+1})) \\ &= \lambda\gamma\|\mathbf{h}_h^{n+1}\|^2 - \lambda(\mathbf{h}_h^{n+1}, D_\tau \mathbf{d}_h^{n+1}). \end{aligned} \tag{16}$$

Besides, we put (16) into (15) to get

$$(D_\tau \tilde{\mathbf{u}}_h^{n+1}, \tilde{\mathbf{u}}_h^{n+1}) + \eta\|\nabla \tilde{\mathbf{u}}_h^{n+1}\|^2 + \lambda\gamma\|\mathbf{h}_h^{n+1}\|^2 = \lambda(\mathbf{h}_h^{n+1}, D_\tau \mathbf{d}_h^{n+1}). \tag{17}$$

For (7), we take the inner product with $\lambda D_\tau \mathbf{d}_h^{n+1}$ in L^2 to get

$$\begin{aligned} &\lambda(\mathbf{h}_h^{n+1}, D_\tau \mathbf{d}_h^{n+1}) + \lambda(\nabla \mathbf{d}_h^{n+1}, \nabla D_\tau \mathbf{d}_h^{n+1}) + \lambda(f_1(\mathbf{d}_h^{n+1}, D_\tau \mathbf{d}_h^{n+1}) \\ &+ \lambda(f_2(\mathbf{d}_h^{n+1}, \hat{\mathbf{d}}_h^{n+1}), D_\tau \mathbf{d}_h^{n+1}) = 0. \end{aligned} \tag{18}$$

Due to

$$\begin{aligned} (f_1(\mathbf{d}_h^{n+1}), D_\tau \mathbf{d}_h^{n+1}) =& \frac{1}{2\tau\epsilon^2}(\|\mathbf{d}_h^{n+1}\|^2 - \|\mathbf{d}_h^n\|^2 + \|2\mathbf{d}_h^{n+1} - \mathbf{d}_h^n\|^2 \\ &- \|2\mathbf{d}_h^n - \mathbf{d}_h^{n-1}\|^2 + \|\mathbf{d}_h^{n+1} - 2\mathbf{d}_h^n + \mathbf{d}_h^{n-1}\|^2), \end{aligned} \tag{19}$$

we derive

$$\begin{aligned} &(f_2(\mathbf{d}_h^{n+1}, \hat{\mathbf{d}}_h^{n+1}), D_\tau \mathbf{d}_h^{n+1}) = \frac{1}{\epsilon^2}((\hat{\mathbf{d}}_h^{n+1})^2 \mathbf{d}_h^{n+1} - 3\hat{\mathbf{d}}_h^{n+1}), D_\tau \mathbf{d}_h^{n+1}) \\ =& \frac{1}{2\tau\epsilon^2}\Big(\int_\Omega \frac{1}{2}(\hat{\mathbf{d}}_h^{n+1})^2[(\mathbf{d}_h^{n+1})^2 - (\mathbf{d}_h^n)^2 + (2\mathbf{d}_h^{n+1} - \mathbf{d}_h^n)^2 - (2\mathbf{d}_h^n - \mathbf{d}_h^{n-1})^2 \\ &+ (\mathbf{d}_h^{n+1} - 2\mathbf{d}_h^n + \mathbf{d}_h^{n-1})^2]d\mathbf{x} + 3(-\frac{1}{2}(\|\mathbf{d}_h^{n+1}\|^2 + \|2\mathbf{d}_h^{n+1} - \mathbf{d}_h^n\|^2 \\ &- 2\|\mathbf{d}_h^{n+1} - \mathbf{d}_h^n\|^2) + \frac{1}{2}(\|\mathbf{d}_h^n\|^2 - \|2\mathbf{d}_h^n - \mathbf{d}_h^{n-1}\|^2 - 2\|\mathbf{d}_h^n - \mathbf{d}_h^{n-1}\|^2)) \end{aligned}$$

$$
\begin{aligned}
&+\frac{3}{2}\|\mathbf{d}_h^{n+1}-2\mathbf{d}_h^n+\mathbf{d}_h^{n-1}\|^2)\\
=&\frac{1}{4\tau\epsilon^2}(\|\hat{\mathbf{d}}_h^{n+1}\mathbf{d}_h^{n+1}\|^2-\|\hat{\mathbf{d}}_h^{n+1}\mathbf{d}_h^{n}\|^2+\|\hat{\mathbf{d}}_h^{n+1}(2\mathbf{d}_h^{n+1}-\mathbf{d}_h^n)\|^2\\
&-\|\hat{\mathbf{d}}_h^{n+1}(2\mathbf{d}_h^{n}-\mathbf{d}_h^{n-1})\|^2+\|(\hat{\mathbf{d}}_h^{n+1}(\mathbf{d}_h^{n+1}-2\mathbf{d}_h^n+\mathbf{d}_h^{n-1})\|^2)\\
&+\frac{3}{2\tau\epsilon^2}(-\frac{1}{2}(\|\mathbf{d}_h^{n+1}\|^2+4\|\mathbf{d}_h^{n+1}\|^2+\|\mathbf{d}_h^{n}\|^2-4\mathbf{d}_h^{n+1}\mathbf{d}_h^n-2\|\mathbf{d}_h^{n+1}\|^2\\
&-2\|\mathbf{d}_h^{n}\|^2+4\mathbf{d}_h^{n+1}\mathbf{d}_h^n)+\frac{1}{2}(\|\mathbf{d}_h^{n}\|^2+4\|\mathbf{d}_h^{n}\|^2+\|\mathbf{d}_h^{n-1}\|^2-4\mathbf{d}_h^{n}\mathbf{d}_h^{n-1}\\
&-2\|\mathbf{d}_h^{n}\|^2-2\|\mathbf{d}_h^{n-1}\|^2+4\mathbf{d}_h^{n}\mathbf{d}_h^{n-1}))+\frac{9}{4\tau\epsilon^2}\|\mathbf{d}_h^{n+1}-2\mathbf{d}_h^n+\mathbf{d}_h^{n-1}\|^2\\
=&\frac{1}{4\tau\epsilon^2}(\|\hat{\mathbf{d}}_h^{n+1}\mathbf{d}_h^{n+1}\|^2-\|\hat{\mathbf{d}}_h^{n+1}\mathbf{d}_h^{n}\|^2+\|\hat{\mathbf{d}}_h^{n+1}(2\mathbf{d}_h^{n+1}-\mathbf{d}_h^n)\|^2\\
&-\|\hat{\mathbf{d}}_h^{n+1}(2\mathbf{d}_h^{n}-\mathbf{d}_h^{n-1})\|^2+\|\hat{\mathbf{d}}_h^{n+1}(\mathbf{d}_h^{n+1}-2\mathbf{d}_h^n+\mathbf{d}_h^{n-1})\|^2)\\
&+\frac{9}{4\tau\epsilon^2}(-\|\mathbf{d}_h^{n+1}\|^2+\|\mathbf{d}_h^{n}\|^2)+\frac{3}{4\tau\epsilon^2}(\|\mathbf{d}_h^{n}\|^2-\|\mathbf{d}_h^{n-1}\|^2)\\
&+\frac{9}{4\tau\epsilon^2}\|\mathbf{d}_h^{n+1}-2\mathbf{d}_h^n+\mathbf{d}_h^{n-1}\|^2\\
=&\frac{1}{4\tau\epsilon^2}(\|\hat{\mathbf{d}}_h^{n+1}\mathbf{d}_h^{n+1}\|^2-\|\hat{\mathbf{d}}_h^{n+1}\mathbf{d}_h^{n}\|^2+\|\hat{\mathbf{d}}_h^{n+1}(2\mathbf{d}_h^{n+1}-\mathbf{d}_h^n)\|^2\\
&-\|\hat{\mathbf{d}}_h^{n+1}(2\mathbf{d}_h^{n}-\mathbf{d}_h^{n-1})\|^2+\|\hat{\mathbf{d}}_h^{n+1}(\mathbf{d}_h^{n+1}-2\mathbf{d}_h^n+\mathbf{d}_h^{n-1})\|^2)\\
&+\frac{9}{4\tau\epsilon^2}((1-\|\mathbf{d}_h^{n+1}\|^2)-(1-\|\mathbf{d}_h^{n}\|^2))+\frac{3}{4\tau\epsilon^2}(\|\mathbf{d}_h^{n}\|^2-\|\mathbf{d}_h^{n-1}\|^2)\\
&+\frac{9}{4\tau\epsilon^2}\|\mathbf{d}_h^{n+1}-2\mathbf{d}_h^n+\mathbf{d}_h^{n-1}\|^2.
\end{aligned}
\tag{20}
$$

Here, the director vector $\mathbf{d}$ is bounded. It is well known that the director vector $\mathbf{d}$ satisfies the following maximum principle [11,13,33]:

"If $|\ \mathbf{d}_0\ |\leq 1$ in Ω, then $|\ \mathbf{d}(t)\ |\leq 1$ in Ω for each $t\in[0,T]$."

The derivation can be found in the Appendix A.

By putting (19) and (20) into (18) and (18) into (17), we have

$$
\begin{aligned}
&(D_\tau\tilde{\mathbf{u}}_h^{n+1},\tilde{\mathbf{u}}_h^{n+1})+\eta\|\nabla\tilde{\mathbf{u}}_h^{n+1}\|^2+\lambda\gamma\|\mathbf{h}_h^{n+1}\|^2+\lambda(\nabla\mathbf{d}_h^{n+1},\nabla D_\tau\mathbf{d}_h^{n+1})\\
&+\frac{\lambda}{2\tau\epsilon^2}(\|\mathbf{d}_h^{n+1}\|^2-\|\mathbf{d}_h^{n}\|^2+\|2\mathbf{d}_h^{n+1}-\mathbf{d}_h^n\|^2-\|2\mathbf{d}_h^{n}-\mathbf{d}_h^{n-1}\|^2\\
&+\|\mathbf{d}_h^{n+1}-2\mathbf{d}_h^n+\mathbf{d}_h^{n-1}\|^2)+\frac{\lambda}{4\tau\epsilon^2}(\|\hat{\mathbf{d}}_h^{n+1}\mathbf{d}_h^{n+1}\|^2-\|\hat{\mathbf{d}}_h^{n+1}\mathbf{d}_h^{n}\|^2\\
&+\|\hat{\mathbf{d}}_h^{n+1}(2\mathbf{d}_h^{n+1}-\mathbf{d}_h^n)\|^2-\|\hat{\mathbf{d}}_h^{n+1}(2\mathbf{d}_h^{n}-\mathbf{d}_h^{n-1})\|^2\\
&+\|\hat{\mathbf{d}}_h^{n+1}(\mathbf{d}_h^{n+1}-2\mathbf{d}_h^n+\mathbf{d}_h^{n-1})\|^2)+\frac{9\lambda}{4\tau\epsilon^2}((1-\|\mathbf{d}_h^{n+1}\|^2)-(1-\|\mathbf{d}_h^{n}\|^2))\\
&+\frac{3\lambda}{4\tau\epsilon^2}(\|\mathbf{d}_h^{n}\|^2-\|\mathbf{d}_h^{n-1}\|^2)+\frac{9\lambda}{4\tau\epsilon^2}\|\mathbf{d}_h^{n+1}-2\mathbf{d}_h^n+\mathbf{d}_h^{n-1}\|^2=0.
\end{aligned}
\tag{21}
$$

According to (10), for any variable $\mathbf{v}$ with $\nabla\cdot\mathbf{v}$ and $\mathbf{v}\cdot\mathbf{n}\ |_{\partial\Omega}=0$, we easily obtain $(\tilde{\mathbf{u}}_h^{n+1},\mathbf{v})=(\mathbf{u}_h^{n+1},\mathbf{v})$. Then, for the first term, we apply the fact that

$$(a-b,a)=\frac{1}{2}(\|a\|^2-\|b\|^2+\|a-b\|^2)$$

to have

$$\begin{aligned}(D_\tau \tilde{\mathbf{u}}_h^{n+1}, \tilde{\mathbf{u}}_h^{n+1}) =&(3\frac{\tilde{\mathbf{u}}_h^{n+1} - \mathbf{u}_h^{n+1}}{2\tau}, \tilde{\mathbf{u}}_h^{n+1}) + (D_\tau \mathbf{u}_h^{n+1}, \mathbf{u}_h^{n+1}) \\ =&(3\frac{\tilde{\mathbf{u}}_h^{n+1} - \mathbf{u}_h^{n+1}}{2\tau}, \tilde{\mathbf{u}}_h^{n+1} - \mathbf{u}_h^{n+1}) + (D_\tau \mathbf{u}_h^{n+1}, \mathbf{u}_h^{n+1}) \\ =&\frac{3}{4\tau}(\|\tilde{\mathbf{u}}_h^{n+1}\|^2 - \|\mathbf{u}_h^{n+1}\|^2) + (D_\tau \mathbf{u}_h^{n+1}, \mathbf{u}_h^{n+1}).\end{aligned} \tag{22}$$

To approach the pressure term, we reformulate (10) as

$$\frac{3}{2\tau}\mathbf{u}_h^{n+1} + \nabla p_h^{n+1} = \frac{3}{2\tau}\tilde{\mathbf{u}}_h^{n+1} + \nabla p_h^n. \tag{23}$$

By taking the square of both sides of the above equation, we obtain

$$\frac{9}{4\tau^2}\|\mathbf{u}_h^{n+1}\|^2 + \|\nabla p_h^{n+1}\|^2 = \frac{9}{4\tau^2}\|\tilde{\mathbf{u}}_h^{n+1}\|^2 + \|\nabla p_h^n\|^2 + \frac{3}{\tau}(\tilde{\mathbf{u}}_h^{n+1}, \nabla p_h^n). \tag{24}$$

It is readily verified that

$$\frac{3}{4\tau}(\|\mathbf{u}_h^{n+1}\|^2 - \|\tilde{\mathbf{u}}_h^{n+1}\|^2) + \frac{\tau}{3}(\|\nabla p_h^{n+1}\|^2 - \|\nabla p_h^n\|^2) = (\tilde{\mathbf{u}}_h^{n+1}, \nabla p_h^n). \tag{25}$$

Noticing the identity

$$(3a - 4b + c, a) = \frac{1}{2}(\|a\|^2 - \|b\|^2 + \|2a - b\|^2 - \|2b - c\|^2 + \|a - 2b + c\|^2),$$

we derive the equality

$$\begin{aligned}(D_\tau \mathbf{u}_h^{n+1}, \mathbf{u}_h^{n+1}) =&\frac{1}{4\tau}(\|\mathbf{u}_h^{n+1}\|^2 - \|\mathbf{u}_h^n\|^2 + \|2\mathbf{u}_h^{n+1} - \mathbf{u}_h^n\|^2 \\ &- \|2\mathbf{u}_h^n - \mathbf{u}_h^{n-1}\|^2 + \|\mathbf{u}_h^{n+1} - 2\mathbf{u}_h^n + \mathbf{u}_h^{n-1}\|^2).\end{aligned} \tag{26}$$

Similarly, we can get

$$\begin{aligned}(\nabla D_\tau \mathbf{d}_h^{n+1}, \nabla \mathbf{d}_h^{n+1}) =&\frac{1}{4\tau}(\|\nabla \mathbf{d}_h^{n+1}\|^2 - \|\nabla \mathbf{d}_h^n\|^2 + \|2\nabla \mathbf{d}_h^{n+1} - \nabla \mathbf{d}_h^n\|^2 \\ &- \|2\nabla \mathbf{d}_h^n - \nabla \mathbf{d}_h^{n-1}\|^2 + \|\nabla \mathbf{d}_h^{n+1} - 2\nabla \mathbf{d}_h^n + \nabla \mathbf{d}_h^{n-1}\|^2).\end{aligned} \tag{27}$$

Hence, combining (21), (22), and (25)–(27), we arrive at

$$\begin{aligned}&\eta\|\nabla \tilde{\mathbf{u}}_h^{n+1}\|^2 + \frac{1}{4\tau}(\|\mathbf{u}_h^{n+1}\|^2 - \|\mathbf{u}_h^n\|^2 + \|2\mathbf{u}_h^{n+1} - \mathbf{u}_h^n\|^2 - \|2\mathbf{u}_h^n - \mathbf{u}_h^{n-1}\|^2 \\ &+ \|\mathbf{u}_h^{n+1} - 2\mathbf{u}_h^n + \mathbf{u}_h^{n-1}\|^2) + \frac{\lambda}{4\tau}(\|\nabla \mathbf{d}_h^{n+1}\|^2 - \|\nabla \mathbf{d}_h^n\|^2 + \|2\nabla \mathbf{d}_h^{n+1} - \nabla \mathbf{d}_h^n\|^2 \\ &- \|2\nabla \mathbf{d}_h^n - \nabla \mathbf{d}_h^{n-1}\|^2 + \|\nabla \mathbf{d}_h^{n+1} - 2\nabla \mathbf{d}_h^n + \nabla \mathbf{d}_h^{n-1}\|^2) + \lambda\gamma\|\mathbf{h}_h^{n+1}\|^2 \\ &+ \frac{\lambda}{2\tau\epsilon^2}(\|\mathbf{d}_h^{n+1}\|^2 - \|\mathbf{d}_h^n\|^2 + \|2\mathbf{d}_h^{n+1} - \mathbf{d}_h^n\|^2 - \|2\mathbf{d}_h^n - \mathbf{d}_h^{n-1}\|^2 \\ &+ \|\mathbf{d}_h^{n+1} - 2\mathbf{d}_h^n + \mathbf{d}_h^{n-1}\|^2) + \frac{\lambda}{4\tau\epsilon^2}(\|\hat{\mathbf{d}}_h^{n+1}\mathbf{d}_h^{n+1}\|^2 - \|\hat{\mathbf{d}}_h^{n+1}\mathbf{d}_h^n\|^2 \\ &+ \|\hat{\mathbf{d}}_h^{n+1}(2\mathbf{d}_h^{n+1} - \mathbf{d}_h^n)\|^2 - \|\hat{\mathbf{d}}_h^{n+1}(2\mathbf{d}_h^n - \mathbf{d}_h^{n-1})\|^2 \\ &+ \|\hat{\mathbf{d}}_h^{n+1}(\mathbf{d}_h^{n+1} - 2\mathbf{d}_h^n + \mathbf{d}_h^{n-1})\|^2) + \frac{9\lambda}{4\tau\epsilon^2}((1 - \|\mathbf{d}_h^{n+1}\|^2) - (1 - \|\mathbf{d}_h^n\|^2)) \\ &+ \frac{3\lambda}{4\tau\epsilon^2}(\|\mathbf{d}_h^n\|^2 - \|\mathbf{d}_h^{n-1}\|^2) + \frac{9\lambda}{4\tau\epsilon^2}\|\mathbf{d}_h^{n+1} - 2\mathbf{d}_h^n + \mathbf{d}_h^{n-1}\|^2 \\ &+ \frac{\tau}{3}(\|\nabla p_h^{n+1}\|^2 - \|\nabla p_h^n\|^2) = 0.\end{aligned} \tag{28}$$

Then, multiplying (28) by 2τ, we can derive

$$\begin{aligned}
&E^{n+1} - E^n + \frac{1}{2}(\|2\mathbf{u}_h^{n+1} - \mathbf{u}_h^n\|^2 - \|2\mathbf{u}_h^n - \mathbf{u}_h^{n-1}\|^2 + \|\mathbf{u}_h^{n+1} - 2\mathbf{u}_h^n + \mathbf{u}_h^{n-1}\|^2) \\
&+ \frac{\lambda}{2}(\|2\nabla\mathbf{d}_h^{n+1} - \nabla\mathbf{d}_h^n\|^2 - \|2\nabla\mathbf{d}_h^n - \nabla\mathbf{d}_h^{n-1}\|^2 + \|\nabla\mathbf{d}_h^{n+1} - 2\nabla\mathbf{d}_h^n + \nabla\mathbf{d}_h^{n-1}\|^2) \\
&+ \frac{\lambda}{\epsilon^2}(\|2\mathbf{d}_h^{n+1} - \mathbf{d}_h^n\|^2 - \|2\mathbf{d}_h^n - \mathbf{d}_h^{n-1}\|^2 + \|\mathbf{d}_h^{n+1} - 2\mathbf{d}_h^n + \mathbf{d}_h^{n-1}\|^2) \\
&+ 2\tau\eta\|\nabla\tilde{\mathbf{u}}_h^{n+1}\|^2 + \frac{\lambda}{2\epsilon^2}(\|\hat{\mathbf{d}}_h^{n+1}(2\mathbf{d}_h^{n+1} - \mathbf{d}_h^n)\|^2 - \|\hat{\mathbf{d}}_h^{n+1}(2\mathbf{d}_h^n - \mathbf{d}_h^{n-1})\|^2 \\
&+ \|\hat{\mathbf{d}}_h^{n+1}(\mathbf{d}_h^{n+1} - 2\mathbf{d}_h^n + \mathbf{d}_h^{n-1})\|^2) + \frac{9\lambda}{2\epsilon^2}((1 - \|\mathbf{d}_h^{n+1}\|^2) - (1 - \|\mathbf{d}_h^n\|^2)) \\
&+ 2\tau\lambda\gamma\|\mathbf{h}_h^{n+1}\|^2 + \frac{3\lambda}{2\epsilon^2}(\|\mathbf{d}_h^n\|^2 - \|\mathbf{d}_h^{n-1}\|^2) + \frac{9\lambda}{2\epsilon^2}\|\mathbf{d}_h^{n+1} - 2\mathbf{d}_h^n + \mathbf{d}_h^{n-1}\|^2 \\
&+ \frac{2\tau^2}{3}(\|\nabla p_h^{n+1}\|^2 - \|\nabla p_h^n\|^2) = 0.
\end{aligned} \tag{29}$$

Due to the definition of Ξ^{n+1}, we have

$$\Xi^{n+1} + 2\tau\eta\|\nabla\tilde{\mathbf{u}}_h^{n+1}\|^2 + 2\tau\lambda\gamma\|\mathbf{h}_h^{n+1}\|^2 \leq \Xi^n. \tag{30}$$

The proof is complete. □

3.2. The Leap Frog Scheme

We now consider the fully discrete version of the leap frog scheme for solving the model, where we use a new convex splitting method. Let S_h be a quasi-uniform triangulation of the domain Ω of mesh size h. We define the spaces as follows:

$$X_h = H_0^1(\Omega),\ \ Y_h = H^1(\Omega),\ \ M = H^1(\Omega) \cap L_0^1(\Omega).$$

Scheme II The initial conditions are $\mathbf{d}_h^0$, $\mathbf{u}_h^0$ and $p_h^0 = 0$. Given $\mathbf{d}_h^n, \mathbf{u}_h^n, p_h^n$ for $n \geq 0$, we can find $(\mathbf{d}_h^{n+1}, \mathbf{u}_h^{n+1}, p_h^{n+1}) \in X_h \times X_h \times Y_h$ by

$$D'_\tau\mathbf{d}_h^{n+1} + \bar{\mathbf{u}}_h^{n+1} \cdot \nabla\mathbf{d}_h^n = \gamma\bar{\mathbf{h}}_h^{n+1}, \tag{31}$$

$$\bar{\mathbf{h}}_h^{n+1} = \Delta\bar{\mathbf{d}}_h^{n+1} - (f_1(\bar{\mathbf{d}}_h^{n+1}) + f_2(\bar{\mathbf{d}}_h^{n+1}, \mathbf{d}_h^n)), \tag{32}$$

$$D'_\tau\mathbf{u}_h^{n+1} + \mathbf{u}_h^n \cdot \nabla\bar{\mathbf{u}}_h^{n+1} = -\nabla\bar{p}_h^{n+1} + \eta\Delta\bar{\mathbf{u}}_h^{n+1} - \lambda\bar{\mathbf{h}}_h^{n+1}\nabla\mathbf{d}_h^n, \tag{33}$$

$$\nabla \cdot \bar{\mathbf{u}}_h^{n+1} = 0, \tag{34}$$

where $D'_\tau\mathbf{d}_h^{n+1} = \dfrac{\mathbf{d}_h^{n+1} - \mathbf{d}_h^{n-1}}{2\tau}$, $D'_\tau\mathbf{u}_h^{n+1} = \dfrac{\mathbf{u}_h^{n+1} - \mathbf{u}_h^{n-1}}{2\tau}$, $\bar{\mathbf{d}}_h^{n+1} = \dfrac{\mathbf{d}_h^{n+1} + \mathbf{d}_h^{n-1}}{2}$, $\bar{\mathbf{u}}_h^{n+1} = \dfrac{\mathbf{u}_h^{n+1} + \mathbf{u}_h^{n-1}}{2}$, $\bar{\mathbf{h}}_h^{n+1} = \dfrac{\mathbf{h}_h^{n+1} + \mathbf{h}_h^{n-1}}{2}$, $\bar{p}_h^{n+1} = \dfrac{p_h^{n+1} + p_h^{n-1}}{2}$, $f_1(\bar{\mathbf{d}}_h^{n+1}) = \dfrac{2}{\epsilon^2}\bar{\mathbf{d}}_h^{n+1}$, $f_2(\bar{\mathbf{d}}_h^{n+1}, \mathbf{d}_h^n) = \dfrac{1}{\epsilon^2}((\mathbf{d}_h^n)^2\bar{\mathbf{d}}_h^{n+1} - 3\mathbf{d}_h^n)$.

Now, we prove that Scheme II is unconditionally stable in terms of energy.

Theorem 2 (Energy Stability). *Let $\{\mathbf{u}_h^{n+1},\ p_h^{n+1},\ \mathbf{d}_h^{n+1}\}$ be the solutions of Scheme II. For all $\tau > 0$ and $1 \leq n \leq N$, Scheme II satisfies unconditional energy stability with respect to the discrete energy*

$$\frac{\Gamma^{n+1} - \Gamma^n}{\tau} \leq -2\eta\|\nabla\bar{\mathbf{u}}_h^{n+1}\|^2 - 2\lambda\gamma\|\bar{\mathbf{h}}_h^{n+1}\|^2 \leq 0, \tag{35}$$

where

$$\Gamma^{n+1} =\frac{1}{2}(\|\mathbf{u}_h^{n+1}\|^2 + \|\mathbf{u}_h^n\|^2) + \frac{\lambda}{2\tau}(\|\nabla \mathbf{d}_h^{n+1}\|^2 + \|\nabla \mathbf{d}_h^n\|^2) \\ + \frac{\lambda}{\epsilon^2}(\|\mathbf{d}_h^{n+1}\|^2 + \|\mathbf{d}_h^n\|^2) + \frac{\lambda}{2\epsilon^2}\|\mathbf{d}_h^{n+1}\mathbf{d}_h^n - 3\|^2.$$

Proof. For (33), we apply the fact that

$$(a-b, a+b) = \|a\|^2 - \|b\|^2,$$

and we take the inner product with $\bar{\mathbf{u}}_h^{n+1}$ in L^2 to get

$$\frac{1}{4\tau}(\|\mathbf{u}_h^{n+1}\|^2 - \|\mathbf{u}_h^{n-1}\|^2) + ((\mathbf{u}_h^n \cdot \nabla)\bar{\mathbf{u}}_h^{n+1}, \bar{\mathbf{u}}_h^{n+1}) - (p_h^{n+1}, \nabla \cdot \bar{\mathbf{u}}_h^{n+1}) \\ + \eta\|\nabla \bar{\mathbf{u}}_h^{n+1}\|^2 = -\lambda(\bar{\mathbf{h}}_h^{n+1}\nabla \mathbf{d}_h^n, \bar{\mathbf{u}}_h^{n+1}) = -\lambda(\bar{\mathbf{h}}_h^{n+1}, \nabla \mathbf{d}_h^n \bar{\mathbf{u}}_h^{n+1}). \tag{36}$$

Then, by putting (31) into the right part of (36), we obtain

$$\lambda(\bar{\mathbf{h}}_h^{n+1}, \nabla \mathbf{d}_h^n \bar{\mathbf{u}}_h^{n+1}) = \lambda(\bar{\mathbf{h}}_h^{n+1}, \gamma(\bar{\mathbf{h}}_h^{n+1} - D_\tau' \mathbf{d}_h^{n+1})) \\ = \lambda\gamma\|\bar{\mathbf{h}}_h^{n+1}\|^2 - \lambda(\bar{\mathbf{h}}_h^{n+1}, D_\tau' \mathbf{d}_h^{n+1}). \tag{37}$$

Similarly, we put (37) into (36) to get

$$\frac{1}{4\tau}(\|\mathbf{u}_h^{n+1}\|^2 - \|\mathbf{u}_h^{n-1}\|^2) + \eta\|\nabla \bar{\mathbf{u}}_h^{n+1}\|^2 + \lambda\gamma\|\bar{\mathbf{h}}_h^{n+1}\|^2 = \lambda(\bar{\mathbf{h}}_h^{n+1}, D_\tau \mathbf{d}_h^{n+1}). \tag{38}$$

By taking the inner product of (32) with $\lambda D_\tau' \mathbf{d}_h^{n+1}$ in the L^2 space, we find

$$\lambda(\bar{\mathbf{h}}_h^{n+1}, D_\tau' \mathbf{d}_h^{n+1}) + \lambda(\nabla \bar{\mathbf{d}}_h^{n+1}, \nabla D_\tau' \mathbf{d}_h^{n+1}) + \lambda(f_1(\bar{\mathbf{d}}_h^{n+1}), D_\tau' \mathbf{d}_h^{n+1}) \\ + \lambda(f_2(\bar{\mathbf{d}}_h^{n+1}, \mathbf{d}_h^n), D_\tau' \mathbf{d}_h^{n+1}) = 0. \tag{39}$$

Due to

$$(\nabla \bar{\mathbf{d}}_h^{n+1}, \nabla D_\tau' \mathbf{d}_h^{n+1}) = \frac{1}{4\tau}(\|\nabla \mathbf{d}_h^{n+1}\|^2 - \|\nabla \mathbf{d}_h^{n-1}\|^2), \tag{40}$$

$$(f_1(\bar{\mathbf{d}}_h^{n+1}), D_\tau' \mathbf{d}_h^{n+1}) = \frac{1}{2\tau\epsilon^2}(\|\mathbf{d}_h^{n+1}\|^2 - \|\mathbf{d}_h^{n-1}\|^2), \tag{41}$$

we have

$$(f_2(\bar{\mathbf{d}}_h^{n+1}, \mathbf{d}_h^n), D_\tau' \mathbf{d}_h^{n+1}) = \frac{1}{\epsilon^2}((\mathbf{d}_h^n)^2 \bar{\mathbf{d}}_h^{n+1} - 3\mathbf{d}_h^n, D_\tau' \mathbf{d}_h^{n+1}) \\ =\frac{1}{2\tau\epsilon^2}(\int_\Omega \frac{1}{2}(\mathbf{d}_h^n)^2((\mathbf{d}_h^{n+1})^2 - (\mathbf{d}_h^{n-1})^2)d\mathbf{x} - 3\int_\Omega \mathbf{d}_h^n(\mathbf{d}_h^{n+1} - \mathbf{d}_h^{n-1})d\mathbf{x}) \\ =\frac{1}{2\tau\epsilon^2}\int_\Omega \frac{1}{2}((\mathbf{d}_h^{n+1}\mathbf{d}_h^n)^2 - (\mathbf{d}_h^n\mathbf{d}_h^{n-1})^2 - 6\mathbf{d}_h^{n+1}\mathbf{d}_h^n + 6\mathbf{d}_h^n\mathbf{d}_h^{n-1})d\mathbf{x} \\ =\frac{1}{4\tau\epsilon^2}\int_\Omega((\mathbf{d}_h^{n+1}\mathbf{d}_h^n - 3)^2 - (\mathbf{d}_h^n\mathbf{d}_h^{n-1} - 3)^2)d\mathbf{x} \\ =\frac{1}{4\tau\epsilon^2}(\|\mathbf{d}_h^{n+1}\mathbf{d}_h^n - 3\|^2 - \|\mathbf{d}_h^n\mathbf{d}_h^{n-1} - 3\|^2). \tag{42}$$

In addition, we put (40)–(42) into (39) and (39) into (38) to have

$$\begin{aligned}&\frac{1}{4\tau}(\|\mathbf{u}_h^{n+1}\|^2-\|\mathbf{u}_h^{n-1}\|^2)+\frac{\lambda}{4\tau}(\|\nabla\mathbf{d}_h^{n+1}\|^2-\|\nabla\mathbf{d}_h^{n-1}\|^2)\\&+\eta\|\nabla\bar{\mathbf{u}}_h^{n+1}\|^2+\lambda\gamma\|\bar{\mathbf{h}}_h^{n+1}\|^2+\frac{\lambda}{2\tau\epsilon^2}(\|\mathbf{d}_h^{n+1}\|^2-\|\mathbf{d}_h^{n-1}\|^2)\\&+\frac{\lambda}{4\tau\epsilon^2}(\|\mathbf{d}_h^{n+1}\mathbf{d}_h^{n}-3\|^2-\|\mathbf{d}_h^{n}\mathbf{d}_h^{n-1}-3\|^2)=0.\end{aligned}\tag{43}$$

Then, multiplying both sides by 2τ in (43), we can deduce

$$\Gamma^{n+1}+2\tau\eta\|\nabla\bar{\mathbf{u}}_h^{n+1}\|^2+2\tau\lambda\gamma\|\bar{\mathbf{h}}_h^{n+1}\|^2\leq\Gamma^{n}.\tag{44}$$

The proof is complete. □

4. Numerical Experiments

In this section, we present several numerical experiments to verify the accuracy, stability, and efficiency of the proposed schemes. All programs were implemented with the free finite element software FreeFem++ 3.28 [34]. Firstly, we investigate the numerical accuracy and conduct a convergence test of the proposed schemes with respect to time and space. Then, we conduct some numerical simulations of liquid crystal flows in two-dimensional space while focusing on the flow-induced defect dynamics, which represent rod-like nematic liquid crystals. Finally, we numerically check the conditional stability, which depends on the trend of diminishing energy, by showing the evolution of the kinetic and elastic energies.

4.1. Accuracy and Convergence Test

We first verify the convergence rates of the two different schemes by conducting two-dimensional simulations, and the computational domain is set to $[-1,1]\times[-1,1]$. By setting some suitable functions, we assume that the initial conditions of the system are as follows:

$$\mathbf{u}=\mathbf{0},\ p=0,\ \mathbf{d}=(sin(2\pi(cosx-siny)),cos(2\pi(cosx-siny))).$$

The convergence rates with respect to the time step τ are calculated with the formula $\frac{\log(E_i/E_{i+1})}{\log(\tau_i/\tau_{i+1})}$, where E_i and E_{i+1} are the relative errors corresponding to the time steps τ_i and τ_{i+1}, respectively.

4.1.1. The Order of Temporal Convergence

We first verified the temporal convergence order. We fixed the grid size to $h=\frac{1}{50}$, so the grid size was small enough and the spatial discretization errors were negligible compared to the time discretization error. In Tables 1–4, we verify the temporal convergence order of Scheme I for different parameter values. In the experiment, we used different time step sizes ($\tau=0.0625, 0.03125, 0.015625$) for the H^1-errors of $\mathbf{u},\mathbf{d}$ and the L^2-errors of p. In Table 1, by fixing the values of the other parameters and taking the values of γ as 0.21 and 0.19 respectively, it was found that the order of convergence was 2. Similarly, we took the values of λ as 0.19 and 0.21, respectively, in Table 2. We took the values of η as 0.19 and 0.21, respectively, in Table 4. We took the values of ϵ as 0.06 and 0.07, respectively, in Table 4. In conclusion, the temporal convergence order of Scheme I was close to 2 in comparison with the different variables $\gamma,\lambda,\eta,\epsilon$ in Tables 1–4. In Tables 5–8, we verify the temporal convergence order of Scheme II for different parameter values. In the experiment, we used different time step sizes ($\tau=0.03125, 0.015625, 0.0078125$) for the H^1-errors of $\mathbf{u},\mathbf{d}$ and the L^2-errors of p. Similarly, different parameter values ($\gamma=0.015,\ 0.02,\lambda=0.25,\ 0.28,\eta=0.45,\ 0.55,\epsilon=0.05, 0.06$) were taken in Tables 5–8, respectively. For Scheme II, we reached the same conclusion with a similar analysis—the temporal convergence order was close to 2. The numerical results were consistent with the accuracy of the proposed schemes, indicating their correctness.

Table 1. The temporal convergence order of Scheme I with different values of γ.

γ	τ	d-Error	Order	u-Error	Order	p-Error	Order
0.21	0.0625	0.34299		0.11631		0.32683	
	0.03125	0.09125	1.8636	0.02967	1.9707	0.08991	1.8620
	0.015625	0.02271	2.0529	0.00753	1.9750	0.02212	2.0226
0.19	0.0625	0.33641		0.10992		0.31852	
	0.03125	0.09317	1.8523	0.02794	1.9757	0.08935	1.8338
	0.015625	0.02426	1.9411	0.00711	1.9747	0.02307	1.9532

Table 2. The temporal convergence order of Scheme I with different values of λ.

λ	τ	d-Error	Order	u-Error	Order	p-Error	Order
0.19	0.0625	0.33956		0.10741		0.30724	
	0.03125	0.09417	1.8503	0.02728	1.9772	0.08539	1.8472
	0.015625	0.02446	1.9447	0.00693	1.9770	0.02151	1.9890
0.21	0.0625	0.34036		0.11892		0.33942	
	0.03125	0.09181	1.8902	0.03023	1.9757	0.09414	1.8502
	0.015625	0.02358	1.9608	0.00771	1.9720	0.02373	1.9876

Table 3. The temporal convergence order of Scheme I with different values of η.

η	τ	d-Error	Order	u-Error	Order	p-Error	Order
0.19	0.0625	0.34019		0.11625		0.31611	
	0.03125	0.08624	1.9799	0.02956	1.9756	0.08799	1.8449
	0.015625	0.02162	1.9956	0.00751	1.9768	0.02239	1.9746
0.21	0.0625	0.33973		0.11023		0.33044	
	0.03125	0.09419	1.8507	0.02809	1.9723	0.09156	1.8516
	0.015625	0.02446	1.9451	0.00713	1.9765	0.02287	2.0014

Table 4. The temporal convergence order of Scheme I with different values of ϵ.

ϵ	τ	d-Error	Order	u-Error	Order	p-Error	Order
0.06	0.0625	0.40213		0.15011		0.41299	
	0.03125	0.10961	1.8753	0.03807	1.9791	0.11633	1.8278
	0.015625	0.02819	1.9588	0.00971	1.9713	0.02835	2.0365
0.07	0.0625	0.33995		0.11316		0.32333	
	0.03125	0.09428	1.8503	0.02880	1.9740	0.08756	1.8846
	0.015625	0.02448	1.9454	0.00734	1.9711	0.02206	1.9883

Table 5. The temporal convergence order of Scheme II with different values of γ.

γ	τ	d-Error	Order	u-Error	Order	p-Error	Order
0.015	0.03125	0.19661		0.42594		0.51343	
	0.015625	0.05368	1.8729	0.10340	2.0424	0.13021	1.9793
	0.0078125	0.01320	2.0237	0.02884	1.8421	0.03388	1.9422
0.02	0.03125	0.28796		0.25789		0.44004	
	0.015625	0.08050	1.8388	0.06252	2.0443	0.12265	1.8431
	0.0078125	0.01959	2.0383	0.01586	1.9784	0.03462	1.8247

Table 6. The temporal convergence order of Scheme II with different values of λ.

λ	τ	d-Error	Order	u-Error	Order	p-Error	Order
0.25	0.03125	0.11689		0.35949		0.40146	
	0.015625	0.02852	2.0352	0.08765	2.0362	0.10130	1.9866
	0.0078125	0.00767	1.8947	0.02301	1.9288	0.02613	1.9546
0.28	0.03125	0.13932		0.54288		0.57504	
	0.015625	0.03389	2.0392	0.12727	2.0927	0.14874	1.9508
	0.0078125	0.00957	1.8239	0.03530	1.8502	0.03792	1.9718

Table 7. The temporal convergence order of Scheme II with different values of η.

η	τ	d-Error	Order	u-Error	Order	p-Error	Order
0.45	0.03125	0.17905		0.82395		0.79063	
	0.015625	0.04531	1.9824	0.20411	2.0132	0.21686	1.8662
	0.0078125	0.01205	1.9098	0.05520	1.8866	0.05943	1.8675
0.55	0.03125	0.14819		0.61768		0.69639	
	0.015625	0.03640	2.0253	0.15156	2.0270	0.18340	1.9249
	0.0078125	0.00994	1.8722	0.04168	1.8621	0.04780	1.9398

Table 8. The temporal convergence order of Scheme II with different values of ϵ.

ϵ	τ	d-Error	Order	u-Error	Order	p-Error	Order
0.05	0.03125	0.16191		0.71126		0.74159	
	0.015625	0.04029	2.0067	0.16924	2.0713	0.18711	1.9867
	0.0078125	0.01138	1.8232	0.04607	1.8771	0.04761	1.9745
0.06	0.03125	0.11519		0.32705		0.37503	
	0.015625	0.02803	2.0388	0.07847	2.0592	0.09197	2.0278
	0.0078125	0.00716	1.9681	0.02139	1.8747	0.02355	1.9651

In addition, using Scheme I, Scheme II, and the scheme in [20] to solve the modified Ericksen–Leslie system, we compared the total CPU usage times with different time steps. As shown in Table 9, Scheme II took less CPU usage time than Scheme I, which indicated that Scheme II was more computationally efficient and had a lower computational cost.

Table 9. The total CPU usage times of different schemes.

τ	Scheme I	Scheme II	Original Method
0.03125	10.253	8.599	36.832
0.015625	20.979	17.55	71.479
0.0078125	41.003	35.749	148.039

In order to better compare the novel convex splitting method proposed in this study with the original convex splitting method, we compared the errors of the scheme in [20] with Scheme II of this study. As shown in Figure 1, the error tended to decrease as the time step decreases.

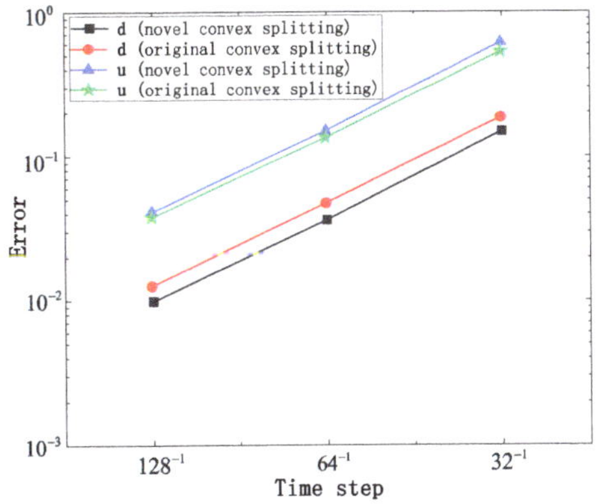

Figure 1. Errors of $\mathbf{u}, \mathbf{d}$ in H^1.

4.1.2. The Order of Spatial Convergence

To verify the spatial convergence order, we fixed the time step $\tau = 0.01$ so that the errors were only dominated by the spatial discretization error. We used different grid sizes ($h = \frac{1}{32}, \frac{1}{64}, \frac{1}{128}$) for the H^1-errors of $\mathbf{u}, \mathbf{d}$ and the L^2-errors of p. In Tables 10–13, we verify the spatial convergence order of Scheme I for different parameter values. In Table 10, by fixing the values of the other parameters and taking the values of γ as 0.8 and 1, respectively, it was found that the order of convergence was 2. Similarly, we took the values of λ as 0.5 and 0.7, respectively, in Table 11. We took the values of η as 0.08 and 0.09, respectively, in Table 12. We took the values of ϵ as 0.07 and 0.08, respectively, in Table 13. In conclusion, the spatial convergence order of Scheme I was close to 2 in comparison with the different variables $\gamma, \lambda, \eta, \epsilon$ in Tables 10–13. In Tables 14–17, we verify the spatial convergence order of Scheme II for different parameter values. Similarly, different parameter values of $\gamma = 0.1, 0.2, \lambda = 1, 0.8, \eta = 0.1, 0.2, \epsilon = 0.07, 0.08$ were taken in Tables 14–17, respectively. For Scheme II, we obtained the same conclusion with a similar analysis—the spatial convergence order was close to 2. These results are in full agreement with the theoretical expectation of accuracy for the $P2$ element of $\mathbf{u}, \mathbf{d}$ and the $P1$ element of p, indicating the correctness of our schemes.

Table 10. The spatial convergence order of Scheme I with different values of γ.

γ	h	d-Error	Order	u-Error	Order	p-Error	Order
0.8	$\frac{1}{32}$	0.03701		0.05387		0.08411	
	$\frac{1}{64}$	0.00968	1.9345	0.01520	1.8254	0.02177	1.9497
	$\frac{1}{128}$	0.00271	1.8376	0.00420	1.8522	0.00545	1.9972
1	$\frac{1}{32}$	0.02756		0.05562		0.08628	
	$\frac{1}{64}$	0.00725	1.9267	0.01569	1.8258	0.02188	1.9791
	$\frac{1}{128}$	0.00198	1.8715	0.00436	1.8468	0.00549	1.9928

Table 11. The spatial convergence order of Scheme I with different values of λ.

λ	h	d-Error	Order	u-Error	Order	p-Error	Order
0.5	$\frac{1}{32}$	0.02442		0.06460		0.10979	
	$\frac{1}{64}$	0.00656	1.8953	0.01743	1.8895	0.02725	2.0102
	$\frac{1}{128}$	0.00181	1.8555	0.00466	1.9018	0.00660	2.0458
0.7	$\frac{1}{32}$	0.02567		0.09305		0.15457	
	$\frac{1}{64}$	0.00714	1.8460	0.02532	1.8774	0.03819	2.0170
	$\frac{1}{128}$	0.00196	1.8640	0.00685	1.8865	0.00931	2.0367

Table 12. The spatial convergence order of Scheme I with different values of η.

η	h	d-Error	Order	u-Error	Order	p-Error	Order
0.08	$\frac{1}{32}$	0.02685		0.04027		0.05563	
	$\frac{1}{64}$	0.01438	1.9518	0.01561	1.8332	0.01456	1.9338
	$\frac{1}{128}$	0.00397	1.8546	0.00398	1.9706	0.00380	1.9366
0.09	$\frac{1}{32}$	0.02678		0.03626		0.05746	
	$\frac{1}{64}$	0.00693	1.9503	0.01016	1.8356	0.01467	1.9693
	$\frac{1}{128}$	0.00193	1.8439	0.00280	1.8574	0.00366	2.0008

Table 13. The spatial convergence order of Scheme I with different values of ϵ.

ϵ	h	d-Error	Order	u-Error	Order	p-Error	Order
0.07	$\frac{1}{32}$	0.02744		0.05073		0.08868	
	$\frac{1}{64}$	0.00723	1.9246	0.01361	1.8979	0.02196	2.0138
	$\frac{1}{128}$	0.00196	1.8817	0.00363	1.9076	0.00530	2.0496
0.08	$\frac{1}{32}$	0.02341		0.03742		0.06559	
	$\frac{1}{64}$	0.00609	1.9404	0.01002	1.9012	0.01639	2.0004
	$\frac{1}{128}$	0.00155	1.9753	0.00265	1.9173	0.00394	2.0575

Table 14. The spatial convergence order of Scheme II with different values of γ.

γ	h	d-Error	Order	u-Error	Order	p-Error	Order
0.1	$\frac{1}{32}$	0.20571		0.01638		0.21204	
	$\frac{1}{64}$	0.05759	1.8366	0.00405	2.0163	0.06053	1.8084
	$\frac{1}{128}$	0.01516	1.9253	0.00097	2.0607	0.01617	1.9041
0.2	$\frac{1}{32}$	0.15486		0.02831		0.18484	
	$\frac{1}{64}$	0.04232	1.8715	0.00744	1.9284	0.05269	1.8105
	$\frac{1}{128}$	0.01128	1.9068	0.00184	2.0145	0.01411	1.9004

Table 15. The spatial convergence order of Scheme II with different values of λ.

λ	h	d-Error	Order	u-Error	Order	p-Error	Order
1	$\frac{1}{32}$	0.04682		0.02348		0.18415	
	$\frac{1}{64}$	0.01237	1.9198	0.00611	1.9428	0.05253	1.8097
	$\frac{1}{128}$	0.00322	1.9421	0.00151	2.0204	0.01398	1.9094
0.8	$\frac{1}{32}$	0.07849		0.09336		0.07836	
	$\frac{1}{64}$	0.02055	1.9335	0.02379	1.9725	0.02232	1.8116
	$\frac{1}{128}$	0.00527	1.9641	0.00576	2.0464	0.00611	1.8689

Table 16. The spatial convergence order of Scheme II with different values of η.

η	h	d-Error	Order	u-Error	Order	p-Error	Order
0.1	$\frac{1}{32}$	0.13489		0.02945		0.18592	
	$\frac{1}{64}$	0.03659	1.8821	0.00749	1.9749	0.04951	1.9086
	$\frac{1}{128}$	0.00956	1.9362	0.00185	2.0193	0.01321	1.9053
0.2	$\frac{1}{32}$	0.17717		0.03014		0.18198	
	$\frac{1}{64}$	0.04683	1.9197	0.00764	1.9795	0.04843	1.9096
	$\frac{1}{128}$	0.01218	1.9422	0.00194	1.9745	0.01276	1.9243

Table 17. The spatial convergence order of Scheme II with different values of ϵ.

ϵ	h	d-Error	Order	u-Error	Order	p-Error	Order
0.07	$\frac{1}{32}$	0.20571		0.02832		0.18484	
	$\frac{1}{64}$	0.05454	1.9152	0.00686	2.0455	0.05269	1.8105
	$\frac{1}{128}$	0.01455	1.9068	0.00162	2.0826	0.01412	1.9004
0.08	$\frac{1}{32}$	0.17718		0.02833		0.18525	
	$\frac{1}{64}$	0.04611	1.9421	0.00698	2.0212	0.04965	1.8996
	$\frac{1}{128}$	0.01219	1.9197	0.00169	2.0458	0.01321	1.9102

Figure 2 illustrates the variation in the error with the grid size for both schemes. It can be seen in the figure that the error became smaller and smaller as the mesh increased.

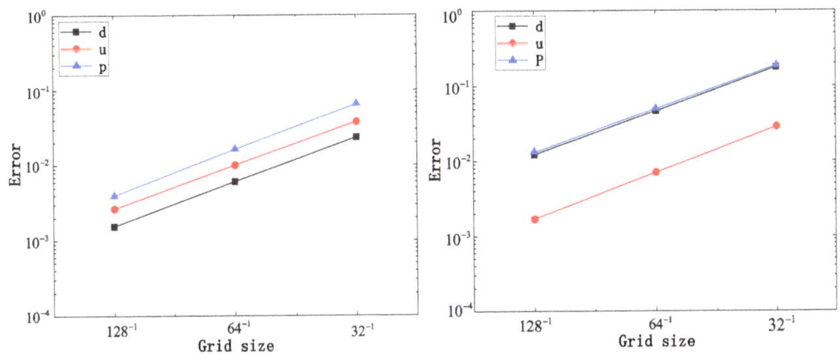

Figure 2. The trend of the errors with the grid size: Scheme I (**left**); Scheme II (**right**).

4.2. Annihilation and Stable Defects

The numerical example was associated with the phenomenon of the annihilation of singularities. We considered many numerical experiences consisting of the motions of the singularity. We simulated evolutions of the director vector **d** field over time under certain conditions. The motion of defect points in liquid crystals can be simulated via the long-time behavior of the harmonic map flow. Moreover, the disappearance of singularity is affected by the direction. Finally, the defects would move toward a steady state. We simulated the dynamic evolution of singularities until the simulation reached the steady state. For the different initial values of **d**, we give the annihilation phenomena of the singularities. A comparison of the annihilation for different initial directors in two schemes is presented. We considered the computational domain in the unit circle $\Omega = (x,y) : x^2 + y^2 < 1$, and the following parameters were chosen: $\tau = 0.05, h = \frac{1}{50}, \gamma = 0.18, \lambda = 0.01, \eta = 0.1$, and $\epsilon = 0.05$.

For Scheme I, we chose the initial conditions as follows:

$$\mathbf{u} = \mathbf{0},\ p = 0,\ \mathbf{d} = (sin(\pi(x^2+y^2)^2), cos(\pi(x^2+y^2)^2)).$$

The evolutions of the director field **d** and the velocity field **u** at different times are displayed in Figures 3 and 4, where $T = 3$ is the stoping time of the iteration.

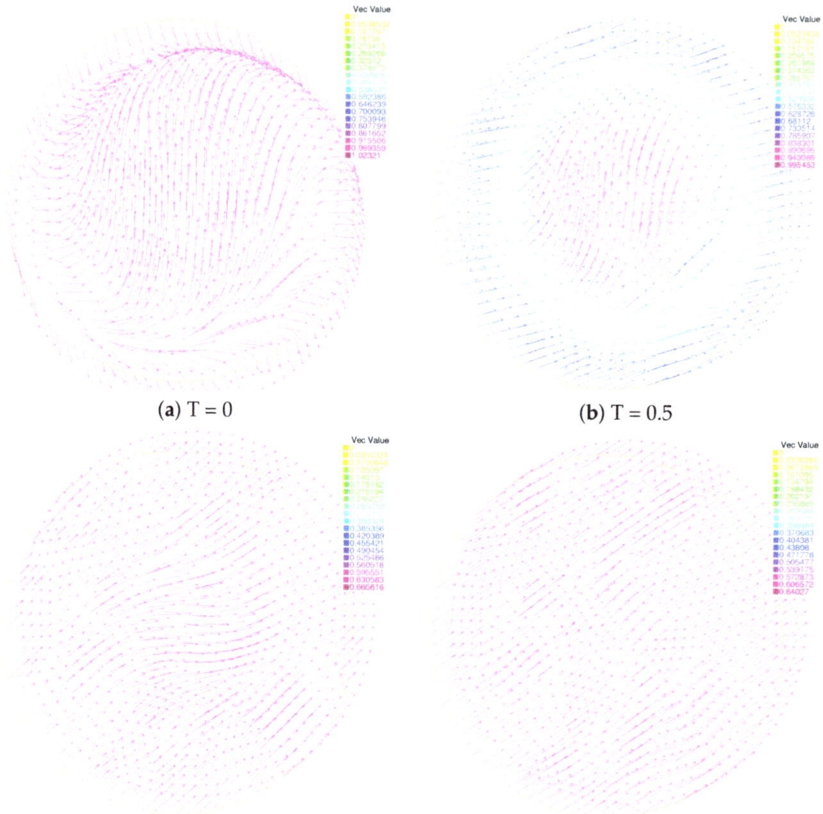

(**a**) T = 0 (**b**) T = 0.5

(**c**) T = 1.5 (**d**) T = 3

Figure 3. Evolution of the director fields of Scheme I: T = 0 (**top left**), T = 0.5 (**top right**), T = 1.5 (**bottom left**), T = 3 (**bottom right**).

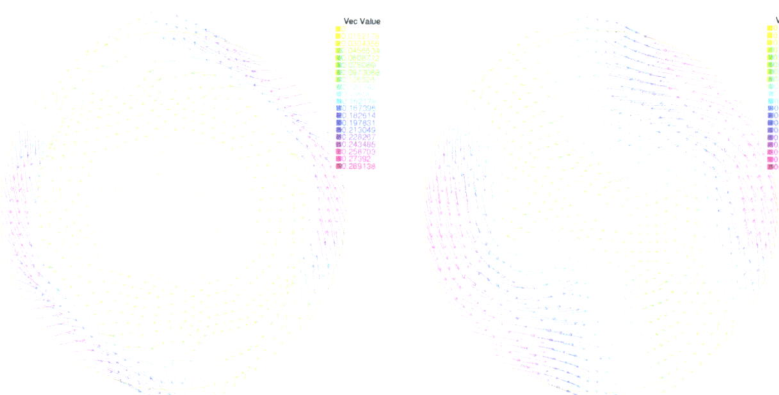

(**a**) $T = 0.05$ (**b**) $T = 0.5$

Figure 4. *Cont.*

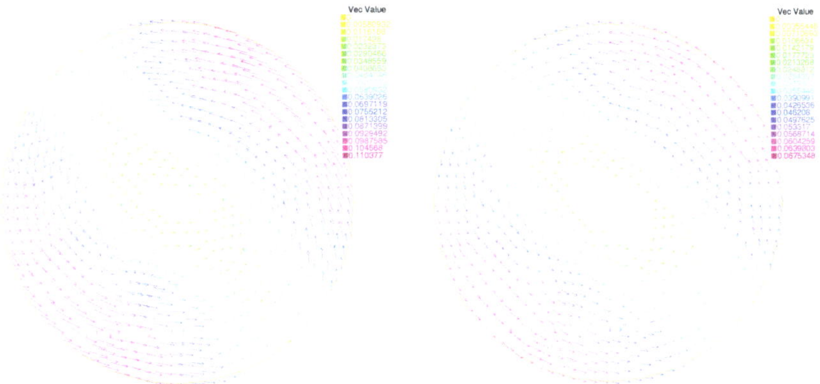

(**c**) $T = 1.5$ (**d**) $T = 3$

Figure 4. Evolution of the velocity fields of Scheme I: T = 0.05 (**top left**), T = 0.5 (**top right**), T = 1.5 (**bottom left**), T = 3 (**bottom right**).

For Scheme II, the initial conditions were taken as follows:

$$\mathbf{u} = \mathbf{0},\ p = 0,\ \mathbf{d} = (sin(2\pi(cosx - siny)), cos(2\pi(cosx - siny))).$$

By changing the initial directors, we present the phenomenon of the annihilation of singularities. We also found a small difference in the molecule orientation near the boundary. Figures 5 and 6 show the simulation results for the annihilation of singularities.

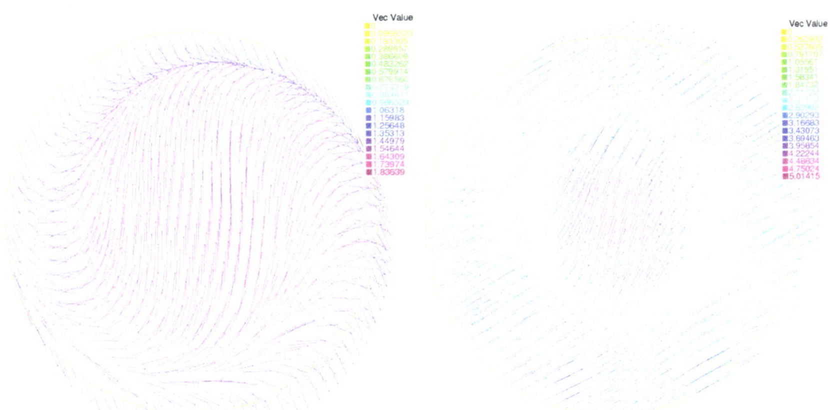

(**a**) $T = 0$ (**b**) $T = 0.5$

Figure 5. *Cont.*

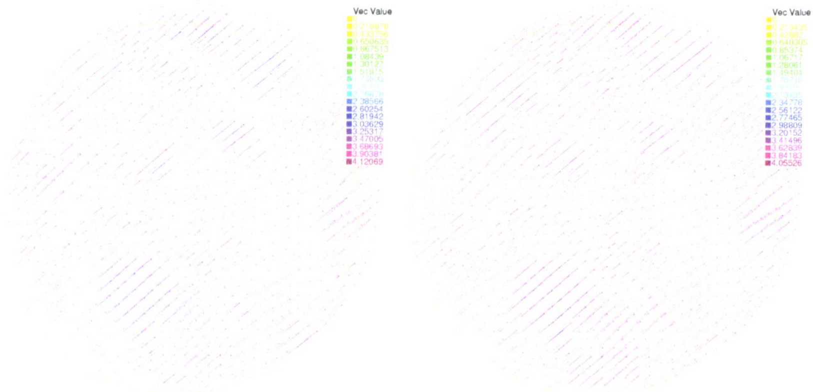

(c) $T = 1.5$ (d) $T = 3$

Figure 5. Evolution of the director fields of Scheme II: T = 0 (**top left**), T = 0.5 (**top right**), T = 1.5 (**bottom left**), T = 3 (**bottom right**).

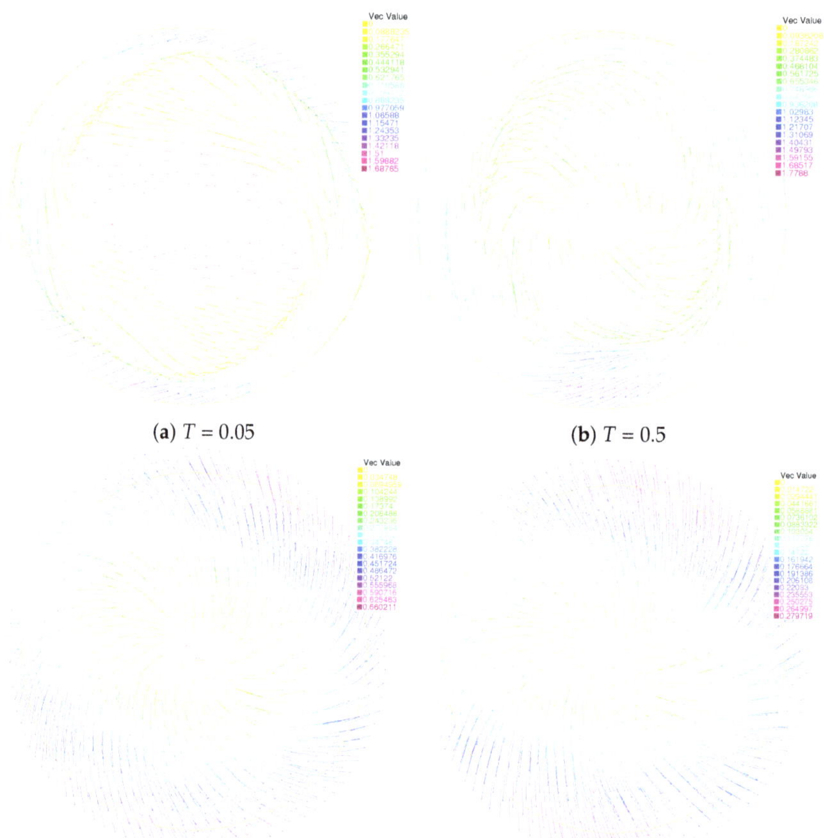

(a) $T = 0.05$ (b) $T = 0.5$

(c) $T = 1.5$ (d) $T = 3$

Figure 6. Evolution of the velocity fields of Scheme II: T = 0.05 (**top left**), T = 0.5 (**top right**), T = 1.5 (**bottom left**), T = 3 (**bottom right**).

'Vec Value' in Figures 3–6 is the abbreviation of 'Vector Value'. The arrows in the figure represent the directions of the molecules, and different colors represent different numerical sizes. In Figure 3, we plot the director field $\mathbf{d}$ at four different times: at $t = 0$, where the singularities are swirled around with the flow; at $t = 0.5$, where the singularities clearly keep on moving with the flow; after $t = 1.5$, where the change trend starts moving in one direction. Figure 5 is the same. In Figure 4, we plot the velocity field $\mathbf{u}$ at four different times: at $t = 0.05$, where the singularities are swirled around with the flow; at $t = 0.5$, where the singularities keep on moving closer and closer to each other with the flow; at $t = 1.5$, with the singularities just prior to annihilation; finally, at $t = 3$, where the steady state is reached. Similarly, we find that the steady state begins to be reached roughly after $t = 1.5$ in Figure 6.

1.3. The Dissipation of Energy

In this section, we describe the test of the energy decay for the proposed schemes. The discrete energy functional for Scheme I can be written as

$$E(\mathbf{u}_h^{n+1}, \mathbf{d}_h^{n+1}) = \int_\Omega (\frac{1}{2} \mid \mathbf{u}_h^{n+1} \mid^2 + \frac{\lambda}{2} \mid \nabla \mathbf{d}_h^{n+1} \mid^2 + \frac{\lambda}{4\epsilon^2} (\mid \mathbf{d}_h^{n+1} \mid^2 - 1)^2) dx.$$

In the test, we considered a numerical experience consisting of the motion of two singularities. In order to simulate the time behavior of different energies interacting in the system, we defined the kinetic and elastic energies as

$$E_{kin} = \frac{1}{2} \|\mathbf{u}\|^2, \qquad E_{ela} = \frac{\lambda}{2} \|\nabla \mathbf{d}\|^2 + \frac{\lambda}{4\epsilon^2} \|\mathbf{d}^2 - 1\|^2.$$

Scheme I of the Ericksen–Leslie hydrodynamic model was computed in the domain $[-1, 1] \times [-1, 1]$, and the initial conditions were

$$\mathbf{u} = \mathbf{0}, \ p = 0, \ \mathbf{d}_0 = (\frac{\bar{\mathbf{d}}}{\sqrt{\mid \bar{\mathbf{d}} \mid^2 + \epsilon^2}}), \ \bar{\mathbf{d}} = (x^2 + y^2 - 0.25, y).$$

The evolution of the kinetic and elastic energies is depicted in Figures 7–10. Here, Figures 7 and 8 show the results of the kinetic energy and elastic energy in comparison with the different time steps. Similarly, it was found that the energies were acceptable for E_{kin} and E_{ela} in comparison with the variables γ, λ, η, and ϵ in Figures 9 and 10, respectively.

In Figures 7 and 8, we also plot the condition parameters in terms of the time step τ for different values of E_{kin} and E_{ela}. No matter how large or small, the elastic energy changed only a little. However, the degree of kinetic energy dissipation became more obvious with the increase in the time step.

It was obvious that the condition parameters of the matrix were not sensitive to γ, λ, η, and ϵ, as shown in Figure 9. The velocity was dissipated, and the elastic energy showed a slow decay.

Furthermore, we found that the kinetic energy reached its maximum level at the annihilation time in Figure 10. The results verified our expectations. Therefore, these numerical results were achieved as expected.

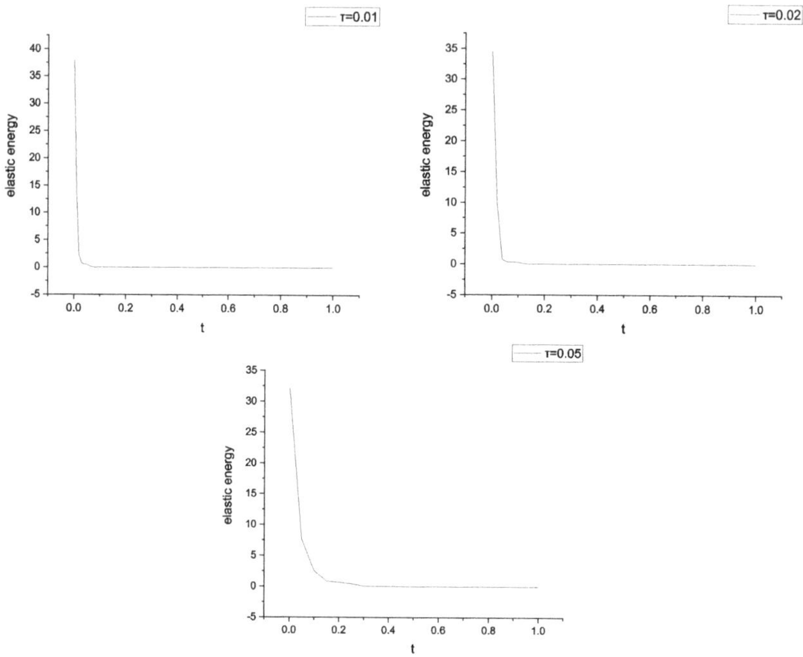

Figure 7. The different time steps of elastic energy.

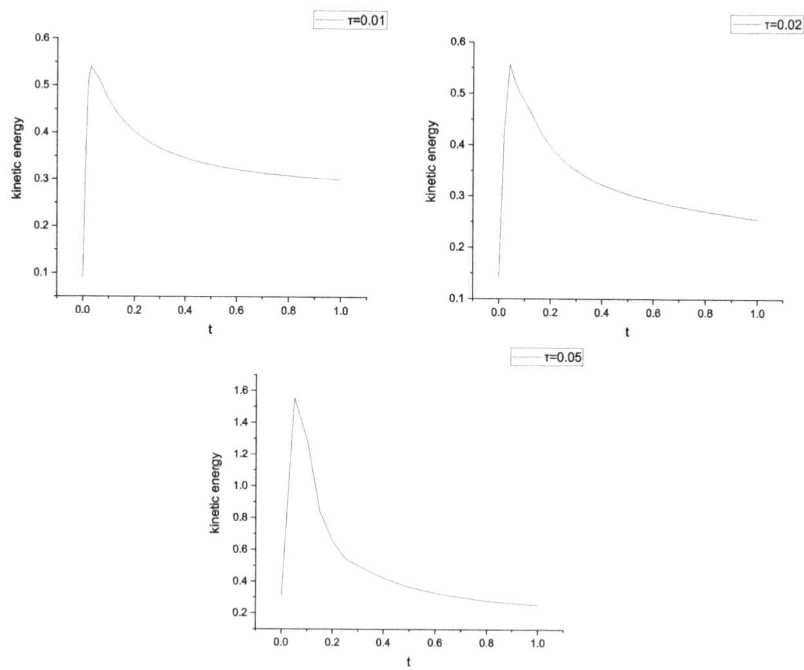

Figure 8. The different time steps of kinetic energy.

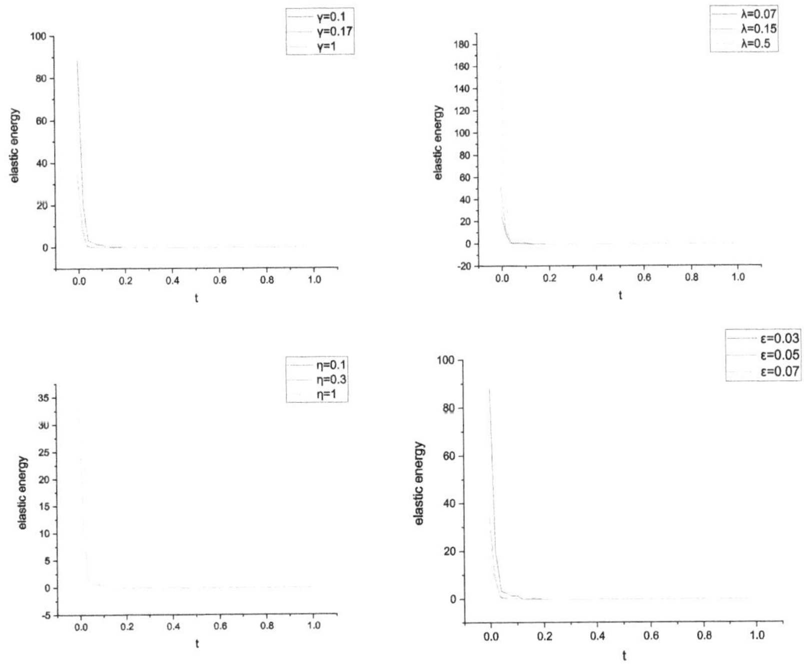

Figure 9. The different parameters of elastic energy.

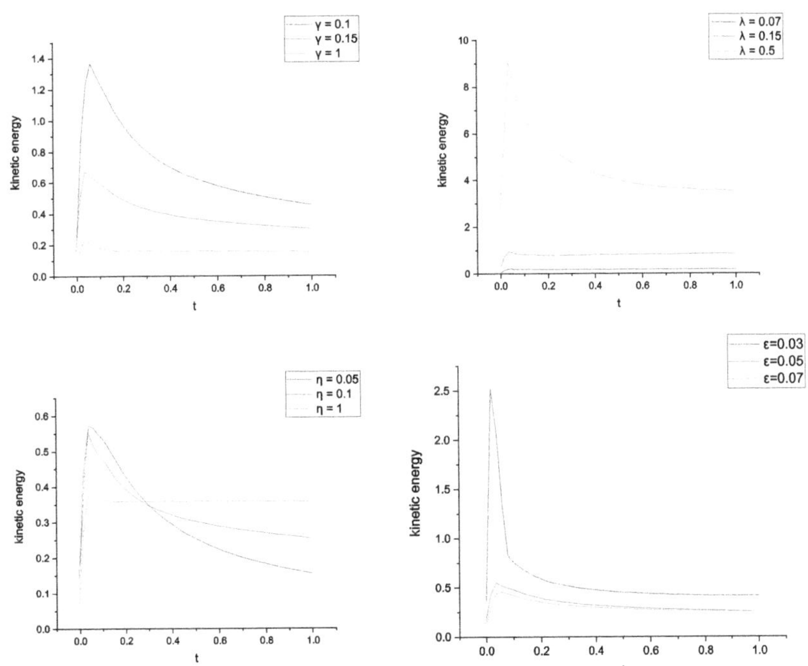

Figure 10. The different parameters of kinetic energy.

5. Conclusions

To study numerical approximations for the modified Ericksen–Leslie model, this study designed two different fully discrete finite element schemes. One was the numerical scheme of the second-order backward differentiation formula, and the other was the leap frog scheme. Their key idea was based on a novel convex splitting method, which was a unique way to skillfully deal with the nonlinear term. We not only rigorously proved the unconditional energy stability, but we also showed a detailed practical implementation for both schemes. A large number of numerical results showed that the order of convergence of the two schemes was of the second order in both time and space. Significantly, the numerical experiments also showed that the leap frog scheme was more computationally efficient than the backward differentiation formula.

Author Contributions: Conceptualization, D.W.; Methodology, D.W.; Software, C.L.; Writing—review & editing, C.L.; Writing—original draft, H.Z. All authors have read and agreed to the published version of the manuscript.

Funding: This study was supported by a research project supported by the Shanxi Scholarship Council of China (2021-029), Shanxi Province Natural Science Foundation (202203021211129).

Data Availability Statement: All data generated or analyzed during this study are included in the published article.

Conflicts of Interest: The authors declare no conflict of interest.

Appendix A. Maximum Principle

"If $|\mathbf{d}_0| \leq 1$ in Ω, then $|\mathbf{d}(t)| \leq 1$ in Ω for each $t \in [0, T]$."

This result is based on the following time-differential inequality satisfied by $|\mathbf{d}|^2$:

$$\frac{1}{2}\partial_t|\mathbf{d}|^2 + \mathbf{u} \cdot \nabla|\mathbf{d}|^2 - \gamma\Delta|\mathbf{d}|^2 + \gamma f(\mathbf{d}) \cdot \mathbf{d} \leq 0 \quad \text{in } Q,$$

which was obtained by making the scalar product of the first two equations in (3) with $\mathbf{d}$ jointly with the property

$$f(\mathbf{d}) \cdot \mathbf{d} \geq 0 \quad \text{if } |\mathbf{d}| \geq 1.$$

References

1. Rey, A.D.; Denn, M.M. Dynamical phenomena in liquid-crystalline materials. *Annu. Rev. Fluid Mech.* **2002**, *34*, 233–266. [CrossRef]
2. Ericksen, J. Hydrostatic theory of liquid crystal. *Arch. Ration. Mech. Anal.* **1962**, *9*, 371–378. [CrossRef]
3. Ericksen, J.L. Conservation laws for liquid crystals. *J. Rheol.* **1961**, *5*, 23–34. [CrossRef]
4. Ericksen, J.L. Liquid Crystals with Variable Degree of Orientation. *IMA Preprint Ser.* **1989**, 559. [CrossRef]
5. Leslie, F.M. Some constitutive equations for liquid crystals. *Arch. Ration. Mech. Anal.* **1968**, *28*, 265–283. [CrossRef]
6. Ball, J.M. Mathematics and liquid crystals. *Mol. Cryst. Liq. Cryst.* **2017**, *647*, 1–27. [CrossRef]
7. Climent-Ezquerra, B.; Guillen-González, F. Convergence to equilibrium for smectic-A liquid crystals in domains without constraints for the viscosity. *Nonlinear Anal.* **2014**, *102*, 208–219. [CrossRef]
8. Liu, C.; Walkington, N.J. Approximation of liquid crystal flows. *SIAM J. Numer. Anal.* **2000**, *37*, 725–741. [CrossRef]
9. Chen, C.J.; Yang, X.F. Fully-decoupled, energy stable second-order time-accurate and finite element numerical scheme of the binary immiscible Nematic-Newtonian model. *Comput. Methods Appl. Mech. Eng.* **2022**, *395*, 114963. [CrossRef]
10. Zhang, X.; Wang, D.X.; Zhang, J.W.; Jia, H.E. Fully decoupled linear BDF2 scheme for the penalty incompressible Ericksen-Leslie equations. *Math. Comput. Simulat.* **2023**, *212*, 249–266. [CrossRef]
11. Lin, F.; Liu, C. Nonparabolic dissipative systems modeling the flow of liquid crystals. *Commun. Pure Appl. Math.* **1995**, *48*, 501–537. [CrossRef]
12. Ping, L.; Liu, C. Simulations of singularity dynamics in liquid crystal flows: A C0 finite element approach. *J. Comput. Phys.* **2006**, *215*, 348–362.
13. Guillen-Gonzalez, F.M.; Gutirrez-Santacreu, J.V. A linear mixed finite element scheme for a nematic EricksenCLeslie liquid crystal model. *ESAIM Math. Model. Numer. Anal.* **2013**, *47*, 1433–1464. [CrossRef]
14. Girault, V.; Guillen-Gonzalez, F. Mixed formulation, approximation and decoupling algorithm for a penalized nematic liquid crystals model. *Math. Comput.* **2011**, *80*, 781–819. [CrossRef]
15. Badia, S.; Guilln-Gonzlez, F.; Gutirrez-Santacreu, J.V. Finite element approximation of nematic liquid crystal flows using a saddle-point structure. *J. Comput. Phys.* **2011**, *230*, 1686–1706. [CrossRef]

16. Bao, X.; Chen, R.; Zhang, H. Constraint-preserving energy-stable scheme for the 2D simplified Ericksen-Leslie system. *J. Comput. Math.* **2021**, *39*, 1. [CrossRef]
17. Wang, D.; Miao, N.; Liu, J. A second-order numerical scheme for the Ericksen-Leslie equation. *AIMS Math.* **2022**, *7*, 15834–15853. [CrossRef]
18. Cheng, K.; Wang, C.; Wise, S.M. An energy stable finite difference scheme for the Ericksen–Leslie system with penalty function and its optimal rate convergence analysis. *Commun. Math. Sci.* **2023**, *21*, 1135–1169. [CrossRef]
19. Wang, D.; Liu, F.; Jia, H.; Zhang, J. Error estimates of a sphere-constraint-preserving numerical scheme for Ericksen-Leslie system with variable density. *Discret. Contin. Dyn. Syst.-B* **2023**, *28*, 5814–5838. [CrossRef]
20. Miao, N.; Wang, D.; Zhang, H.; Liu, J. A second-order BDF convex splitting numerical scheme for the ericksen-leslie equation. *Numer. Algorithms* **2023**, *94*, 293–314. [CrossRef]
21. Ren, Y.; Liu, D. Pressure correction projection finite element method for the 2D/3D time-dependent thermomicropolar fluid problem. *Comput. Math. Appl.* **2023**, *136*, 136–150. [CrossRef]
22. Wang, S.; Zhu, M.; Cao, H.; Xie, X.; Li, B.; Guo, M.; Li, H.; Xu, Z.; Tian, J.; Ma, D. Contact Pressure Distribution and Pressure Correction Methods of Bolted Joints under Mixed-Mode Loading. *Coatings* **2022**, *12*, 1516. [CrossRef]
23. Yang, X.F. Linear, first and second-order, unconditionally energy stable numerical schemes for the phase field model of homopolymer blends. *J. Comput. Phys.* **2016**, *327*, 294–316. [CrossRef]
24. Shen, J.; Xu, J.; Yang, J. The scalar auxiliary variable (SAV) approach for gradient flows. *J. Comput. Phys.* **2018**, *353*, 407–416. [CrossRef]
25. Shen, J.; Xu, J.; Yang, J. A new class of efficient and robust energy stable schemes for gradient flows. *SIAM Rev.* **2019**, *61*, 474–506. [CrossRef]
26. Guilln-Gonzlez, F.; Tierra, G. On linear schemes for a Cahn Hilliard diffuse interface model. *J. Comput. Phys.* **2013**, *234*, 140–171. [CrossRef]
27. Xu, X.; Van Zwiete, G.J.; van der Zee, K.G. Stabilized second-order convex splitting schemes for cahn-hilliard models with application to diffuse-interface tumor-growth models. *Int. J. Numer. Methods Biomed. Eng.* **2014**, *30*, 180–203.
28. Shen, J.; Wang, C.; Wang, S.; Wang, X. Second-order convex splitting schemes for gradient flows with ehrlich-schwoebel type energy: Application to thin film epitaxy. *SIAM J. Numer. Anal.* **2012**, *50*, 105–125. [CrossRef]
29. Elliott, C.M.; Stuart, A.M. The global dynamics of discrete semilinear parabolic equations. *SIAM J. Numer. Anal.* **1993**, *30*, 1622–1663. [CrossRef]
30. Eyre, D.J. Unconditionally gradient stable time marching the Cahn-Hilliard equation. *MRS Online Proc. Libr. (OPL)* **1998**, *529*, 39–46. [CrossRef]
31. Chandrasekhar, S. *Liquid Crystals*; Cambridge University Press: Cambridge, UK, 1992.
32. de Gennes, P.G. *The Physics of Liquid Crystals*; Oxford University Press: London, UK, 1974.
33. Ezquerra, M.B.C.; González, F.M.G.; Medar, M.A.R. Reproductivity for a nematic liquid crystal model. *Z. FüR Angew. Math. Und Phys. Zamp* **2006**, *57*, 984–998. [CrossRef]
34. Hecht, F.; Pironneau, O.; Ohtsuka, K. FreeFEM++. 2010. Available online: http://www.freefem.org/ff++/ (accessed on 16 February 2024).

mathematics

MDPI

Article

Accuracy Verification of a 2D Adaptive Mesh Refinement Method by the Benchmarks of Lid-Driven Cavity Flows with an Arbitrary Number of Refinements

Rajnesh Lal [1,*], Zhenquan Li [2] and Miao Li [3]

[1] School of Mathematical and Computing Sciences, Fiji National University, Lautoka P.O. Box 5529, Fiji
[2] School of Computing, Mathematics and Engineering, Charles Sturt University, Thurgoona, NSW 2640, Australia; jali@csu.edu.au
[3] School of Computing, Mathematics and Engineering, Charles Sturt University, Bathurst, NSW 2795, Australia; mli@csu.edu.au
* Correspondence: rajnesh.lal@fnu.ac.fj

Abstract: The lid-driven cavity flow problem stands as a widely recognized benchmark in fluid dynamics, serving to validate CFD algorithms. Despite its geometric simplicity, the lid-driven cavity flow problem exhibits a complex flow regime primarily characterized by the formation of vortices at the centre and corners of the square domain. This study evaluates the accuracy of the 2D velocity-driven adaptive mesh refinement (2D VDAMR) method in estimating vortex centres in a steady incompressible flow within a 2D square cavity. The VDAMR algorithm allows for an arbitrary number of finite mesh refinements. Increasing the number of successive mesh refinements results in more accurate outcomes. In this paper, the initial coarse uniform grid mesh was refined ten times for Reynolds numbers $100 \leq Re \leq 7500$. Results show that VDAMR accurately identifies vortex centres, with its findings closely aligning with benchmark data from six literature sources.

Keywords: adaptive mesh refinement; VDAMR; lid-driven cavity; centre of vortices

MSC: 76M10

1. Introduction

Computational fluid dynamics (CFD) has evolved into a powerful tool for simulating fluid flow, heat transfer, and other related phenomena in diverse engineering applications. Discretizing the computing domain through a mesh is crucial to accurate and robust CFD simulations. Mesh refinement, a crucial aspect of this discretization process, involves adjusting the grid resolution to capture fine details and complex flow features and elevating computational accuracy without severely impacting computational cost.

High-quality mesh generation and mesh adaptivity remain major obstacles in the CFD workflow. Ensuring consistent and reliable flow solvers and residual values convergence presents challenges across various industrial contexts [1,2]. While many CFD software packages can achieve convergence in more straightforward scenarios, they often encounter difficulties with flows involving complex physics and geometries, such as those found in high-lift aircraft configurations. Existing solver techniques frequently need more robustness to ensure reliable convergence in such situations. Adaptive mesh refinement (AMR), another term for h-refinement, is a computational approach that enables users to optimize their simulations by dynamically adjusting the resolution of the computational mesh based on evolving flow characteristics and phenomena, thereby reducing computational costs. AMR techniques typically refine the computational mesh during the time-stepping process, selectively enhancing resolution in areas of interest or where refinement is deemed necessary [3]. Despite the potential of AMR strategies to enhance accuracy at a reduced computational cost, concerns regarding robustness, error estimation, management of complex geometries, and software complexity have limited their widespread adoption [1].

In addressing the challenges of accurately modelling fluid flow while preserving computational efficiency, the AMR technique has undergone significant evolution, driven by contributions from various researchers in the field of CFD. The origins of adaptive mesh refinement for CFD can be traced back to the 1980s and 1990s, encompassing seminal contributions from researchers like Berger and Oliger [4], Bell et al. [5], Friedel et al. [6], and Berger and Leveque [7]. Subsequently, the advancement of AMR has progressed alongside improvements in numerical techniques, computer hardware and software, and its application to various problems in fluid dynamics and computational science.

Li [8] introduced and presented a 2D AMR method derived from the qualitative theory of differential equations. This method refines a computational mesh based on numerically computed velocity fields. Henceforth, we refer to the 2D AMR approach introduced in [8] as the 2D velocity-driven adaptive mesh refinement (VDAMR) method. The efficacy and accuracy of the VDAMR method have been verified through the accurate locations of singular points, asymptotic lines, and closed streamlines [9], as well as through comparisons with established CFD benchmark experiments up to two refinements, including lid-driven cavity flow [10], 2D unsteady flow past a square cylinder [11], backward-facing step flow [12], and 2D flow over a wall-mounted plate [13]. In particular, the VDAMR method has been shown to be useful for capturing localized flow features, such as identifying accurate locations of the centre of vortices within refined cells [10,13]. The accuracy of the VDAMR method depends solely on the accuracy of the numerical methods used. The VDAMR method is a low-cost and robust method applicable to all incompressible fluid flows [10,11]. Li [14] analysed the computational cost of the 2D VDAMR method by applying it to a 2D lid-driven cavity flow. For a Reynolds number (Re) of 1000, the results in [14] indicated that a single application of mesh refinement reduces the computational cost to approximately 17.6% of that required for a uniform mesh to achieve similar accuracy in the velocity field. When the refinement method is applied twice, the cost is further reduced to about 3.5%. This efficiency is attributed to the refinement method's focus on refining cells only around vortex centres, separation curves, and boundaries.

The lid-driven cavity flow problem stands as a widely recognized fluid dynamics benchmark, validating CFD algorithms [15–26]. Despite its geometric simplicity, the lid-driven cavity flow problem exhibits a complex flow regime primarily characterized by the formation of vortices at the centre and corners of the square domain. The combination of its simple geometry, the presence of various corner singularities, and the difficulty in approximating the exact solution made the lid-driven cavity one of the most common benchmarks in CFD.

Numerous benchmark results are documented in the literature, including the works of Ghia et al. [21], Barragy and Carey [22], Botella and Peyret [23], Erturk et al. [24], Shapeev and Lin [25], and Perumal and Dass [26], among others. Ghia et al. [21] used the vorticity–stream function formulation of the 2D incompressible Navier–Stokes (NS) equations to study the effectiveness of the coupled strongly implicit multigrid method. They have presented solutions for several Reynolds numbers as high as $Re = 10{,}000$ with the uniform grid mesh of resolution 129×129. Barragy and Carey [22] have used a p-type finite element scheme for the fully coupled stream function–vorticity formulation of the NS equations. With this, they have presented solutions for $Re \leq 12{,}500$ on a 257×257 strongly graded and refined element mesh. Botella and Peyret [23] reported the solutions for the lid-driven cavity flow for $Re = 1000$, computed by a Chebyshev collocation method with a grid mesh of $N = 160$ (polynomial degree). Erturk et al. [24] have used the NS equations in stream function and vorticity formulation, which are solved numerically using a fine uniform grid mesh of 601×601. The solution for flows computed with several high $Re \leq 21{,}000$ are reported. Shapeev and Lin [25] employed the stream function formulation of the NS equations for the solution of the lid-driven cavity flow with several Reynolds numbers (Re). In [25], the problem is approached using a high-order finite element technique featuring exponential mesh refinement in proximity to the corners, coupled with analytical asymptotics of the flow near the corners. For $Re \leq 25{,}000$, results using 49,156 triangular elements are presented in [25]. Perumal and Dass [26] have simulated the cavity flow using the lattice Boltzmann method with a single-relaxation-time (LBM-SRT) and a multi-relaxation-time (LBM-MRT) model. They provided solutions for $Re \leq 7500$, obtained with a 201×201 lattice. The findings in [26] confirmed that the LBM-MRT model produces qualitatively accurate results and exhibits significantly fewer spatial oscillations near geometric singularities in higher Reynolds number flows.

In the early works, e.g., [10,13], we examined the accuracy of the 2D VDAMR method with two refinements and used the finite volume methods to solve the NS equations numerically. As the 2D VDAMR technique can be iteratively applied, greater accuracy in locating vortex centres can be achieved if numerical velocity fields are sufficiently accurate and more refinements are implemented. Hence, the present study further verifies the accuracy of a 2D VDAMR method in estimating the locations of the centre of vortices for a steady incompressible flow in a 2D lid-driven square cavity using more mesh refinements. A finite element method is used to solve the NS equations numerically and compute steady-driven cavity flows. The range of Re considered in this study is $100 \leq Re \leq 7500$, which, according to several studies [15,16,21–25], is well in the steady-state range. We consider an initial coarse uniform grid mesh with a resolution of 20×20 for $Re = 100$, 400 and 1000; 50×50 for $Re = 2500$ and 5000; and 80×80 for $Re = 7500$. We perform ten mesh refinements for each of the six cases using the 2D VDAMR method. The accuracy of the 2D VDAMR method in identifying the locations of the centre of vortices is validated against the corresponding benchmark results presented in [21–26].

2. Materials and Methods

This section describes the governing equations, the computational domain and the mesh structure, the flow solver, and briefly, the 2D AMR method.

2.1. The Governing Equations and Computational Domain

The present study considers the finite element discretizations of the 2D steady, incompressible NS equations, which are governed by the continuity equation and the momentum equations in two directions defined by

$$\begin{aligned} \nabla \cdot \mathbf{V} &= 0, \\ -\nu \nabla^2 \mathbf{V} + \mathbf{V} \cdot \nabla \mathbf{V} + \frac{1}{\rho} \nabla P &= 0, \end{aligned} \tag{1}$$

where $\mathbf{V} = (u, v)$ denotes the velocity field in 2D with u and v as the velocity components in the $x-$ and $y-$ directions, respectively, ν is the kinematic viscosity, ρ is the fluid density, and P represents the scalar pressure.

The lid-driven cavity consists of a square cavity with the dimensions of L. At the top boundary, a tangential unit velocity ($u = 1, v = 0$) is applied to drive the fluid flow in the cavity. The remaining three rigid walls are imposed with no-slip boundary conditions ($u = v = 0$). The origin of the cartesian coordinate is located at the left lower corner of the cavity. The geometry of the computational domain is shown in Figure 1. The Reynolds number is defined as $Re = UL/\nu$, where U is the velocity of the lid, L is the length of the cavity, and ν is the kinematic viscosity of the fluid.

2.2. Computational Mesh and the Flow Solver

For the case with $Re = 100$, 400, and 1000, the initial mesh (Mesh_0) is a uniform grid mesh with a resolution of 20×20, i.e., Mesh_0 has 441 computational nodes. This corresponds to 1323 degrees of freedom (DOF). The DOF is given by the number of nodes multiplied by the number of dependent variables. For $Re = 2500$ and 5000, Mesh_0 is a uniform grid mesh with a resolution of 50×50, corresponding to 2601 computational nodes and 7803 DOF. Mesh$_0$ for $Re = 7500$ is a finer initial mesh with a resolution of 80×80, corresponding to 6561 computational nodes and 19,683 DOF.

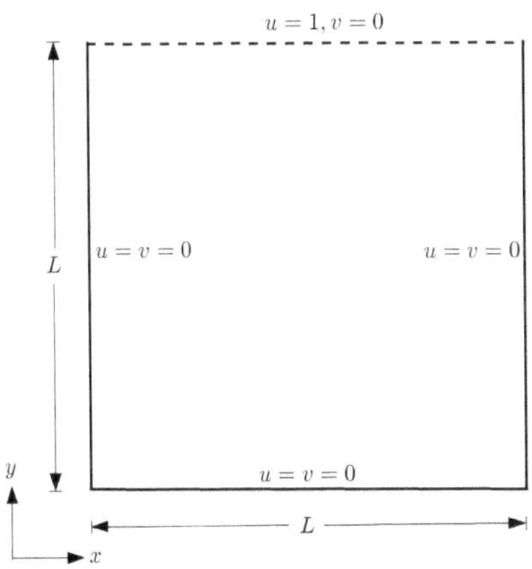

Figure 1. Cavity flow geometry and boundary conditions.

The Finite Element Analysis simulation Toolbox (FEATool, version 1.16.3, https://www.featool.com/, accessed on 3 March 2024) in MATLAB (Version 23.2.0, R2023b) was used to numerically solve the steady 2D Navier–Stokes equations. We assumed that the convergence is achieved when the numerical solutions (velocity fields) are computed with residuals smaller than 10^{-12}.

2.3. The 2D Adaptive Mesh Refinement Method

In the present study, we apply the same AMR method from [13]. We summarise the 2D AMR method and further refer the reader to Section 3 of [13] for a detailed description of the method.

Let $\mathbf{V}_l = \mathbf{AX} + \mathbf{b}'$ be defined as a vector field on a triangle obtained through linear interpolation of vectors at the three vertices of the triangle in the domain of the velocity field, where

$$\mathbf{A} = \begin{pmatrix} a_{11} & a_{12} \\ a_{21} & a_{22} \end{pmatrix}, \ \mathbf{b}' = \begin{pmatrix} b_1' \\ b_2' \end{pmatrix}, \text{ and } \mathbf{X} = \begin{pmatrix} x_1 \\ x_2 \end{pmatrix}$$

are a matrix of constants, a vector of constants, and a vector of spatial variables, respectively.

For the interpolated vector field $\mathbf{V}_l$ to satisfy the continuity equation for incompressible or steady-state flow, the equation $\nabla \cdot \mathbf{V}_l = \text{trace}(\mathbf{A}) = 0$ must be satisfied. However, the interpolated numerical velocity vector field generally does not satisfy the continuity equation. Hence, it is assumed that $f\mathbf{V}_l$ satisfies the continuity equation, where f is an unknown scalar function of the spatial variables x_1 and x_2. A differential equation is obtained when $f\mathbf{V}_l$ is substituted into the vector field $\mathbf{V}$ of the continuity equation $\nabla \cdot \mathbf{V} = 0$, resulting in $\nabla \cdot f\mathbf{V}_l = 0$. Solving the resulting differential equation for the four different Jacobian forms of the constant matrix $\mathbf{A}$ results in four distinct expressions of the function f. Table 1 shows the summary of the Jacobian forms of the constant matrix $\mathbf{A}$ with their corresponding distinct expressions of the function f for the four distinct cases in which the linear interpolations of the vector fields over triangular domains do not satisfy the law of mass conservation.

In Table 1, $(y_1, y_2)^T = \mathbf{V}^{-1}\mathbf{X}$ and $(b_1, b_2)^T = \mathbf{V}^{-1}\mathbf{b}$ where $\mathbf{V}$ satisfies $\mathbf{AV} = \mathbf{VJ}$, and $\mathbf{J}$ is one of the Jacobian matrices in the table. For $f \notin \{0, \infty\}$, the vectors $\mathbf{V}_l$ and $f\mathbf{V}_l$ produce the same streamlines (for more details we refer the readers to Section 2.2 of [9]). Consequently, mass conservation (MC) conditions are that the computed functions f in Table 1 are not equal to zero or infinity at any point on the triangular domains.

Table 1. Jacobian forms of the constant matrix **A** and the corresponding distinct expressions of the function f ($C \neq 0$) for all possible cases of a non-mass conservative linear field. The value of C is set to 1 when the conditions (MC) are implemented in MATLAB (Version 23.2.0, R2023b).

Case	Jacobian	f
1	$\begin{pmatrix} r_1 & 0 \\ 0 & r_2 \end{pmatrix}$ $(0 \neq r_1 \neq r_2 \neq 0)$	$\frac{C}{\left(y_1+\frac{b_1}{r_1}\right)\left(y_2+\frac{b_2}{r_2}\right)}$
2	$\begin{pmatrix} r_1 & 0 \\ 0 & 0 \end{pmatrix}$ $(r_1 \neq 0)$	$\frac{C}{y_1+\frac{b_1}{r_1}}$
3	$\begin{pmatrix} r_1 & 0 \\ 0 & r_1 \end{pmatrix}$ $(r_1 \neq 0)$	$\frac{C}{\left(y_1+\frac{b_1}{r_1}\right)^2}$
4	$\begin{pmatrix} \mu & \lambda \\ -\lambda & \mu \end{pmatrix}$ $(\mu \neq 0, \lambda \neq 0)$	$\frac{C}{\left(y_1+\frac{\mu b_1-\lambda b_2}{\mu^2+\lambda^2}\right)^2+\left(y_2+\frac{\lambda b_1+\mu b_2}{\mu^2+\lambda^2}\right)^2}$

A cell-by-cell AMR approach is followed on the quadrilateral grid meshes. A quadrilateral cell on which one of the conditions MC is not satisfied is subdivided. A cell is refined by connecting the mid-points of opposite sides into four equally smaller quadrilateral cells. Applying the AMR method to the initial mesh, $Mesh_0$, produces the first refined mesh, $Mesh_1$, and by repeating the procedure nine more times, we obtain the tenth refined mesh, $Mesh_{10}$. The coordinates of the centre of the isolated refined cells in the area of interest are then taken as an estimate of the centre of vortices.

Figure 2 summarises the process by which an initial mesh ($Mesh_0$) is transformed into $Mesh_2$ through the application of the flow solver and the mesh refinement algorithm VDMAR. For illustrative purposes, in Figure 2, $Mesh_0$ is a uniform grid mesh with a resolution of 5×5. This iterative procedure is repeated, with each successive mesh being refined, until the final mesh ($Mesh_{10}$) is obtained.

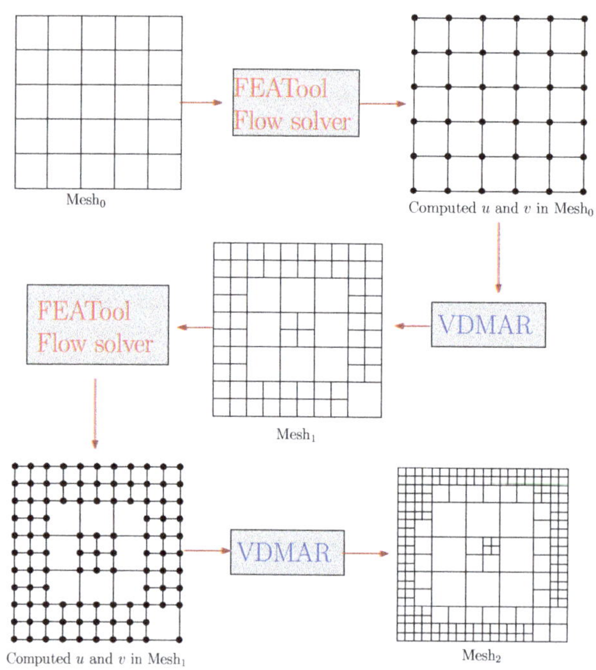

Figure 2. Summary of the process by which an initial mesh ($Mesh_0$) is transformed into $Mesh_2$ through the application of the flow solver and VDMAR.

3. Accuracy Verification and Numerical Results

This section presents the tenth refined mesh, $Mesh_{10}$, and the location of vortices estimated in a driven cavity flow for an *Re* of 100, 400, 1000, 2500, 5000, and 7500. The computed velocity fields are compared with established benchmark data from the literature to verify local accuracy. The abbreviations BR, BL, and TL denote the bottom right, bottom left, and top left vortices, respectively. The numbers that follow these abbreviations indicate the vortices' order of size, from largest to smallest. The primary vortex is abbreviated as PV.

3.1. Accuracy Verification

To validate the local accuracy of the numerically computed velocity fields for the cases with $100 < Re < 7500$, through Figures 3–8, we present the u-velocity profile along a vertical line and the v-velocity profile along a horizontal line passing through the geometric centre of the cavity. It can be seen from Figures 3–8 that the velocity profiles for all cases agree very well with those obtained by Erturk et al. [24], with a grid mesh of 601×601 using the stream function–vorticity method. The agreement between the present velocity profiles and the results of Erturk et al. [24] verifies the accuracy of the flow solver used in this study.

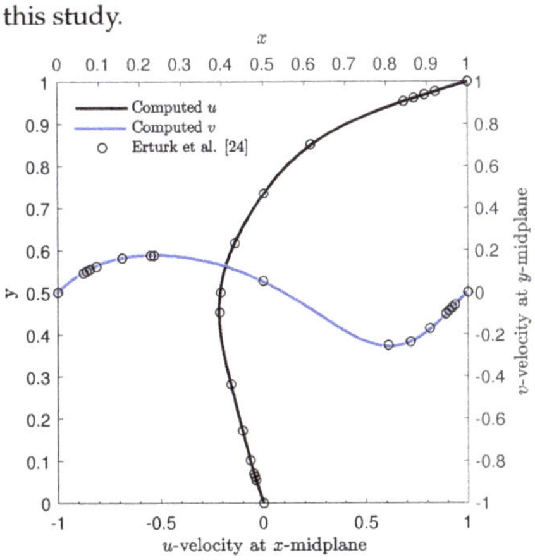

Figure 3. Computed $u-$ and $v-$ velocity profiles along a vertical line and a horizontal line, respectively, passing through the geometric centre of the cavity for the flow with $Re = 100$.

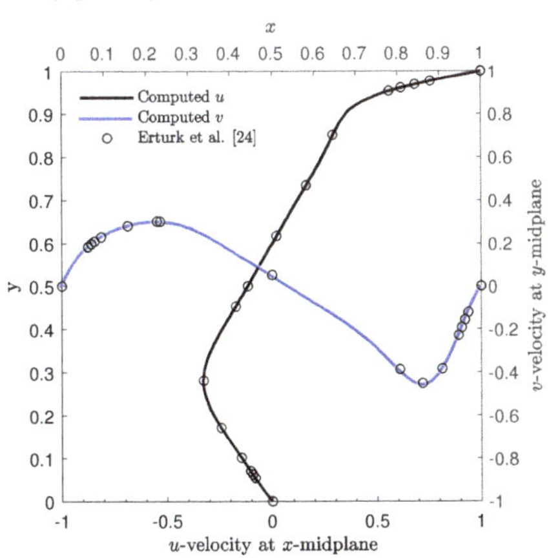

Figure 4. Computed $u-$ and $v-$ velocity profiles along a vertical line and a horizontal line, respectively, passing through the geometric centre of the cavity for the flow with $Re = 400$.

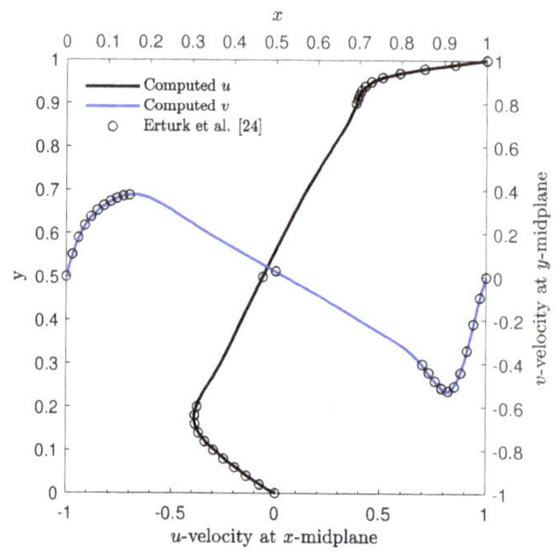

Figure 5. Computed $u-$ and $v-$ velocity profiles along a vertical line and a horizontal line, respectively, passing through the geometric centre of the cavity for the flow with $Re = 1000$.

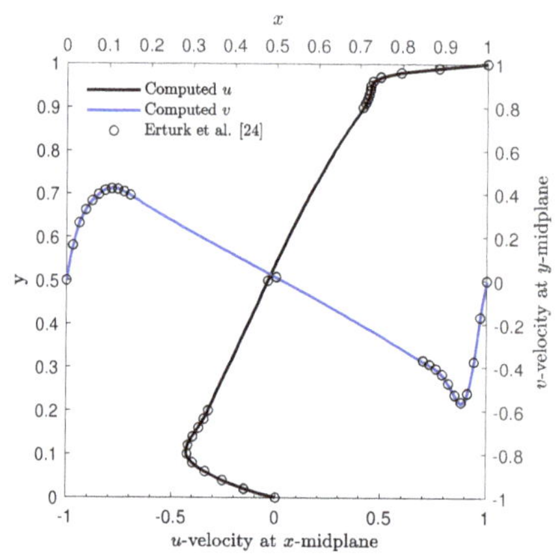

Figure 6. Computed $u-$ and $v-$ velocity profiles along a vertical line and a horizontal line, respectively, passing through the geometric centre of the cavity for the flow with $Re = 2500$.

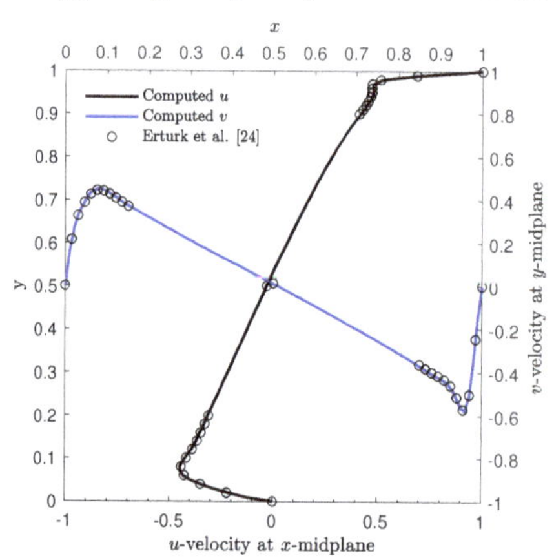

Figure 7. Computed $u-$ and $v-$ velocity profiles along a vertical line and a horizontal line, respectively, passing through the geometric centre of the cavity for the flow with $Re = 5000$.

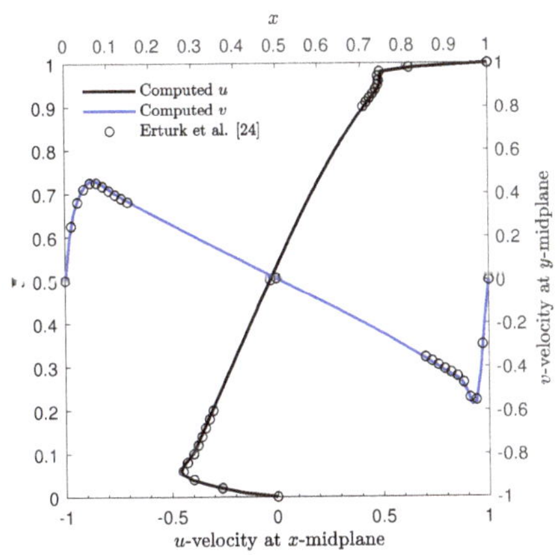

Figure 8. Computed $u-$ and $v-$ velocity profiles along a vertical line and a horizontal line, respectively, passing through the geometric centre of the cavity for the flow with $Re = 7500$.

3.2. The Refined Meshes, $Mesh_{10}$

Figure 9 shows the tenth refined mesh, Mesh_{10}, for the flow with $Re = 100$. As seen in Mesh_{10}, the mesh is refined mostly near the boundaries and at the bottom in the vicinity of the vortices BR1 and BL1. The refinements also identify the location of the PV. For the flow with $Re = 400$, a similar mesh refinement pattern as for the flow with $Re = 100$ was observed. Mesh_{10} for $Re = 400$ identified the location of two additional secondary vortices, BR2 and BL2, which appeared near the bottom right and left corners, respectively.

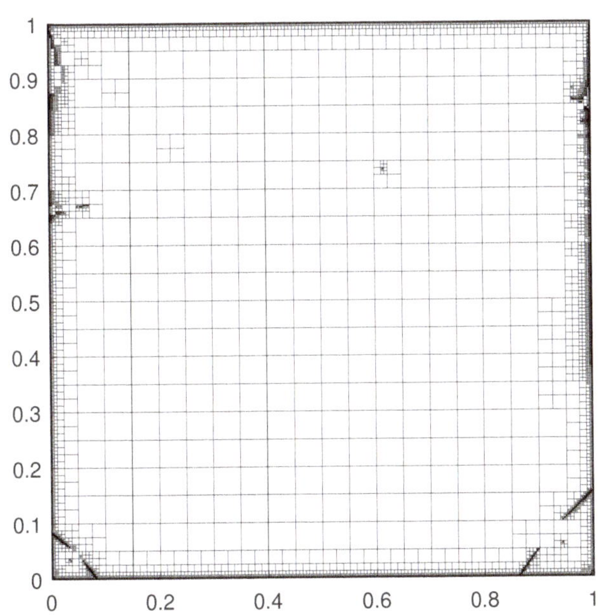

Figure 9. The tenth refined mesh, Mesh_{10}, for the flow with $Re = 100$.

Figure 10 presents Mesh_{10} for the flow with $Re = 1000$. Additionally, for this case, Figure 11a–e provides zoomed-in views highlighting the isolated refined cells containing the centres of the vortices PV, BR, and BL. In these zoomed-in sections, red circles are used for illustrative purposes to mark the locations of the vortex centres. Specifically, they indicate the positions of PV, BR1, BL1, BR2, and BL2 for $Re = 1000$.

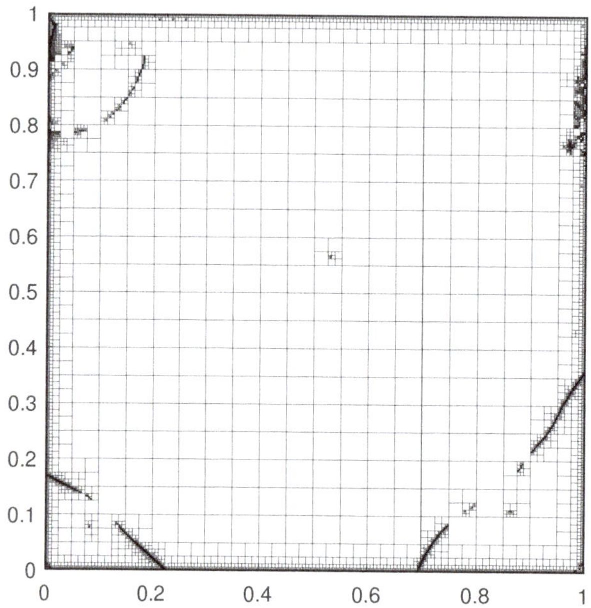

Figure 10. The tenth refined mesh, $Mesh_{10}$, for the flow with $Re = 1000$.

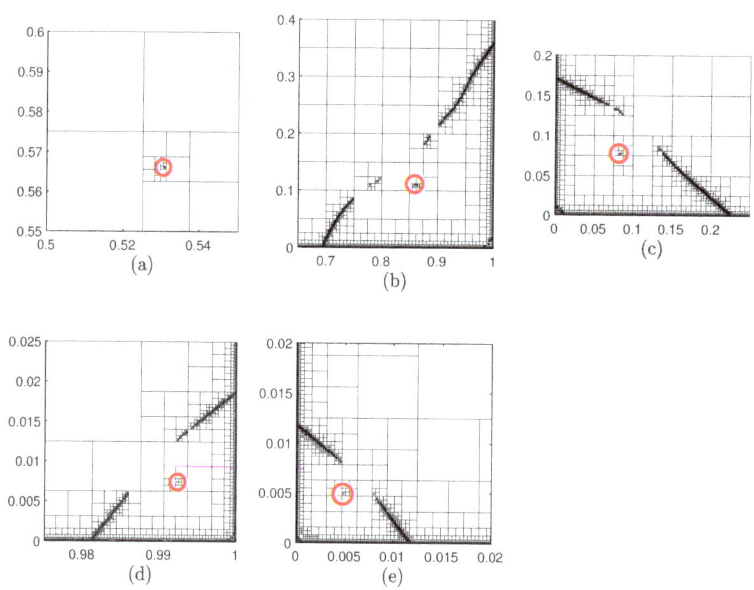

Figure 11. Zoomed-in sections of PV, BR, and BL for $Re = 1000$. Red circles contain the location of the centres of (**a**) PV, (**b**) BR1, (**c**) BL1, (**d**) BR2, and (**e**) BL2.

For the flow with $Re = 2500$, a mesh refinement pattern similar to that of the flow with $Re = 1000$ was observed. However, the refined mesh $Mesh_{10}$ for $Re = 2500$ identified the location of an additional secondary vortex, TL1, which appears near the top left corner.

$Mesh_{10}$ for the flow with $Re = 5000$ is presented in Figure 12. Compared to the case with $Re = 2500$, the refined mesh in Figure 12 identifies the location of additional secondary vortices, BR3 and BL3, which appear near the bottom right and left corners, respectively. For the flow with $Re = 7500$, a mesh refinement pattern similar to that of the flow with $Re = 5000$ was observed. $Mesh_{10}$ for the flow with $Re = 7500$ is shown in Figure 13.

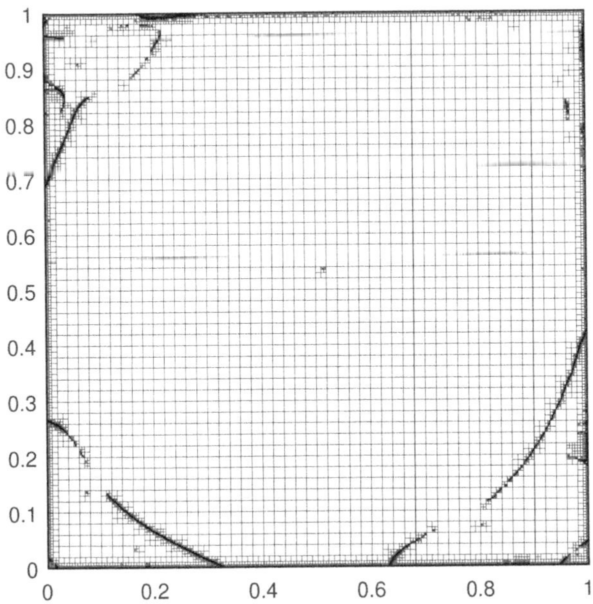

Figure 12. The tenth refined mesh, $Mesh_{10}$, for the flow with $Re = 5000$.

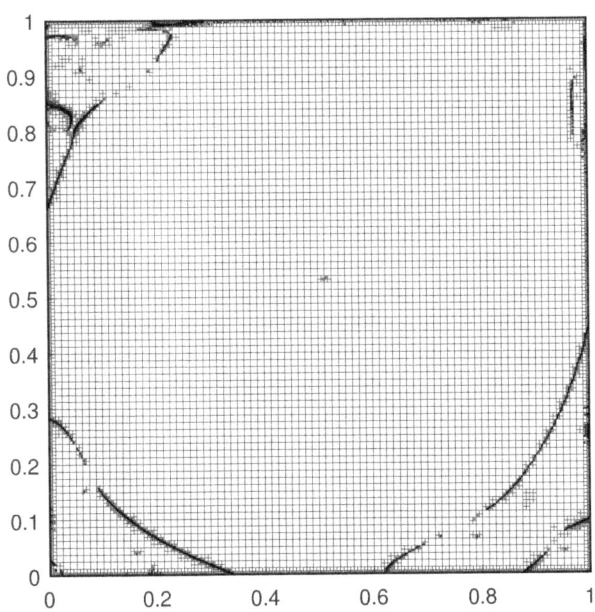

Figure 13. The tenth refined mesh, $Mesh_{10}$, for the flow with $Re = 7500$.

3.3. Vortex Centre Locations

Table 2 presents the estimated coordinates of vortex centres for the cases with $100 \leq Re \leq 7500$. The table compares the VDAMR estimated coordinates with the six reference centre locations reported by Ghia et al. [21], Barragy and Carey [22], Botella and Peyret [23], Erturk et al. [24], Shapeev and Lin [25], and Perumal and Dass [26]. The vortex centres reported in Table 2 by Perumal and Dass [26] were obtained using the LBM-MRT model. Additionally, the parameters, such as the grid resolution in terms of DOF for Mesh_{10}, along with the grid mesh size and DOF from the corresponding references, are presented in Table 2. For each case, the errors relative to the reference vortex centres were computed as $\|(x_1, y_1) - (x_{\text{ref}}, y_{\text{ref}})\| / \|(x_{\text{ref}}, y_{\text{ref}})\|$, where (x_1, y_1) are the VDAMR estimated coordinates and $(x_{\text{ref}}, y_{\text{ref}})$ are the reference vortex centres. The summarised relative errors are presented in Table 3.

Our results for $Re = 100$ align closely with those reported by Ghia et al. [21] and Perumal and Dass [26]. The relative errors in the estimated coordinates of the vortex centres underscore the precision of our findings. Specifically, the relative error in the centre location of PV and BR1 is less than 0.0073 compared to results reported by Ghia et al. [21] and Perumal and Dass [26]. A minor discrepancy exists for the estimated centre location of BL1, where the relative error is slightly higher, approaching 0.09. However, our overall results remain highly consistent with those reported in [21,26], reinforcing the robustness and accuracy of our computational approach in capturing the flow dynamics at $Re = 100$.

The results for the flow at $Re = 400$ also show a good agreement with the findings of Ghia et al. [21] and Perumal and Dass [26]. The relative errors in the centre locations of PV, BR1, and BR2 are remarkably low, with discrepancies of less than 0.007 compared to the result reported in [21,26]. This indicates a high level of precision in the VDAMR method. Additionally, the relative error in the centre location of BL1 is similarly minimal, being under 0.04. However, a significant deviation is observed in the centre location of BL2, where our results exhibit a relative error of 0.2238. This significant difference suggests a divergence in the detection of BL2 between our study and Ghia et al. [21], highlighting a potential area for further investigation.

The results for $Re = 1000$ demonstrate a high level of agreement with the findings of Botella and Peyret [23], Erturk et al. [24], Shapeev and Lin [25], and Perumal and Dass [26]. The relative errors in the centre locations of PV and secondary vortices (BR1, BR2) are impressively low, all being under 0.0035. For the secondary vortices BL1 and BL2, the relative error is slightly higher but remains under 0.025. Notably, our findings align most closely with those reported by Shapeev and Lin [25], where the relative errors for the centre locations of all vortices are consistently below 0.008. This agreement suggests that our methodology and computational approach are robust and in agreement with the results of Shapeev and Lin [25] for $Re = 1000$.

For $Re = 2500$, the VDAMR results show a remarkable agreement with those reported by Barragy and Carey [22], Erturk et al. [24], and Shapeev and Lin [25]. The comparison reveals that the relative errors in the centre locations of PV, BR1, BL1, BR2, and TL1 between our work and the studies mentioned above are consistently under 0.0086. Even though the location of BL2 exhibits a slightly higher relative error, it remains under 0.08. Among the reference studies, the closest alignment is observed with the results of Shapeev and Lin [25], where the relative errors for all VDAMR estimated centre locations are impressively less than 0.006.

Table 2. The estimated location of the centre of vortices for the flow with $100 \leq Re \leq 7500$ using the 2D VDAMR method and comparison of the present results with corresponding benchmark reference data.

Re	Vortex	Present ($Mesh_{10}$) DOF: 557,922 ($Re = 100$) DOF: 575,820 ($Re = 400$) DOF: 615,669 ($Re = 1000$) DOF: 1,660,092 ($Re = 2500$) DOF: 1,751,523 ($Re = 5000$) DOF: 2,745,150 ($Re = 7500$)	Ghia et al. [21] grid size: 129 × 129 DOF: 33,282	Barragy and Carey [22] grid size: 257 × 257 DOF: 132,098	Botella and Peyret [23] grid size: 160 × 160 DOF: 76,164	Erturk et al. [24] grid size: 601 × 601 DOF: 722,402	Shapeev and Lin [25] DOF: 226,574	Perumal and Dass [26] lattice size: 201 × 201 DOF: 121,203
100	PV	(0.615723, 0.737402)	(0.6172, 0.7344)					(0.6156, 0.7366)
	BR1	(0.942969, 0.0617188)	(0.9453, 0.0625)					(0.9405, 0.0681)
	BL1	(0.0335938, 0.0351562)	(0.0313, 0.0391)					(0.032, 0.0371)
400	PV	(0.554004, 0.605762)	(0.5547, 0.6055)					(0.5534, 0.6039)
	BR1	(0.884912, 0.12251)	(0.8906, 0.1250)					(0.8896, 0.1247)
	BL1	(0.0507812, 0.0476562)	(0.0508, 0.0469)					(0.0501, 0.05)
	BR2	(0.992578, 0.00742187)	(0.9922, 0.0078)					–
	BL2	(0.00302734, 0.00302734)	(0.0039, 0.0039)					–
1000	PV	(0.530762, 0.566113)	(0.5313, 0.5625)		(0.5308, 0.5652)	(0.5300, 0.5650)	(0.530790112, 0.565240557)	(0.5302, 0.5635)
	BR1	(0.862109, 0.112109)	(0.8594, 0.1094)		(0.8640, 0.1118)	(0.8633, 0.1117)	(0.86404006, 0.11180617)	(0.8612, 0.1112)
	BL1	(0.0833008, 0.0780273)	(0.0859, 0.0781)		(0.0833, 0.0781)	(0.0833, 0.0783)	(0.08327318, 0.078095725)	(0.0826, 0.0776)
	BR2	(0.992578, 0.00742187)	(0.9922, 0.0078)		(0.99232, 0.00765)	(0.9917, 0.0067)	(0.992324852, 0.007650979)	–
	BL2	(0.00488281, 0.00488281)	–		(0.00490, 0.00482)	(0.0050, 0.0050)	(0.0048426963, 0.0048452406)	–
2500	PV	(0.519629, 0.544043)		(0.5188822, 0.5434181)		(0.5200, 0.5433)	(0.5197769, 0.5439244)	
	BR1	(0.833438, 0.090625)		(0.834232, 0.0907512)		(0.8333, 0.0900)	(0.8344014, 0.09075692)	
	BL1	(0.0841992, 0.110918)		(0.08439557, 0.1109646)		(0.0833, 0.1117)	(0.08424181, 0.1110061)	
	BR2	(0.9904594, 0.009384439)		(0.990370, 0.00932132)		(0.9900, 0.0083)	(0.9904594, 0.009384439)	
	BL2	(0.00613281, 0.00621094)		(0.00602392, 0.00621139)		(0.0067, 0.0067)	(0.006129716, 0.006158831)	
	TL1	(0.0434375, 0.889062)		(0.0432916, 0.8890354)		(0.0433, 0.8900)	(0.04300225, 0.8893601)	
5000	PV	(0.514648, 0.535664)	(0.5117, 0.5352)	(0.5151064, 0.5358696)		(0.5150, 0.5350)	(0.5150937, 0.5352620)	(0.5147, 0.5331)
	BR1	(0.801758, 0.0730859)	(0.8086, 0.0742)	(0.8041016, 0.07248652)		(0.8050, 0.0733)	(0.8046254, 0.07274733)	(0.8051, 0.0733)
	BL1	(0.0727539, 0.136621)	(0.0703, 0.1367)	(0.07248652, 0.1370297)		(0.0733, 0.1367)	(0.07285071, 0.1370629)	(0.0733, 0.1367)
	BR2	(0.978359, 0.0188281)	(0.9805, 0.0195)	(0.9786017, 0.01881959)		(0.9783, 0.0183)	(0.9783735, 0.01877724)	(0.9801, 0.0194)
	BL2	(0.0078125, 0.00796875)	(0.0117, 0.0078)	(0.0078985, 0.007898571)		(0.0083, 0.0083)	(0.007849997, 0.007996012)	(0.0075, 0.0069)
	BR3	(0.998828, 0.001172)	–	(0.9987615, 0.001172679)		(0.9983, 0.0017)	(0.9987908, 0.001208945)	–
	BL3	(0.000468, 0.000468)	–	(0.0005185267, 0.0004534772)		–		–
	TL1	(0.0636719, 0.909141)	(0.0625, 0.9102)	(0.063488808, 0.9092488)		(0.0633, 0.9100)	(0.06335428, 0.9092566)	(0.0615, 0.9071)

Table 2. *Cont.*

Re	Vortex	Present ($Mesh_{10}$) DOF: 557,922 ($Re = 100$) DOF: 575,820 ($Re = 400$) DOF: 615,669 ($Re = 1000$) DOF: 1,660,092 ($Re = 2500$) DOF: 1,751,523 ($Re = 5000$) DOF: 2,745,150 ($Re = 7500$)	Ghia et al. [21] grid size: 129 × 129 DOF: 33,282	Barragy and Carey [22] grid size: 257 × 257 DOF: 132,098	Botella and Peyret [23] grid size: 160 × 160 DOF: 76,164	Erturk et al. [24] grid size: 601 × 601 DOF: 722,402	Shapeev and Lin [25] DOF: 226,574	Perumal and Dass [26] lattice size: 201 × 201 DOF: 121,203
7500	PV	(0.512842, 0.53208)	(0.5117, 0.5322)	(0.5132184, 0.532095)		(0.5133, 0.5317)	(0.5130967, 0.5318922)	(0.5107, 0.5308)
	BR1	(0.788037, 0.0648926)	(0.7813, 0.0625)	(0.790025, 0.06483485)		(0.79, 0.065)	(0.7903051, 0.06516917)	(0.7898, 0.0646)
	BL1	(0.064209, 0.15249)	(0.0645, 0.1504)	(0.06416178, 0.1525889)		(0.065, 0.1517)	(0.06425712, 0.1529439)	(0.0638, 0.1542)
	BR2	(0.950586, 0.0431641)	(0.9492, 0.043)	(0.9517405, 0.04218909)		(0.9517, 0.0417)	(0.9515559, 0.04215257)	(0.9474, 0.0475)
	BL2	(0.0109863, 0.0116699)	(0.0117, 0.0117)	(0.01117058, 0.01178644)		(0.0117, 0.0117)	(0.01106468, 0.01177737)	(0.0129, 0.0134)
	BR3	(0.997217, 0.0027832)	(0.9961, 0.0039)	(0.997342, 0.0026578)		(0.9967, 0.0033)	(0.9972834, 0.002715411)	–
	BL3	(0.000634766, 0.000634766)	–	(0.0006488255, 0.0007140747)		–	(0.000688091, 0.0006881077)	–
	TL1	(0.0636719, 0.911328)	(0.0664, 0.9141)	(0.06685477, 0.9116328)		(0.0667, 0.9133)	(0.06665739, 0.9114901)	(0.0652, 0.9071)

Table 3. Summary of errors relative to the benchmark reference vortex centres from six reference studies in the literature. The errors are computed as $\|(x_1, y_1) - (x_{\text{ref}}, y_{\text{ref}})\| / \|(x_{\text{ref}}, y_{\text{ref}})\|$, where (x_1, y_1) are the VDAMR estimated coordinates and $(x_{\text{ref}}, y_{\text{ref}})$ are the reference vortex centres.

Re	Vortex	Ghia et al. [21]	Barragy and Carey [22]	Botella and Peyret [23]	Erturk et al. [24]	Shapeev and Lin [25]	Perumal and Dass [26]
100	PV	0.0035					0.0008
	BR1	0.0026					0.0073
	BL1	0.0911					0.0513
400	PV	0.0009					0.0024
	BR1	0.0069					0.0058
	BL1	0.0109					0.0345
	BR2	0.0005					–
	BL2	0.2238					–
1000	PV	0.0047		0.0012	0.0017	0.0011	0.0035
	BR1	0.0044		0.0022	0.0014	0.0022	0.0015
	BL1	0.0224		0.0006	0.0024	0.0006	0.0072
	BR2	0.0005		0.0003	0.0011	0.0003	–
	BL2	–		0.0095	0.0234	0.0080	–
2500	PV		0.0013		0.0011	0.0003	
	BR1		0.0010		0.0008	0.0012	
	BL1		0.0014		0.0086	0.0007	
	BR2		0.0001		0.0012	0.0000	
	BL2		0.0126		0.0790	0.0060	
	TL1		0.0002		0.0011	0.0006	
5000	PV	0.0040	0.0007		0.0010	0.0008	0.0035
	BR1	0.0085	0.0030		0.0040	0.0036	0.0041
	BL1	0.0160	0.0032		0.0036	0.0029	0.0036
	BR2	0.0023	0.0002		0.0005	0.0001	0.0019
	BL2	0.2767	0.0099		0.0502	0.0041	0.1093
	BR3	–	0.0001		0.0007	0.0001	–
	BL3	–	0.0763		–	0.0212	–
	TL1	0.0017	0.0002		0.0010	0.0004	0.0033
7500	PV	0.0016	0.0005		0.0008	0.0004	0.0034
	BR1	0.0091	0.0025		0.0025	0.0028	0.0024
	BL1	0.0129	0.0007		0.0068	0.0027	0.0105
	BR2	0.0015	0.0016		0.0019	0.0015	0.0057
	BL2	0.0432	0.0134		0.0432	0.0082	0.1387
	BR3	0.0016	0.0037		0.0007	0.0001	–
	BL3	–	0.0002		–	0.0775	–
	TL1	0.0042	0.0035		0.0039	0.0032	0.0049

The comparison of the present results for $Re = 5000$ with those reported by Ghia et al. [21], Barragy and Carey [22], Erturk et al. [24], Shapeev and Lin [25], and Perumal and Dass [26] reveals a high level of agreement in the estimated locations of the vortex centres, with relative errors in the centre locations of PV, BR1, BR2, BR3, and TL1 being less than 0.009, and less than 0.016 for BL1. This indicates a consistent alignment across these studies, showcasing the robustness and reliability of the VDAMR method. Notably, a significant discrepancy is observed in the centre location of BL2 when compared to the result reported by Ghia et al. [21] and Perumal and Dass [26]. However, the VDAMR method's estimated centre location of BL2 aligns closely with the findings of Barragy and Carey [22] and Shapeev and Lin [25], with relative errors of 0.0099 and 0.0041, respectively. This underscores the compatibility and accuracy of VDAMR in relation to these studies. Additionally, the centre location of BL3, which is only reported by Barragy and Carey [22] and Shapeev and Lin [25], shows good agreement with the VDAMR estimates, evidenced by relative errors of 0.0763 and 0.0212, respectively. Overall, the closest and hence the best agreement of the present results for $Re = 5000$ is observed with the results of Shapeev and Lin [25], where the relative errors for the centre locations of PV, BR1, BL1, BR2, BR3, and TL1 are all under 0.004, and for BL3, the relative error is 0.0212. This comparison underscores the precision and efficacy of VDAMR in capturing vortex centre locations accurately, aligning well with the values reported in the literature.

For the case with $Re = 7500$, the VDAMR estimated centre locations of PV, BR1, BR2, and TL show good agreement with the results of Ghia et al. [21], Barragy and Carey [22], Erturk et al. [24], Shapeev and Lin [25], and Perumal and Dass [26]. The relative errors in the estimated PV, BR1, BR2, and TL centre locations are all less than 0.009. The estimated centre location of BL1 aligns closely with that reported by Barragy and Carey [22], with a relative error of 0.0007. There is a significant discrepancy in the estimated centre location of BL2 compared to the results reported by Perumal and Dass [26], with a relative error of 0.1387. The present location of BL2 aligns most closely with those reported by Barragy and Carey [22] and Shapeev and Lin [25], with relative errors of 0.0134 and 0.0082, respectively. Moreover, the present estimated centre location of BL3 is also in good agreement with the literature, with results only reported by Barragy and Carey [22] and Shapeev and Lin [25] showing a relative error of less than 0.08. The closest alignment of the present results for the case with $Re = 7500$ is observed with those presented in [25].

Figures 14–19 illustrate the streamlined contours and the flow characteristics near the vortex centres for flows with $Re = 100$, $Re = 400$, $Re = 1000$, $Re = 2500$, $Re = 5000$, and $Re = 7500$, respectively. In these figures, the red dots, added for illustrative purposes, mark the locations of the vortex centres as estimated using the VDAMR method.

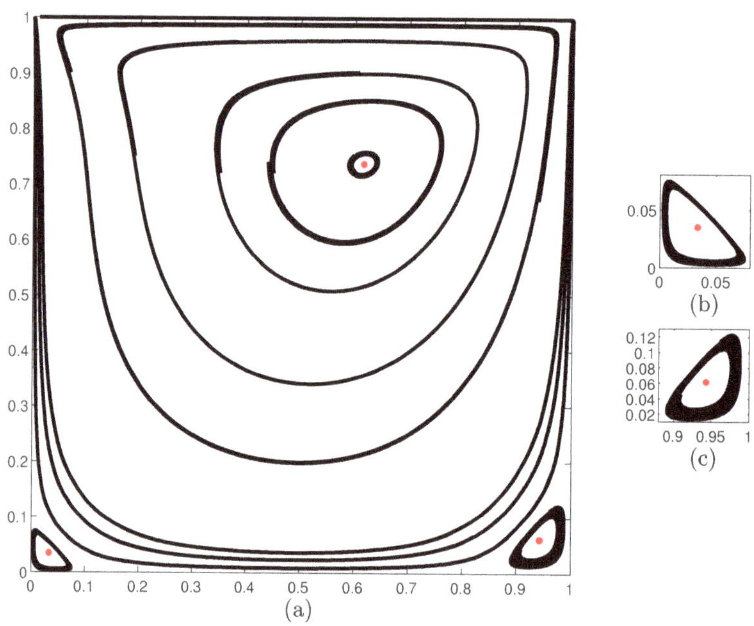

Figure 14. (**a**) $Re = 100$: streamline contours and the location of centres of PV, BR1, and BL1. The zoomed-in sections of BL and BR show (**b**) BL1 and (**c**) BR1, respectively.

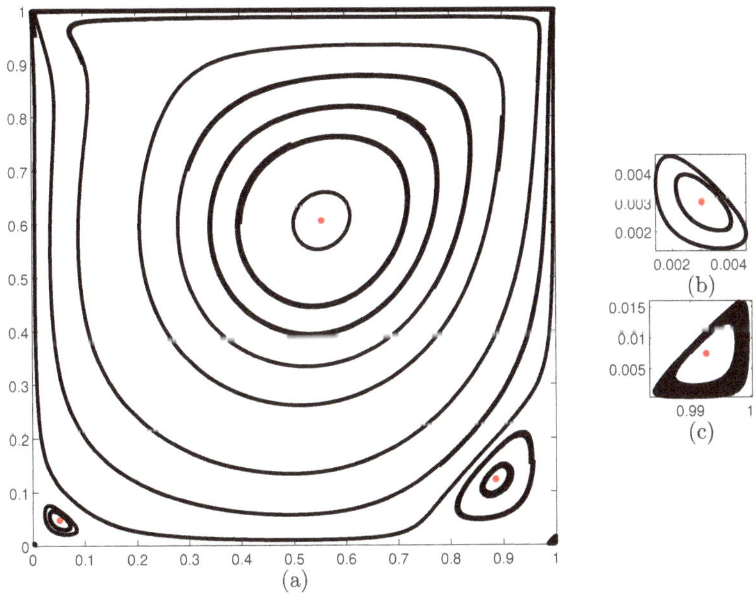

Figure 15. (**a**) $Re = 400$: streamline contours and the location of centres of PV, BR1, BL1, BR2, and BL2. The zoomed-in sections of BL and BR show (**b**) BL2 and (**c**) BR2, respectively.

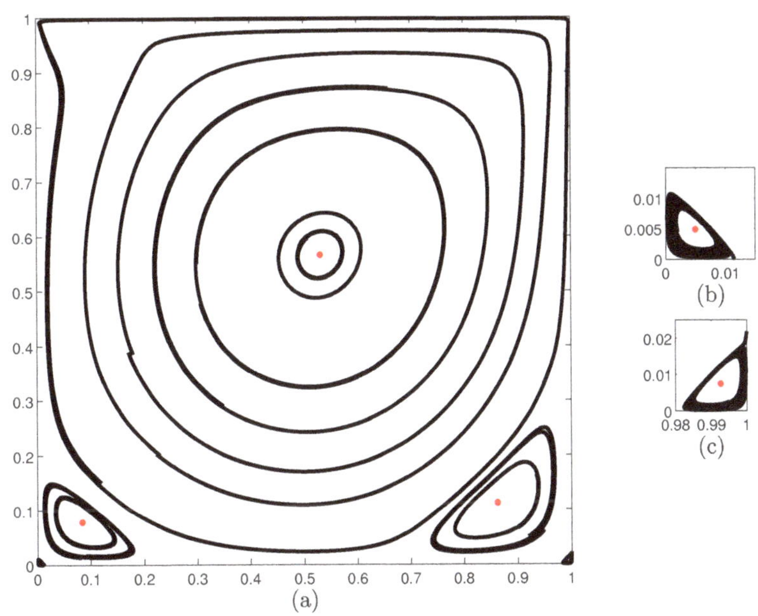

Figure 16. (a) $Re = 1000$: streamline contours and the location of centres of PV, BR1, BL1, BR2, and BL2. The zoomed-in sections of BL and BR show (**b**) BL2 and (**c**) BR2, respectively.

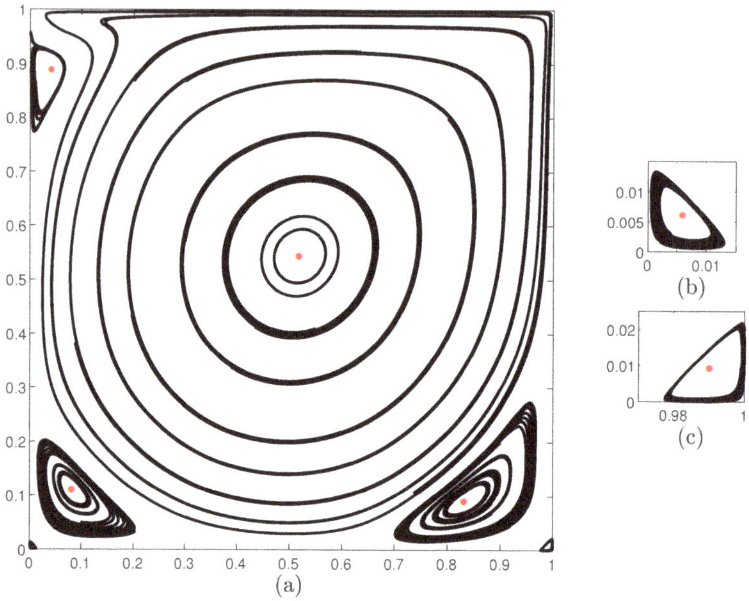

Figure 17. (a) $Re = 2500$: streamline contours and the location of centres of PV, BR1, BL1, BR2, BL2, and TL1. The zoomed-in sections of BL and BR show (**b**) BL2 and (**c**) BR2, respectively.

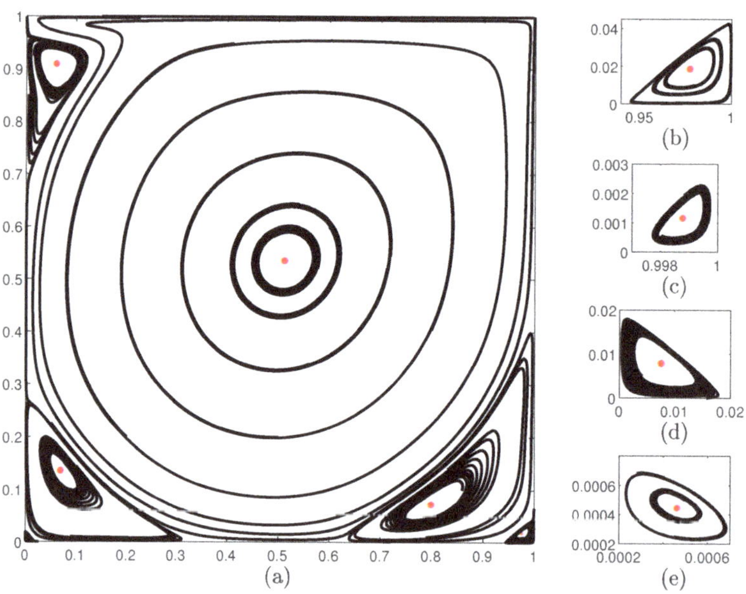

Figure 18. (a) $Re = 5000$: streamline contours and the location of centres of PV, BR1, BL1, BR2, BL2, BR3, BL3, and TL1. The zoomed-in sections of BR and BL show (**b**) BR2, (**c**) BR3, (**d**) BL2, and (**e**) BL3, respectively.

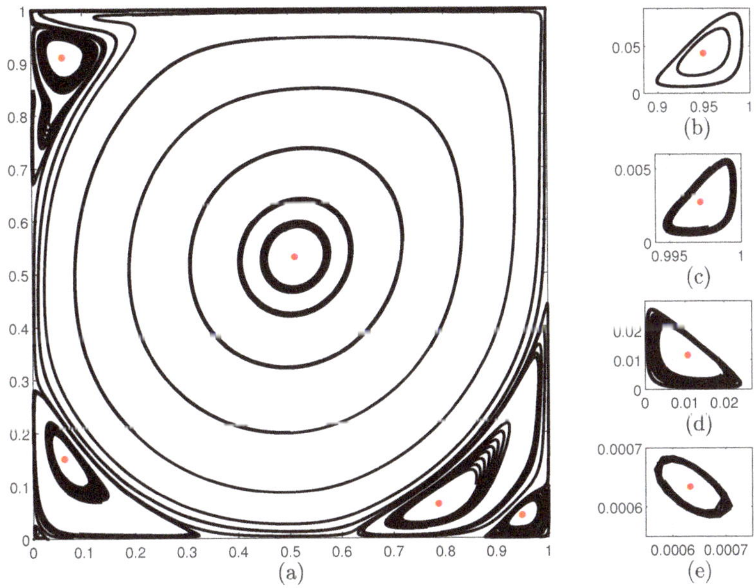

Figure 19. (**a**) $Re = 7500$: streamline contours and the location of centres of PV, BR1, BL1, BR2, BL2, BR3, BL3, and TL1. The zoomed-in sections of BR and BL show (**b**) BR2, (**c**) BR3, (**d**) BL2, and (**e**) BL3, respectively.

4. Discussion

The agreement between the VDAMR method's estimated vortex centre locations and the reference data from Ghia et al. [21], Barragy and Carey [22], Botella and Peyret [23], Erturk et al. [24], and Shapeev and Lin [25] is notably strong. Across a range of Reynolds numbers (*Re*), the estimated locations of the vortex centres align closely with the benchmark reference values, demonstrating the robustness and accuracy of the VDAMR method. The only significant deviations occur for the BL2 vortex centres at $Re = 400$ and $Re = 5000$, where there is a marked discrepancy with the results reported by Ghia et al. [21]. However, this disagreement is specific to the findings of Ghia et al. [21], as the VDAMR estimations for BL2 align well with the results from Barragy and Carey [22], Botella and Peyret [23], Erturk et al. [24], and Shapeev and Lin [25]. This consistency with multiple reference studies underscores the reliability of the VDAMR method across various Reynolds numbers. Moreover, the adaptive mesh refinement inherent in the VDAMR method allows for enhanced resolution in critical regions, ensuring precise capture of complex flow structures. The minor discrepancies can be attributed to differences in numerical schemes and boundary conditions in the six reference studies [21–26].

Building on the success of the 2D VDAMR method in accurately estimating vortex centres, future work will explore its application to flows with higher Reynolds numbers, where more complex and turbulent phenomena are present. In our previous works [27,28], we successfully verified the accuracy of the 3D VDAMR using analytical velocity fields. Future work will focus on evaluating the accuracy of the VDAMR using 3D computational velocity fields. This includes adapting the method to handle 3D flow problems, requiring additional refinement in the mesh adaptation process and further validation against 3D benchmark data. Additionally, investigating the method's performance in real-world engineering applications, such as aerodynamic simulations or industrial fluid dynamics, will be a key focus. These extensions aim to enhance the method's versatility and applicability to a broader range of fluid dynamics problems.

5. Conclusions

The accuracy of the 2D VDAMR method was rigorously validated through the analysis of six distinct cases of 2D lid-driven cavity flow, spanning a Reynolds number range of $100 \leq Re \leq 7500$. A very coarse initial mesh was iteratively refined ten times. The resulting estimated vortex centre locations demonstrated a high level of agreement with established benchmarks across six references. This agreement was further supported by the numerically computed $u-$ and $v-$ velocity profiles, which fit very well with the benchmark data. The main conclusions that can be drawn are as follows:

- The present results, along with the errors relative to the benchmark reference vortex centres, affirm the robustness and precision of the 2D VDAMR method in estimating the centres of vortices.
- This study demonstrates that applying the VDAMR method improves estimation accuracy with more refinements. Since 2D VDAMR can be applied a finite number of times, further refinements can be made if the results are not accurate enough in certain cases.
- The VDAMR method's performance confirms its potential in applications for simulating fluid dynamics problems, mainly where detailed vortex dynamics are crucial.

Author Contributions: Conceptualization, R.L. and Z.L.; methodology, R.L. and Z.L.; software, R.L. and Z.L.; validation, R.L. and M.L.; formal analysis, R.L. and M.L.; writing—original draft preparation, R.L.; writing—review and editing, R.L., Z.L. and M.L.; visualization, R.L. All authors have read and agreed to the published version of the manuscript.

Funding: This research received no external funding.

Data Availability Statement: All data are included in the manuscript as tables and figures.

Conflicts of Interest: The authors declare no conflicts of interest.

References

1. Slotnick, J.P.; Khodadoust, A.; Alonso, J.; Darmofal, D.; Gropp, W.; Lurie, E.; Mavriplis, D.J. *CFD Vision 2030 Study: A Path to Revolutionary Computational Aerosciences*; NASA: Washington, DC, USA, 2013.
2. George, P.L.; Borouchaki, H.; Alauzet, F.; Laug, P.; Loseille, A.; Marcum, D.; Maréchal, L. Mesh generation and mesh adaptivity: Theory and techniques. In *Encyclopedia of Computational Mechanics*; Stein, E., Borst, R., Hughes, T.J.R., Eds.; John Wiley & Sons, Ltd.: Sussex, UK, 2017.
3. Plewa, T.; Linde, T.J.; Weirs, V.G. Adaptive mesh refinement-theory and applications. In Proceedings of the Chicago Workshop on Adaptive Mesh Refinement Methods, Chicago, IL, USA, 3–5 September 2003.
4. Berger, M.; Oliger, J. Adaptive mesh refinement for hyperbolic partial differential equations. *J. Comput. Phys.* **1984**, *53*, 484–512. [CrossRef]
5. Bell, J.; Berger, M.; Saltzman, J. Three-dimensional adaptive mesh refinement for hyperbolic conservation laws. *SIAM J. Sci. Comput.* **1994**, *15*, 127–138. [CrossRef]
6. Friedel, H.; Grauer, R.; Marliani, C. Adaptive mesh refinement for singular current sheets in incompressible magnetohydrodynamic flows. *J. Comput. Phys.* **1997**, *134*, 190–198. [CrossRef]
7. Berger, M.J.; Leveque, R.J. Adaptive mesh refinement using wave-propagation algorithms for hyperbolic systems. *SIAM J. Numer. Anal.* **1998**, *35*, 2298–2316. [CrossRef]
8. Li, Z. An adaptive two-dimensional mesh refinement method based on the law of mass conservation. *J. Flow Visual. Image Process.* **2008**, *15*, 17–33. [CrossRef]
9. Li, Z.; Wood, R. Accuracy analysis of an adaptive mesh refinement method using benchmarks of 2-D steady incompressible lid-driven cavity flows and coarse meshes. *J. Comput. Appl. Math.* **2015**, *275*, 262–271. [CrossRef]
10. Lal, R.; Li, Z. Sensitivity analysis of a mesh refinement method using the numerical solutions of 2-D steady incompressible driven cavity flow. *J. Math. Chem.* **2015**, *53*, 844–867. [CrossRef]
11. Li, Z. Analysis of 2D unsteady flow past a square cylinder at low Reynolds numbers with CFD and a mesh refinement method. *WSEAS Trans. Fluid Mech.* **2017**, *12*, 150–157.
12. Li, Z.; Li, M. Accuracy verification of a 2D adaptive mesh refinement method using backward-facing step flow of low Reynolds numbers. *Int. J. Comput. Methods* **2021**, *18*, 2041012. [CrossRef]
13. Li, Z.; Lal, R. Application of 2D adaptive mesh refinement method to estimation of the center of vortices for flow over a wall-mounted plate. *Int. J. Comput. Methods* **2023**, *20*, 2143012. [CrossRef]

14. Li, Z. Computational complexity of the algorithm for a 2D adaptive mesh refinement method using lid-driven cavity flows. *Comput. Therm. Sci.* **2017**, *9*, 395–403. [CrossRef]
15. Wahba, E.M. Steady flow simulations inside a driven cavity up to Reynolds number 35,000. *Comput. Fluids* **2012**, *66*, 85–97. [CrossRef]
16. Bourantas, G.C.; Zwick, B.F.; Joldes, G.R.; Loukopoulos, V.C.; Tavner, A.C.R.; Wittek, A.; Miller, K. An explicit meshless point collocation solver for incompressible Navier-Stokes equations. *Fluids* **2019**, *3*, 164. [CrossRef]
17. Boroujerdi, A.A.; Hamzeh, M. Comparison of varieties of numerical methods applied to lid-driven cavity flow: Coupling algorithms, staggered grid vs. collocated grid, and FUDS vs. SUDS. *Int. J. Mech. Mater. Eng.* **2019**, *14*, 1–19. [CrossRef]
18. Khorasanizade, S.; Sousa, J.M. A detailed study of lid-driven cavity flow at moderate Reynolds numbers using incompressible SPH. *Int. J. Numer. Methods Fluids* **2014**, *10*, 653–668. [CrossRef]
19. Kim, J.; Moin, P. Application of a fractional-step method to incompressible Navier-Stokes equations. *J. Comput. Phys.* **1985**, *59*, 308–323. [CrossRef]
20. Perumal, D.A.; Dass, A.K. A Review on the development of lattice Boltzmann computation of macro fluid flows and heat transfer. *Alex. Eng. J.* **2015**, *54*, 955–971. [CrossRef]
21. Ghia, U.K.N.G.; Ghia, K.N.; Shin, C.T. High-Re solutions for incompressible flow using the Navier-Stokes equations and a multigrid method. *J. Comput. Phys.* **1982**, *48*, 387–411. [CrossRef]
22. Barragy, E.; Carey, G.F. Stream function-vorticity driven cavity solution using p finite elements. *Comput. Fluids* **1997**, *26*, 453–468. [CrossRef]
23. Botella, O.; Peyret, R. Benchmark spectral results on the lid-driven cavity flow. *Comput. Fluids* **1998**, *27*, 421–433. [CrossRef]
24. Erturk, E.; Corke, T.C.; Gökçöl, C. Numerical solutions of 2-D steady incompressible driven cavity flow at high Reynolds numbers. *Int. J. Numer. Methods Fluids* **2005**, *48*, 747–774. [CrossRef]
25. Shapeev, A.V.; Lin, P. An asymptotic fitting finite element method with exponential mesh refinement for accurate computation of corner eddies in viscous flows. *SIAM J. Sci. Comput.* **2009**, *31*, 1874–1900. [CrossRef]
26. Perumal, D.A.; Dass, A.K. Application of lattice Boltzmann method for incompressible viscous flows. *Appl. Math. Model.* **2013**, *37*, 4075–4092. [CrossRef]
27. Li, Z. An adaptive three-dimensional mesh refinement method based on the law of mass conservation. *J. Flow Visual. Image Process.* **2007**, *14*, 375–395. [CrossRef]
28. Li, Z.; Lal, R. An evaluation of accuracy and efficiency of a 3D adaptive mesh refinement method with analytical velocity fields. *Int. J. Comput. Methods* **2023**, 2341001. [CrossRef]

mathematics

MDPI

Article

Numerical Modeling of Two-Phase Fluid Filtration for Carbonate Reservoir in Two-Dimensional Formulation

Ravil M. Uzyanbaev [1,2,*], Yuliya O. Bobreneva [2], Yury A. Poveshchenko [3], Viktoriia O. Podryga [3], Sergey V. Polyakov [3], Parvin I. Rahimly [3] and Irek M. Gubaydullin [2]

1 Department of Digital Technologies and Modeling, Graduate School of Information and Social Technologies, Ufa State Petroleum Technological University, Kosmonavtov Street 1, 450062 Ufa, Russia
2 Institute of Petrochemistry and Catalysis, Russian Academy of Sciences, Pr. Oktyabrya Street 141, 450075 Ufa, Russia; yu.o.bobreneva@gmail.com (Y.O.B.); irekmars@mail.ru (I.M.G.)
3 Keldysh Institute of Applied Mathematics, Russian Academy of Sciences, Miusskaya Square 4, 125047 Moscow, Russia; hecon@mail.ru (Y.A.P.); pvictoria@list.ru (V.O.P.); polyakov@imamod.ru (S.V.P.); pervin@rehimli.info (P.I.R.)
* Correspondence: ravil-11@mail.ru

Abstract: This work considers the isothermal process of incompressible viscous fluid filtration in an oil-saturated, fractured-porous reservoir. A study of the pressure and water saturation distribution process is carried out for a case in which a production well is put into operation. For this problem, i.e., a mathematical model in a two-dimensional formulation, a numerical method and a parallel algorithm are proposed. The mathematical model of two-phase filtration is written in accordance with the classical laws of continuum mechanics and Darcy's law and also includes a function of fluid exchange between low-permeability pores and high-permeability natural fractures within the framework of the Warren–Root model. The numerical solution is based on the finite-difference method and a splitting scheme of physical processes and spatial coordinates. For a split system with respect to piezoconductivity, an implicit finite-difference scheme with fixed saturations is constructed, and with respect to saturation transfer, explicit and implicit difference schemes are constructed. For parallel implementation of the developed numerical approach, a method based on geometric parallelism is selected. Testing of the developed method is performed using the example of calculating liquid mass transfer for a wide range of parameters. To verify the model, the obtained calculated pressure curves are compared with field data recorded by a deep-well measuring device. The results allow for estimation of the distribution of reservoir pressure and water saturation depending on the permeability of the fracture set and the pore part. The obtained results allow for monitoring of well operations, reducing unexpected accident risks and optimizing the development system in order to increase oil production in fractured-porous reservoirs. Computational experiments confirm the efficiency of the developed numerical algorithm and its parallel implementation.

Keywords: mathematical modeling; two-phase filtration; fracture system; pressure; saturation; implicit finite-difference schemes; geometric parallelism

MSC: 65Y05; 00A71; 35M10; 65N06; 76S05

1. Introduction

In the modern world, any industrial activity is directly related to mathematical modeling. Modeling is especially relevant for the oil and gas industry, where constant calculations of various types are required in real time. For engineers involved in field development and management, information on the current energy state of the reservoir, as well as the predicted pressure value under various operating conditions, is important. This information is necessary to understand the operation of the facility, conduct geological and technical measurements, and further new drilling in order to minimize dangerous risks and increase hydrocarbon production [1–4].

The development of new methods and technologies expands the scope of hydrocarbon exploration, which makes it possible to discover deposits with complex geological conditions. Now objects with deteriorated filtration properties are often encountered, requiring the development of alternative approaches to well drilling and operation. In this regard, there is an increasing need for a deep study of fluid movement in such reservoirs.

This work considers a complex geological object related to a carbonate reservoir. In carbonate rocks, the pore system is highly heterogeneous, with secondary voids predominating. Secondary voids include fractures that arise under the influence of tectonic stresses and caverns formed as a result of chemical reactions [5–7]. The length and size of fractures can significantly exceed the size of primary pores. The network of natural fractures in such formations forms complex paths for hydrocarbon movement, affecting well productivity and formation characteristics. These features of the reservoir require modification of the classical theory of fluid filtration in formations [8–10]. Namely, it is necessary to take into account the simultaneous occurrence of processes in different environments, namely in the system of natural fractures and in the porous part of the reservoir (matrix). Moreover, each environment has its own filtration-capacitive properties [11–18].

The modeling of filtration processes in carbonate reservoirs leads to difficulties such as a large number of variables; the presence of two phases (oil and water), resulting in nonlinearity of the main equations of mass transfer; and the impossibility of obtaining complete information about the process due to the labor intensity of conducting experimental studies [19,20].

Modern computer technologies open up new possibilities for such problems to be solved. To achieve success, an efficient numerical algorithm that is adapted to the architecture of large computing clusters and supercomputers is needed.

A large number of software products have been developed in worldwide to solve problems of hydrodynamics and multiphase fluid flow in wells. These include PipeSim (Schlumberger, Moscow, Russia, version 22.1) [21], which models multiphase flow to optimize oil production. However, the calculation package is aimed at designing and optimizing the structure of the well network, modeling optimal well completions, and increasing production by selecting a pump based on the entire system. It allows for calculation of the movement of multiphase fluid in vertical and horizontal wells. However, there are no detailed models of mass transfer flow in fracture-porous formations.

Another widely used software product is Petex Prosper (Pe Limited, Edinburgh, UK, version 13.5) [22], which allows for the design and optimization of well operations. The program models the hydrodynamic properties of the fluid in pipes and its temperature. The range of problem solving is huge, but it does not enable modeling of the flow in formations with complex structures.

The Gidrozond (Yamalpromgeofizika, Urengoy, Russia, version 578) [23] software product includes special algorithms for the processing of data from hydrodynamic studies obtained during the development of low-yield wells (compressor, swab, and ejector pump). However, it is also intended for the interpretation of simple models of the reservoir and well, that is, a model of fluid flow in a fractured reservoir is not provided.

The HydraTest (NPP GETEK, Russia, Kamerton, version 578) [24] module is designed for quantitative processing of the results of hydrodynamic studies of oil and gas wells under difficult conditions. The main emphasis is on algorithms for unstable wells and wells significantly influenced by the wellbore, namely during compression, swabbing, and pumping operations. The module has a wide functional range, but models of a fracture-porous reservoir are not included.

Avton (Autograph, Yoshkar-Ola, Russia, version 4.6.0.29) software [25] ensures the implementation and processing of data from various types of reservoir studies and allows for the joint use of field research data and hydrodynamic research data. This software also does not contain a module for analysis of processes in fracture-porous reservoirs.

The HydroGeoSphere (Aquanty Inc., Ontario, Canada, version 2732) simulator [26] is a three-dimensional integrated simulator of surface and subsurface water flow. It allows for three-dimensional modeling of variably saturated fractured or porous aquifers, which is beyond the scope of our research.

The TOUGH3 (Berkeley National Laboratory, Berkeley, CA, USA, version 1.0) simulator [27] is designed for numerical modeling of multidimensional fluid and heat flows of multiphase, multicomponent fluid mixtures in porous and fractured media. It solves mass and energy balance equations that describe fluid and heat flow in general multiphase, multicomponent systems. It also allows for the efficient solution of strongly coupled nonlinear algebraic equations. This package is the closest to modeling the processes that interest us in the presented work, but it has several disadvantages. One of them is the orientation of the calculation code toward the use of Newton–Raphson iterative processes. This technique is good in the case of smooth coefficients of the basic system of differential equations and under stable flow regimes. In our case, we allow for discontinuity of properties and focus on the calculation of substantially nonequilibrium flows in porous reservoirs. Therefore, the property of smoothness of coefficients cannot be used. Another disadvantage is the high computational capacity of the Newton–Raphson method with the inclusion of processes of varying degrees of singularity in the general matrix of the system, which leads to a significant increase in the number of conditions and, accordingly, a larger number of iterations at a given accuracy. In addition to this, the number of unknowns in the grid nodes is also unreasonably high.

Thus, the above-mentioned packages only partially help to solve the problem under consideration. Therefore, in our work, we revised the traditional approach to solving problems of this class. As a result, we present a modified mathematical model of filtration mass transfer processes in multiphase calculations (oil and water) in fracture-porous reservoirs with dual porosity. An original numerical method was developed, and a software package was created for it. The comprehensive solution developed is characterized by the following innovations: (1) splitting of the differential model by physical processes, with the allocation of piezoconductivity blocks and saturation transfer processes in the pore matrix and fracture network; (2) implementation of the split model at the discrete level carried out based on the support operator method, with the property of complete conservatism; (3) the solution of the obtained nonlinear system of difference equations based on decomposition into a singular piezoconductive block of small dimensions and a regular block of saturation transfer in fractures; (4) an iterative algorithm tp solve the obtained difference equations, divided into blocks and involving the use of the alternating direction method for the singular part; and (5) a saturation transfer block that allows solutions to be found explicitly.

In the practical use of this approach, we achieved a general acceleration of the method by 4–5 times compared to the traditional method implemented, for example, in the TOUGH3 package. In particular, in the TOUGH3 package, due to the use of the Newton–Raphson method, four variables are used (two saturation variable and two pressure variables in the pore matrix and fractures) in each grid node, but in our software package, only one variable (pressure in fractures) is used in each grid node for the solved system of algebraic equations. Thus, in TOUGH3, the Newton–Raphson method is automatically applied to a problem of any complexity due to the lack of information on its simplification. However, if we reduce the size of the problem, simplify its implementation, and simplify vector and matrix operations, then one node contains not four variables but only one, and the main processor time is spent only on the piezoconductive block, as implemented in our work.

In previous work, we considered the isothermal and non-isothermal processes of mass transfer of a two-phase liquid in a fracture-pore collector in a one-dimensional formulation [28–30]. An original implicit finite-difference scheme on an uneven spatial grid and a parallel algorithm are proposed for numerical implementation. The conducted numerical experiments confirm the effectiveness of the proposed algorithm and its parallel implementation.

This work presents a complete mathematical model describing the isothermal process of the filtration of a two-phase liquid in a two-dimensional setting. The idea is that two media (the pore part and the set of natural fractures) have different properties (porosity and permeability). At the same time, natural fractures are more highly permeable than the pore part of the reservoir, and the main filtration of fluid occurs on them. The pore part, in turn, is a certain source of fluid that feeds the fractures. Therefore, classical filtration equations are supplemented with a source function that describes fluid exchange between the fracture set and the pore space. We consider a case in which a reservoir in an equilibrium state is opened by a production well.

To solve thus problem, an efficient numerical solution algorithm is proposed and implemented using the method of splitting by physical processes. Within this framework, a special approximation of grid functions in time is used, which ensures the correctness and consistency of fluxes in the fracture system and the porous reservoir and allows for the simplification and speeding up of the calculation process without sacrificing the accuracy of the solution. The selected model problem reflects the real spatio-temporal characteristics of an industrial reservoir in which longitudinal distances reach hundreds of meters, fracture thicknesses fluctuate in the range of several millimeters to tens of centimeters, and the development times of filtration processes range from several hours to several weeks. As a result, the full modeling cycle leads to significant computational costs. This prompted the development of a parallel algorithm to solve the problem, as well as for the creation of the corresponding program code. The parallel algorithm is based on the principle of geometric parallelism, as well as the parallel matrix sweep method. The program was implemented in C++ language using the MPI standard. The final parallel program can be executed on computing systems with either shared or distributed memory. As part of program testing, an analysis of the parallelization efficiency was conducted, and the optimal number of processes for solving the system of difference equations was determined depending on the size of the grid. Precision calculations allowed us to estimate the distribution of reservoir pressure and water saturation depending on the permeability of the fracture set and the pore part.

Finding a solution to the problem will allow us to analyze the hydrodynamic regime of the formation and determine the optimal scenario for well operation and further development based on multivariate calculations of the pressure front distribution around the well and within its vicinity. This information on the pressure distribution is also important when carrying out geological and technical measurements in order to reduce possible risks.

2. Statement of the Problem

The mathematical model for the problem of two-phase fluid filtration is described by mass transfer equations taking into account fluid exchange between the set of natural fractures and the pore part of the reservoir. The system is represented by the following nonlinear partial differential equations:

$$\frac{\partial(\phi^\alpha \rho_o^\alpha S_o^\alpha)}{\partial t} + div(\rho_o^\alpha \vec{U}_o^\alpha) + q_o^\alpha = 0,\ q_o^m = -q_o^f = -\rho_o^m \sigma \lambda_o^m (P^f - P^m), \tag{1}$$

$$\frac{\partial(\phi^\alpha \rho_w^\alpha S_w^\alpha)}{\partial t} + div(\rho_w^\alpha \vec{U}_w^\alpha) + q_w^\alpha = 0,\ q_w^m = -q_w^f = -\rho_w^m \sigma \lambda_w^m (P^f - P^m), \tag{2}$$

$$\lambda_o^m = \frac{k^m k_{ro}(S_o^m)}{\mu_o},\ \lambda_w^m = \frac{k^m k_{rw}(S_w^m)}{\mu_w}. \tag{3}$$

Systems (1)–(3) are closed by the generalized Darcy law, which is described by Equation (4).

$$\vec{U}_o^\alpha = -\frac{k^\alpha k_{ro}(S_o^\alpha)}{\mu_o} gradP^\alpha, \ \vec{U}_w^\alpha = -\frac{k^\alpha k_{rw}(S_w^\alpha)}{\mu_w} gradP^\alpha. \tag{4}$$

In (1)–(4) the following notations, $\alpha = f, m$; index f denotes the fracture system; index m denotes the matrix system; index o denotes oil; index w denotes water; P^f is the formation pressure in the fracture system (Pa); P^m is the formation pressure in the matrix (Pa); ϕ^f is the porosity in the fracture system; ϕ^m is the porosity in the matrix; ρ_o^α is the density of oil (g/m^3); ρ_w^α is the density of water (g/m^3); S_o^f and S_w^f are the saturations of oil and water in the fracture system, respectively; S_o^m and S_w^m are the saturations of oil and water in the matrix, respectively; $\vec{U}_o^\alpha$ and $\vec{U}_w^\alpha$ are the flow velocities of oil and water, respectively; q_o^α and q_w^α are the functions of redistribution of the oil and water between the matrix and the fractures, respectively; σ is the coefficient of fractured rock (1/m^2); k^α is the absolute permeability (m^2); k_{rw} and k_{ro} are the relative phase permeabilities of water and oil, respectively; μ_o is the viscosity of oil (Pa·s); and μ_w is the viscosity of water (Pa·s).

The change in density for water and oil is recorded taking into account pressure, as represented by Equation (5).

$$\rho_w^\alpha = \rho_{w0}^\alpha + C_w(P^\alpha - P_0), \ \rho_o^\alpha = \rho_{o0}^\alpha + C_o(P^\alpha - P_0), \tag{5}$$

where C_w and C_o are the compressibility coefficients or water and oil, respectively; ρ_{w0}^α and ρ_{o0}^α are the densities of water and oil at atmospheric pressure, respectively; and P_0 is the atmospheric pressure.

It should be noted that the production well under consideration is not affected by the operating environment, and the formation is characterized as infinite. Based on this, zero fluxes at the boundaries ($x = 0$, $x = l$, $y = 0$, and $y = l$) and a constant bottom-hole pressure of P_b in the center of the region (x_c, y_c) are set. For the initial condition, reservoir pressures (P_0) in the matrix and fractures at the initial moment of time are used.

$$\begin{gathered} P^m|_{t=0} = P^f|_{t=0} = P_0, P^f(x_c; y_c) = P_b, \\ \frac{\partial P^f}{\partial x}|_{x=0} = \frac{\partial P^f}{\partial x}|_{x=l} = 0, \frac{\partial P^f}{\partial y}|_{y=0} = \frac{\partial P^f}{\partial y}|_{y=l} = 0, \end{gathered} \tag{6}$$

where P_0 and P_b are the initial and bottom-hole pressures, respectively.

Systems (1)–(5), taking into account the initial and boundary conditions (2), represent a complex system of equations of mathematical physics of mixed type. To solve this system, we will use the numerical approaches described in [20–30] and generalize to the two-dimensional case.

To solve the system of Equations (1) and (2), we discretize the spatial differential operators on a Cartesian grid using the finite-difference method.

To obtain an economical and absolutely stable scheme, in the studied range of parameters, we use the method of splitting by physical processes. Splitting allows us to break complex problems (1) and (2) into two simple problems of lower dimensions. Note that the split discrete model is equivalent to the difference approximation of the general system [19,31]. As a result of splitting, we obtain two mutually independent linear difference problems of the second order. The first system describes changes in pressure in the collector, while the describes changes in transfer of saturations. In Section 3, we provide a description and discuss the results of the application of the splitting method.

3. Construction of a Difference Scheme

The first group of equations, where the only unknown parameter is pressure, is obtained by fixing the saturations of oil and water in the original system of Equations ((1)–(4)). By means of simple mathematical operations, saturations are taken out from under the time derivative sign. As a result, we obtain a new system (7) describing the pressure distribution in the fractures and matrix.

$$
\begin{aligned}
&\frac{S_o^f}{\rho_o^f}\frac{\partial(\phi^f\rho_o^f)}{\partial t}+\frac{S_w^f}{\rho_w^f}\frac{\partial(\phi^f\rho_w^f)}{\partial t}+DIG^f=0,\\
DIG^f=&\frac{div(\rho_o^f\vec{U}_o^f)}{\rho_o^f}+\frac{div(\rho_w^f\vec{U}_w^f)}{\rho_w^f}+\sigma(P^f-P^m)\left(\frac{\rho_o^m}{\rho_o^f}\lambda_o^m+\frac{\rho_w^m}{\rho_w^f}\lambda_w^m\right),\\
&\frac{S_o^m}{\rho_o^m}\frac{\partial(\phi^m\rho_o^m)}{\partial t}+\frac{S_w^m}{\rho_w^m}\frac{\partial(\phi^m\rho_w^m)}{\partial t}+DIG^m=0,\\
&DIG^m=-\sigma(P^f-P^m)(\lambda_o^m+\lambda_w^m).
\end{aligned}
\tag{7}
$$

The second group of equations, where the unknown parameter is saturation, is formed by taking into account the condition of $S_w^f+S_o^f=1$. This condition allows one of the two obtained equations to remain one equation relative to water saturation. Oil saturation is obtained by recalculation. The group of equations relative to saturation transfer is represented by system (8).

$$
\begin{aligned}
&\frac{\partial(\phi^f\rho_w S_w^f)}{\partial t}+\nabla(\rho_w\vec{U}_w^f)+q_w^f=0,\\
&\frac{\partial(\phi^m\rho_w S_w^m)}{\partial t}+q_w^m=0.
\end{aligned}
\tag{8}
$$

To solve the obtained systems, numerical schemes are proposed that have a number of important properties, such as the existence and uniqueness of the solution and the non-negativity of the density, as well as resistance to errors in the initial data.

Let us now consider the discretization of Equations (7) and (8) in the spatially two-dimensional case. For discretization, we use the finite-difference method on a uniform space-time grid. Note that the version of discrete equations described below is also suitable for solving a spatially three-dimensional problem. The use of a non-uniform grid is also allowed.

In order for the difference approximation of the split model comprising (7) and (8) to be equivalent to the difference approximation of Equations (1)–(4) written in divergent form, we introduce time layers t and $\widehat{t}=t+\tau$, where τ is the time step, as well as derivatives and time averages, in accordance with the following approximation and interpolation rules (9):

$$
a_t=(\widehat{a}-a)/\tau,\ a^{(\delta_1)}=\delta_1\widehat{a}+(1-\delta_1)a,
\tag{9}
$$

where a_t is the difference derivative with respect to time, a and $\widehat{a}$ are arbitrary functions on adjacent time layers (t and $\widehat{t}$, respectively), and $a^{(\delta_1)}$ is time interpolation with weight δ_1 of grid function a.

The interpolation weight (δ_1) may depend on the spatial grid node and, for our case, is represented by Equation (10).

$$
\delta_1=\frac{\sqrt{(\widehat{\phi})}}{\sqrt{(\widehat{\phi})}+\sqrt{(\phi)}},
\tag{10}
$$

where $\bar{\phi} = \hbar_{xy}\phi$, ϕ is the porosity at the node multiplied by the spatial step ($\hbar_{xy}$), and $\widehat{\bar{\phi}}$ is the value in the time layer ($\widehat{t}$).

When discretizing Equations (7) and (8), well known approximations of spatially differential operators on a Cartesian grid are used. The corresponding difference equations represent a system of nonlinear algebraic equations for the solution of which we can use either linearization or iterative methods such as the Newton method. In this case, a modified Newton method is used.

Applying Newton's method to the equations of piezoconductivity in fractures (7), we obtain Equation (11).

$$\begin{gathered}
\frac{(S_w^f)^{(\delta 1f)\approx}}{(\rho_w^f)^{(\delta 1f)\approx}}(\bar{\phi}^f\rho_w^f)'^s_{pf}\delta P^f + \frac{(1-S_w^f)^{(\delta 1f)\approx}}{(\rho_o^f)^{(\delta 1f)\approx}}\left(\bar{\phi}^f\rho_o^f\right)'^s_{pf}\delta P^f + \\
+\tau\delta(DIG^{f\approx}) = 0 - F^{fs}, \\
\tau\delta(DIG^{f\approx}) = \frac{-\tau}{(\rho_w^f)^{(\delta 1f)\approx}} DIN\left[\left(\frac{\rho_w^f k^f}{\mu_w^f}\right)^s k_{rw}^{ups} GRAN\delta P^f\right] + \\
+\frac{-\tau}{(\rho_o^f)^{(\delta 1f)\approx}} DIN\left[\left(\frac{\rho_o^f k^f}{\mu_o^f}\right)^s k_{ro}^{ups} GRAN\delta P^f\right] + \\
\frac{\tau(\rho_w^m\bar{\sigma}(\lambda_w^m))^s}{(\rho_w^f)^{(\delta 1f)\approx}}(\delta P^f - \delta P^m) + \frac{\tau(\rho_o^m\bar{\sigma}(\lambda_o^m))^s}{(\rho_o^f)^{(\delta 1f)\approx}}(\delta P^f - \delta P^m),
\end{gathered} \tag{11}$$

where difference operation DIN : $(\Omega) \rightarrow \omega$ denotes the approximation of the divergence (dv $\cdot$ div) acting on the functions in the cells (Ω), $a^{\sim}$ denotes arbitrary time interpolation of grid functions a and $\widehat{a}$, F^{fs} is the difference approximation of the left side of the equation of piezoconductivity in fractures multiplied by τ, a'_{pf} is the pressure derivative, $\bar{\sigma} = \sigma\hbar_{xy}$ is the coefficient of fractured rock at the node multiplied by the spatial step ($\hbar_{xy}$), δP is the pressure residual, GRAN : $(\omega) \rightarrow (\Omega)$ denotes the approximation of the gradient in cells (Ω) acting on grid functions in nodes (ω), and $k_{rw\Omega}^{ups}$ is the relative phase permeability of water in cell Ω taken from the $\omega(\Omega)$ of this cell located upwind (up) from the implicit layer in time. In grid approximations $(a^{\approx})$, the values in the implicit layer $(\widehat{t})$ are taken as $s+1$ of the already calculated iteration if they are related to pressure (P^{s+1}) and at s-th iteration if they are related to water saturation (S_w^s).

After linearization of the split equations of piezoconductivity in the pore part of the collector, we obtain System (12).

$$\begin{gathered}
\frac{(S_w^m)^{(\delta 1m)\approx}}{(\rho_w^m)^{(\delta 1m)\approx}}(\bar{\phi}^m\rho_w^m)'^s_{pm}\delta P^m + \frac{(1-S_w^m)^{(\delta 1m)\approx}}{(\rho_o^m)^{(\delta 1m)\approx}}(\bar{\phi}^m\rho_o^m)'^s_{pm}\delta P^m + \\
+\tau\delta(DIG^{m\approx}) = 0 - F^{ms}, \\
\tau\delta(DIG^{m\approx}) = \frac{-\tau(\rho_w^m\bar{\sigma}(\lambda_w^m))^s}{(\rho_w^m)^{(\delta 1m)\approx}}(\delta P^f - \delta P^m) + \\
+\frac{-\tau(\rho_o^m\bar{\sigma}(\lambda_o^m))^s}{(\rho_o^m)^{(\delta 1m)\approx}}(\delta P^f - \delta P^m).
\end{gathered} \tag{12}$$

where F^{ms} is the difference in approximation of the left part of the piezoconductivity equation in the pore part of the collector multiplied by τ.

After transformations, Equations (11) and (12) after can be represented in the form of the following system of linear algebraic equations (SLAEs) with respect to pressure increments in fractures:

$$
\begin{aligned}
&-A^{y}_{p(k,j)}\delta P^{f*}{}_{(k,j-1)} + (C^{*}_{p(k,j)} + C^{**}_{p(k,j)} + C^{y}_{p(k,j)})\delta P^{f*}{}_{(k,j)} - \\
&\qquad - B^{y}_{p(k,j)}\delta P^{f*}{}_{(k,j+1)} = \Phi_{p(k,j)}, \\
&-A^{x}_{p(k,j)}\delta P^{f}_{(k-1,j)} + (C^{*}_{p(k,j)} + C^{**}_{p(k,j)} + C^{x}_{p(k,j)})\delta P^{f}_{(k,j)} - B^{x}_{p(k,j)}\delta P^{f}_{(k+1,j)} = \Phi^{*}_{p(k,j)}.
\end{aligned} \tag{13}
$$

The coefficients (13) have the following form:

$$
\begin{aligned}
A^{x}_{p(k,j)} = &\frac{\iota}{\left[(\rho^{f}_{w})^{(\delta_{1f})}\right]^{\approx}_{(k,j)}}\left\{\frac{1}{h_{x(k-1/2,j)}}\left(\frac{\rho^{f}_{w}k^{f}}{\mu^{f}_{w}}\right)^{s}_{(k-1/2,j)} k^{ups_x}_{rw(k-1/2,j)}\right\} + \\
&\frac{\tau}{\left[(\rho^{f}_{o})^{(\delta_{1f})}\right]^{\approx}_{(k,j)}}\left\{\frac{1}{h_{x(k-1/2,j)}}\left(\frac{\rho^{f}_{o}k^{f}}{\mu^{f}_{o}}\right)^{c}_{(k-1/2,j)} k^{ups_x}_{ro(k-1/2,j)}\right\},
\end{aligned}
$$

$$
\begin{aligned}
B^{x}_{p(k,j)} = &\frac{\tau}{\left[(\rho^{f}_{w})^{(\delta_{1f})}\right]^{\approx}_{(k,j)}}\left\{\frac{1}{h_{x(k+1/2,j)}}\left(\frac{\rho^{f}_{w}k^{f}}{\mu^{f}_{w}}\right)^{s}_{(k+1/2,j)} k^{ups_x}_{rw(k+1/2,j)}\right\} + \\
&\frac{\tau}{\left[(\rho^{f}_{o})^{(\delta_{1f})}\right]^{\approx}_{(k,j)}}\left\{\frac{1}{h_{x(k+1/2,j)}}\left(\frac{\rho^{f}_{o}k^{f}}{\mu^{f}_{o}}\right)^{s}_{(k+1/2,j)} k^{ups_x}_{ro(k+1/2,j)}\right\},
\end{aligned}
$$

$$
\begin{aligned}
A^{y}_{p(k,j)} = &\frac{\tau}{\left[(\rho^{f}_{w})^{(\delta_{1f})}\right]^{\approx}_{(k,j)}}\left\{\frac{1}{h_{y(k,j-1/2)}}\left(\frac{\rho^{f}_{w}k^{f}}{\mu^{f}_{w}}\right)^{s}_{(k,j-1/2)} k^{ups_y}_{rw(k,j-1/2)}\right\} + \\
&\frac{\tau}{\left[(\rho^{f}_{o})^{(\delta_{1f})}\right]^{\approx}_{(k,j)}}\left\{\frac{1}{h_{y(k,j-1/2)}}\left(\frac{\rho^{f}_{o}k^{f}}{\mu^{f}_{o}}\right)^{s}_{(k,j-1/2)} k^{ups_y}_{ro(k,j-1/2)}\right\},
\end{aligned}
$$

$$
\begin{aligned}
B^{y}_{p(k,j)} = &\frac{\tau}{\left[(\rho^{f}_{w})^{(\delta_{1f})}\right]^{\approx}_{(k,j)}}\left\{\frac{1}{h_{y(k,j+1/2)}}\left(\frac{\rho^{f}_{w}k^{f}}{\mu^{f}_{w}}\right)^{s}_{(k,j+1/2)} k^{ups_y}_{rw(k,j+1/2)}\right\} + \\
&\frac{\tau}{\left[(\rho^{f}_{o})^{(\delta_{1f})}\right]^{\approx}_{(k,j)}}\left\{\frac{1}{h_{y(k,j+1/2)}}\left(\frac{\rho^{f}_{o}k^{f}}{\mu^{f}_{o}}\right)^{s}_{(k,j+1/2)} k^{ups_y}_{ro(k,j+1/2)}\right\},
\end{aligned}
$$

$$
\begin{aligned}
C_{p(k,j)} = \frac{(S_w^f)^{(\delta_{1f})\approx}}{(\rho_w^f)^{(\delta_{1f})\approx}}\left(\bar{\phi}^f\rho_w^f\right)'^s_{pf} + \frac{(1-S_w^f)^{(\delta_{1f})\approx}}{(\rho_o^f)^{(\delta_{1f})\approx}}\left(\bar{\phi}^f\rho_o^f\right)'^s_{pf} + \\
\frac{\tau}{\left[(\rho_w^f)^{(\delta_{1f})}\right]^{\approx}_{(k,j)}}\left\{\frac{1}{h_{x(k+\frac{1}{2},j)}}\left(\frac{\rho_w^f k^f}{\mu_w^f}\right)^s_{(k+\frac{1}{2},j)} k^{ups}_{rw(k+\frac{1}{2},j)} + \frac{1}{h_{x(k-\frac{1}{2},j)}}\left(\frac{\rho_w^f k^f}{\mu_w^f}\right)^s_{(k-\frac{1}{2},j)} k^{ups}_{rw(k-\frac{1}{2},j)}\right\} + \\
\frac{\tau}{\left[(\rho_o^f)^{(\delta_{1f})}\right]^{\approx}_{(k,j)}}\left\{\frac{1}{h_{x(k+\frac{1}{2},j)}}\left(\frac{\rho_o^f k^f}{\mu_o^f}\right)^s_{(k+\frac{1}{2},j)} k^{ups}_{ro(k+\frac{1}{2},j)} + \frac{1}{h_{x(k-\frac{1}{2},j)}}\left(\frac{\rho_o^f k^f}{\mu_o^f}\right)^s_{(k-\frac{1}{2},j)} k^{ups}_{ro(k-\frac{1}{2},j)}\right\} + \\
\frac{\tau}{\left[(\rho_w^f)^{(\delta_{1f})}\right]^{\approx}_{(k,j)}}\left\{\frac{1}{h_{y(k,j+\frac{1}{2})}}\left(\frac{\rho_w^f k^f}{\mu_w^f}\right)^s_{(k,j+\frac{1}{2})} k^{ups}_{rw(k,j+\frac{1}{2})} + \frac{1}{h_{y(k,j-\frac{1}{2})}}\left(\frac{\rho_w^f k^f}{\mu_w^f}\right)^s_{(k,j-\frac{1}{2})} k^{ups}_{rw(k,j-\frac{1}{2})}\right\} + \\
\frac{\tau}{\left[(\rho_o^f)^{(\delta 1f)}\right]^{\approx}_{(k,j)}}\left\{\frac{1}{h_{y(k,j+\frac{1}{2})}}\left(\frac{\rho_o^f k^f}{\mu_o^f}\right)^s_{(k,j+\frac{1}{2})} k^{ups}_{ro(k,j+\frac{1}{2})} + \frac{1}{h_{y(k,j-\frac{1}{2})}}\left(\frac{\rho_o^f k^f}{\mu_o^f}\right)^s_{(k,j-\frac{1}{2})} k^{ups}_{ro(k,j-\frac{1}{2})}\right\} + \\
\left\{\frac{\tau}{(\rho_w^f)^{(\delta_{1f})\approx}}(\rho_w^m\bar{\sigma}\lambda_w^m)^s(1-\pi_m^s)\right\}_{(k,j)} + \left\{\frac{\tau}{(\rho_o^f)^{(\delta_{1f})\approx}}(\rho_o^m\bar{\sigma}\lambda_o^m)^s(1-\pi_m^s)\right\}_{(k,j)},
\end{aligned}
$$

$$
C^*_{p(k,j)} = \frac{(S_w^f)^{(\delta_{1f})\approx}}{(\rho_w^f)^{(\delta_{1f})\approx}}\left(\bar{\phi}^f\rho_w^f\right)'^s_{pf} + \frac{(1-S_w^f)^{(\delta_{1f})\approx}}{(\rho_o^f)^{(\delta_{1f})\approx}}\left(\bar{\phi}^f\rho_o^f\right)'^s_{pf},
$$

$$
C^{**}_{p(k,j)} = \left\{\frac{\tau}{(\rho_w^f)^{(\delta_{1f})\approx}}(\rho_w^m\bar{\sigma}\lambda_w^m)^s(1-\pi_m^s)\right\}_{(k,j)} + \left\{\frac{\tau}{(\rho_o^f)^{(\delta_{1f})\approx}}(\rho_o^m\bar{\sigma}\lambda_o^m)^s(1-\pi_m^s)\right\}_{(k,j)},
$$

$$
C^y_{p(k,j)} = A^y_{p(k,j)} + B^y_{p(k,j)}, C^x_{p(k,j)} = A^x_{p(k,j)} + B^x_{p(k,j)},
$$

$$
\Phi_{p(k,j)} = -F^{fs} - \left(\frac{(\rho_w^m\bar{\sigma}\lambda_w^m)^s}{(\rho_w^f)^{(\delta_{1f})\approx}} + \frac{(\rho_o^m\bar{\sigma}\lambda_o^m)^s}{(\rho_o^f)^{(\delta_{1f})\approx}}\right)\tau\Phi^{ms},
$$

$$
\Phi^*_{p(k,j)} = -F^{fs*} - \left(\frac{(\rho_w^m\bar{\sigma}\lambda_w^m)^s}{(\rho_w^f)^{(\delta_{1f})\approx}} + \frac{(\rho_o^m\bar{\sigma}\lambda_o^m)^s}{(\rho_o^f)^{(\delta_{1f})\approx}}\right)\tau\Phi^{ms*},
$$

where (k,j) represent indexing in the nodes by x and y, respectively, and $(k \pm 1/2, j \pm 1/2)$ represent indexing in the cells by x and y, respectively. The corresponding blocks from the total diagonal coefficient $(C^x_{p(k,j)}, C^y_{p(k,j)})$ are allocated to the coefficients $(C_{p(k,j)})$ in accordance with the principle of constructing the additive difference scheme. The value of F^{fs} is taken from (11). The values of Φ^{ms} and π^{ms} are determined by (12). The values of $k_{rw}^{ups_x}$, $k_{rw}^{ups_y}$, $k_{ro}^{ups_x}$, and $k_{ro}^{ups_y}$ are the relative phase permeabilities of water and oil on the face of the cell (Ω), taken from the node $\omega(\Omega)$ of this cell, located upwind (ups_x, ups_y) along the x and y axes from the previous iteration (s).

Having solved the system (13), we obtain the pressures in the fracture system and in the matrix. Recall that calculations are performed at fixed saturations.

Next, we consider a group of equations regarding saturation transfer. Considering that $S_w^f + S_o^f = 1$, the system can be represented in the form of Equation (14).

$$
\begin{aligned}
\frac{L^f}{\tau} = [\bar{\phi}^f\rho_w^f S_w^f]_t + DIN(\rho_w^f\vec{U}_w^f)^{\sim} + q_w^{f\sim} = 0, \\
\frac{L^m}{\tau} = [\bar{\phi}^m\rho_w^m S_w^m]_t + q_w^{m\sim} = 0.
\end{aligned} \quad (14)
$$

As a result of linearization (14) and multiplication by τ, we obtain the following:

$$(\bar{\phi}^f \rho_w^f)^{s+1} \delta S_w^f + \tau\delta[DIN(\rho_w^f \vec{U}_w^f)^{\approx}] + \tau\delta q_w^{f\approx} = 0 - L^{f\approx},$$

$$(\bar{\phi}^m \rho_w^m)^{s+1} \delta S_w^m + \tau\delta q_w^{m\approx} = 0 - L^{m\approx}, \tag{15}$$

where

$$(\rho_w^f \vec{U}_w^f)_{\Omega}^{\approx} = -\left(\frac{\rho_w^f k^f}{\mu_w^f}\right)_{\Omega}^{\approx} k_{rw\Omega}^{up\approx} GRANP^{f\approx}. \tag{16}$$

where δS_w^f and δS_w^m are the saturation increments in the fracture and matrix, respectively. The notations used in the equations are similar to those for System (12) with respect to pressure.

In the spatial grid node (k,j), we introduce the following notations:

$$C_{S_{w(k,j)}}^m \delta S_{w(k,j)}^m = 0 - L_{(k,j)}^{m\approx},$$

$$C_{S_{w(k,j)}}^m = (\bar{\phi}^m \rho_w^m)_{(k,j)}^{s+1} - \tau\left[\rho_w^m \bar{\sigma}(P^f - P^m)\frac{k^m}{\mu_w^m}\right]_{(k,j)}^{s+1} [(k_{rw})'_{S_w^m}]_{(k,j)}^s. \tag{17}$$

For convenience, we denote the following:

$$E_{S_{w(k,j)}} = \tau\left[\rho_w^m \bar{\sigma}(P^f - P^m)\frac{k^m}{\mu_w^m}\right]_{(k,j)}^{s+1} [(k_{rw})'_{S_w^m}]_{(k,j)}^s. \tag{18}$$

Next, we determine the saturations for the system of fractures. Taking into account the above, we obtain a system represented by Equation (19).

$$\begin{gathered}
-A_{S_{w(k,j)}}^{yf} \delta S_{w(k,j-1)}^{f^*} + (C_{S_{w(k,j)}}^{f^*} + C_{S_{w(k,j)}}^{yf}) \delta S_{w(k,j)}^{f^*} - B_{S_{w(k,j)}}^{yf} \delta S_{w(k,j+1)}^{f^*} \\
+ E_{S_{w(k,j)}} \delta S_{w(k,j)}^{m^*} = 0 - L^{f\approx}, \\
-A_{S_{w(k,j)}}^{xf} \delta S_{w(k-1,j)}^{f} + (C_{S_{w(k,j)}}^{f^*} + C_{S_{w(k,j)}}^{xf}) \delta S_{w(k,j)}^{f} - B_{S_{w(k,j)}}^{xf} \delta S_{w(k+1,j)}^{f} \\
+ E_{S_{w(k,j)}} \delta S_{w(k,j)}^{m} = 0 - L^{f\approx *}, \\
S_{w(k,j)}^{f^*} = S_{w(k,j)}^{sf} + \delta S_{w(k,j)}^{f^*}, \; S_{w(k,j)}^{m^*} = S_{w(k,j)}^{sm} + \delta S_{w(k,j)}^{m^*}, \\
L^{f\approx *} = L^{f\approx}(S_{w(k,j)}^{f^*}, S_{w(k,j)}^{m^*}), \; L^{m\approx *} = L^{m\approx}(S_{w(k,j)}^{m^*}).
\end{gathered} \tag{19}$$

The coefficients for the system of Equation (19) are expressed as follows:

$$A_{S_{w(k,j)}}^{yf} = -\tau\left\{\left[\rho_w^f \frac{k^f}{\mu_w^f}\frac{1}{h_y}\right]_{(k,j-\frac{1}{2})}^{s+1} (P_{(k,j)}^f - P_{(k,j-1)}^f)^{s+1} \left[(k_{rw})'_{S_{w(k,j-1)}^f}\right]_{up}^s\right\},$$

if $P_{(k,j)}^f < P_{(k,j-1)}^f$, $A_{S_{w(k,j)}}^{yf} \geq 0$ and zero otherwise.

$$A_{S_{w(k,j)}}^{xf} = -\tau\left\{\left[\rho_w^f \frac{k^f}{\mu_w^f}\frac{1}{h_x}\right]_{(k-\frac{1}{2},j)}^{s+1} (P_{(k,j)}^f - P_{(k-1,j)}^f)^{s+1} \left[(k_{rw})'_{S_{w(k-1,j)}^f}\right]_{up}^s\right\}, \tag{20}$$

if $P^f_{(k,j)} < P^f_{(k-1,j)}, A^{xf}_{S_{w(k,j)}} \geq 0$ and zero otherwise.

$$B^{yf}_{S_{w(k,j)}} = \tau \left\{ \left[\rho^f_w \frac{k^f}{\mu^f_w} \frac{1}{h_y} \right]^{s+1}_{(k,j+\frac{1}{2})} (P^f_{(k,j+1)} - P^f_{(k,j)})^{s+1} \left[(k_{rw})'_{S^f_{w(k,j+1)}} \right]^s_{up} \right\},$$

if $P^f_{(k,j)} < P^f_{(k,j+1)}, B^{yf}_{S_{w(k,j)}} \geq 0$ and zero otherwise.

$$B^{xf}_{S_{w(k,j)}} = \tau \left\{ \left[\rho^f_w \frac{k^f}{\mu^f_w} \frac{1}{h_x} \right]^{s+1}_{(k+\frac{1}{2},j)} (P^f_{(k+1,j)} - P^f_{(k,j)})^{s+1} \left[(k_{rw})'_{S^f_{w(k+1,j)}} \right]^s_{up} \right\}, \tag{21}$$

if $P^f_{(k,j)} < P^f_{(k+1,j)}, B^{xf}_{S_{w(k,j)}} \geq 0$ and zero otherwise.

$$\begin{aligned} C^f_{S_{w(k,j)}} &= C^{f*}_{S_{w(k,j)}} + C^{xf}_{S_{w(k,j)}} + C^{yf}_{S_{w(k,j)}} = (\bar{\phi}^f \rho^f_w)^{s+1}_{(k,j)} - \\ &- \tau \left[\left\{ \left[\rho^f_w \frac{k^f}{\mu^f_w} \frac{1}{h_x} \right]^{s+1}_{(k+\frac{1}{2},j)} (P^f_{(k+1,j)} - P^f_{(k,j)})^{s+1} \right\} \left[(k_{rw})'_{S^f_{w(k,j)}} \right]^s_{up} \right] + \\ &+ \tau \left[\left\{ \left[\rho^f_w \frac{k^f}{\mu^f_w} \frac{1}{h_x} \right]^{s+1}_{(k-\frac{1}{2},j)} (P^f_{(k,j)} - P^f_{(k-1,j)})^{s+1} \right\} \left[(k_{rw})'_{S^f_{w(k,j)}} \right]^s_{up} \right] - \\ &- \tau \left[\left\{ \left[\rho^f_w \frac{k^f}{\mu^f_w} \frac{1}{h_y} \right]^{s+1}_{(k,j+\frac{1}{2})} (P^f_{(k,j+1)} - P^f_{(k,j)})^{s+1} \right\} \left[(k_{rw})'_{S^f_{w(k,j)}} \right]^s_{up} \right] + \\ &+ \tau \left[\left\{ \left[\rho^f_w \frac{k^f}{\mu^f_w} \frac{1}{h_y} \right]^{s+1}_{(k,j-\frac{1}{2})} (P^f_{(k,j)} - P^f_{(k,j-1)})^{s+1} \right\} \left[(k_{rw})'_{S^f_{w(k,j)}} \right]^s_{up} \right] > 0. \end{aligned} \tag{22}$$

where only the terms in which the diagonal pressure value ($P^f_{(k,j)}$) is greater than the corresponding non-diagonal value are taken into consideration and the contributions of these terms are zero otherwise. (k, j) represent indexing in nodes by x and y, respectively; $(i \pm 1/2, j \pm 1/2)$ represent indexing in cells by x and y, respectively; and h_x and h_y are the spatial steps of the difference grid by x and y, respectively.

The following value is also entered:

$$C^{f^*}_{S_{w(k,j)}} = (\bar{\phi}^f \rho^f_w)^{s+1}_{(k,j)}.$$

Furthermore, in the iterative process, similar to the system with respect to pressure distribution [9], splitting is performed along spatial directions (with the allocation of coefficients $C^{xf}_{S_w(k,j)}$ and $C^{yf}_{S_{w(k,j)}}$) but taking into account non-zero contributions to the sweep coefficients only upwind, as presented in (20)–(22), that is, coefficients $C^{xf}_{S_{w(k,j)}}$ and $C^{yf}_{S_{w(k,j)}}$, are allocated to the corresponding blocks from the total diagonal coefficient ($C^f_{S_{w(k,j)}}$) in accordance with the principle of constructing an additive difference scheme.

To solve the system of Equation (13) with a block-tridiagonal matrix, the matrix sweep algorithm is used, since it is relatively simple to parallelize [30]. To solve Equation (19) with respect to saturations, implicit and explicit difference schemes are considered. The implicit method using saturations (hereafter referred to as IMPIS) requires additional calculations and is more difficult to implement than the explicit method (hereafter referred to as IMPES).

Figure 1 shows the main steps of the program algorithm for one iteration. The explicit algorithm is not described in detail because it is a simplified (part of) version of the implicit algorithm.

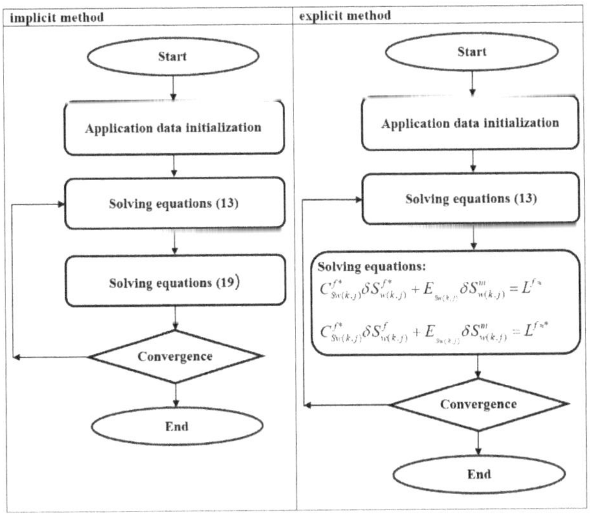

Figure 1. Basic steps of the program algorithm for one iteration.

Implicit and explicit methods differ in their approaches to choosing the time step. In the explicit method, the implementation of each time step requires iterative convergence, but we can specify larger time steps. On the other hand, in the implicit algorithm, each time step is not required to converge, but in order for the solution to be accurate, we have to choose a smaller time step.

The applied iterative process uses implicit iterative terms of the non-stationary part on the implicit layer. Convergence is checked by comparing the values between adjacent iterations. Closeness to the solution is determined when a small difference between iterations is achieved, which is considered sufficient to declare an implicit time layer. Usually, five iterations are enough. If convergence is not achieved, the time step is reduced, and the iteration block is restarted.

It is difficult to find an analytical solution to this problem, so an approach based on nested grid calculations is used to assess the accuracy of the solution. The convergence and accuracy of the method are tested here by performing calculations on a fine reference grid and coarser grids with a gradually decreasing spatial step.

A grid with a time step of 0.0001 is considered as a reference. The problem with this grid is solved in one iteration. With a time step of 0.1, it is solved in six to seven iterations, and with a time step of 0.01 s it is solved in two to three iterations.

The data on convergence when refining the spatial grid are presented in Table 1. A grid with a spatial step of 0.001 m is considered as a reference. The maximum absolute error (dmax, deviation from the reference solution) is given for grids with spatial steps of 0.002, 0.004, and 0.006 m (see Figure 2), decreasing by 6, 4, and 2 times, respectively, demonstrating spatial convergence.

Table 1. Errors of solution for different spatial grids.

Step-Through Space	dmax, Pa	Relative Error, %
0.001	0	0
0.006	57,910.6	0.25
0.004	35,082.1	0.15
0.002	11,800.1	0.05

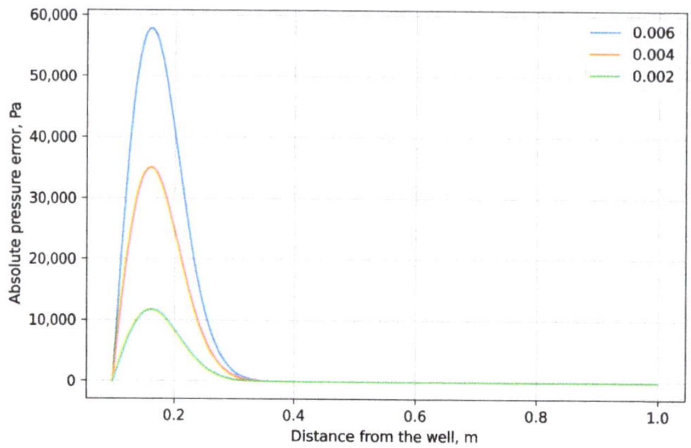

Figure 2. Spatial distribution of absolute error of pressure at the time of 100 s. Blue color indicates the grid with a spatial step of 0.006 m, orange corresponds to a spatial step of −0.004 m, and green indicates a spatial step of −0.002 m.

4. Parallel Part

For efficient implementation of the constructed difference schemes on detailed grids, a parallel computation algorithm based on the principle of geometric parallelism was developed. This principle is considered the most efficient for solving multidimensional problems in systems with both shared and distributed memory [32]. It involves dividing the computational domain into equal subdomains according to the number of processor cores in the computing system. In this problem, we used two types of decomposition, namely linear and quadratic decomposition. Linear decomposition is applied to elongated areas and is performed along one coordinate, and quadratic decomposition is applied to square or close-to-square areas and is performed along two coordinates. The decomposition type affects the configuration of the parallel algorithm and the structure of data exchange between processors. Maximum efficiency is achieved when the structure of the computing system is similar to the structure of the computational grid.

For a more detailed description of the parallel algorithm, we use the following abstract form of recording the resulting algebraic problems (13): (19):

$$\begin{gathered}
\widehat{\vec{Y}}_{i_1,i_2} - \Lambda_h\widehat{\vec{Y}} = \vec{Y}_{i_1,i_2} + \tau\vec{F}_{i_1,i_2}, \Lambda_h\widehat{\vec{Y}} = \Lambda_x\widehat{\vec{Y}} + \Lambda_y\widehat{\vec{Y}}, \\
\Lambda_x\widehat{\vec{Y}} = \vec{B}_{x,i_1,i_2}(\widehat{\vec{Y}}_{i_1+1,i_2} - \widehat{\vec{Y}}_{i_1,i_2}) - \vec{A}_{x,i_1,i_2}(\widehat{\vec{Y}}_{i_1,i_2} - \widehat{\vec{Y}}_{i_1-1,i_2}), \\
\Lambda_y\widehat{\vec{Y}} = \vec{B}_{y,i_1,i_2}(\widehat{\vec{Y}}_{i_1,i_2+1} - \widehat{\vec{Y}}_{i_1,i_2}) - \vec{A}_{y,i_1,i_2}(\widehat{\vec{Y}}_{i_1,i_2} - \widehat{\vec{Y}}_{i_1,i_2-1}),
\end{gathered} \tag{23}$$

and

$$\begin{gathered}
\widehat{\vec{Y}}_{i_1,i_2} = \vec{Y}_{i_1,i_2} + \Lambda_h\vec{Y} + \tau\vec{F}_{i_1,i_2}, \Lambda_h\vec{Y} = \Lambda_x\vec{Y} + \Lambda_y\vec{Y}, \\
\Lambda_x\vec{Y} = \vec{B}_{x,i_1,i_2}(\vec{Y}_{i_1+1,i_2} - \vec{Y}_{i_1,i_2}) - \vec{A}_{x,i_1,i_2}(\vec{Y}_{i_1,i_2} - \vec{Y}_{i_1-1,i_2}), \\
\Lambda_y\vec{Y} = \vec{B}_{y,i_1,i_2}(\vec{Y}_{i_1,i_2+1} - \vec{Y}_{i_1,i_2}) - \vec{A}_{y,i_1,i_2}(\vec{Y}_{i_1,i_2} - \vec{Y}_{i_1,i_2-1}).
\end{gathered} \tag{24}$$

where $\widehat{\vec{Y}}$ and $\vec{Y}$ are the vectors of dimension 2 corresponding to the desired functions (pressures or saturations) on the lower and upper layers in time; $\vec{A}_{x,i_1,i_2}$, $\vec{B}_{x,i_1,i_2}$, $\vec{A}_{y,i_1,i_2}$, and $\vec{B}_{y,i_1,i_2}$ are the matrix coefficients with 2×2 dimensions; and indices i_1 and i_2 run through many grid nodes along the corresponding coordinate ($i_1 = 0, ..., N_1, i_2 = 0, ..., N_2$). It is understood that at the boundaries, changes in system indices (23) and (24) naturally transform into the corresponding boundary conditions. τ is the time step, $\vec{F}_{i_1,i_2}$ is the right-hand side of the equations, and Λ is an approximation of the differential elliptic operator.

System (23) is resolved using the iterative matrix method of alternating directions and is written in the following form:

$$\begin{gathered}
\hat{\vec{Y}}^{s+1/2}_{i_1,i_2} - \alpha_1 \Lambda_x \hat{\vec{Y}}^{s+1/2}_{i_1,i_2} = \hat{\vec{Y}}^{s}_{i_1,i_2} + \alpha_1 \Lambda_y \hat{\vec{Y}}^{s} + \alpha_1 \vec{G}_{i_1,i_2}, \\
\hat{\vec{Y}}^{s+1}_{i_1,i_2} - \alpha_2 \Lambda_y \hat{\vec{Y}}^{s+1}_{i_1,i_2} = \hat{\vec{Y}}^{s+1/2}_{i_1,i_2} + \alpha_1 \Lambda_x \hat{\vec{Y}}^{s+1/2} + \alpha_2 \vec{G}_{i_1,i_2}, \\
\vec{G}_{i_1,i_2} \equiv \vec{Y}_{i_1,i_2} + \tau \vec{F}_{i_1,i_2}, \ s = 0,1,2,\ldots, \ \hat{\vec{Y}}^{0}_{i_1,i_2} = \vec{Y}_{i_1,i_2},
\end{gathered} \tag{25}$$

where $\alpha_1, \alpha_2 \subset (0,1)$ represents the iteration parameters.

Each stage of iterative scheme (14) implies the use of parallel sweeping (the parallel running algorithm is described in Appendix A) in the corresponding direction. As a result, the parallelism resource turns is another grid index that is not used during parallelization. In fact, at each stage, it is necessary to implement an independent $N_2 + 1$ or $N_1 + 1$ parallel matrix sweep. Due to the non-stationary nature of the problem and the relatively slow development of the flow, the number of iterations in this algorithm is small (usually no more than 10, dropping to 1 when the solution reaches a stationary state). As a result, the efficiency of such parallelization is high, although, of course, it depends on the dimensions (N_1, N_2) of the grid and the number of parallel processes (p_1, p_2) in the grid, as well as the speed of the interconnection.

Information matching in the explicit algorithm is achieved by using a non-overlapping distribution of grid cells among the calculators and forwarding the missing data between neighbors at each integration step. Information matching in the implicit algorithm uses the same technique, but at the local one-dimensional calculation step. In this case, two variants of the scheme can be implemented—without iterations and with iterations. In the first variant, all nonlinearity is taken from the lower layer, i.e., the scheme is explicit–implicit. Then, using two blocks of spatially one-dimensional sweeps, the final solution is obtained in the next layer. When parallelizing, an exact sweep algorithm is used, which does not affect the accuracy of the scheme. In the second variant, when using a completely implicit scheme, an iterative process for nonlinearity is implemented, which, when using the operator linearization procedure, again, leads to the possibility of using two sweep blocks at each iteration. The sweeps themselves, again, do not affect the convergence of the iterations or the scheme as a whole. The convergence of iterations is controlled by the criterion of smallness of the solution difference norm (Y) in adjacent iterations. The criterion is met if the error norm does not exceed the approximation error of the scheme (Ψ), with a coefficient of 0.01. As a result, the following convergence formula is applied:

$$||Y^{s+1} - Y^s|| \leq 0.01 \cdot ||\Psi||, ||\Psi|| \leq C(h_x^2 + h_y^2 + \tau^2),$$

where C is a constant.

The constant (C) depends on the third derivatives of the solution with respect to space and time. If the solution is unknown, it can be estimated from above by some number. Our estimates show that this value can be of the order of 10 or more. We used $C = 100$. In this case, the dimensionless steps of the grid in space are of the order of 0.001, and the dimensionless step in time satisfies the condition of asymptotic stability. As a result, the final constant obtained in the convergence criterion is $\varepsilon = 0.01 \times 100 \times 0.001^2 = 10^{-6}$.

$$||Y^{s+1} - Y^s|| \leq \varepsilon.$$

To achieve parallelism, we launch additional MPI processes on the nodes of the computing cluster. The following MPI functions were used in this work. MPI_Init, MPI_Comm _size, MPI_Comm_rank, and MPI_Get_processor_name were used to initialize the MPI environment and determine the number of processes, the rank of each process and the processor name, respectively; MPI_Bcast was used to broadcast model parameters to all processes; MyRange was used to distribute the computational domain between processes; MPI_Isend/MPI_Irecv was used to exchange data between neighboring processes; and MPI_Allreduce was used to aggregate data from all processes.

Thus, the parallel algorithm for solving a two-dimensional problem generally repeats the structure of the one-dimensional algorithm described in [30]. However, the two-dimensional case differs in the decomposition of the two-dimensional computational grid into a lattice of domains. At each time step, the algorithm sequentially solves two spatial subproblems; for pressures, it uses an implicit iterative matrix algorithm, and for saturations, it uses an explicit non-iterative or implicit iterative matrix algorithm.

Testing of the parallel algorithm and all model calculations were performed on the K100 supercomputer at the Shared Resource Center of the Keldysh Institute of Applied Mathematics of the Russian Academy of Sciences [33]. The K100 supercomputer specifications are listed as follows: 2xCPU Intel Xeon X5670, 2.93 GHz, 12 cores per node, and 64 nodes in total (the equipment was obtained from Kvant Scientific Research Company, Moscow, Russia). The following software was used: Centos 7.6 and GNU gcc 4.3 compilers, and an MPICh 1.2 parallel interface. Only standard libc and libmpi libraries were used in program implementation. The test results are presented in the next paragraph.

5. Results

Based on the developed program code (sequential and parallel), a series of calculations was performed. The following condition for the problem was considered. A production well on an unlimited reservoir was launched into operation. At the initial moment of time, the reservoir was undisturbed and had an initial reservoir pressure in fractures and matrix of $P^f = P^m = P_0 = 31.6$ (MPa). At the moment of starting up the well, the bottom-hole pressure was $P_b = 14.6$ (MPa). The formation and fluid parameters were set to the following values $\phi^f = 0.01$, $\rho_w = 1110$ (kg/m^3), $\rho_o = 780$ (kg/m^3), $S_w^\alpha = 0.24$, $\sigma = 0.32$ (1/m^2), $k^f = 1 \cdot 10^{-12}$ (m^2), $k^m = 1 \cdot 10^{-17}$ (m^2), $k_{rw} = 7.7(S_w^\alpha)^4 - 12.07(S_w^\alpha)^3 + 6.9(S_w^\alpha)^2 - 1.8(S_w^\alpha) + 0.2$, $k_{ro} = (S_w^\alpha)^2 0.03 + 0.002(S_w^\alpha) + 0.0002$, $\mu_o = 0.87 \cdot 10^{-3}$ (Pa$\cdot$ s), and $\mu_w = 0.36 \cdot 10^{-3}$ (Pa$\cdot$ s).

The input parameters were set and varied based on field studies conducted on wells of carbonate deposits. The production data were obtained from deep-well measuring equipment installed at the pump intake and recording the bottom-hole pressure throughout the entire period of well operation. The discreteness of recording pressure points was one measurement per 5 min. The sizes of the computational grid were determined by constant spatial steps of $hx = 0.1$ m and $hy = 0.1$ m, with a total count of $N = 200$, for a total time of 20 m. The time step was set equal to $\tau = 0.1$ s.

To verify the model, the calculated pressure curves were compared with the field data recorded by the measuring device (Figure 3).

Figure 3 describes the dynamics of the pressure drop at the bottom hole after the well was put into operation. The calculated curves in the fracture system (P^f) and the matrix (P^m) and field data (P^e) are presented, which were recorded for 7 days. The error of the calculated data relative to the field data does not exceed 8%. For practice in real conditions, an error of 10% was allowed, so the obtained results achieve good consistency. The difference between the pressures in the fracture and the matrix in the section from 0 to 200,000 s is explained by the fact that after the well was put into operation, the fluid flowed only through the fractures, and the matrix was connected later. It is also worth paying attention to the behavior of the pressure in the fracture and matrix. Having obtained good consistency with the field experiment, a number of calculations were carried out.

The mathematical model under consideration is most sensitive to changes in parameters such as permeability. Even a slight change in permeability leads to a change in the pressure distribution in the system. The remaining parameters do not result in significant changes when varied. Therefore, the distribution of the pressure front depending on permeability plays an important role in practice. The development system will depend on the distribution rate, or permeability value, for example, how wells will be located at cluster sites, the bottom-hole pressure at which the wells operate, and how soon it is necessary to introduce a reservoir pressure maintenance system. The general goal of these tasks is to optimally locate the wells and maintain a high level of hydrocarbon production with minimal costs.

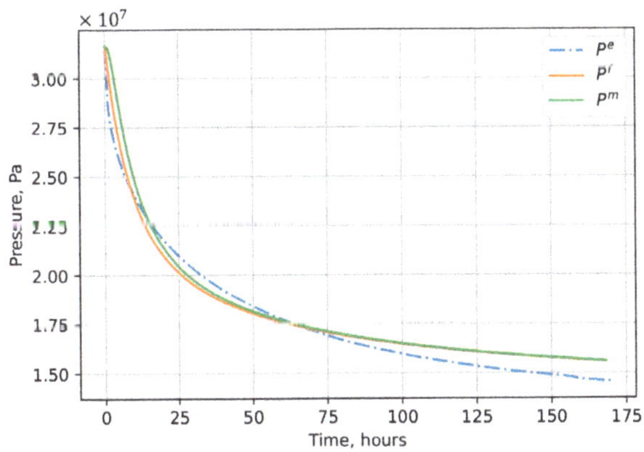

Figure 3. Pressure-drop curve based on calculated (fracture (P^f) and matrix (P^m)) and field data (P^e).

Figure 4 shows the distributions of pressure in the fracture system near the well at the final moment of time with absolute permeability values of $k^f = 10^{-10}$ (m^2) and $k^f = 10^{-12}$ (m^2). A change in absolute permeability by two orders of magnitude significantly affects the rate of distribution of pressure. The higher the value of k^f, the faster the redistribution process occurs.

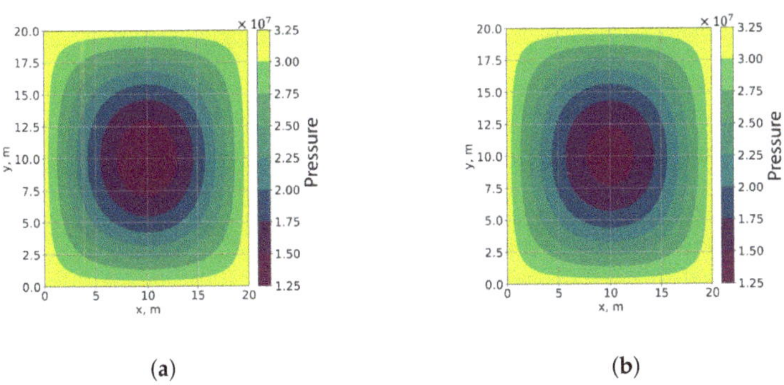

Figure 4. Distribution of pressure near the well at the final moment of time with values of absolute permeability pf $k^f = 10^{-10}$ (m^2) (**a**) and $k^f = 10^{-12}$ (m^2) (**b**).

Figure 5 shows the change in water saturation near the well in space at the final moment of time with absolute values of permeability in fractures of $k^f = 10^{-10}$ (m^2) and $k^f = 10^{-12}$ (m^2). The graphs show that the increase in water saturation at high values of permeability in fractures at $k^f = 10^{-10}$ (m^2) occurs faster.

Figure 6 shows the distribution of pressure in the fracture system at a distance of 100 m from the well bottom for periods of 5 and 10 days. From the figures, we can see how the distribution of pressure occurred after 5 days of well operation. With an increase in the duration of well operation, the depression funnel increases. Such calculations allow us to model the dynamics of pressure at a distance from the well, which makes it possible to estimate the drainage radius and the time at which the influence will reach neighboring wells.

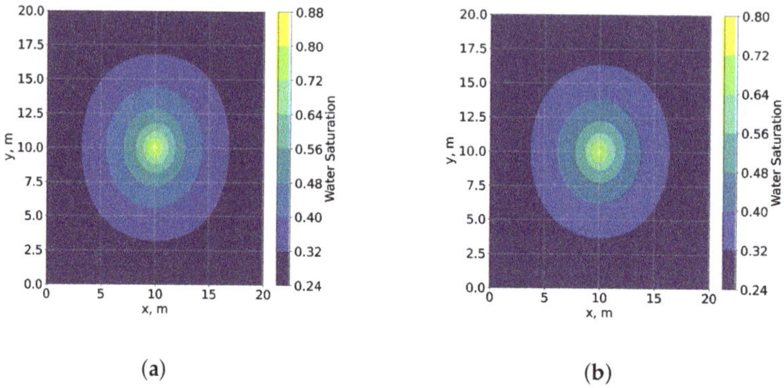

Figure 5. Distribution of water saturation near the well at the final moment of time with values of absolute permeability of $k^f = 10^{-10}$ (m^2) (**a**) and $k^f = 10^{-12}$ (m^2) (**b**).

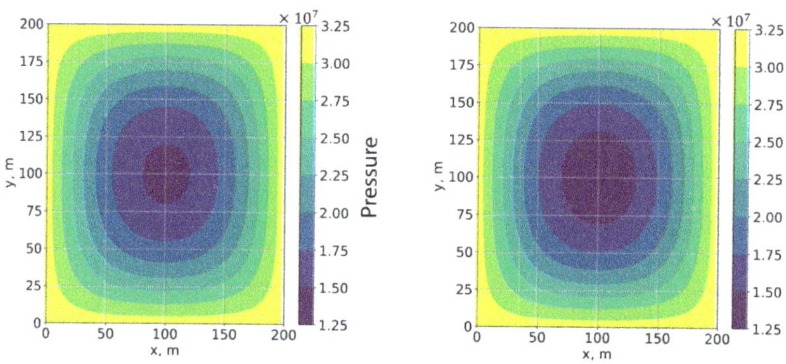

Figure 6. Distribution of pressure at a distance of 100 m from the well after 5 (**left**) and 10 (**right**) days of operation.

The calculations were performed for the explicit and implicit algorithms on the K100 supercomputer at the Center of Collective Usage of the Keldysh Institute of Applied Mathematics of the Russian Academy of Sciences. To study the properties of the developed parallel algorithms and compare them with sequential algorithms and with each other, we characteristics such as the speedup (S_m) and efficiency (E_m) coefficients.

$$S_m = \frac{T_1}{T_m}, \tag{26}$$

$$E_m = \frac{S_m}{m} \cdot 100\%, \tag{27}$$

where T_m is the execution time of the parallel program on m processes and T_1 is the execution time of the sequential program.

In our work, we use a rectangular grid topology with parameters p_1 and p_2 a total of $p_1 * p_2$ parallel processes.

The obtained speedup and efficiency coefficients (see Figure 7) show that for the implicit algorithm, the best result for the computational grid with parameters of $N_1 = 1000$ and $N_2 = 1000$ is achieved on the $p_1 * p_2 = 5 * 5 = 25$ configuration (three K100 nodes are used). The calculation time is accelerated by 14 times, but the efficiency drops to 56%. For the explicit algorithm, the best parallelization result is achieved with the $p_1 * p_2 = 6 * 6 = 36$ configuration. The calculation time is accelerated by 26 times, but the efficiency drops to 73%.

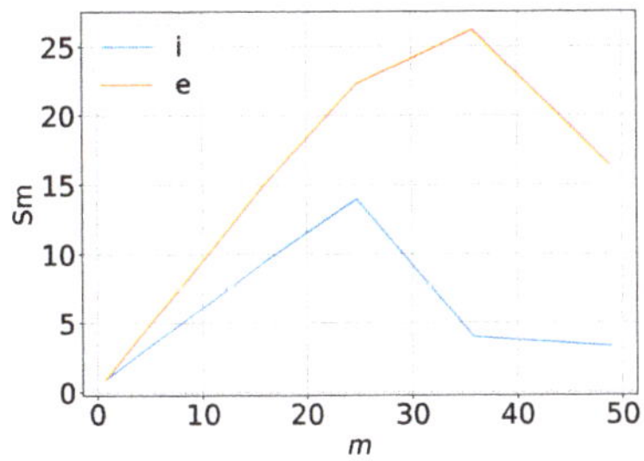

(**a**)

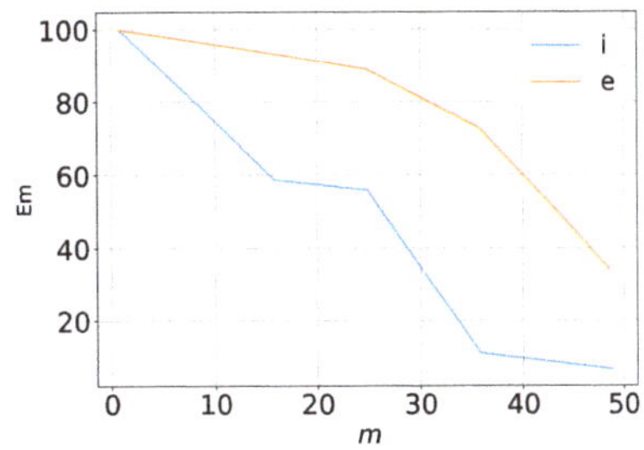

(**b**)

Figure 7. Speedup (**a**) and efficiency (**b**) of calculation for explicit (e) and implicit (i) algorithms.

Figure 8 presents data on the strong scalability of the developed parallel algorithm for two grid dimensions (1000 × 1000 and 2000 × 2000). They show that the program created on its basis still requires considerable resources to optimize the parallelization technique. However, this optimization was not the main goal of the presented work.

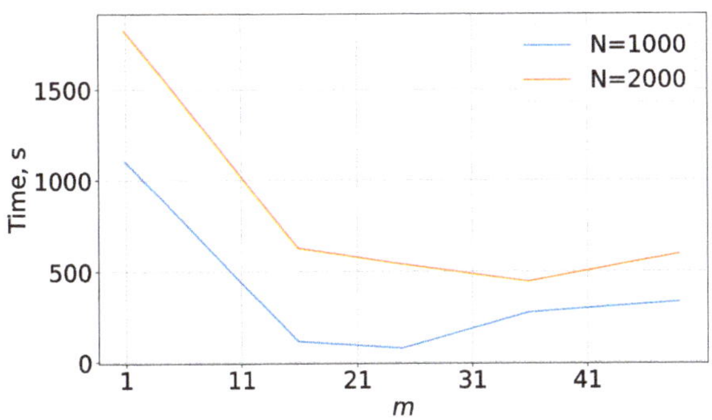

Figure 8. Dependence of the calculation time for 1000 steps of the scheme on the number of parallel processes for two grid dimensions (1000 × 1000 and 2000 × 2000).

6. Conclusions

In this work, we studied the isothermal process of viscous fluid filtration in an oil-saturated, fracture-porous reservoir. A mathematical model of two-phase fluid mass transfer was developed, taking into account the exchange function between the media in a two-dimensional formulation. An effective method was proposed and implemented based on the splitting scheme by physical processes. This approach allowed for the simplification of a complex system of equations without sacrificing the accuracy of the solution, which accelerated the process of solving the problem in the considered range of parameters. The following finite-difference schemes were used for the numerical solution: an implicit scheme for piezoconductive equations and an explicit and implicit scheme with respect to the transfer of saturations. The resulting systems of equations were solved using a parallel algorithm of block-parallel sweeping based on geometric parallelism. The results of a series of computational experiments confirm the efficiency of the developed numerical algorithm and its parallel implementation. The error of the calculated data relative to industry data did not exceed 8%. The choices of the optimal configuration of the region-partitioning topology and the method of interprocessor exchanges were determined by the ratio of the sizes of the computational grid and the grid of parallel processes. There are optimal exchange topologies and an numbers of processes (25 or 36) that provide the fastest solutions to the problem for a fixed computational grid ($N_1 = 1000$, $N_2 = 1000$). The speedup provided by the implicit and explicit algorithms is 14 and 26 times, but efficiency drops to 56% and 73%, respectively. When choosing the optimal configuration of the process grid, the calculation time for the explicit and implicit schemes could be close at a fixed number of steps. Based on the developed software module, the pressure distribution around the operating production well was constructed both at different points in the time of operation and at different distances from the well with variations in the absolute permeability of fractures. Calculations were performed to determine the change in water saturation near the well at different values of permeability in fractures. Estimation of the pressure behavior allowed for monitoring of the well operation and the reduction of unforeseen risks. In the future, we plan to introduce a finer partitioning in the grid cells for a detailed study of filtration flows in areas of abrupt changes in the parameters of the porous medium, as well as to take into account the different scales of processes in the main reservoir massif and in irregularly located well clusters.

Author Contributions: Conceptualization, Y.O.B., R.M.U. and I.M.G.; methodology, Y.A.P.; formal analysis, S.V.P.; software, R.M.U.; validation, Y.O.B. and R.M.U.; investigation, V.O.P.; writing—original draft preparation, Y.O.B. and R.M.U.; writing—review and editing, P.I.R.; supervision, Y.A.P., V.O.P. and S.V.P.; data curation, Y.O.B. and I.M.G. All authors have read and agreed to the published version of the manuscript.

Funding: The work of Bobreneva Yu.O. (conceptualization, validation, original draft preparation, and data curation), Uzyanbaev R.M. (conceptualization, software, validation, and original draft preparation), and Gubaydullin I.M. (conceptualization and data curation) was supported by the Russian Science Foundation (project №21-71-20047; project URL: https://rscf.ru/en/project/21-71-20047/ (accessed on 18 September 2024)). The work of Poveshchenko Yu.A. (methodology and supervision), Podryga V.O. (investigation and supervision), Polyakov S.V. (formal analysis and supervision), and Rahimly P.I. (review and editing) was carried out within the framework of the state assignment of KIAM RAS. Numerical experiments were performed on the K100 hybrid supercomputer installed at the Center of Collective Usage of KIAM RAS.

Data Availability Statement: The original contributions presented in the study are included in the article, further inquiries can be directed to the corresponding author.

Conflicts of Interest: The authors declare no conflicts of interest.

Abbreviations

The following abbreviations are used in this manuscript:

CPU	Central Processing Unit
MPI	Message-Passing Interface

Appendix A

Let us explain our parallel approach using a simple algebraic problem as an example.

$$-A_i y_{i-1} + C_i y_i - B_i y_{i+1} = F_i, 1 \leq i \leq N-1. \tag{A1}$$

$$C_0 y_0 - B_0 y_1 = F_0, C_N y_N - A_N y_{N-1} = F_N.$$

Problem (A1) can be solved using the following sequential sweep algorithm:

$$\alpha_0 = \frac{B_0}{C_0}, \beta_0 = \frac{F_0}{C_0}, \alpha_i = \frac{B_i}{C_i - A_i \alpha_{i-1}}, \beta_i = \frac{F_i + A_i \beta_{i-1}}{C_i - A_i \alpha_{i-1}}, i = N-1, ..., 0. \tag{A2}$$

$$y_N = \beta_N, y_i = \alpha_i y_{i+1} + \beta_i, i = N-1, ..., 0.$$

A parallel sweep algorithm for p computers assumes that a uniform linear partition of the index set ($\Omega = \{0, 1, ..., N\}$) into adjacent disjoint subsets ($\Omega_m = \{i_1^m, ..., i_2^m\}$ $(m = 0, ..., p-1)$ is the logical number of the process (see Figure A1).

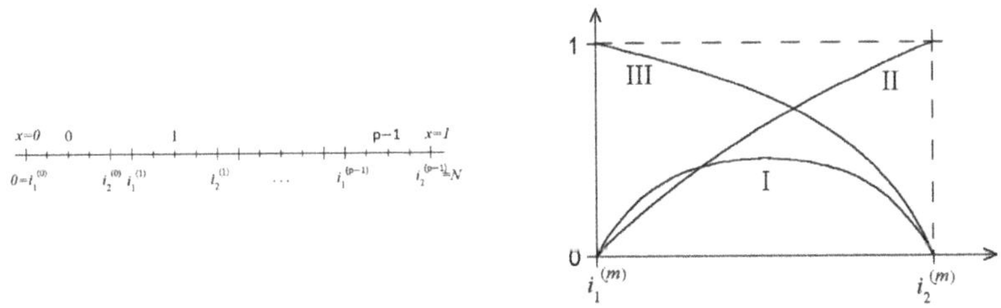

Figure A1. Parallel sweep algorithm.

As a result of such a partition, process m processe $(i_2^{(m)} - i_1^{(m)} + 1)$ points. Let us represent the solution for each internal process $(0 < m < p-1)$ in the following form:

$$y_i = y_i^{(m)} = y_i^{(I,m)} + y_{i_1^{(m)}} y_i^{(III,m)} + y_{i_2^{(m)}} y_i^{(II,m)}, \tag{A3}$$

where $y_i^{(\alpha,m)}$ $(\alpha = I, II, III)$ are defined on Ω_m and play the role of a basis and the values of the function on the boundary $(\Omega_m - y_{i_1^{(m)}})$ and $y_{i_2^{(m)}}$ are not yet known. At the internal nodes (Ω_m), the function expressed as $y_i^{(I,m)}$ is determined according to Equation (A1), and the functions expressed as $y_i^{(II,m)}$ and $y_i^{(III,m)}$ are determined according to Equation (A1) with zero right-hand side.

The boundary conditions for $y_i^{(\alpha,m)}$ are expressed as follows:

$$y_{i_1^{(m)}}^{(I,m)} = 0, y_{i_2^{(m)}}^{(I,m)} = 0, y_{i_1^{(m)}}^{(II,m)} = 0, y_{i_2^{(m)}}^{(II,m)} = 1, y_{i_1^{(m)}}^{(III,m)} = 1, y_{i_2^{(m)}}^{(III,m)} = 0. \tag{A4}$$

On the zero and last processes,

$$y_i^{(0)} = y_i^{(I,0)} + y_{i_2^0} y_i^{(II,0)}, y_i^{p-1} = y_i^{(I,p-1)} + y_{i_1^{(p-1)}} y_i^{(III,p-1)}. \tag{A5}$$

The boundary conditions are

$$\begin{aligned} C_0 y_0^{(I,0)} - B_0 y_1^{(I,0)} = F_0, y_{i_2^{(0)}}^{(I,0)} = 0, y_{i_1^{(0)}}^{(I,p-1)} = 0,& \\ C_N y_N^{(I,p-1)} - A_N y_{N-1}^{(I,p-1)} = F_N, C_0 y_0^{(II,0)} - B_0 y_1^{(II,0)} = 0, y_{i_2^{(0)}}^{(II,0)} = 1,& \\ y_{i_1^{(0)}}^{(III,p-1)} = 1, C_N y_N^{(III,p-1)} - A_N y_{N-1}^{(III,p-1)} = 0.& \end{aligned} \tag{A6}$$

Finding the values at the boundary nodes of subdomains leads us to the following so-called "short" system:

$$\begin{aligned} -A_{i_2^{(m)}} y_{i_2^{(m)}-1} + C_{i_2^{(m)}} y_{i_2^{(m)}} - B_{i_2^{(m)}} y_{i_2^{(m)}+1} = F_{i_2^{(m)}},& \\ -A_{i_1^{(m+1)}} y_{i_1^{(m+1)}-1} + C_{i_1^{(m+1)}} y_{i_1^{(m+1)}} - B_{i_1^{(m+1)}} y_{i_1^{(m+1)}+1} = F_{i_1^{(m+1)}}.& \end{aligned} \tag{A7}$$

If we take into account the obvious connections in these equations,

$$\begin{aligned} y_{i_2^{(m)}-1} = y_{i_2^{(m)}-1}^{(I,m)} + y_{i_1^{(m)}} y_{i_2^{(m)}-1}^{(III,m)} + y_{i_2^{(m)}} y_{i_2^{(m)}-1}^{(II,m)}, y_{i_2^{(m)}+1} = y_{i_1^{m+1}},& \\ y_{i_1^{(m+1)}-1} = y_{i_2^{(m)}}, y_{i_1^{(m+1)}+1} = y_{i_1^{(m+1)}+1}^{(I,m)} + y_{i_1^{(m+1)}} y_{i_1^{(m+1)}+1}^{(III,m)} + y_{i_2^{(m+1)}} y_{i_1^{(m+1)}+1}^{(II,m)},& \end{aligned}$$

we obtain

$$
\begin{gathered}
-\tilde{A}_{i_2^{(m)}} y_{i_1^{(m)}} + \tilde{C}_{i_2^{(m)}} y_{i_2^{(m)}} - \tilde{B}_{i_2^{(m)}} y_{i_1^{(m+1)}} = \tilde{F}_{i_2^{(m)}}, \\
-\tilde{A}_{i_1^{(m+1)}} y_{i_2^{(m)}} + \tilde{C}_{i_1^{(m+1)}} y_{i_1^{(m+1)}} - \tilde{B}_{i_1^{(m+1)}} y_{i_2^{(m+1)}} = \tilde{F}_{i_1^{(m+1)}},
\end{gathered} \quad \text{(A8)}
$$

with the following coefficients:

$$
\begin{gathered}
\tilde{A}_{i_2^{(m)}} = A_{i_2^{(m)}} y^{(III,m)}_{i_2^{(m)}-1}, \tilde{B}_{i_2^{(m)}} = B_{i_2^{(m)}}, \tilde{C}_{i_2^{(m)}} = C_{i_2^{(m)}} - A_{i_2^{(m)}} y^{(II,m)}_{i_2^{(m)}-1}, \\
\tilde{F}_{i_2^{(m)}} = F_{i_2^{(m)}} + A_{i_2^{(m)}} y^{(I,m)}_{i_2^{(m)}-1}, \tilde{A}_{i_1^{(m+1)}} = A_{i_1^{(m+1)}}, \tilde{B}_{i_1^{(m+1)}} = B_{i_1^{(m+1)}} y^{(II,m+1)}_{i_1^{(m+1)}+1}, \\
\tilde{C}_{i_1^{(m+1)}} = C_{i_2^{(m+1)}} - B_{i_1^{(m+1)}} y^{(III,m+1)}_{i_1^{(m+1)}+1}, \tilde{F}_{i_1^{(m+1)}} = F_{i_1^{(m+1)}} + B_{i_1^{(m+1)}} y^{(I,m+1)}_{i_1^{(m+1)}+1}.
\end{gathered}
$$

As a result, we obtain the following system of $2p-2$ equations for $2p-2$ unknowns:

$$
-\tilde{A}_i y_{i-1} + \tilde{C}_i y_i - \tilde{B}_i y_{i+1} = \tilde{F}_i, i \in \tilde{\Omega} = \{i_2^{(0)}, i_1^{(1)}, i_2^{(1)}, \ldots, i_1^{(p-1)}\}, \quad \text{(A9)}
$$

where index $i \pm 1$ indicates the transition to the corresponding neighboring element from the set expressed as $\tilde{\Omega}$. At boundary nodes $i_2^{(0)}$ and $i_1^{(p-1)}$, Equation (A9) takes a form similar to that of (A1).

References

1. Méndez, J.N.; Jin, Q.; González, M.; Zhang, X.; Lobo, C.; Boateng, C.D.; Zambrano, M. Fracture characterization and modeling of karsted carbonate reservoirs: A case study in tahe oilfield, Tarim basin (Western China). *Mar. Pet. Geol.* **2020**, *112*, 104104. [CrossRef]
2. Yan, B.; Mi, L.; Chai, Z.; Wang, Y.; Killough, J.E. An enhanced discrete fracture network model for multiphase flow in fractured reservoirs. *J. Pet. Sci. Eng.* **2018**, *161*, 667–682. [CrossRef]
3. Andersen, P.Ø. A simplified modelling approach for petroleum recovery by spontaneous imbibition in naturally fractured reservoirs. *J. Nat. Gas Sci. Eng.* **2019**, *63*, 95–114. [CrossRef]
4. Barros-Galvis, N.; Fernando Samaniego, V.; Cinco-Ley, H. Fluid dynamics in naturally fractured tectonic reservoirs. *J. Pet. Explor. Prod. Technol.* **2018**, *8*, 1–16. [CrossRef]
5. Barenblatt, G.I.; Entov, V.M.; Ryzhik, V.M. *Movement of Fluids and Gases in Natural Reservoirs*; Nedra: Moscow, Russia, 1984; p. 211.
6. Kotyakhov, F.I. *Physics of Oil and Gas Reservoirs*; Nedra: Moscow, Russia, 1977; p. 287.
7. Aguilera, R. *Naturally Fractured Reservoirs*; Pennwell Corp: Tulsa, OK, USA, 1980.
8. Denk, S.O. *Problems of Fractured Productive Objects*; Electronic publishing: Perm, Russia, 2004; p. 334.
9. Cholovsky, I.P. *Handbook: Oil and Gas Geologist's Companion*; Nedra: Moscow, Russia, 1989.
10. Golf-Racht, T.D. *Fundamentals of Fractured Reservoir Engineering*; Elsevier Scientific Publishing Company: Amsterdam, The Netherlands, 1982.
11. Jia, P.; Cheng, L.; Huang, S.; Wu, Y. A semi-analytical model for the flow behavior of naturally fractured formations with multi-scale fracture networks. *J. Hydrol.* **2016**, *537*, 208–220. [CrossRef]
12. Wu, Z.; Cui, C.; Trivedi, J.; Ai, N.; Tang, W. Pressure analysis for volume fracturing vertical well considering Low-velocity non-darcy flow and stress sensitivity. *Geofluids* **2019**, *2019*, 2046061. [CrossRef]
13. Xu, J.; Sun, B.; Chen, B. A hybrid embedded discrete fracture model for simulating tight porous media with complex fracture systems. *J. Pet. Sci. Eng.* **2019**, *174*, 131–143. [CrossRef]
14. Basquet, R.; Bourbiaux, B.J.; Cohen, C.E. Fracture flow property identification: An optimized implementation of discrete fracture network models. In Proceedings of the SPE Middle East Oil and Gas Show and Conference, Manama, Bahrain, 12–15 March 2005; Society of Petroleum Engineers: London, UK, 2005.
15. Sarda, S.; Jeannin, L.; Basquet, R.; Bourbiaux, B. Hydraulic characterization of fractured reservoirs: Simulation on discrete fracture models. *Spe Reserv. Eval. Eng.* **2002**, *5*, 154–162. [CrossRef]
16. Cao, R.; Fang, S.; Jia, P.; Cheng, L.; Rao, X. An efficient embedded discrete-fracture model for 2D anisotropic reservoir simulation. *J. Pet. Sci. Eng.* **2019**, *174*, 115–130. [CrossRef]
17. Soleimani, M. Naturally fractured hydrocarbon reservoir simulation by elastic fracture modeling. *Pet. Sci.* **2017**, *14*, 286–301. [CrossRef]
18. Vaughan, R.; Hicks, J.; Chasqui, E.; Velarde, J. History matching of naturally fractured reservoirs using pressure transient analysis and a case study. In Proceedings of the SPE Trinidad and Tobago Section Energy Resources Conference, Port of Spain, Trinidad and Tobago, 25–26 June 2018; Society of Petroleum Engineers: Port of Spain, Trinidad and Tobago, 2018.

19. Aziz, H.; Settari, E. *Mathematical Modeling of Reservoir Systems*; Institute for Computer Research: Moscow-Izhevsk, Russia, 2004.
20. Bobreneva, Y.O.; Rahimly, P.I.; Poveshchenko, Y.A.; Podryga, V.O.; Enikeeva, L.V. On one method of numerical modeling of piezoconductive processes of a two-phase fluid system in a fractured-porous reservoir. *J. Phys. Conf. Ser.* **2021**, *2131*, 0220021. [CrossRef]
21. PipeSim Software. Available online: https://digital.slb.ru/products/pipesim/flow_modeling/#tab_section114 (accessed on 20 October 2024).
22. Engineering and Structural Geology Software. Available online: https://www.petex.com/pe-engineering/ipm-suite/prosper (accessed on 20 October 2024).
23. Gidrozond Software. Available online: https://yapg.ru/?page_id=524 (accessed on 20 October 2024).
24. HydraTest Module. Available online: http://www.getek.ru/hydratest.html (accessed on 20 October 2024).
25. Avton Complexes for Automation of Field Operations. Available online: https://avtprom.ru/kompleksy-avton-dlya-avtomatizatsii-prom (accessed on 20 October 2024).
26. Manual Documents HydroGeoSphere (HGS) Version 2732. Available online: https://aquanty-artifacts-public.s3.amazonaws.com/hgs/hydrosphere_theory.pdf (accessed on 20 October 2024).
27. TOUGH3 Software. Available online: https://tough.lbl.gov/software/tough3/(accessed on 20 October 2024).
28. Bobreneva, Y.O. Modeling the Piezoconductivity Process of a Two-Phase Fluid System in a Fractured-Porous Reservoir. *Math. Model. Comput. Simulations* **2022**, *4*, 645–653. [CrossRef]
29. Uzyanbaev, R.; Bobreneva, Y.; Poveshchenko, Y.; Podryga, V.; Polyakov, S. Modeling of two-phase fluid flow processes in a fractured-porous type reservoir using parallel computations. In *Parallel Computational Technologies. PCT 2022*; Sokolinsky, L., Zymbler, M., Eds.; Springer: Cham, Switzerland, 2022; pp. 276–292.
30. Uzyanbaev, R.M.; Poveshchenko, Y.A.; Podryga, V.O.; Polyakov, S.V.; Bobreneva, Y.O.; Gubaydullin, I.M. Analysis of parallel algorithm efficiency for numerical solution of mass transfer problem in fractured-porous reservoir. *Lect. Notes Comput. Sci.* **2022**, *13708*, 33–47.
31. Marchuk, G.I. *Splitting Methods*; Nauka: Moscow, Russia, 1988.
32. MPI: A Message-Passing Interface Standard. Available online: http://www.mpi-forum.org/docs/ (accessed on 4 June 2024).
33. Center of Collective Usage of the Keldysh Institute of Applied Mathematics of RAS. Available online: http://ckp.kiam.ru (accessed on 4 June 2024).

mathematics

MDPI

Article

Energy Efficacy Enhancement in a Reactive Couple-Stress Fluid Induced by Electrokinetics and Pressure Gradient with Variable Fluid Properties

Peace O. Banjo [1,*], Ramoshweu S. Lebelo [2,3], Samuel O. Adesanya [1,3,4] and Emmanuel I. Unuabonah [5,6]

1 Department of Mathematics and Statistics, Faculty of Natural Sciences, Redeemer's University, Ede 232101, Nigeria; adesanyas@run.edu.ng
2 Applied Physical Sciences Department, Vaal University of Technology, Private Bag X021, Vanderbijlpark 1911, South Africa; sollyl@vut.ac.za
3 Environmental Hydrology Unit, African Center of Excellence for Water and Environmental Research (ACEWATER), Redeemer's University, PMB 230, Ede 232101, Nigeria
4 Education Department, Vaal University of Technology, Private Bag X021, Vanderbijlpark 1911, South Africa
5 Department of Chemical Sciences, Redeemer's University, PMB 230, Ede 232101, Nigeria; unuabonahe@run.edu.ng
6 Environmental Science and Technology Unit, African Center of Excellence for Water and Environmental Research (ACEWATER), Redeemer's University, PMB 230, Ede 232101, Nigeria
* Correspondence: banjop@run.edu.ng

Abstract: This study presents a mathematical analysis of the collective effect of chemical reactions, variable fluid properties, and thermal stability of a hydromagnetic couple-stress fluid flowing through a microchannel driven by electro-osmosis and a pressure gradient. The viscosity of the biofluid is assumed to depend on the temperature, while the electrical conductivity is assumed to be a linear function of the drift velocity. The governing equations are derived non-dimensionalized, and numerical solutions are obtained using the spectral Chebyshev collocation method. The numerical solution is validated using the shooting Runge–Kutta method. The effects of varying the parameters on the thermal stability, temperature, velocity, and entropy profiles are discussed with adequate interpretations using tables and graphs. The results reveal that the chemical reactions and viscosity parameter increase the fluid temperature, while the Hartmann number decreases the temperature and increases the flow velocity and entropy generation. It was also observed that the chemical reactions and viscosity parameter increased the entropy at the channel walls, while the Hartmann number decreased the entropy at the core center of the channel. This study has tremendous empirical significance, including but not limited to biophysical applications of devices, engineering applications such as control systems, and thermo-fluidic transport.

Keywords: electro-osmotic flow; chemical reactions; variable fluid properties; thermal stability

MSC: 76A05

1. Introduction

Due to its applications in many real-life situations, significant progress has been made in studies related to electro-osmotic flow (EOF) with or without pressure gradients. This is due to the fact that electro-osmotic principles are helpful in water treatment, soil percolation, chemical separation analysis, microfluidics apparatus, and scientific, engineering, and industrial applications that deal with electrolysis. Some vital literature on EOF includes that of Elbaighdriri et al. [1], who investigated the EOF of Williamson nanofluids through a convergent tube experiencing double diffusivity with a constant heat source. In [2], Reddy et al. conducted a thermal investigation of the EOF of a nanofluid with wave-like movement through an asymmetrical channel. The study by Tripathi et al. [3] highlighted the collective impacts of peristalsis and electro-osmosis on unsteady electrokinetic fluid flow in a microchannel. Other references related to electro-osmotic flow can be found in [4–7].

Chemical reactions are significant in energy production, forensic investigations, pool testing equipment, waste management, and metabolism. It also has industrial applications in combustion processes, metal production, and many other applications that have not been mentioned. Based on the foregoing, Raju et al. [8] studied the bearing of binary chemical reactions with activation energy on the convective Maxwell fluid flow through a rotating medium full of porous materials. Tanveer et al. [9] explored the interactions of homogenous and heterogeneous chemical reactions with the electro-osmotic flow of Jeffrey fluid with peristalsis. Prashanth and Rao [10] examined the effect of DuFour and Soret on the equilibrium of the magnetohydrodynamic flow of a chemically reactive nanofluid using the Keller Box technique. Other notable literature has been written on chemical reactions [11–14].

Recent findings [15–21] have shown that variable fluid properties are more appropriate for describing many complex fluids. In actual sense, these properties: viscosity, density, electrical conductivity, porous permeability, and many others vary with time, space, temperature, and velocity. The temperature-dependent viscosity and velocity-dependent electrical conductivity of the fluid are of interest here. In [15], Prasad et al. reported the outcome of varying thermal and viscosity conductivities on steady hydromagnetic flow over a stretched surface. Adeyemo et al. [16] addressed the fully developed nonlinear flow of an incompressible fluid bounded by a vertical channel saturated with permeable materials without heat transfer at the walls; the fluid's viscosity was assumed to be linearly dependent on temperature. Wu and Pruess [17] applied the integral method to obtain analytic solutions to a transient movement of a compressible fluid across a porous medium, with the permeability taken as a function of pressure.

The thermal stability of fluids is the ability of a reactive fluid to resist spontaneous ignition due to heat generation and dissipation. The auto-ignition temperature is the lowest temperature at which fluids will self-combust. The study of the thermal stability of materials has become increasingly important due to its various applications in energy storage and conversion, safe working environments, medical electronic devices, pharmaceuticals, and chemical processes, for example, in the production of polymers. Given these different applications, numerous authors [22–28] have investigated and discussed the thermal stability of various reactive fluids. Adeosun and Ukaegbu [22] performed a thermal criticality analysis of squeezed fluid flowing along parallel plates with variable electrical conductivity. The study by Salawu et al. [23] reported the thermal stability of Williamson reactive fluid with combined isotropic nanoparticles under thin radiation. Adesanya et al. [24] examined the thermal stability of a reactive fluid flowing through a porous medium and demonstrated the role of heat dissipation in stability control.

The originality of our work lies in the inclusion of reaction kinetics (in the form of Arrhenius, Sensitized, and Bimolecular), temperature-dependent viscosity, and velocity-dependent electrical conductivity, which were not considered in the previous study [7]. Our study provides a broad-based approach to biophysical systems and thermal engineering. Additionally, the inclusion of thermal stability analysis in the combustible exothermic system introduces a novel perspective not extensively addressed in earlier works. From an application viewpoint, physical fluid properties are not constant in many real-life situations. For instance, electrical conductivity varies with ion size, temperature [29], and, most importantly, drift velocity, even in biofluids like blood [30]. This is especially true when the working fluid has haphazardly oriented and rigid particles and substructures, which are features of a couple of stress fluids. For other related works, refer [31–33]. These variations are expected to better approximate the electro-osmotic flow, especially in many thermal engineering applications involving flow rate and varying temperature due to chemical interactions. In addition, after an exhaustive survey of the literature on electro-osmotic flows of a couple of stress fields, there is no report on chemical reactions and variable electrical conductivity, which varies with drift velocity; this highlights the significance of the research. The study outcomes for the temperature, velocity, and entropy profiles are displayed pictorially, and the physical interpretations are reported comprehensively. The results for validating the solution, convergence, and thermal stability are tabulated for varying parameters. Furthermore, the results reveal that the temperature and flow velocity magnitude increase when the variable viscosity parameter increases.

2. Model Derivation

We examine the steady flow of a non-compressible EMHD couple-stress fluid along an unending horizontal channel at $z = -H \; and \; z = H$, which can be seen in Figure 1.

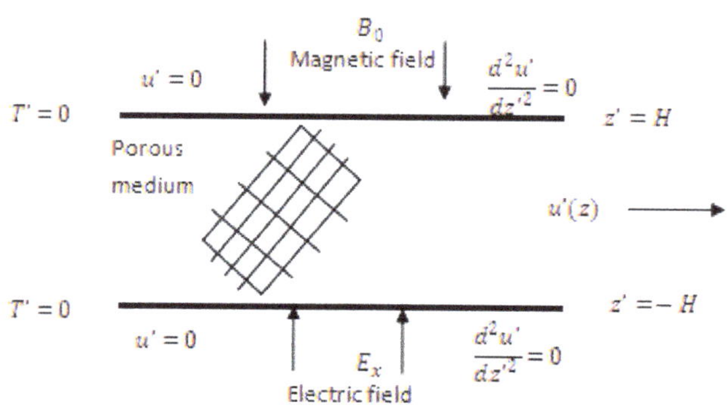

Figure 1. Flow geometry.

2.1. Derivation of Potential Distribution

To drive the fluid flow in the axial direction, we need to determine the potential distribution within the system. The electrochemical potential, which is the combination of the electrical and chemical potential, is given as,

$$\mu = \mu_0 + k_B \; T \; In(n) + Z \; e \; \psi' \tag{1}$$

where, μ_0 is the reference potential, n is the number density (concentration), T is the room temperature, Z is the valency, e is the protonic charge, ψ' is the electric potential, k_B is the Boltzmann constant.

Imposing the electrochemical equilibrium condition on (1), we obtain the following Boltzmann distribution equation,

$$n = n_0 e^{-\frac{Z \, e \, \psi'}{k_B \, T}} \tag{2}$$

where the positive and negative ions, positive and negative valency are respectively given as,

$$n^{+} = n_0 e^{-\frac{Z^{+}\,e\,\psi'}{k_B\,T}},\ n^{-} = n_0 e^{-\frac{Z^{-}\,e\,\psi'}{k_B\,T}},\ Z^{+} = Z,\ Z^{-} = -Z \tag{3}$$

Applying the Gauss' Law to relate the charge density with the electric field, we obtain

$$\varepsilon_0 \oint_S \vec{E}\bullet d\vec{S} = \int_V (\rho_e)_{total} dV = \int_V \left[-\nabla\bullet\left(\varepsilon_0\,\chi\,\vec{E}\right) + \rho_e\right] dV \tag{4}$$

with

$$\begin{aligned} (\rho_e)_{total} &= (\rho_e)_{free} + (\rho_e)_{bound} \\ &= (\rho_e)_{free} - \nabla\bullet\vec{P} \\ &= (\rho_e)_{free} - \nabla\bullet\varepsilon_0\,\chi\,\vec{E} \end{aligned} \tag{5}$$

By applying the Gauss' divergence theorem, we obtain the Poisson-type equation,

$$\nabla\bullet\left[\varepsilon\,\vec{E}\right] = \rho_e \tag{6}$$

where $\vec{E}$: Electric field, ε_0 : free space permittivity, $d\vec{S}$: surface element, $(\rho_e)_{total}$: total volumetric charge density, dV : volume element, $\vec{P}$: polarization vector, χ : susceptibility of the medium. $\varepsilon = \varepsilon_0\,(1+\chi)$: total permittivity.

Using $\vec{E} = -\nabla\,\psi'$, we obtain the Laplacian equation,

$$\nabla^2\psi' = \frac{-\rho_e}{\varepsilon} \tag{7}$$

The free charge density is the sum total of negative and positive ions, $\rho_e = \sum Ze\,n_i,\ (i = 1,2,\ )$ therefore,

$$\varepsilon\frac{d^2\psi'}{dz'^2} = (n^{-} - n^{+})Ze \tag{8}$$

$$\varepsilon\frac{d^2\psi'}{dz'^2} = n_0 Ze\left[e^{\frac{Z\,e\,\psi'}{k_B\,T}} - e^{-\frac{Z\,e\,\psi'}{k_B\,T}}\right] = 2n_0\,Z\,e\,sinh\left[\frac{Z\,e\,\psi'}{k_B\,T}\right] \tag{9}$$

The nonlinear equation above is called the Poisson-Boltzmann equation. By using the Debye–Hückel linearization for $\frac{Z\,e\,\psi'}{k_B\,T} << 1$, that is, $sinh\left[\frac{Z\,e\,\psi'}{T_a k_B}\right] \approx \frac{Z\,e\,\psi'}{T_a k_B}$, we obtain

$$\frac{d^2\psi'}{dz'^2} = \frac{2n_0\,Z^2\,e^2}{\varepsilon k_B\,T_a}\psi' = k^2\psi' \tag{10}$$

together with the symmetric and slip conditions to solve the equation.

$$\left.\frac{d\psi'}{dz'}\right|_{z'=0} = 0 \quad and \quad \psi'|_{z'=H} = \zeta \text{ and} \tag{11}$$

where k : inverse Debye Length, $\zeta = Max\,[\psi']$: zeta potential.

Finally, the solution of (10) subject to (11) satisfies,

$$\rho_e(z') = \frac{-\varepsilon k^2\zeta\cosh(kz')}{\cos\text{h}(kH)} \tag{12}$$

2.2. Conservation of Mass and Momentum

In this work, the steady flow of reactive couple-stress fluid through a porous medium is considered. The flow is driven by electro-osmotic force together with a pressure gradient. We also examine the effect of variable porous permeability, viscosity, and electrical conductivity. The viscosity of the flow and porous permeability are assumed to be dependent on the width of the microchannel. The electrical conductivity also depends on the flow velocity (Sivaraj and Kumar [21]). The biofluid considered in this study is blood, whose viscosity depends on temperature.

For this model, we have the following assumptions

- The flow is steady, hydrodynamically and thermally fully developed,
- The flow is unidirectional, hence $\vec{u} = (u'(z'), 0, 0)$ and $\overline{T} = (T'(z'), 0, 0)$
- The electric field $\vec{E} = (E_x, E_y, 0)$ is applied along the $x\prime$ and $y\prime$ directions.
- The magnetic field $\vec{B} = (0,\ 0, B_0)$ is imposed along the $z\prime$ direction.
- $\vec{J} = \sigma\left(\vec{E} + \vec{u} \times \vec{B}\right)$

The modified momentum equation, therefore, becomes

$$-\frac{dP}{dx'} + \frac{d}{dz'}\left(\mu(T)\frac{du'}{dz'}\right) - \eta\frac{d^4u'}{dz'^4} - \frac{\varepsilon k^2 E_x \zeta \cosh(kz')}{\cosh(kH)} + \sigma_e E_y B_0 - \sigma_e {B_0}^2 u' = 0 \tag{13}$$

with the no-slip and non-moving wall conditions given as,

$$u'(z')\big|_{z'=\pm H} = 0 \qquad and \qquad \left.\frac{d^2u'}{dz'^2}\right|_{z'=\pm H} = 0 \qquad \text{and} \tag{14}$$

where

$$\sigma_e = \sigma_0 u,\ \mu(T') = \mu_0 e^{\alpha'\ (T_0 - T')} \tag{15}$$

To make the equation dimensionless, we use the following parameters,

$$\left.\begin{array}{l} U_{HS} = \frac{\varepsilon E_x \zeta}{\mu_0},\ z = \frac{z'}{H},\ u = \frac{u'}{U_{HS}},\ \kappa = kH,\ \Omega = -\frac{H^2}{\mu_0\, U_{HS}}\frac{dP}{dx'}, \\ Ha = B_0 H\sqrt{\frac{\sigma_0}{\mu_0}},\ S = \frac{E_y H}{U_{HS}}\sqrt{\frac{\sigma_0}{\mu_0}},\ \gamma = \sqrt{\frac{\mu_0\, H^2}{\eta}} \end{array}\right\} \tag{16}$$

Applying these parameters above, we obtain the dimensionless equation,

$$\left.\begin{array}{l} \Omega + \frac{d}{dz}\left[e^{-\alpha_1\theta}\frac{du}{dz}\right] - \frac{1}{\gamma^2}\frac{d^4u}{dz^4} - \kappa^2\frac{\cosh(\kappa z)}{\cosh(\kappa)} + S\ Ha\ u - Ha^2u^2 = 0 \\ u(\pm 1) = 0,\quad \left.\frac{d^2u}{dz^2}\right|_{z=\pm 1} = 0 \end{array}\right\} \tag{17}$$

Evidently, the exact solution to the above boundary-value problem is only possible when both α_1 and Ha approach zero.

2.3. Conservation of Energy

The total energy in the control volume is the sum of the kinetic energy and nonlinear internal heat energy. With the addition of chemical reaction term to the model, we arrive at the energy equation,

$$0 = k_f\left(\frac{d^2T'}{dz'^2}\right) + QC_0A\left(\frac{hT'}{vl}\right)^m e^{\frac{-E}{RT'}} + \mu(T')\left(\frac{du'}{dz'}\right)^2 + \eta\left(\frac{d^2u'}{dz'^2}\right)^2 + \sigma_e\left({E_x}^2 + {E_y}^2 - 2E_yB_0u\prime + {B_0}^2u'^2\right) \tag{18}$$

and the boundary conditions, $T'(z')|_{z'=\pm H} = T_0$.

We make use of the following dimensionless parameters to non-dimensionalize the energy equation.

$$\left.\begin{array}{l}\theta = \frac{E(T'-T_0)}{RT_0^2},\ \alpha_1 = \frac{\alpha' RT_0^2}{E},\ s_x = \frac{\sigma_0 E_x^2 H^2}{\mu_0 U_{HS}^2},\ s_y = \frac{\sigma_0 E_y^2 H^2}{\mu_0 U_{HS}^2}, \\ \beta = \frac{RT_0}{E},\ \lambda = \frac{QC_0AEH^2}{k_f RT_0^2}\left(\frac{hT_0}{\upsilon l}\right)^m e^{\frac{-E}{RT_0}},\ \delta = \frac{\mu_0 U_{HS}^2}{QC_0AH^2}\left(\frac{\upsilon l}{hT_0}\right)^m e^{\frac{E}{RT_0}}\end{array}\right\} \tag{19}$$

The dimensionless form of the modified combustion equation is given as,

$$\left.\begin{array}{l}\frac{d^2\theta}{dz^2} + \lambda\left[(1+\beta\theta)^m e^{\frac{\theta}{1+\beta\theta}} + \delta\left(e^{-\alpha_1\theta}\left(\frac{du}{dz}\right)^2 + \frac{1}{\gamma^2}\left(\frac{d^2u}{dz^2}\right)^2 + (s_x+s_y)u - 2\,S\,Ha\,u^2 + Ha^2u^3\right)\right] = 0 \\ \theta(\pm 1) = 0\,.\end{array}\right\} \tag{20}$$

The shear stress and wall heat flux are respectively defined as,

$$\tau_w = \mu(T')\frac{du'}{dz'} - \eta\frac{d^3u'}{dz'^3}\bigg|_{z=-1} \qquad q_w = -k_f\frac{dT'}{dz'}\bigg|_{z=-1} \tag{21}$$

2.4. Entropy Generation Analysis

The local volumetric rate of entropy generation is expressed as

$$E_G = \frac{k_f}{T_0{}^2}\left(\frac{dT'}{dz'}\right)^2 + \frac{1}{T_0}\left[\mu(T')\left(\frac{du'}{dz'}\right)^2 + \eta\left(\frac{d^2u'}{dz'^2}\right)^2 + \sigma_e\left(E_x{}^2 + E_y{}^2 - 2E_yB_0u' + B_0{}^2u'^2\right)\right] \tag{22}$$

The non-dimensional entropy generation is given as,

$$N_S = \underbrace{\left(\frac{d\theta}{dz}\right)^2}_{N_{HT}} + \underbrace{\frac{\lambda\delta}{\beta}\left[e^{-\alpha_1\theta}\left(\frac{du}{dz}\right)^2 + \frac{1}{\gamma^2}\left(\frac{d^2u}{dz^2}\right)^2 + (s_x+s_y)u - 2\,SHa\,u^2 + Ha^2u^3\right]}_{N_{VD}} \tag{23}$$

We introduce the Bejan number, Be, to evaluate the effect of each parameter on the entropy generation profile. It is given as,

$$Be = \frac{N_{HT}}{N_S} \tag{24}$$

A total of 14 non-dimensional parameters are used in this study, namely, Hartmann number, activation energy parameter, electric field parameter, (Ha, β, S), coefficient of viscosity, couple-stress parameter, electrokinetic width, (α_1, γ, K), velocity, temperature and pressure gradient, (u, θ, Ω), Frank-Kameneskii parameter, entropy generation, (λ, N_S), viscous dissipation parameter, Joule heat parameters (δ, s_x, s_y) respectively.

3. Method of Solution

The solutions to the nonlinear Equations (17) and (20) are obtained via the spectral collocation method. The spectral Chebyshev collocation method is chosen for its high accuracy and efficiency in solving complex boundary-value problems. This method is particularly effective for problems involving sharp gradients, as it minimizes computational error and achieves rapid convergence. Validation using the shooting Runge–Kutta method confirms the robustness of this approach, as shown in Tables 1 and 2.

Table 1. (a) Validation for velocity when $\beta = 0.1$; $m = 0.5$; $S = 1$; $R = 1$; $H = 0.2$; $\Lambda = 1$; $\gamma = 1$; $\lambda = 0.1$; $\alpha_1 = 0.01$; $s_1 = 0.02$; $\delta = 3$; $\kappa = 1$; (b) Validation for temperature when $\beta = 0.1$; $m = 0.5$; $S = 1$; $R = 1$; $H = 0.2$; $\Lambda = 1$; $\gamma = 1$; $\lambda = 0.1$; $\alpha_1 = 0.01$; $s_1 = 0.02$; $\delta = 3$; $\kappa = 1$.

		(a)	
z	$u(z)_{SCCM}$	$u(z)_{RK4}$	$\lvert u(z)_{SCCM} - u(z)_{RK4}\rvert$
-1	$1.278457061874004 \times 10^{-17}$	0.	$1.374898306521335 \times 10^{-18}$
-0.75	0.0629067528195136	0.06290675639956234	$1.212604495981484 \times 10^{-9}$
-0.5	0.11300454429091983	0.11300454648432434	$1.801353691210927 \times 10^{-9}$
-0.25	0.14291696897585213	0.14291696903977355	$3.64452736045795 \times 10^{-9}$
0.0	0.14993371862224614	0.1499337180703369	$4.460718419641019 \times 10^{-9}$
0.25	0.13487591971840526	0.13487591943819496	$7.535644719336432 \times 10^{-9}$
0.5	0.10117000646607631	0.10117000659895337	$1.110966178774486 \times 10^{-8}$
0.75	0.05407250188183676	0.05407250280453991	$1.011271340278785 \times 10^{-8}$
1.0	$8.037935726473451 \times 10^{-19}$	$1.538216525204596 \times 10^{-9}$	$6.650356695509854 \times 10^{-10}$
		(b)	
z	$\theta(z)_{SCCM}$	$\theta(z)_{RK4}$	$\lvert\theta(z)_{SCCM} - \theta(z)_{RK4}\rvert$
-1	$8.347506626484343 \times 10^{-18}$	0.	$6.650507319668297 \times 10^{-18}$
-0.75	0.03058197395534581	0.030581968580185397	$3.975948570378307 \times 10^{-9}$
-0.5	0.05284437821144731	0.05284437008583946	$4.714958777574107 \times 10^{-9}$
-0.25	0.06602942949986432	0.066029424266624	$2.094374902672502 \times 10^{-9}$
0.0	0.06989972223532497	0.06989971497358342	$7.650101385703323 \times 10^{-10}$
0.25	0.06470574644977296	0.0647057366257331	$2.431655009293987 \times 10^{-9}$
0.5	0.05096126175034675	0.050961251931184746	$4.9188363451802 \times 10^{-9}$
0.75	0.029232629710794485	0.029232620363145338	$6.575776253375798 \times 10^{-9}$
1.0	$-3.288932058159692 \times 10^{-18}$	$-6.386044694272373 \times 10^{-9}$	$7.039165616692663 \times 10^{-9}$

Table 2. Exact Solution versus Numerical Solution $\beta = 0.1$; $m = 0.5$; $S = 1$; $R = 1$; $H = 0$; $\Lambda = 1$; $\gamma = 1$; $\lambda = 0.1$; $\alpha_1 = 0$; $s_1 = 0.02$; $\delta = 3$; $\kappa = 1$.

z	$u(z)_{Exact}$	$u(z)_{SCCM}$	$u(z)_{Exact} - u(z)_{SCCM}$
-1	0.	$-3.325780086847037 \times 10^{-18}$	$3.325780086847037 \times 10^{-18}$
-0.75	0.06218675003473847	0.062186750034738315	$1.52655665885959 \times 10^{-16}$
-0.5	0.11167226783139574	0.11167226783139575	$1.387778780781445 \times 10^{-17}$
-0.25	0.14117656707847842	0.14117656707847837	$5.551115123125783 \times 10^{-17}$
0.0	0.14805427366388543	0.14805427366388538	$5.551115123125783 \times 10^{-17}$
0.25	0.13314676750126822	0.13314676750126817	$5.551115123125783 \times 10^{-17}$
0.5	0.09985338386132184	0.09985338386132184	0.
0.75	0.053363321317313625	0.053363321317313556	$6.938893903907228 \times 10^{-17}$
1.0	0.	$-1.578342750457657 \times 10^{-17}$	$1.578342750457657 \times 10^{-17}$

Assume admissible trial polynomials of the form $\Psi_k(z)$ with

$$\left.\begin{aligned} u(z) &\approx u^N(z) = \sum_{k=0}^{N} b_k \Psi_k(z), \\ \theta(z) &\approx \theta^N(z) = \sum_{k=0}^{N} c_k \Psi_k(z) \end{aligned}\right\} \tag{25}$$

In (25), $\Psi_k(z)$ is the spectral Chebyshev polynomial with the unknown constants (b_k, c_k) satisfying boundary conditions. Substituting (25) into the boundary-value problem (17) and (20) gives the subsequent residues that must be solved at specific grid points,

$$\left.\begin{aligned} R_1 &= \Omega + \left(e^{-\alpha_1 \theta^N} u_z^N\right)' - \frac{1}{\gamma^2} u^N_{z\,z\,z\,z} - \frac{\kappa^2 \cosh(\kappa z)}{\cosh(\kappa)} + SHa\, u^N - Ha^2 u^{2N}, \\ R_2 &= \theta^N_{z\,z} + \lambda \left[\left(1 + \beta \theta^N\right)^m e^{\frac{\theta^N}{1+\beta\theta^N}} + \delta \left(e^{-\alpha_1 \theta^N} \left(u_z^N\right)^2 + \frac{1}{\gamma^2} \left(u^N_{z\,z}\right)^2 + \left(s_x + s_y\right) u^N - 2\, S\, Ha\, u^{2N} + Ha^2 u^{3N} \right) \right] \end{aligned}\right\} \tag{26}$$

with boundary conditions

$$u^N(-1) = 0 = u^N(1),\ u^N_{zz}\Big|_{z=-1} = 0 = u^N_{zz}\Big|_{z=1},\ \theta^N(-1) = 0 = \theta^N(1) \tag{27}$$

where z_k are points within $[-1,1] = [z_{0,} z_N]$. Then the Gauss-Lobato collocation points are given as

$$z_k = \left(-\cos\left(\frac{i\pi}{N}\right)\right), \quad i = 0,1,2,\ ,N \tag{28}$$

The residues are solved at the points

$$R_1(z_k) = 0, \text{ and } R_2(z_k) = 0,\ k = 0,1,2,\ ,N \tag{29}$$

and the lth-derivatives for dependent variables are obtained as

$$\frac{d^l u}{dz^l} = \sum_{i=0}^{N} b_i \frac{d^l u_i}{dz^l} \text{ and } \frac{d^l \theta}{dz^l} = \sum_{i=0}^{N} c_i \frac{d^l \theta_i}{dz^l} \tag{30}$$

with the differentiation matrix at each collocation point given as

$$\begin{array}{lcl} \frac{d\overline{u}}{dz} = D^{(1)}\overline{u} = D\overline{u} & & \frac{d\overline{\theta}}{dz} = D^{(1)}\overline{\theta} = D\overline{\theta} \\ \frac{d^2\overline{u}}{dz^2} = D^{(2)}\overline{u} = D^2\overline{u} & and & \frac{d^2\overline{\theta}}{dz^2} = D^{(2)}\overline{\theta} = D^2\overline{\theta} \\ \cdots\ \cdots\ \cdots\ \cdots & & \cdots\ \cdots\ \cdots\ \cdots \\ \frac{d^l\overline{u}}{dz^l} = D^{(l)}\overline{u} = D^l\overline{u} & & \frac{d^l\overline{\theta}}{dz^l} = D^{(l)}\overline{\theta} = D^l\overline{\theta} \end{array} \tag{31}$$

The vector form of the equations is defined as

$$\left.\overline{u} = (u(z_0), u(z_1),\ , u(z_N))^T, \overline{\theta} = (\theta(z_0), \theta(z_1),\ , \theta(z_N))^T\right\} \tag{32}$$

The set of algebraic equations derived from the nonlinear boundary-value problem was converted into and solved using the Wolfram Mathematica symbolic package via the shooting-Runge–Kutta method on the NDSolve algorithm.

4. Code Validation

The accuracy of the spectral Chebyshev collocation solution is validated using the shooting Runge–Kutta method with the NDSolve algorithm in Wolfram Mathematica 13.3. The pointwise validations for $u(z)$, $\theta(z)$ are presented in Tables 1 and 2.

From Table 1a,b, it can be seen that the numerical solutions are convergent, leading to a minima absolute difference of the order of 10^{-9} within the interior points and order of 10^{-18} at the boundary points. This shows the superimposition of the convergent solutions.

To further verify the numerical solutions obtained through the spectral Chebyshev collocation method, comparisons have been made with exact solutions for the velocity profile. This comparison, presented in Table 2, confirms the accuracy and robustness of the numerical approach employed in this study.

It is crucial to test for the convergence of the numerical scheme (25), as can be seen in Table 3. A critical look at Table 3 shows that the true value of λ_c is 0.842179204, even when $N = 15$ convergence is suspected but confirmed when $N = 20$. In contrast, the convergence of the Nusselt number is suspected at $N = 15$ but confirmed at $N = 20$ to 9 decimal places. The true value of the Nusselt number is 2.608270652. The table reveals that the critical value λ_c has a fast convergence up to 9 decimal places. This shows the strength of SCCM in handling the nonlinear problem.

Table 3. Order of Approximation. $\gamma = 1; S = 1; \delta = 3; \alpha_1 = 0.1; s_1 = 0.02.$

N	β	κ	Ha	γ	m	λ_c	Nu
5	0.1	1	0.1	1	0.5	0.859747754	2.526044368
10	0.1	1	0.1	1	0.5	0.842181180	2.608235465
15	0.1	1	0.1	1	0.5	0.842179328	2.608271531
20	0.1	1	0.1	1	0.5	0.842179204	2.608270652
25	0.1	1	0.1	1	0.5	0.842179204	2.608270652
30	0.1	1	0.1	1	0.5	0.842179204	2.608270652

The second row in Table 4 shows the reference data. From Table 4, it can be observed that an increase in the Hartmann number causes a decrease in the thermal critical values. This shows that the Lorentz force in the magnetic field reduces the flow velocity. This observation is true due to the fact that a rise in Hartmann's number brings about a corresponding decrease in the flow velocity and its powers. As a result, an increase in the Hartmann number is expected to have an increasing effect on the heat source. Therefore, the spontaneous heating of the fluid is accelerated.

As is seen from Table 4, increasing values of the coefficient of viscosity stabilizes the thermal stability of the fluid. This is due to the fact that as the fluid increases in thickness, its resistance to flow is increased, thereby reducing the velocity of the fluid. Consequently, the spontaneous heating of the fluid is delayed, causing it to stabilize. From Table 4, it can be seen that increasing values of the viscous heating parameter, δ destabilizes the thermal stability of the fluid. This is due to the fact that decreasing velocity and its derivatives in the microchannel suppresses the stabilizing effect of the coefficient of viscosity. It is observed from Equation (17) that as the joule heat parameters increase, the velocity, its derivatives, and powers increase, which in turn causes the temperature of the fluid to increase; therefore, thermal ignition is sped up; hence, as seen in Table 4, this destabilizes the fluid.

We can see from Equation (17) that as the electrokinetic width increases, the velocity, its derivatives, and powers decrease; therefore, the temperature falls, which means that thermal ignition is accelerated; hence, as seen in Table 4, this destabilizes the fluid. As can be seen from Table 4, increasing the values of the couple-stress inverse parameter destabilizes the thermal stability of the fluid. This is because the couple-stress fluid is a non-Newtonian fluid; hence, this reduces the velocity of the fluid; therefore, spontaneous heating of the fluid is accelerated, causing it to destabilize. From Table 4, it can be observed that an increase in the activation energy parameter causes an increase in the thermal critical values. This observation is true due to the fact that a rise in activation energy brings about a corresponding decrease in the flow velocity and its powers. As a result, the thermal ignition of the fluid is delayed.

Table 4. Thermal stability with values when $N = 30; m = 0.5; \kappa = 1$.

Ha	α_1	δ	S	κ	γ	β	λ_c
0	0.05	3	2	1	0.5	0.05	0.8101958114944492
1	0.05	3	2	1	0.5	0.1	0.8084489921845223
2	0.05	3	2	1	0.5	0.1	0.8069508609286701
0	0.10	3	2	1	0.5	0.1	0.8414049673721098
0	0.15	3	2	1	0.5	0.1	0.8772991474595369
0	0.05	5	2	1	0.5	0.1	0.7617201487125268
0	0.05	7	2	1	0.5	0.1	0.7208157852683288
0	0.05	3	1	1	0.5	0.1	0.8101958114944492
0	0.05	3	0	1	0.5	0.1	0.8101958114944492
0	0.05	3	2	5	0.5	0.1	0.6519506043881368
0	0.05	3	2	6	0.5	0.1	0.5529606777180318
0	0.05	3	2	1	0.8	0.1	0.7284496140669078
0	0.05	3	2	1	1.0	0.1	0.6835096763560569
0	0.05	3	2	1	0.5	0.07	0.8221977660661939
0	0.05	3	2	1	0.5	0.10	0.8414049673721098

5. Results and Discussion

We observe from Figure 2 that the Frank-Kameneskii parameter has a negligible effect on the velocity of the fluid. This is due to the slight variations in the viscosity profile as a result of the thermal effect. The result behaves well since changes in viscosity usually do not have significant changes in flow velocity. This aligns with theoretical expectations, as variations in viscosity due to temperature primarily affect temperature profiles rather than velocity. The effect of the Frank-Kamenetskii parameter on the velocity is small because the temperature is not captured as one of the body forces.

In Figure 3, we see the relationship between temperature and the Frank-Kameneskii parameter. From this plot, an increase in the Frank-Kameneskii parameter is seen to significantly enhance the fluid temperature. In an actual sense, when an exothermic reaction occurs, it transfers heat energy to the surrounding fluid, causing the fluid temperature to rise. This occurs because the reaction releases excess energy in the form of heat, which is then absorbed by the fluid, leading to a temperature increase.

In Figure 4, we see that when the Frank-Kameneskii number increases, the entropy generation increases. Entropy is the rate of disorder in the fluid particles. Therefore, for an exothermic chemical reaction, the liberated heat will encourage the randomness and mobility of ions, which in turn increases the entropy of the system.

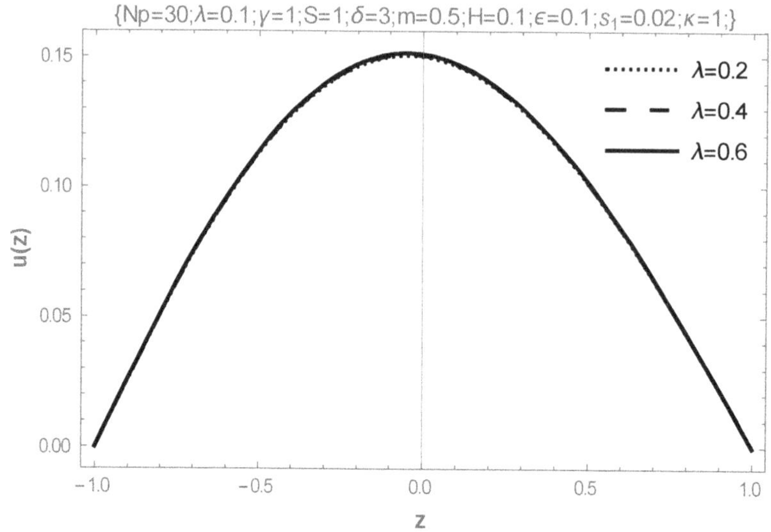

Figure 2. Effect of chemical reactions on the velocity profile.

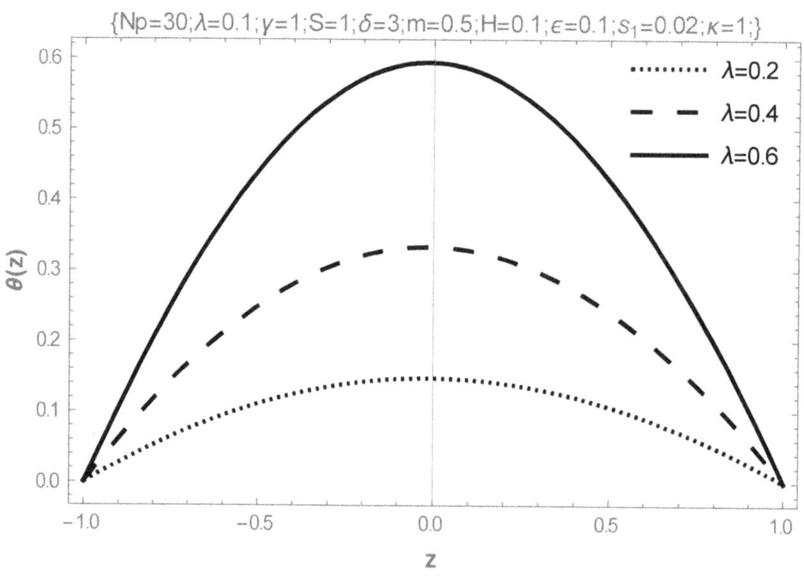

Figure 3. Effect of chemical reactions on temperature distribution.

In Figure 5, we see that when the Frank-Kameneskii number increases, both the temperature and the Bejan number increase. This indicates that the entropy generation contributed by fluid friction is lesser in comparison to that by heat transfer due to an increase in the exothermic chemical reactions in the microchannel, except at the walls where irreversibility arising from fluid friction attains its maximum.

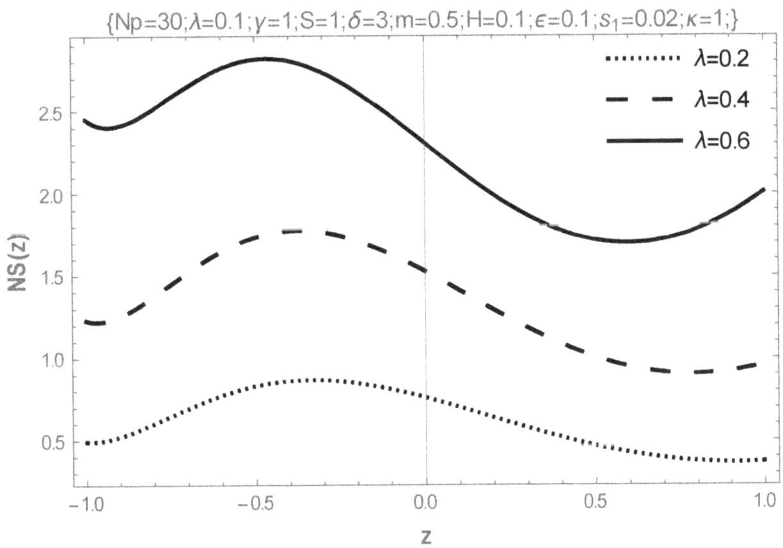

Figure 4. Effect of chemical reactions on entropy generation.

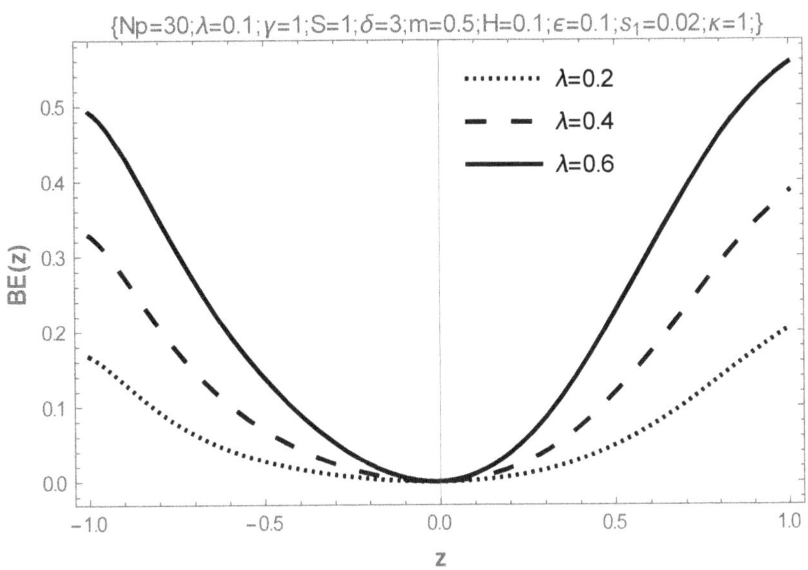

Figure 5. Effect of chemical reactions on Bejan number.

In Figure 6, we see that when the fluid viscosity increases, the effect on the velocity is small. This is a result of the term $e^{-\alpha_1\theta}$ in Equation (17) approaching zero as α_1 increases. Therefore, the variation in the fluid velocity is expected to be small in the microchannel. The impact of viscosity variation is subtle, as inertial forces dominate the viscosity at the microscale.

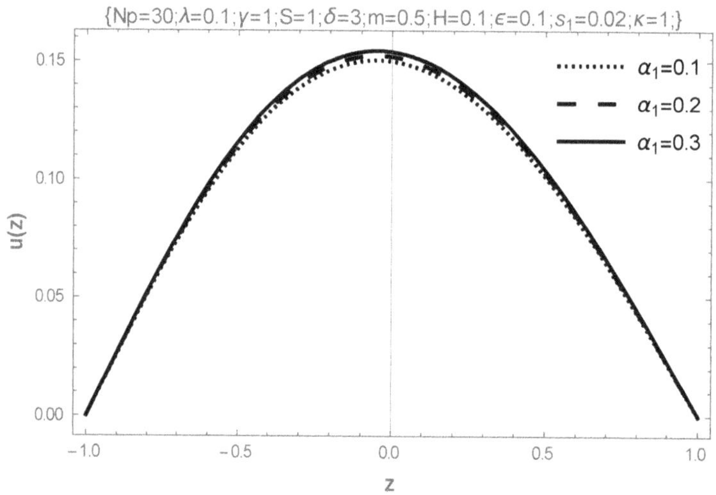

Figure 6. Effect of variable viscosity on velocity profile.

The net effect of viscosity on the temperature distribution is presented in Figure 7. The results revealed a significant change with a small increase in the viscosity variation parameter. This is correct since the velocity and its gradients contribute more to the heat source in the microchannel.

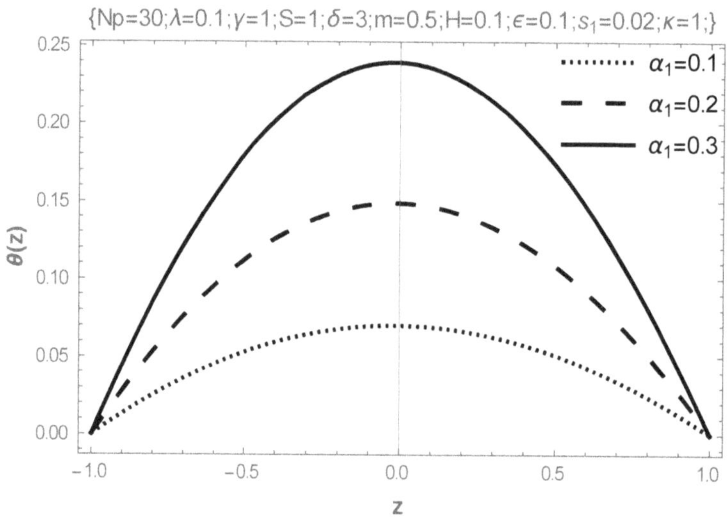

Figure 7. Effect of variable viscosity on temperature distribution.

Figure 8 shows the entropy profile with changes in the viscosity variation parameter. From the plot, it is observed that for increasing values of the viscosity parameter, both the fluid velocity and temperature improve, which in turn encourages entropy due to increased randomness in fluid particles. However, a symmetrical distribution is observed in the microchannel due to the drift velocity.

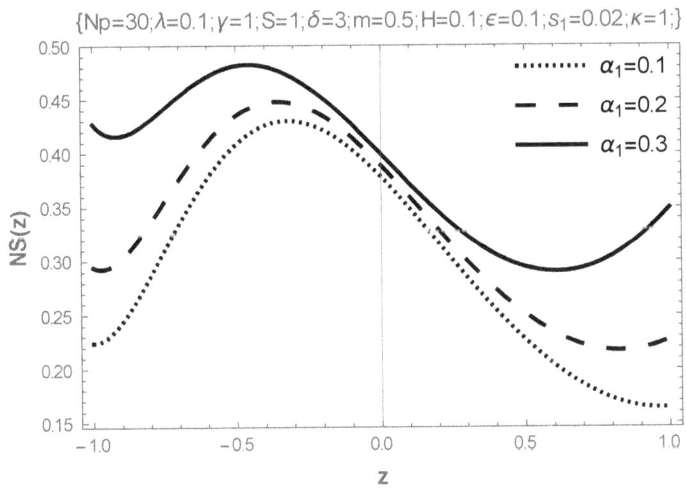

Figure 8. Effect of variable viscosity on entropy generation.

Figure 9 shows the profile of the Bejan number when α_1 is varied. From the plot, when α_1 is 0.1, it is observed that the Bejan values at the centerline are zero and near zero at the walls. This means that the heat irreversibility from fluid friction is at a maximum and very small at the walls. However, as the viscosity parameter value increases, the core center is invariant to changes but attains a maximum of 0.5 at walls when $\alpha_1 = 0.3$. At this point that $Be = 0.5$, then $N_{VD} = N_{HT}$ and a further increase in the values of α_1 weakens fluid friction irreversibility.

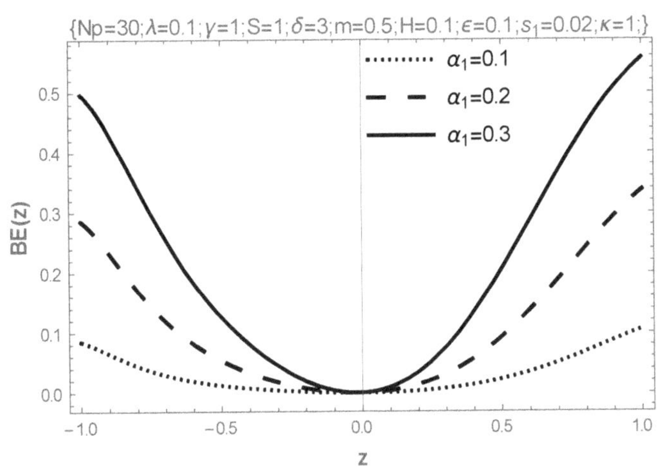

Figure 9. Effect of variable viscosity on Bejan number.

Figure 10 shows the effect of the drift velocity with the reactive couple-stress fluid. As seen from the graph, a rise in the Hartmann number elevates the flow velocity due to the fact that the charged fluid particle experiences the Lorentz force and moves in the direction of flow. This automatically enhances the flow, as shown here. With a low Hartmann number, which implies a weak magnetic field, the flow is less suppressed, which leads to higher velocity gradients.

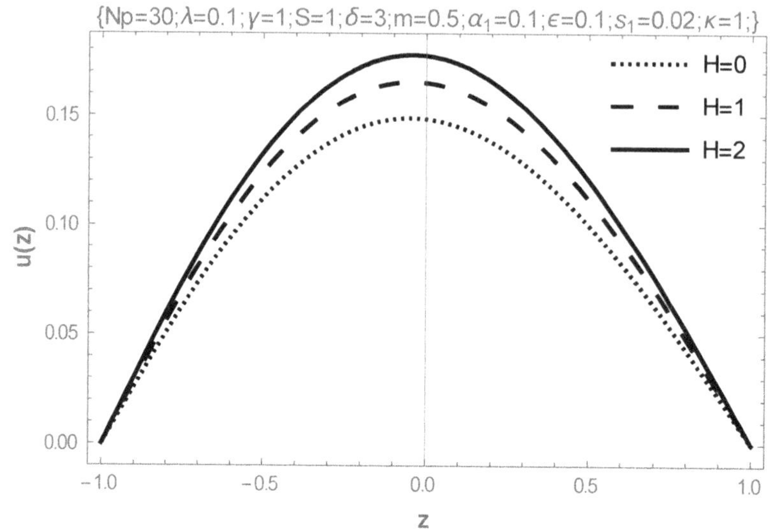

Figure 10. Effect of Hartmann number on the velocity profile.

Figure 11 shows that when the Hartmann number increases, the temperature decreases. This is due to the fact that as the Hartmann number increases, the velocity of the fluid increases, as seen in Figure 10. The magnitude is, however, small with $u_{\max} < 0.2$. Consequently, the temperature of the fluid decreases as the Hartmann number increases, as shown in Figure 11. The effect of the Hartmann number on temperature is limited due to the competing effects of Lorentz force damping and viscous dissipation.

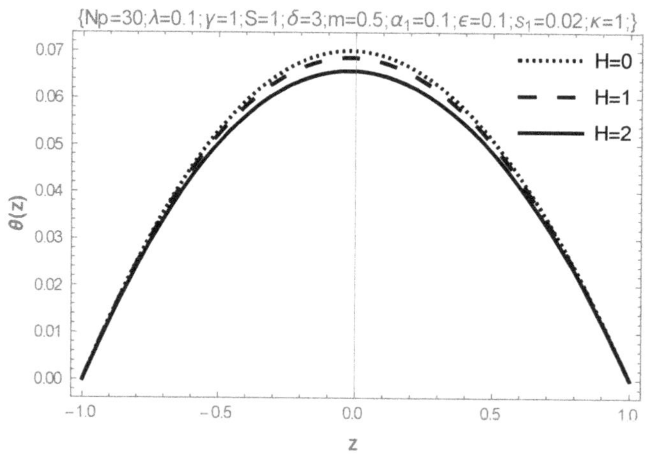

Figure 11. Effect of the Hartmann number on the temperature distribution.

As observed in Figures 10 and 11, an increase in the Hartmann number increases the flow velocity while decreasing the fluid temperature. The net effect of this behavior is shown in Figure 12 as the entropy generation profile. From the graph, entropy increases at the channel walls, while it drops at the core center of the microchannel. Additionally, the influence of the Hartmann number is more pronounced, as shown in Figures 10–12, where it is observed to decrease temperature while increasing velocity. A weaker magnetic field (low Ha) enhances the velocity, which may decrease the temperature gradients, leading to lower entropy generation in certain regions of the flow. This behavior highlights the interplay between magnetic forces and thermal effects in controlling entropy generation.

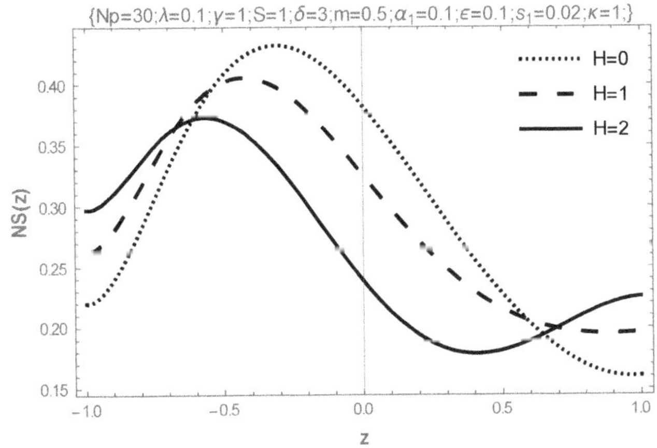

Figure 12. Effect of the Hartmann number on entropy generation.

The hydrodynamic case when H = 0 shows that the Bejan number is zero at the core center due to the maximum irreversibility from the fluid friction and about 0.1 at the walls. This shows that the irreversibility arising from fluid friction is the lowest at the walls. A further increase in the values of H results in a further decrease at the walls. This can be observed in Figure 13.

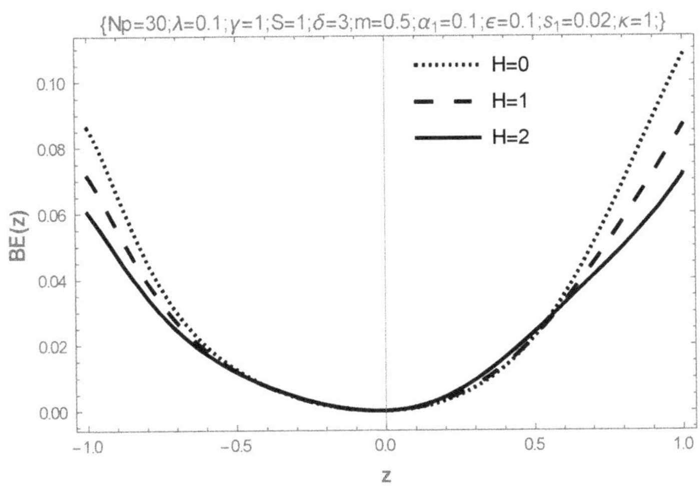

Figure 13. Effect of Hartmann number on Bejan number.

An electric field affects the velocity of a charged particle by accelerating it, thereby increasing the speed. This can be observed in Figure 14, where the drift velocity increases at the center of the channel as the electric field parameter increases.

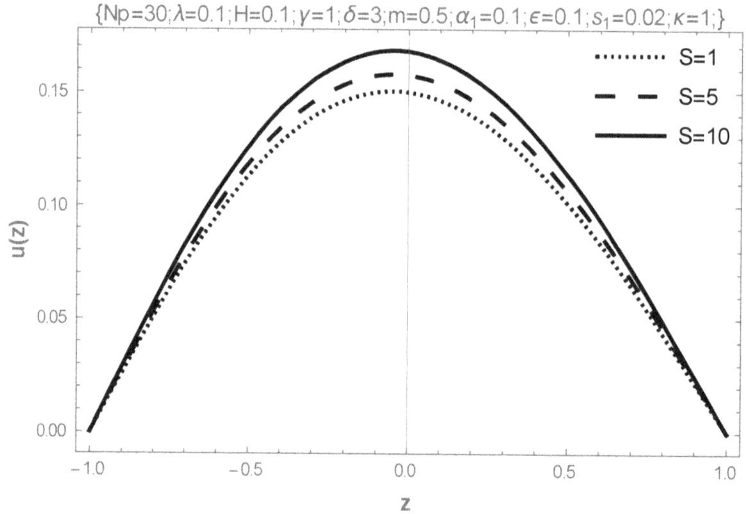

Figure 14. Effect of electric field parameter on the velocity profile.

In Figure 15, we observe that the electric field parameter has a negligible decreasing effect on the temperature distribution. This is due to the term $-2SHau^2$ in Equation (20), which diminishes the temperature of the fluid, but the effect is small, as other terms in the equation dominate over it.

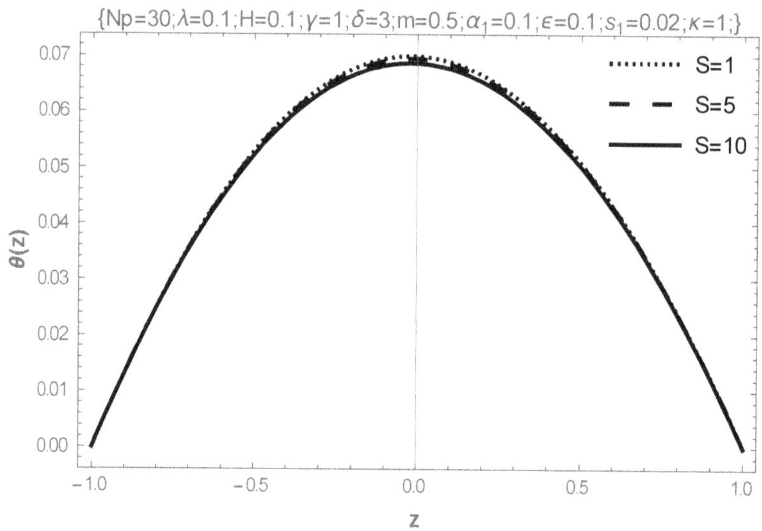

Figure 15. Effect of electric field parameter on temperature distribution.

In Figure 16, we see that when the electric field parameter increases, the entropy generation in the system increases at the wall; however, at the center of the channel, between $z = -0.4975$ and $z = 0.5567$, the entropy decreases, which is the net effect of an increase in the flow velocity (Figure 14) and a decrease in the fluid temperature (Figure 15) for increasing values of S. A similar trend is observed in Figure 12, with an increase in the Hartmann number.

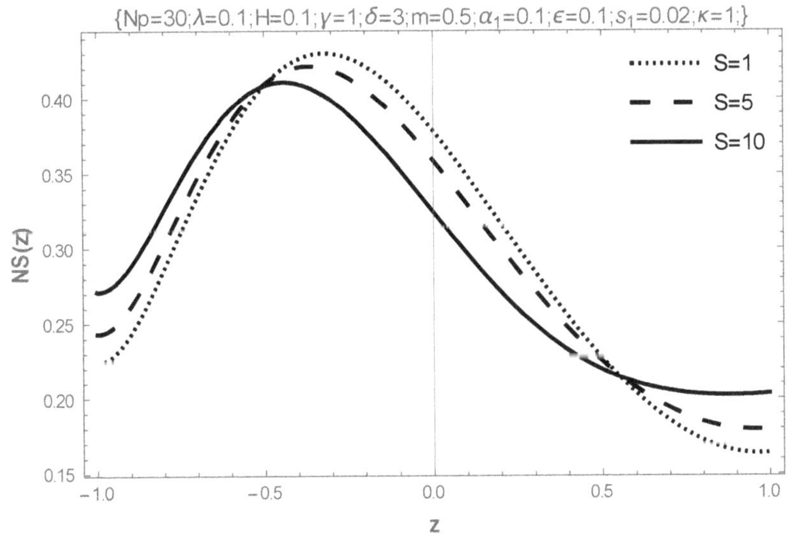

Figure 16. Effect of electric field parameter on entropy generation.

It is observed from Figure 17 that the Bejan number is zero at the core center due to the maximum irreversibility from the fluid friction and about 0.1 at the walls. This shows that irreversibility arising from fluid friction is at its lowest at the walls. A further increase in the values of the electric field parameter results in a further decrease at the walls. An identical behavior is observed in Figure 13.

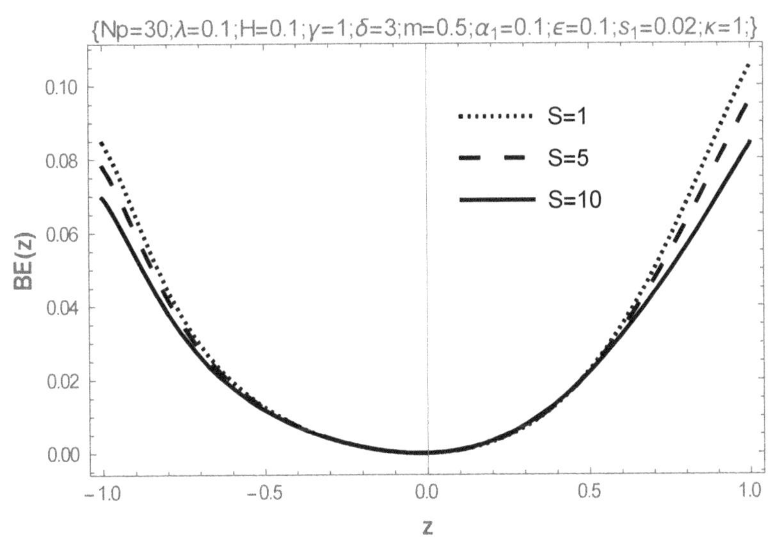

Figure 17. Effect of electric field parameter on Bejan number.

In Figure 18, the thermal criticality for the biomolecular flow is shown to be maximum at $\lambda_C = 0.842179$. It is observed that when $\lambda_C = 0.842179$, the temperature will have one solution, and for $\lambda_C < 0.842179$, it will have two solutions, and when $\lambda_C > 0.842179$, auto-ignition occurs and the solution disappears, which is a typical combustion process.

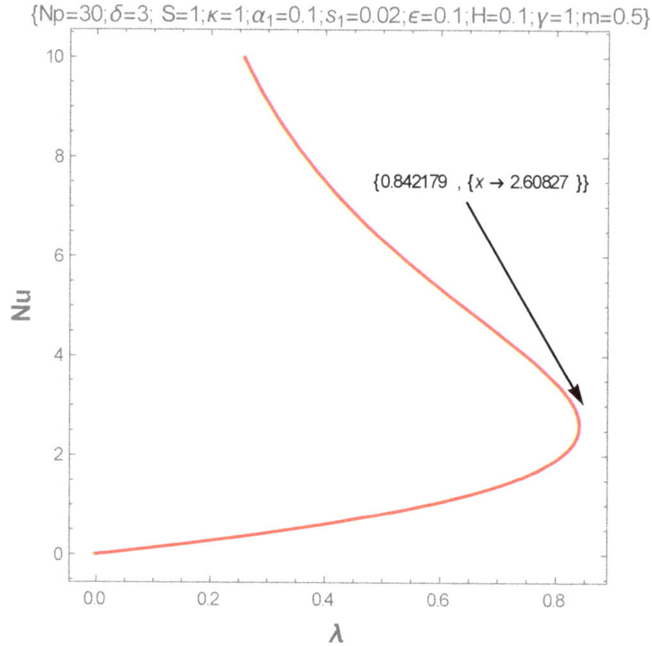

Figure 18. Thermal criticality.

6. Conclusions

In this paper, the effects of drift velocity, chemical reactions, and variable properties on the electrokinetic flow of reactive couple-stress fluid were examined. A computational approach was adopted to derive solutions to the momentum, energy, and entropy equations using the spectral Chebyshev collocation method and validated using the Runge–Kutta method. The solutions of the two methods were in agreement, demonstrating the accuracy of the methods. The following are the significant contributions to knowledge:

i. The increasing values of the Hartmann number, electrokinetic width, electric field parameter, joule heat parameters, and the couple-stress parameter destabilize the flow, while the coefficient of viscosity and the activation energy parameter stabilize the flow.
ii. The rising values of the Hartmann number, the coefficient of viscosity, and the electric field parameter enhance the flow of fluid, while the Frank-Kameneskii parameter does not have an effect on the flow velocity.
iii. In addition, intensifying the values of the Frank-Kameneskii parameter and the coefficient of viscosity elevates the temperature of the fluid, while the Hartmann number reduces the temperature.

The limitations of the model include the neglect of three-dimensional effects, convective cases, and other variable physical properties. This model is most applicable to small-scale systems where these assumptions hold true, such as microfluidic devices or controlled laboratory environments. It may require adjustments when applied to large-scale industrial processes or highly dynamic systems.

Author Contributions: Conceptualization, S.O.A.; Data curation, E.I.U.; Formal analysis, P.O.B.; Funding acquisition, R.S.L.; Investigation, R.S.L.; Methodology, S.O.A.; Resources, R.S.L.; Supervision,

S.O.A.; Validation, P.O.B.; Writing—original draft, P.O.B.; Writing—review and editing, E.I.U. All authors have read and agreed to the published version of the manuscript.

Funding: This research received no external funding.

Data Availability Statement: The original contributions presented in this study are included in the article. Further inquiries can be directed to the corresponding author.

Conflicts of Interest: The authors do not have any conflicts of interest.

Nomenclature

u	dimensionless velocity	θ	dimensionless temperature
z	Horizontal coordinate	Ha	Hartmann number
β	activation energy parameter	m	Exponential Factor
J_x, J_y	Joule heat parameters	ϑ	Viscous Dissipation Parameter
N_S	dimensionless entropy generation	S	electric field parameter
κ	electrokinetic width	γ	Couple-stress parameter
Ω	pressure gradient	λ	Frank Kameneskii parameter
α_1	coefficient of viscosity		

References

1. Elboughdiri, N.; Javid, K.; Shehzad, M.Q.; Benguerba, Y. Influence of chemical reaction on electro-osmotic flow of nanofluid through convergent multi-sinusoidal passages. *Case Stud. Therm. Eng.* **2024**, *54*, 103955. [CrossRef]
2. Reddy, M.G.; Reddy, K.V.; Souayeh, B.; Fayaz, H. Numerical entropy analysis of MHD electro-osmotic flow of peristaltic movement in a nanofluid. *Heliyon* **2024**, *10*, e27185. [CrossRef] [PubMed]
3. Tripathi, D.; Bhushan, S.; Beg, O.A. Unsteady viscous flow driven by the combined effects of peristalsis and electro-osmosis. *Alex. Eng. J.* **2018**, *57*, 1349–1359. [CrossRef]
4. Sakinder, S.; Salahuddin, T. A numerical study of electro-osmosis Williamson nanofluid flow in a permeable tapered channel. *Alex. Eng. J.* **2023**, *81*, 620–625. [CrossRef]
5. Nazeer, M.; Hussain, F.; Ghafar, M.M.; Javed, M.A. Investigation of electro-osmotic flow of Hafnium particles mixed-up with Casson fluid in convergent geometry: Theoretical study of multiphase flow. *Partial. Differ. Equ. Appl. Math.* **2022**, *6*, 100448. [CrossRef]
6. Abdul-Wahab, M.S.; Al-Saif, A.J. Studying the effects of electro-osmotic and several parameters on blood flow in stenotic arteries using CAGHPM. *Partial. Differ. Equ. Appl. Math.* **2024**, *11*, 100767. [CrossRef]
7. Siva, T.; Jangili, S.; Kumbhakar, B. Analytical solution to optimise the energy generation in EHMD flow of non-Newtonian fluid through a microchannel. *Pramana J. Phys.* **2022**, *96*, 168. [CrossRef]
8. Raju, U.; Rangabashyam, S.; Alhazmi, H.; Khan, I. Irreversible and reversible chemical reaction impacts on convective Maxwell fluid flow over a porous media with activation energy. *Case Stud. Therm. Eng.* **2024**, *61*, 104821. [CrossRef]
9. Tanveer, A.; Jarral, S.; Saleem, S. Dynamic interactions in MHD Jeffrey fluid: Exploring peristalsis; electro osmosis and homogeneous/heterogeneous chemical reactions. *Alex. Eng. J.* **2024**, *94*, 354–365. [CrossRef]
10. Prashanth, M.; Rao, V.S. The impact of soret, Dufour, and chemical reaction on MHD nanofluid over a stretching sheet. *Partial. Differ. Equ. Appl. Math.* **2024**, *10*, 100674. [CrossRef]
11. Vijayalakshmi, K.; Chandulal, A.; Alhazmi, H.; Aljohani, A.F.; Khan, I. Effect of chemical reaction and activation energy on Riga plate embedded in a permeable medium over a Maxwell fluid flow. *Case Stud. Therm. Eng.* **2024**, *59*, 104457. [CrossRef]
12. Iranian, D.; Karthik, S.; Seethalakshmy, A. Heat generation effects on Magnetohydrodynamic Powell-Eyring fluid flow along a vertical surface with a Chemical reaction. *Forces Mech.* **2023**, *12*, 100212. [CrossRef]
13. Adesanya, S.O.; Adeosun, A.T.; Lebelo, R.S.; Tisdell, C.C. Numerical investigation of reaction driven magneto-convective flow of Sisko fluid. *Numer. Heat Transf. Part A Appl.* **2024**, *85*, 1–14. [CrossRef]
14. He, Z.; Arain, M.B.; Usman; Khan, W.A.; Alzahrani, A.R.; Muhammad, T.; Hendy, A.S.; Ali, M.R. Theoretical exploration of heat transport in a stagnant power-law fluid flow over a stretching spinning porous disk filled with homogeneous-heterogeneous chemical reactions. *Case Stud. Therm. Eng.* **2023**, *50*, 103406. [CrossRef]
15. Prasad, K.V.; Vajravelu, K.; Datti, P.S. The effects of variable fluid properties on the hydro-magnetic flow and heat transfer over a non-linearly stretching sheet. *Int. J. Therm. Sci.* **2010**, *49*, 603–610. [CrossRef]
16. Adeyemo, A.S.; Sibanda, P.; Goqo, S.P. Analysis of heat and mass transfer of a non-linear convective heat generating fluid flow in a porous medium with variable viscosity. *Sci. Afr.* **2024**, *24*, e02140. [CrossRef]
17. Wu, Y.; Pruess, K. Integral solutions for transient fluid flow through a porous medium with pressure dependent permeability. *Int. J. Rock Mech. Min. Sci.* **2000**, *37*, 51–61. [CrossRef]

18. Jalili, B.; Azar, A.A.; Jalili, P.; Ganji, D.D. Impact of variable viscosity on asymmetric fluid flow through the expanding/contracting porous channel: A thermal analysis. *Case Stud. Therm. Eng.* **2023**, *52*, 103672. [CrossRef]
19. Obalalu, A.M.; Ajala, O.A.; Adeosun, A.T.; Akindele, A.O.; Oladapo, O.A.; Olajide, O.A.; Adegbite, P. Significance of variable electrical conductivity on non-Newtonian fluid flow between two vertical plates in the coexistence of Arrhenius energy and exothermic chemical reaction. *Partial. Differ. Equ. Appl. Math.* **2021**, *4*, 100184. [CrossRef]
20. Ramakrishna, O.; Falodun, B.O.; Akinremi, O.J.; Omole, E.O.; Ismail, A.S.; Amoyedo, F.E. Thermodynamics of variable thermophysical properties of non-Newtonian fluids with the exploration of antiviral and antibacterial mechanisms using silver nanoparticles. *Int. J. Thermofluids* **2024**, *22*, 100648. [CrossRef]
21. Sivaraj, R.; Kumar, B.R. Viscoelastic fluid flow over a moving vertical cone and flat plate with variable electric conductivity. *Int. J. Heat Mass Transf.* **2013**, *61*, 119–128. [CrossRef]
22. Adeosun, A.T.; Ukaegbu, J.C. Effect of the variable electrical conductivity on the thermal stability of the MHD reactive squeezed fluid flow through a channel by a spectral collocation approach. *Partial. Differ. Equ. Appl. Math.* **2022**, *5*, 100256. [CrossRef]
23. Salawu, S.O.; Obalalu, A.M.; Shamshuddin, M.D.; Fatunmbi, E.O.; Ajilore, O.J. Thermal stability of magneto-hybridized silicon and aluminum oxides nanoparticle in $C3H_8O_2$-Williamson exothermic reactive fluid with thin radiation for perovskite solar power. *Kuwait J. Sci.* **2024**, *51*, 100284. [CrossRef]
24. Adesanya, S.O.; Falade, J.A.; Ukaegbu, J.C.; Makinde, O.D. Adomian-Hermite-Padé approximation approach to thermal criticality for a reactive third grade fluid flow through porous medium. *Theor. Appl. Mech.* **2016**, *43*, 133–144. [CrossRef]
25. Alireza, N.; Javad, A.S.; Amin, S.N.; Hamidreza, H.; Majid, V. Influence of monoethanolamine on thermal stability of starch in water based drilling fluid system. *Petrol. Explor. Develop.* **2018**, *45*, 167–171.
26. Lebelo, R.S.; Mahlobo, R.K.; Adesanya, S.O. Reactant consumption and thermal decomposition analysis in a two-step combustible slab. *Defect Diffus. Forum* **2019**, *393*, 59–72. [CrossRef]
27. Doninelli, M.; Marcoberardino, G.D.; Alessandri, I.; Invernizzi, C.M.; Iora, P. Fluorobenzene as new working fluid for high-temperature heat pumps and organic Rankine cycles: Energy analysis and thermal stability test. *Energy Convers. Manag.* **2024**, *321*, 119023. [CrossRef]
28. Salawu, S.O.; Hassan, A.R.; Abolarinwa, A.; Oladejo, N.K. Thermal stability and entropy generation of unsteady reactive hydromagnetic Powell-Eyring fluid with variable electrical and thermal conductivities. *Alex. Eng. J.* **2019**, *58*, 519–529. [CrossRef]
29. Adesanya, S.O.; Banjo, P.O.; Lebelo, R.S. Exergy analysis for combustible third-grade fluid flow through a medium with variable electrical conductivity and porous permeability. *Mathematics* **2023**, *11*, 1882. [CrossRef]
30. Hoetink, A.E.; Faes, T.J.C.; Visser, K.R.; Heethaar, R.M. On the flow dependency of the electrical conductivity of blood. *IEEE Trans. Bio-Med. Eng.* **2004**, *51*, 1251–1261. [CrossRef] [PubMed]
31. Khan, A.; Farooq, M.; Nawaz, R.; Ayaz, M.; Ahmad, H.; Abu-Zinadah, H.; Chu, Y.M. Analysis of couple stress fluid flow with variable viscosity using two homotopy-based methods. *Open Phys.* **2021**, *19*, 134–145. [CrossRef]
32. Baranovskii, E.S.; Prosviryakov, E.Y.; Ershkov, S.V. Mathematical analysis of steady non-isothermal flows of a micropolar fluid. *Nonlinear Anal. Real World Appl.* **2025**, *84*, 104294. [CrossRef]
33. Baranovskii, E.S.; Ershkov, S.V.; Prosviryakov, E.Y.; Yudin, A.V. Exact solutions to the Oberbeck-Boussinesq equations for describing three-dimensional flows of micropolar liquids. *Symmetry* **2024**, *16*, 1669. [CrossRef]

mathematics

MDPI

Article

Irreversibility Analysis of Hydromagnetic Casson Fluid Flow Through an Inclined Channel with Isothermal Boundary Conditions

Bernard Ejugu Njor [1,*], Ramoshweu Solomon Lebelo [2] and Samuel Olumide Adesanya [1,3]

[1] Department of Mathematics and Statistics, Redeemer's University, Ede 232101, Nigeria
[2] Applied Physical Sciences Department, Vaal University of Technology, Private Bag X021, Vanderbijlpark 1911, South Africa; sollyl@vut.ac.za
[3] Education Department, Vaal University of Technology, Private Bag X021, Vanderbijlpark 1911, South Africa
* Correspondence: njorb@run.edu.ng

Abstract: Fluid flow along an inclined channel phenomenon is crucial in several geophysical, environmental, engineering, biological, and industrial processes, and in aerodynamics and hemodynamics. This present study examines the effect of a constant magnetic field on the entropy production rate in a steady flow of Casson fluid along an inclined heated channel. The governing equations for the flow of velocity, temperature, and entropy generation are formulated based on the Casson constitutive relations and thermodynamics' first and second laws. The exact solutions are constructed for the dimensionless equations and validated with previous results in the literature. The effects of various fluid parameters on the flow, heat transfer, and entropy production rate are conducted and reported graphically with adequate discussion. The impact of the Hartmann number parameter reveals a decrease in both flow velocity and entropy generation rate, meanwhile it also enhances the fluid temperature distribution across the inclined channel. An opposite trend is, however, observed with the Casson fluid parameter.

Keywords: hydromagnetic; inclined channel; entropy generation; Casson fluid

MSC: 76-10

1. Introduction

Recently, remarkable progress has been made in studies on heat exchange and work potentials based on thermodynamics' first and second laws. These laws characterize the friction loss and heat exchange rate in a system [1,2]. Bejan [3] pioneered the entropy minimization in thermal designs. Over the years, this idea has been explored in investigations associated with irreversible energy losses in different fluid streams; for instance, Qayyum et al. [4] explored this approach in analyzing the dissipative Williamson fluid flow between two rotating disks with thermal radiation. The volumetric entropy and irreversibility ratio were accounted for in their analysis. Moreover, Khan et al. [5] investigated the minimization of entropy production of a viscous fluid flow and heat transportation through a thin needle. More recently, Yusuf et al. [6] examined the slip effect on the flow of a micropolar fluid, featuring the analysis of the second law of thermodynamics. Furthermore, other surveys are presented in references [7–9]. Obalalu et al. [10] examined aluminum alloy–titanium alloy/ethylene glycol hybrid nanofluid in the flow of non-Newtonian Oldroyd-B through a parabolic trough surface collector located in a solar water pump. Sanni et al. [11] studied entropy generation optimization in a couple stress fluid flows with variable viscosity and aligned magnetic fields. Chen et al. [12] studied minimum entropy generation paths for generalized radiative heat transfer processes with heat leakage.

Real fluids exhibit non-Newtonian behavior due to their complex rheological properties. One of the subclasses of these liquids is Casson fluid, which behaves like a solid when shear stress lower than the yield stress is applied to the fluid, whereas it flows when shear stress greater than the yield stress is used. Examples include honey, tomato paste, and many more. Owing to the vast applications of this liquid, the magneto-hydrodynamics stream of Casson fluid has proved to be essential in machinery-related fields. The stream of Casson fluid through various geometries has been accounted for recently. Chui-On [13] investigates the influence of electro-osmotic Casson fluid flow in a slit microchannel. Mohyud-Din and Khan examined the squeezed flow of Casson fluid between parallel disks with nonlinear thermal radiation [14]. Ramesh and Devakar examined the exact solutions for the flow of Casson fluid over a slippery surface [15]. Recently, Atlas et al. [16] numerically investigated the irreversibility analysis on the transient flow of Casson fluid between equally distant plates with nonlinear heat and mass flux. In their study, Priam and Nasrin [17] numerically appraised the time-dependent peristaltic duct of Casson fluid by applying the finite element method of Galerkin's residual technique in obtaining a numerical solution. Nadeem et al. [18] analyzed a mathematical model of non-Newtonian Casson nanofluid, and Abbas et al. [19] investigated the application of heat and mass transfer to the convective flow of Casson fluids in a microchannel with the Caputo–Fabrizio derivative approach.

Numerous investigators have looked at studies on flow with a slantwise geometry. The analysis of fluid flow induced by physical forces such as gravity-driven flow with nonzero inclinations is being accounted for, particularly in the study of heat transfer, e.g., solar collective technology. Komurgoz et al. [20] employed a semi-analytical approach in investigating the entropy generation on a steady flow with non-isothermal walls. Hayat et al. [21] scrutinized the joint behavior of an inclined magnetic field and viscous dissipation on a peristaltic flow of Williamson fluid through an inclined symmetric channel. Dar and Elangovan examined the peristaltic flow of a micropolar fluid down an aligned channel with an aligned magnetic field [22]. Abbas et al. [23] studied the magnetohydrodynamic (MHD) flow and heat transfer of two immiscible fluids in an inclined channel. Lerisson et al. [24], Turkyilmazoglu [25], and Adesanya et al. [26] are among investigators who have recently examined the film flow and heat transfer down a slantwise substrate. Vaddemani et al. [27] addressed the effects of Soret on an unsteady free convection flow of viscous incompressible fluid through a porous medium with high porosity bounded by a vertical infinite moving plate under the influence of chemical reaction, heat source, and thermal diffusion. Hafez et al. [28] discussed the impact of heat and mass transfer on the MHD peristaltic flow of Casson fluid in a rotating inclined plane, and Mopuri et al. [29] also recently contributed by examining the characteristics of MHD Jeffery fluid on an inclined vertical plate.

Furthermore, Adesanya et al. [30] studied the steady flow of non-Newtonian fluids through an isothermal impervious wall, neglecting magnetic field interaction. Abbas et al. [31] studied the analysis of entropy generation on peristaltic phenomena of MHD in a diverging tube. Naz et al. [32] investigated the entropy generation optimization in MHD pseudoplastic fluid using a cylindrical (tube) channel and the Williamson fluid model. Jha and Yusuf [33] studied steady incompressible fluid flow through leaky walls without the effect of a magnetic field. Khalid et al. [34] studied an unsteady MHD free convection flow of Casson fluid over an oscillating vertical plate embedded in a porous medium. Awais et al. [35] studied heat and mass transfer phenomena for the dynamics of Casson fluid through a porous medium over a shrinking wall subject to Lorentz force and a heat source/sink. MHD free convective non-Newtonian Casson fluid flows over an oscillating vertical plate were investigated by Prameela and his team [36]. Vishalakshi et al. [37] investigated the MHD Casson fluid flow with a porous medium. Just recently, Adel et al. [38] used the Adomian decomposition method (ADM) solution approach to investigate the behavior of a slippery nanofluid flowing over a permeable stretched sheet under the influence of MHD forces.

Despite the huge number of studies [1–38] around entropy generation, inclined channel, and Casson fluid, nothing much has been performed regarding monitoring the entropy generation around hydromagnetic Casson fluid flow down a heated inclined channel despite its huge applications in a good number of medical, industrial, and engineering applications. As a result, the main objective of this study is to extend the work by Jha and Yusuf [33] to its non-Newtonian case with a good number of applications in metallurgical and industrial engineering. In the following section, the model will be formulated based on Casson constitutive relation and magneto-hydrodynamics. In section three, the solution procedure will be described, in section four the graphical description of the solutions will be presented and explained, while section five concludes the study.

2. Problem Formulation

The steady flow of an electrically conducting Casson fluid down an inclined heated porous channel is considered in this work. The flow is assumed to be fully developed and the Cartesian coordinate is chosen in such a way that the x-axis aligns with the axial flow while the y-direction is taken perpendicular to it, as shown in the flow configuration (Figure 1). The constant wall temperatures are kept at T_1 which is greater than the inlet condition for it to be of heat transfer interest, i.e., $T_1 > T_0$.

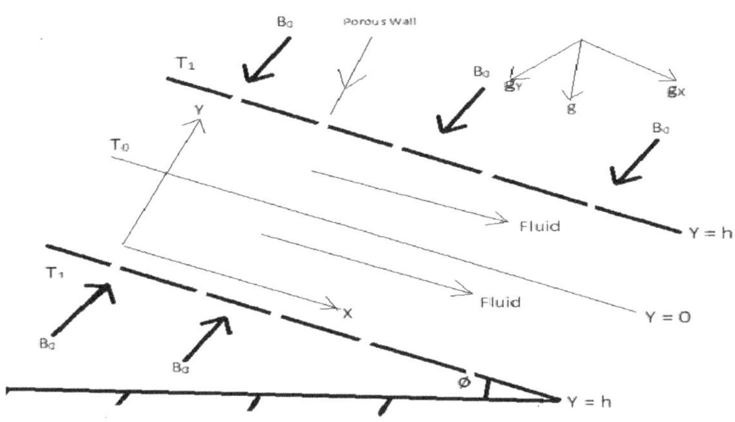

Figure 1. Flow configuration.

Neglecting the pressure drop since the gravitational force is much stronger, the equation governing the flow with constant fluid properties can be written as follows:

$$-\rho v_0 \frac{du'}{dy'} = \rho g Sin\phi + \mu\left(1+\frac{1}{\beta}\right)\frac{d^2u'}{dy'^2} - \sigma B_0^2 u'. \quad (1)$$

The no-slip and the non-moving wall conditions are as follows:

$$u'(\pm h) = 0 \quad (2)$$

Since the walls are heated at constant temperature, the heat transfer due to temperature difference between the heated walls (T_1) and the fluid inlet temperature (T_0) during the process is irreversible. As a result, the balanced energy equation for the heat flow can be written from the heat conservation law as follows, together with the inlet and the porous walls conditions:

$$\begin{array}{c}\rho C_p\left(u'\frac{\partial T}{\partial x'} - v_0\frac{\partial T}{\partial y'}\right) = k\frac{\partial^2 T}{\partial y'^2};\\ T(0,y) = T_0\,, \quad T(x,\pm h) = T_w\end{array} \tag{3}$$

When heat is transferred from the heated walls to the core area of the channel containing viscous fluid it comes with entropy transfer at a molecular level due to the increase in the kinetic energy of the fluid. This disorderliness of the fluid particle is expected due to the non-inviscid nature of the fluid. Also, due to the fact that heat transfer to viscous fluid is an irreversible process, the decay in the work potential in the thermal system due to a non-negative entropy change as postulated in the second law can be written as follows:

$$\dot{S}_{gen} = \frac{k}{T_0^2}\left(\left(\frac{\partial T}{\partial x'}\right)^2 + \left(\frac{\partial T}{\partial y'}\right)^2\right) + \frac{\mu}{T_0}\left(1+\frac{1}{\beta}\right)\left(\frac{du'}{dy'}\right)^2 + \frac{\sigma B_0^2 u'^2}{T_0} \tag{4}$$

As a consequence of the second law, $\dot{S}_{gen} > 0$ implies that $(k,\mu,\sigma) > 0$ must be strictly satisfied for (4) to make any sense in physics. The wall skin friction and the heat transfer rate are given by the following:

$$\tau_{xy} = \mu\left(1+\frac{1}{\beta}\right)\frac{du'}{dy'}\bigg|_{y=-h}, \quad Nu_x = \frac{hq}{k(T_w - T_0)}; \; q = -k\frac{dT'}{dy'}\bigg|_{y=-h} \tag{5}$$

To make Equations (1)–(5) dimensionless, the following variables and parameters are used:

$$\begin{array}{l} y = \frac{y'}{h}, x = \frac{\alpha\mu x'}{\rho g h^4 \sin\phi}, u = \frac{\mu u'}{\rho g h^2 \sin\phi} = \frac{u'}{v_0}, \; Ha^2 = \frac{\sigma B_0^2 h^2}{\mu}, \\ \Pr = \frac{\nu}{\alpha}, \alpha = \frac{k}{\rho C p}, S = \frac{\rho v_0 h}{\mu}, Ns = \frac{S_G h^2 T_0^2}{k(T_w - T_0)^2}, Pe = \frac{\rho g h^3 \sin\phi}{\alpha\mu} \\ \theta = \frac{T - T_0}{T_w - T_0}, \; \Omega = \frac{T_w - T_0}{T_0}, \; Br = Ec.\Pr = \frac{\mu v_0^2}{k(T_w - T_0)}, Ec = \frac{v_0^2}{Cp(T_w - T_0)}, \end{array} \tag{6}$$

The resulting boundary-value problems are given by the following:

$$\left.\begin{array}{ll} 0 = 1 + \left(1+\frac{1}{\beta}\right)\frac{d^2u}{dy^2} + S\frac{du}{dy} - Ha^2 u\,; & u(\pm 1) = 0 \\ u\frac{\partial\theta}{\partial x} = \frac{\partial^2\theta}{\partial y^2} + \Pr S\frac{\partial\theta}{\partial y}; & \theta(0,y) = 0\,,\; \theta(x,\pm 1) = 1 \end{array}\right\} \tag{7}$$

While the dimensionless skin friction and wall Nusselt number are given by the following:

$$SF = \mu\left(1+\frac{1}{\beta}\right)\frac{du}{dy}\bigg|_{y=-1}, \quad Nu_x = -\frac{d\theta}{dy}\bigg|_{y=-1} \tag{8}$$

With the (7) and (8) known, the positive definite total entropy produced along the heated inclined channel becomes the following:

$$\begin{array}{l} Ns = \left(\frac{1}{Pe^2}\left(\frac{\partial\theta}{\partial x}\right)^2 + \left(\frac{\partial\theta}{\partial y}\right)^2\right) + \frac{Br}{\Omega}\left(\left(1+\frac{1}{\beta}\right)\left(\frac{du}{dy}\right)^2 + Ha^2u^2\right) \\ \quad = N_x + N_y + N_{FF} + N_{OH} \end{array} \tag{9}$$

where the first term in (9) represents the entropy generation due to heat transfer along the x-direction, the second term represents the entropy produced due to heat transfer along the y-coordinate, the third term is the entropy generated due to viscous fluid interaction, and the last term is the entropy produced due to electric heating effect of the transverse magnetic field (ohmic heating of the fluid).

Another important tool is the Bejan number, which is the ratio of heat transfer to the total entropy generated along the inclined heated channel, and is given as follows:

$$Be = \frac{\frac{1}{Pe^2}\left(\frac{\partial\theta}{\partial x}\right)^2 + \left(\frac{\partial\theta}{\partial y}\right)^2}{\left(\frac{1}{Pe^2}\left(\frac{\partial\theta}{\partial x}\right)^2 + \left(\frac{\partial\theta}{\partial y}\right)^2\right) + \frac{Br}{\Omega}\left(\left(1+\frac{1}{\beta}\right)\left(\frac{du}{dy}\right)^2 + Ha^2u^2\right)} \tag{10}$$

3. Method of Solution

The system of Equation (7) is not coupled; hence the solution for the non-homogeneous velocity field $u(y)$ can be obtained by using the method of undetermined coefficient to arrive at, which is as follows:

$$u(y) = \frac{1}{Ha^2} + A_1e^{my} + A_2e^{ny} \tag{11}$$

Using (11) in the partial differential equation, then the separation of variables approach suggests that Equation (8) can be written as follows:

$$\frac{\partial\theta}{\partial x} = \frac{1}{u}\left(\frac{\partial^2\theta}{\partial y^2} + PrS\frac{\partial\theta}{\partial y}\right) = \lambda \tag{12}$$

From (12), we obtain the following differential equations by separation of variables:

$$\left.\begin{array}{l} \frac{\partial\theta}{\partial x} = \lambda\,, \\ \frac{d^2\theta}{dy^2} + PrS\frac{d\theta}{\partial y} - \lambda u = 0. \end{array}\right\} \tag{13}$$

So that the nontrivial solution of (12) is assumed to be of the following form:

$$\theta(x,y) = \lambda x + \theta(\mathrm{y}) \tag{14}$$

where $\theta(\mathrm{y})$ satisfies

$$\theta(y) = -\frac{\lambda y}{Ha^2PrS} + \frac{Ke^{PrSy}}{PrS} + L + \frac{\lambda A_1e^{my}}{m(m-PrS)} + \frac{\lambda A_2e^{ny}}{n(n-PrS)} \tag{15}$$

In view of (14) and (15) and the thermal boundary conditions, the exact solution for $\theta(x,y)$ is given by the following:

$$\theta(x,y) = \frac{e^{m+n}\left(e^{2PrS}-1\right)Ha^2mnPrS(m-PrS)(n-PrS)x}{\xi(\mathrm{x},\mathrm{y})}$$

where

$$\xi(\mathrm{x},\mathrm{y}) = e^n\left(e^{m+my} - e^{2m} - e^{m+2PrS+my} + e^{2PrS} + e^{PrS(1+y)}\left(e^{2m}-1\right)\right)Ha^2nPrS(n-PrS)A_1$$
$$+e^m m(m-PrS)\left(\begin{array}{l} e^n n(n-PrS)\left(1-2e^{PrS(1+y)} - Ha^2PrSx - y + e^{2PrS}\left(1+Ha^2PrSx+y\right)\right) \\ -Ha^2PrS\left(e^{2n} - e^{2PrS} + e^{n+ny}\left(e^{2PrS}-1\right) - 2e^{n+PrS(1+y)}Sinh(n)\right)A_2 \end{array}\right)$$

For values of $A_1, A_2, m, n, L, K,$ and λ please see Appendix A on page 11–14.

4. Discussion of Results

In this section, the graphical examination of the exact solutions $u(y), \theta(x,y)$ are presented here with emphasis on some important fluid parameters. The range of values adopted in this study is based on the associated theoretical and experimental analysis reported in different literature.

Figures 2–5 examine the behavior of the magnetic field on profiles of the velocity, temperature, entropy generation, and Bejan number, respectively. Figure 2 shows that a rise in the magnetic field intensity parameter decreases the velocity profile due to increasing magnetic field induction and its retarding effect of fluid motion across the inclined channel.

Meanwhile, kinetic energy is generated from frictional interaction in the moving fluid layers due to increased bonding strength and fluid viscosity. As a result, fluid temperature is expected to rise, as shown in Figure 3. As seen in Figure 4, the entropy generation rate is reduced due to the decreasing effect of the Hartmann number (Ha) on the velocity profile since inter-particle collision at the molecular level will decrease with decreasing flow velocity. From Figure 2, velocity decreases with an increasing magnetic field intensity parameter (Hartmann number). The fluid friction decreases accordingly. This is because a rise in magnetic field intensity parameter implies a reduction in viscosity. Moreover, in Figure 3, Ha has been represented as an increasing function of temperature. Therefore, the effect is seen in Figure 4, where Ha decreases the entropy generation rate with the heated inclined channel. Figure 4 suggests the dominance of heat transfer irreversibility over friction fluid irreversibility since the maximum is approximately one, which is only possible when $\frac{Br}{\Omega} \approx 0$. Therefore, the effect of the magnetic field intensity parameter on the irreversibility ratio is seen to be very weak. The magnitude of the entropy production significantly declines as the magnetic field intensity parameter increases. The influence of the parameter on the Bejan number is depicted in Figure 5. The Bejan number monitors the quantity of heat transfer irreversibility to the overall heat transfer by the fluid friction. The dominance of heat transfer to the irreversibility ratio is observed to have an increasing impact on the heated walls of the aligned channel. It gradually declines as it moves towards the center. However, the irreversibility due to heat transfer controls the flow system at the heated walls.

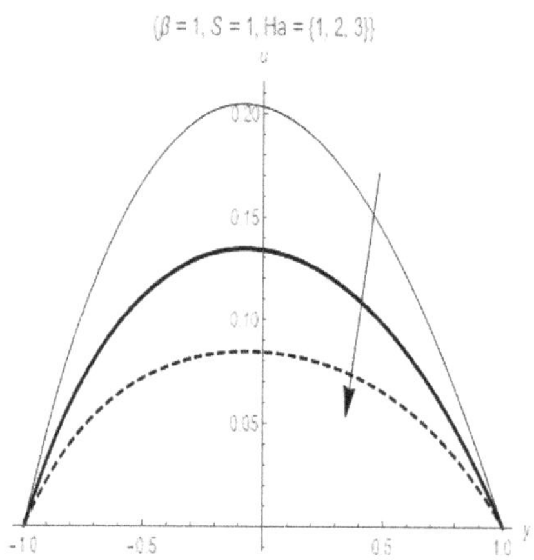

Figure 2. Velocity profile for $\{Ha = 1, 2, 3\}$.

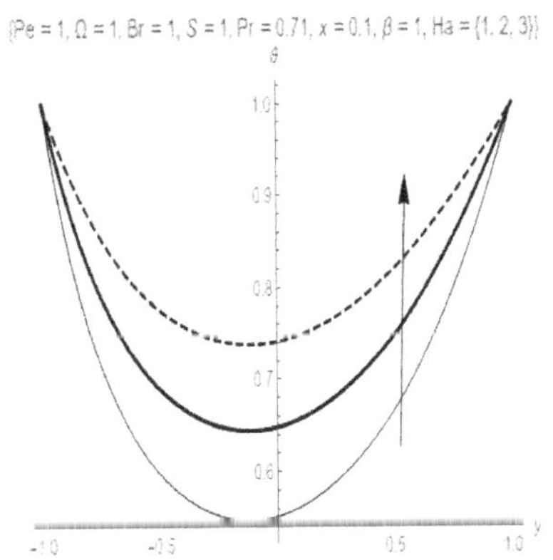

Figure 3. Temperature profile for $\{Ha = 1, 2, 3\}$.

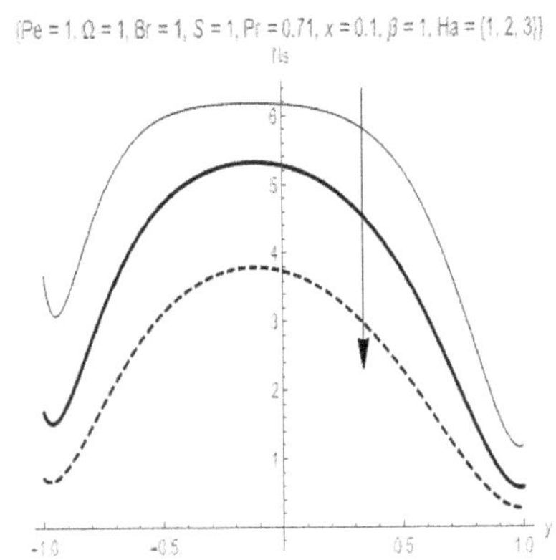

Figure 4. Entropy generation profile for $\{Ha = 1, 2, 3\}$.

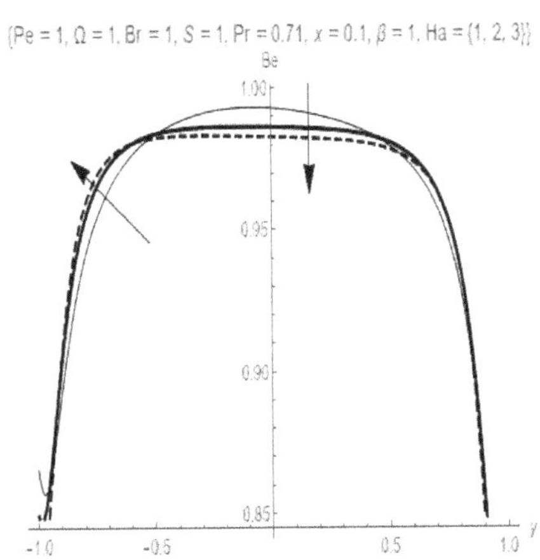

Figure 5. Bejan number for $\{Ha = 1, 2, 3\}$.

The response of the Casson fluid parameter against the profile of velocity, temperature, rate of entropy generation, and the irreversibility ratio is established in Figures 6–9. The result in Figure 6 depicts that increasing the value of the Casson fluid parameter upsurges the velocity profile. This reveals that the magnitude of the non-Newtonian fluid motion is lower than that of the viscous fluid's velocity. An increase in β leads to an increase in the velocity maximum, which approaches the Newtonian limit. Figure 7 describes the response of temperature distribution to variation in the Casson fluid parameter. Here, an increase in the Casson fluid parameter causes a decrease in the temperature distribution throughout the channel, whereas the fluid velocity is enhanced with increasing values of β. As displayed in Figure 8, an enhancement in the Casson fluid parameter improves the entropy production rate. The viscous dissipation and ohmic heating contribution are more excellent at the walls than heat transfer. This is a result of an increase in velocity in Figure 6 and a decrease in temperature in Figure 7. The fluid friction irreversibility contribution to heat transfer irreversibility is slightly noticed at both ends of the heated walls. In contrast, an enhanced value in the Casson fluid parameter influences the dominance of fluid friction over heat transfer irreversibility at the middle of the channel, as shown in Figure 9. The Bejan number attains a maximum of one when the heat transfer irreversibility effect is dominant. There is no effect on friction fluid irreversibility or ohmic heating. It reaches a value of 0.5 when the impact of heat transfer irreversibility is equal to the effect of friction fluid irreversibility and ohmic heating. In contrast, the value tends towards zero when the effect of the combination of friction fluid irreversibility and ohmic heating dominates over heat transfer irreversibility. This implies that heat transfer irreversibility is more substantial at the core area of the channel.

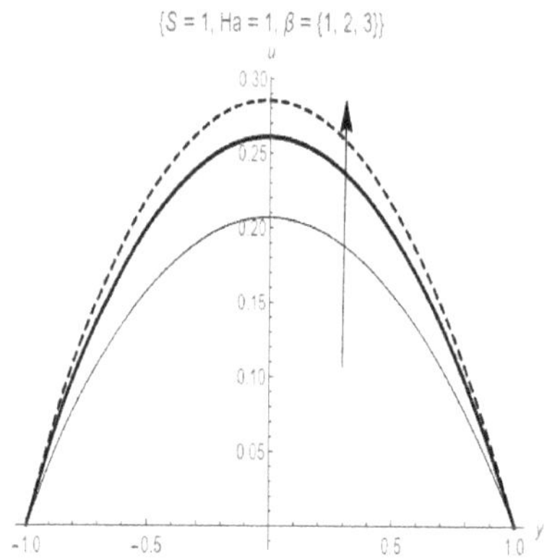

Figure 6. Velocity profile for $\{\beta = 1, 2, 3\}$.

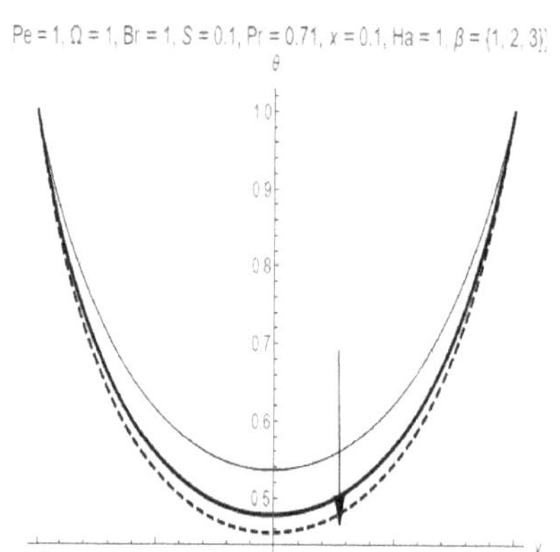

Figure 7. Temperature profile for $\{\beta = 1, 2, 3\}$.

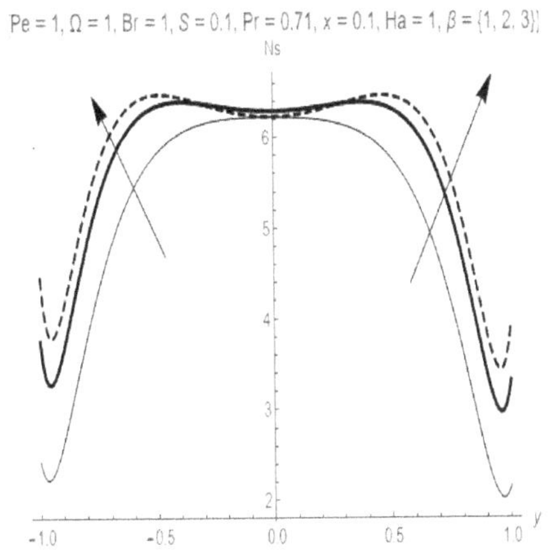

Figure 8. Entropy generation profile for $\{\beta = 1, 2, 3\}$.

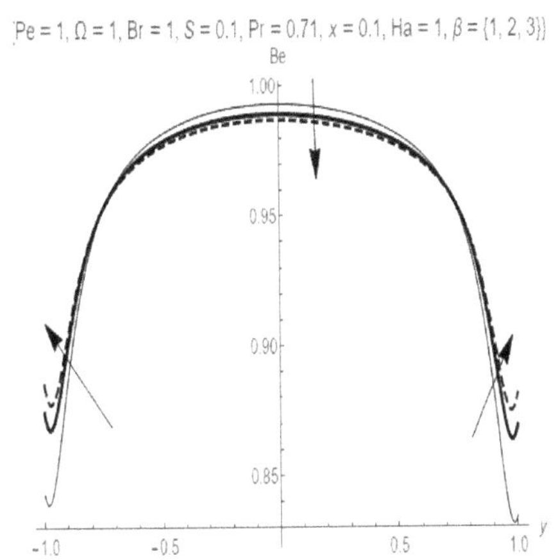

Figure 9. Bejan number for $\{\beta = 1, 2, 3\}$.

5. Conclusions

In the present study, analytical simulation for MHD Casson fluid flow down an inclined channel with isothermal boundary conditions was examined. Exact solution of dimensionless equations are obtained in a straightforward manner and are used to compute the entropy generation rate and irreversibility ratio. Some significant outcomes of the current study are highlighted below:

- The Casson fluid parameter increases fluid flow velocity and entropy generation rate while it decreases the fluid temperature profile.
- The Hartmann number parameter decreases fluid flow velocity and entropy generation rate while it increases the fluid temperature profile.
- The Casson fluid parameter causes the fluid friction irreversibility to dominate at the ends of the wall but weakens the dominance at the core area of the channel.
- The Hartmann number parameter influences the dominance of heat transfer irreversibility at the heated walls and decreases the dominance at the center of the channel.

Author Contributions: Conceptualization, S.O.A.; Methodology, S.O.A.; Validation, B.E.N.; Formal analysis, B.E.N.; Investigation, R.S.L.; Resources, R.S.L.; Writing—original draft, B.E.N.; Supervision,

S.O.A.; Funding acquisition, R.S.L. All authors have read and agreed to the published version of the manuscript.

Funding: This research received no external funding.

Data Availability Statement: Data will be made available on request.

Conflicts of Interest: The authors declare no conflict of interest.

Nomenclature

(v_0, ρ)	constant vertical velocity and fluid density,
$\left(u', \phi\right)$	axial velocity and inclination angle,
(μ, β)	dynamic viscosity, Casson material
(σ, B_0)	electrical conductivity and constant magnetic induction.
(g, k)	gravitational acceleration and thermal conductivity
(C_p, T)	specific heat capacity, fluid temperature
(x', y')	cartesian coordinate
$(\boldsymbol{x}, \boldsymbol{y})$	dimensionless cartesian coordinate
(T_0, T_1)	fluid and heated wall temperatures.
(u, θ)	dimensionless velocity and temperature
(Ha, S)	magnetic field and suction/injection
$(\Pr, \alpha)$	Prandtl number and kinematic viscosity
(Pe, Ec)	Peclet and Eckert numbers
(Ω, Br)	temperature difference and Brinkman number
Ns	dimensionless entropy generation rate
Be	Bejan Number (irreversibility)

Appendix A

Where

$$A_1 = \frac{e^m\left(e^{2n} - 1\right)}{\left(e^{2m} - e^{2n}\right)\text{Ha}^2}$$

$$A_2 = \frac{e^n\left(e^{2m} - 1\right)}{\left(e^{2n} - e^{2m}\right)\text{Ha}^2}$$

$$m = \frac{1}{2}\left[-\frac{S\beta}{1+\beta} - \frac{\sqrt{\beta}\sqrt{4\text{Ha}^2 + 4\text{Ha}^2\beta + S^2\beta}}{1+\beta}\right]$$

$$n = \frac{1}{2}\left[-\frac{S\beta}{1+\beta} + \frac{\sqrt{\beta}\sqrt{4\text{Ha}^2 + 4\text{Ha}^2\beta + S^2\beta}}{1+\beta}\right]$$

$$
\begin{aligned}
L = -\Bigg(\Bigg(&\left(-\frac{y}{\mathrm{Ha}^2\mathrm{Pr}S}-\frac{e^{my}A_1}{m(m+\mathrm{Pr}S)}-\frac{e^{ny}A_2}{n(n+\mathrm{Pr}S)}\right)\Bigg(\frac{e^{-\mathrm{Pr}Sy}\left(\frac{1}{\mathrm{Ha}^2\mathrm{Pr}S}+x+\frac{e^{m}A_1}{m(m+\mathrm{Pr}S)}+\frac{e^{n}A_2}{n(n+\mathrm{Pr}S)}\right)}{\mathrm{Pr}S}\\
&-\frac{e^{-\mathrm{Pr}S}\left(\frac{y}{\mathrm{Ha}^2\mathrm{Pr}S}+\frac{e^{my}A_1}{m(m+\mathrm{Pr}S)}+\frac{e^{ny}A_2}{n(n+\mathrm{Pr}S)}\right)}{\mathrm{Pr}S}\Bigg)\\
&-\Bigg(-\frac{y}{\mathrm{Ha}^2\mathrm{Pr}S}-\frac{e^{my}A_1}{m(m+\mathrm{Pr}S)}\\
&-\frac{e^{ny}A_2}{n(n+\mathrm{Pr}S)}\Bigg)\Bigg(\frac{e^{-\mathrm{Pr}Sy}\left(-\frac{1}{\mathrm{Ha}^2\mathrm{Pr}S}+x+\frac{e^{-m}A_1}{m(m+\mathrm{Pr}S)}+\frac{e^{-n}A_2}{n(n+\mathrm{Pr}S)}\right)}{\mathrm{Pr}S}\\
&-\frac{e^{\mathrm{Pr}S}\left(\frac{y}{\mathrm{Ha}^2\mathrm{Pr}S}+\frac{e^{my}A_1}{m(m+\mathrm{Pr}S)}+\frac{e^{ny}A_2}{n(n+\mathrm{Pr}S)}\right)}{\mathrm{Pr}S}\Bigg)\Bigg)\\
&/\Bigg(\Bigg(\frac{1}{\mathrm{Ha}^2\mathrm{Pr}S}-x+\frac{y}{\mathrm{Ha}^2\mathrm{Pr}S}-\frac{e^{-m}A_1}{m(m+\mathrm{Pr}S)}+\frac{e^{my}A_1}{m(m+\mathrm{Pr}S)}-\frac{e^{-n}A_2}{n(n+\mathrm{Pr}S)}\\
&+\frac{e^{ny}A_2}{n(n+\mathrm{Pr}S)}\Bigg)\Bigg(\frac{e^{-\mathrm{Pr}Sy}\left(\frac{1}{\mathrm{Ha}^2\mathrm{Pr}S}+x+\frac{e^{m}A_1}{m(m+\mathrm{Pr}S)}+\frac{e^{n}A_2}{n(n+\mathrm{Pr}S)}\right)}{\mathrm{Pr}S}\\
&-\frac{e^{-\mathrm{Pr}S}\left(\frac{y}{\mathrm{Ha}^2\mathrm{Pr}S}+\frac{e^{my}A_1}{m(m+\mathrm{Pr}S)}+\frac{e^{ny}A_2}{n(n+\mathrm{Pr}S)}\right)}{\mathrm{Pr}S}\Bigg)\\
&-\Bigg(-\frac{1}{\mathrm{Ha}^2\mathrm{Pr}S}-x+\frac{y}{\mathrm{Ha}^2\mathrm{Pr}S}-\frac{e^{m}A_1}{m(m+\mathrm{Pr}S)}+\frac{e^{my}A_1}{m(m+\mathrm{Pr}S)}-\frac{e^{n}A_2}{n(n+\mathrm{Pr}S)}\\
&+\frac{e^{ny}A_2}{n(n+\mathrm{Pr}S)}\Bigg)\Bigg(\frac{e^{-\mathrm{Pr}Sy}\left(-\frac{1}{\mathrm{Ha}^2\mathrm{Pr}S}+x+\frac{e^{-m}A_1}{m(m+\mathrm{Pr}S)}+\frac{e^{-n}A_2}{n(n+\mathrm{Pr}S)}\right)}{\mathrm{Pr}S}\\
&-\frac{e^{\mathrm{Pr}S}\left(\frac{y}{\mathrm{Ha}^2\mathrm{Pr}S}+\frac{e^{my}A_1}{m(m+\mathrm{Pr}S)}+\frac{e^{ny}A_2}{n(n+\mathrm{Pr}S)}\right)}{\mathrm{Pr}S}\Bigg)\Bigg)\Bigg)
\end{aligned}
$$

$$
\begin{aligned}
K = -\Big(\Big(&e^{\mathrm{Pr}S+\mathrm{Pr}Sy}\mathrm{Pr}S\Big(2e^{m+n}m^2n^2+2e^{m+n}m^2n\mathrm{Pr}S+2e^{m+n}mn^2\mathrm{Pr}S+2e^{m+n}mn\mathrm{Pr}^2S^2\\
&-e^{n}\mathrm{Ha}^2n^2\mathrm{Pr}SA_1+e^{2m+n}\mathrm{Ha}^2n^2\mathrm{Pr}SA_1-e^{n}\mathrm{Ha}^2n\mathrm{Pr}^2S^2A_1\\
&+e^{2m+n}\mathrm{Ha}^2n\mathrm{Pr}^2S^2A_1-e^{m}\mathrm{Ha}^2m^2\mathrm{Pr}SA_2+e^{m+2n}\mathrm{Ha}^2m^2\mathrm{Pr}SA_2\\
&-e^{m}\mathrm{Ha}^2m\mathrm{Pr}^2S^2A_2+e^{m+2n}\mathrm{Ha}^2m\mathrm{Pr}^2S^2A_2\Big)\Big)/\big(-2e^{m+n+\mathrm{Pr}S}m^2n^2\\
&+e^{m+n+\mathrm{Pr}Sy}m^2n^2+e^{m+n+2\mathrm{Pr}S+\mathrm{Pr}Sy}m^2n^2-2e^{m+n+\mathrm{Pr}S}m^2n\mathrm{Pr}S\\
&+e^{m+n+\mathrm{Pr}Sy}m^2n\mathrm{Pr}S+e^{m+n+2\mathrm{Pr}S+\mathrm{Pr}Sy}m^2n\mathrm{Pr}S-2e^{m+n+\mathrm{Pr}S}mn^2\mathrm{Pr}S\\
&+e^{m+n+\mathrm{Pr}Sy}mn^2\mathrm{Pr}S+e^{m+n+2\mathrm{Pr}S+\mathrm{Pr}Sy}mn^2\mathrm{Pr}S-2e^{m+n+\mathrm{Pr}S}mn\mathrm{Pr}^2S^2\\
&+e^{m+n+\mathrm{Pr}Sy}mn\mathrm{Pr}^2S^2+e^{m+n+2\mathrm{Pr}S+\mathrm{Pr}Sy}mn\mathrm{Pr}^2S^2-e^{m+n+\mathrm{Pr}Sy}\mathrm{Ha}^2m^2n^2\mathrm{Pr}Sx\\
&+e^{m+n+2\mathrm{Pr}S+\mathrm{Pr}Sy}\mathrm{Ha}^2m^2n^2\mathrm{Pr}Sx-e^{m+n+\mathrm{Pr}Sy}\mathrm{Ha}^2m^2n\mathrm{Pr}^2S^2x\\
&+e^{m+n+2\mathrm{Pr}S+\mathrm{Pr}Sy}\mathrm{Ha}^2m^2n\mathrm{Pr}^2S^2x-e^{m+n+\mathrm{Pr}Sy}\mathrm{Ha}^2mn\mathrm{Pr}^3S^3x\\
&+e^{m+n+2\mathrm{Pr}S+\mathrm{Pr}Sy}\mathrm{Ha}^2mn\mathrm{Pr}^3S^3x+e^{m+n+\mathrm{Pr}Sy}m^2n^2y-e^{m+n+2\mathrm{Pr}S+\mathrm{Pr}Sy}m^2n^2y\\
&+e^{m+n+\mathrm{Pr}Sy}m^2n\mathrm{Pr}Sy-e^{m+n+2\mathrm{Pr}S+\mathrm{Pr}Sy}m^2n\mathrm{Pr}Sy+e^{m+n+\mathrm{Pr}Sy}mn^2\mathrm{Pr}Sy\\
&-e^{m+n+2\mathrm{Pr}S+\mathrm{Pr}Sy}mn^2\mathrm{Pr}Sy+e^{m+n+\mathrm{Pr}Sy}mn\mathrm{Pr}^2S^2y\\
&-e^{m+n+2\mathrm{Pr}S+\mathrm{Pr}Sy}mn\mathrm{Pr}^2S^2y+e^{n+\mathrm{Pr}S}\mathrm{Ha}^2n^2\mathrm{Pr}SA_1\mathrm{Ha}^2n^2\mathrm{Pr}SA_1\\
&+e^{2m+n+2\mathrm{Pr}S+\mathrm{Pr}Sy}\mathrm{Ha}^2n^2\mathrm{Pr}SA_1+e^{m+n+my+\mathrm{Pr}Sy}\mathrm{Ha}^2n^2\mathrm{Pr}SA_1\\
&-e^{2m+n+\mathrm{Pr}S}\mathrm{Ha}^2n^2\mathrm{Pr}SA_1-e^{n+\mathrm{Pr}Sy}-e^{m+n+2\mathrm{Pr}S+my+\mathrm{Pr}Sy}\mathrm{Ha}^2n^2\mathrm{Pr}SA_1\\
&+e^{n+\mathrm{Pr}S}\mathrm{Ha}^2n\mathrm{Pr}^2S^2A_1-e^{2m+n+\mathrm{Pr}S}\mathrm{Ha}^2n\mathrm{Pr}^2S^2A_1-e^{n+\mathrm{Pr}Sy}\mathrm{Ha}^2n\mathrm{Pr}^2S^2A_1\\
&+e^{2m+n+2\mathrm{Pr}S+\mathrm{Pr}Sy}\mathrm{Ha}^2n\mathrm{Pr}^2S^2A_1+e^{m+n+my+\mathrm{Pr}Sy}\mathrm{Ha}^2n\mathrm{Pr}^2S^2A_1\\
&-e^{m+n+2\mathrm{Pr}S+my+\mathrm{Pr}Sy}\mathrm{Ha}^2n\mathrm{Pr}^2S^2A_1+e^{m+\mathrm{Pr}S}\mathrm{Ha}^2m^2\mathrm{Pr}SA_2\\
&-e^{m+2n+\mathrm{Pr}S}\mathrm{Ha}^2m^2\mathrm{Pr}SA_2-e^{m+\mathrm{Pr}Sy}\mathrm{Ha}^2m^2\mathrm{Pr}SA_2\\
&+e^{m+2n+2\mathrm{Pr}S+\mathrm{Pr}Sy}\mathrm{Ha}^2m^2\mathrm{Pr}SA_2+e^{m+n+ny+\mathrm{Pr}Sy}\mathrm{Ha}^2m^2\mathrm{Pr}SA_2\\
&-e^{m+n+2\mathrm{Pr}S+ny+\mathrm{Pr}Sy}\mathrm{Ha}^2m^2\mathrm{Pr}SA_2+e^{m+\mathrm{Pr}S}\mathrm{Ha}^2m\mathrm{Pr}^2S^2A_2\\
&-e^{m+2n+\mathrm{Pr}S}\mathrm{Ha}^2m\mathrm{Pr}^2S^2A_2-e^{m+\mathrm{Pr}Sy}\mathrm{Ha}^2m\mathrm{Pr}^2S^2A_2\\
&+e^{m+2n+2\mathrm{Pr}S+\mathrm{Pr}Sy}\mathrm{Ha}^2m\mathrm{Pr}^2S^2A_2+e^{m+n+ny+\mathrm{Pr}Sy}\mathrm{Ha}^2m\mathrm{Pr}^2S^2A_2\\
&-e^{m+n+2\mathrm{Pr}S+ny+\mathrm{Pr}Sy}\mathrm{Ha}^2m\mathrm{Pr}^2S^2A_2\big)\big)
\end{aligned}
$$

$$\lambda = \Big(\big(-e^{m+n+\mathrm{Pr}Sy} + e^{m+n+2\mathrm{Pr}S+\mathrm{Pr}Sy}\big)\mathrm{Ha}^2 mn\mathrm{Pr}S(m+\mathrm{Pr}S)(n+\mathrm{Pr}S) \Big) / \big(-2e^{m+n+\mathrm{Pr}S}m^2n^2$$
$$+e^{m+n+\mathrm{Pr}Sy}m^2n^2 + e^{m+n+2\mathrm{Pr}S+\mathrm{Pr}Sy}m^2n^2 - 2e^{m+n+\mathrm{Pr}S}m^2n\mathrm{Pr}S$$
$$+e^{m+n+\mathrm{Pr}Sy}m^2n\mathrm{Pr}S + e^{m+n+2\mathrm{Pr}S+\mathrm{Pr}Sy}m^2n\mathrm{Pr}S - 2e^{m+n+\mathrm{Pr}S}mn^2\mathrm{Pr}S$$
$$+e^{m+n+\mathrm{Pr}Sy}mn^2\mathrm{Pr}S + e^{m+n+2\mathrm{Pr}S+\mathrm{Pr}Sy}mn^2\mathrm{Pr}S - 2e^{m+n+\mathrm{Pr}S}mn\mathrm{Pr}^2S^2$$
$$+e^{m+n+\mathrm{Pr}Sy}mn\mathrm{Pr}^2S^2 + e^{m+n+2\mathrm{Pr}S+\mathrm{Pr}Sy}mn\mathrm{Pr}^2S^2 - e^{m+n+\mathrm{Pr}Sy}\mathrm{Ha}^2m^2n^2\mathrm{Pr}Sx$$
$$+e^{m+n+2\mathrm{Pr}S+\mathrm{Pr}Sy}\mathrm{Ha}^2m^2n^2\mathrm{Pr}Sx - e^{m+n+\mathrm{Pr}Sy}\mathrm{Ha}^2m^2n\mathrm{Pr}^2S^2x$$
$$+e^{m+n+2\mathrm{Pr}S+\mathrm{Pr}Sy}\mathrm{Ha}^2m^2n\mathrm{Pr}^2S^2x - e^{m+n+\mathrm{Pr}Sy}\mathrm{Ha}^2mn^2\mathrm{Pr}^2S^2x$$
$$+e^{m+n+2\mathrm{Pr}S+\mathrm{Pr}Sy}\mathrm{Ha}^2mn^2\mathrm{Pr}^2S^2x - e^{m+n+\mathrm{Pr}Sy}\mathrm{Ha}^2mn\mathrm{Pr}^3S^3x$$
$$+e^{m+n+2\mathrm{Pr}S+\mathrm{Pr}Sy}\mathrm{Ha}^2mn\mathrm{Pr}^3S^3x + e^{m+n+\mathrm{Pr}Sy}m^2n^2y - e^{m+n+2\mathrm{Pr}S+\mathrm{Pr}Sy}m^2n^2y$$
$$+e^{m+n+\mathrm{Pr}Sy}m^2n\mathrm{Pr}Sy - e^{m+n+2\mathrm{Pr}S+\mathrm{Pr}Sy}m^2n\mathrm{Pr}Sy + e^{m+n+\mathrm{Pr}Sy}mn^2\mathrm{Pr}Sy$$
$$-e^{m+n+2\mathrm{Pr}S+\mathrm{Pr}Sy}mn^2\mathrm{Pr}Sy + e^{m+n+\mathrm{Pr}Sy}mn\mathrm{Pr}^2S^2y$$
$$-e^{m+n+2\mathrm{Pr}S+\mathrm{Pr}Sy}mn\mathrm{Pr}^2S^2y + e^{n+\mathrm{Pr}S}\mathrm{Ha}^2n^2\mathrm{Pr}SA_1 - e^{2m+n+\mathrm{Pr}S}\mathrm{Ha}^2n^2\mathrm{Pr}SA_1$$
$$-e^{n+\mathrm{Pr}Sy}\mathrm{Ha}^2n^2\mathrm{Pr}SA_1 + e^{2m+n+2\mathrm{Pr}S+\mathrm{Pr}Sy}\mathrm{Ha}^2n^2\mathrm{Pr}SA_1$$
$$+e^{m+n+my+\mathrm{Pr}Sy}\mathrm{Ha}^2n^2\mathrm{Pr}SA_1 - e^{m+n+2\mathrm{Pr}S+my+\mathrm{Pr}Sy}\mathrm{Ha}^2n^2\mathrm{Pr}SA_1$$
$$+e^{n+\mathrm{Pr}S}\mathrm{Ha}^2n\mathrm{Pr}^2S^2A_1 - e^{2m+n+\mathrm{Pr}S}\mathrm{Ha}^2n\mathrm{Pr}^2S^2A_1 - e^{n+\mathrm{Pr}Sy}\mathrm{Ha}^2n\mathrm{Pr}^2S^2A_1$$
$$+e^{2m+n+2\mathrm{Pr}S+\mathrm{Pr}Sy}\mathrm{Ha}^2n\mathrm{Pr}^2S^2A_1 + e^{m+n+my+\mathrm{Pr}Sy}\mathrm{Ha}^2n\mathrm{Pr}^2S^2A_1$$
$$-e^{m+n+2\mathrm{Pr}S+my+\mathrm{Pr}Sy}\mathrm{Ha}^2n\mathrm{Pr}^2S^2A_1 + e^{m+\mathrm{Pr}S}\mathrm{Ha}^2m^2\mathrm{Pr}SA_2$$
$$-e^{m+2n+\mathrm{Pr}S}\mathrm{Ha}^2m^2\mathrm{Pr}SA_2 - e^{m+\mathrm{Pr}Sy}\mathrm{Ha}^2m^2\mathrm{Pr}SA_2$$
$$+e^{m+2n+2\mathrm{Pr}S+\mathrm{Pr}Sy}\mathrm{Ha}^2m^2\mathrm{Pr}SA_2 + e^{m+n+ny+\mathrm{Pr}Sy}\mathrm{Ha}^2m^2\mathrm{Pr}SA_2$$
$$-e^{m+n+2\mathrm{Pr}S+ny+\mathrm{Pr}Sy}\mathrm{Ha}^2m^2\mathrm{Pr}SA_2 + e^{m+\mathrm{Pr}S}\mathrm{Ha}^2m\mathrm{Pr}^2S^2A_2$$
$$-e^{m+2n+\mathrm{Pr}S}\mathrm{Ha}^2m\mathrm{Pr}^2S^2A_2 - e^{m+\mathrm{Pr}Sy}\mathrm{Ha}^2m\mathrm{Pr}^2S^2A_2$$
$$+e^{m+2n+2\mathrm{Pr}S+\mathrm{Pr}Sy}\mathrm{Ha}^2m\mathrm{Pr}^2S^2A_2 + e^{m+n+ny+\mathrm{Pr}Sy}\mathrm{Ha}^2m\mathrm{Pr}^2S^2A_2$$
$$-e^{m+n+2\mathrm{Pr}S+ny+\mathrm{Pr}Sy}\mathrm{Ha}^2m\mathrm{Pr}^2S^2A_2\big)$$

References

1. Bejan, A. *Entropy Generation Through Heat and Fluid Flow*; Wiley: New York, NY, USA, 1982.
2. Bejan, A. A study of entropy generation in fundamental convective heat-transfer. *J. Heat Transf.* **1979**, *101*, 718–725.
3. Bejan, A. Second-law analysis in heat transfer and thermal design. *Adv. Heat Transf.* **1982**, *15*, 1–58.
4. Qayyum, S.; Khan, M.I.; Hayat, T.; Alsaedi, A.; Tamoor, M. Entropy generation in dissipative flow of Williamson fluid between two rotating disks. *Int. J. Heat Mass. Transf.* **2018**, *127*, 933–942.
5. Khan, M.W.A.; Khan, M.I.; Hayat, T.; Alsaedi, A. Entropy generation minimization (EGM) of nanofluid flow by a thin moving needle with nonlinear thermal radiation. *Phys. B Condens. Matter* **2018**, *534*, 113–119.
6. Yusuf, T.A.; Naveen Kumar, R.; Prasannakumara, B.C.; Adesanya, S.O. Irreversibility analysis in micropolar fluid film along an incline porous substrate with slip effects. *Int. Commun. Heat Mass. Transf.* **2021**, *126*, 105357.
7. Rehman, A.U.; Mehmood, R.; Nadeem, S. Entropy analysis of radioactive rotating nanofluid with thermal slip. *Appl. Therm. Eng.* **2017**, *112*, 832–840. [CrossRef]
8. Eegunjobi, A.S.; Makinde, O.D. Irreversibility analysis of hydromagnetic flow of couple stress fluid with radiative heat in a channel filled with a porous medium. *Results Phys.* **2017**, *7*, 459–469.
9. Yusuf, T.; Mabood, F. Slip Effects and Entropy generation on inclined MHD flow of Williamson fluid through a permeable wall with chemical reaction via DTM. *Math. Model. Eng. Probl.* **2020**, *7*, 1–9. [CrossRef]
10. Obalalu, A.M.; Memon, M.A.; Saleem, S.; Abbas, A.; Olayemi, O.A.; Ali, M.R.; Sadat, R.; Hendy, A.S. Thermal performance of Oldroy-B hybrid nanofluid in solar energy-based water pumping systems and entropy generation minimization. *Case Stud. Therm. Eng.* **2023**, *51*, 103476. [CrossRef]
11. Saini, G.; Hanumagowda, B.N.; Mulki, H.; Raju, S.S.K.; Varma, S.V.K.; Barghout, K.; Murshid, N.; Al-Kouz, W. Entropy generation optimization in couple stress fluid flow with variable viscosity and aligned magnetic field. *Sustainability* **2023**, *15*, 2493. [CrossRef]
12. Chen, L.; Xia, S.; Shi, S. Minimum entropy generation paths for generalized radiative heat transfer processes with heat leakage. *Results Eng.* **2024**, *21*, 101759. [CrossRef]
13. Ng, C.-O. Combined pressure-driven and electroosmotic flow of Casson fluid through a slit microchannel. *J. Non-Newton. Fluid Mech.* **2013**, *198*, 1–9. [CrossRef]
14. Mohyud-Din, S.T.; Khan, S.I. Nonlinear radiation effects on squeezing flow of a Casson fluid between parallel disks. *Aerosp. Sci. Technol.* **2016**, *48*, 186–192. [CrossRef]

15. Ramesh, K.; Devakar, M. Some analytical solutions for flows of Casson fluid with slip boundary conditions. *Ain Shams Eng. J.* **2015**, *6*, 967–975. [CrossRef]
16. Atlas, M.; Hussain, S.; Sagheer, M. Entropy generation and unsteady Casson fluid flow squeezing between two parallel plates subject to Cattaneo-Christov heat and mass flux. *Eur. Phys. J. Plus* **2019**, *134*, 33. [CrossRef]
17. Shadman Sakib, P.; Nasrin, R. Numerical appraisal of time-dependent peristaltic duct flow using Casson fluid. *Int. J. Mech. Sci.* **2022**, *233*, 107676. [CrossRef]
18. Nadeem, S.; Ishtiaq, B.; Hamida, M.B.B.; Almutairi, S.; Ghazwani, H.A.; Eldin, S.M.; Al-Shafay, A.S. Reynolds nanofluid model for Casson fluid flow conveying exponential nanoparticles through a slandering sheet. *Sci. Rep.* **2023**, *13*, 1953. [CrossRef]
19. Abbas, S.; Nisa, Z.U.; Nazar, M.; Amjad, M.; Ali, H.; Jan, A.Z. Application of heat and mass transfer to convective flow of Casson fluid in a microchannel with Caputo-Fabrizio derivative approach. *Arab. J. Sci. Eng.* **2024**, *49*, 1275–1286. [CrossRef]
20. Komurgoz, G.; Arikoglu, A.; Turker, E.; Ozkol, I. Second-law analysis for an inclined channel containing porous-clear fluid layers by using the differential transform method. *Numer. Heat Transf. Part. A* **2010**, *57*, 603–623. [CrossRef]
21. Hayat, T.; Shahida, B.; Rafiq, M.; Alsaedi, A.; Abbasi, F.M. Effect of an inclined magnetic field on peristaltic flow of Williamson fluid in an inclined channel with convective conditions. *J. Magn. Magn. Mater.* **2016**. [CrossRef]
22. Dar, A.A.; Elangovan, K. Influence of an inclined magnetic field and rotation on the peristaltic flow of a micropolar fluid in an inclined channel. *New J. Sci.* **2016**, 5717542. [CrossRef]
23. Abbas, Z.; Hasnaina, J.; Sajid, M. Hydromagnetic mixed convective two-phase flow of couple stress and viscous fluids in an inclined channel. *Z. Naturforsch.* **2014**, *69a*, 553–561. [CrossRef]
24. Lerisson, G.; Ledda, P.G.; Balestra, G.; Gallaire, F. Instability of a thin viscous film flowing under an inclined substrate: Steady patterns. *J. Fluid Mech.* **2020**, *898*, A6. [CrossRef]
25. Turkyilmazoglu, M. Nanoliquid film flow due to a moving substrate and heat transfer. *Eur. Phys. J. Plus* **2020**, *135*, 1–13. [CrossRef]
26. Adesanya, S.O.; Egere, A.C.; Ukaegbu, J.C.; Lebelo, R.S. Influence of temperature-dependent properties on a gravity-driven thin film along inclined plate. *Nonlinear Eng.* **2020**, *9*, 118–123. [CrossRef]
27. Vaddemani, R.R.; Kodi, R.; Mopuri, O. Characteristics of MHD Casson fluid past an inclined vertical porous plate. *Mater. Today Proc.* **2022**, *49 Pt 5*, 2136–2142. [CrossRef]
28. Hafeez, N.M.; Abd-Alla, A.M.; Metwaly, T.M.N. Influences of rotation and mass and heat transfer on MHD peristaltic transport of Casson fluid through inclined plane. *Alex. Eng. J.* **2023**, *68*, 665–692. [CrossRef]
29. Mopuri, O.; Sailakumari, A.; Ganjikunta, A.; Sudhakara, E.; VenkateswaraRajus, K.; Ramesh, P.; Ganteda, C.; Reddy, B.R.; Varma, S.V.K. Characteristics of MHD Jeffery fluid past an inclined vertical porous plate. *CFD Lett.* **2024**, *16*, 68–89. [CrossRef]
30. Adesanya, S.O.; Souayeh, B.; Rahimi-Gorji, M.; Khan, M.N.; Adeyemi, O.G. Heat irreversibility analysis for a couple stress fluid flow in an inclined channel with isothermal boundaries. *J. Taiwan Inst. Chem. Eng.* **2019**, *101*, 251–258. [CrossRef]
31. Abbas, Z.; Rafiq, M.Y.; Alshomrani, A.S.; Ullah, M.Z. Analysis of entropy generation on peristaltic phenomena of MHD slip flow of viscous fluid in a diverging tube. *Case Stud. Therm. Eng.* **2021**, *23*, 100817. [CrossRef]
32. Naz, R.; Noor, M.; Shah, Z.; Sohail, M.; Kumam, P.; Thounthong, P. Entropy generation optimization in MHD pseudoplastic fluid comprising motile microorganisms with stratification effect. *Alex. Eng. J.* **2020**, *59*, 485–496. [CrossRef]
33. Jha, B.K.; Yusuf, T.S. Entropy generation in an inclined porous channel with suction/injection. *Nonlinear Eng.* **2020**, *9*, 94–101. [CrossRef]
34. Khalid, A.; Khan, I.; Khan, A.; Shafie, S. Unsteady MHD free convection flow of Casson fluid past over an oscillating vertical plate embedded in a porous medium. *Eng. Sci. Technol. Int. J.* **2015**, *18*, 309–317. [CrossRef]
35. Awais, M.; Raja, M.A.Z.; Awan, S.E.; Shoaib, M.; Ali, H.M. Heat and mass transfer phenomenon for the dynamics of Casson fluid through porous medium over shrinking wall subject to Lorentz force and heat source/sink. *Alex. Eng. J.* **2021**, *60*, 1355–1363. [CrossRef]
36. Prameela, M.; Gangadhar, K.; Reddy, G.J. MHD free convective non-Newtonian Casson fluid flow over an oscillating vertical plate. *Partial Differ. Equ. Appl. Math.* **2022**, *5*, 100366. [CrossRef]
37. Vishalakshi, A.B.; Mahabaleshwar, U.S.; Ahmad, M.H.; Sharifpur, M. An MHD Casson fluid flow past a porous stretching sheet with threshold Non-Fourier heat flux model. *Alex. Eng. J.* **2023**, *69*, 727–737. [CrossRef]
38. Adel, M.; Khader, M.M.; Ahmad, H. MHD nanofluid flow and heat transfer caused by a stretching sheet that is heated convectively: An approximate solution using ADM. *Case Stud. Therm. Eng.* **2024**, *60*, 104683. [CrossRef]

Σ mathematics

MDPI

Article

Stability Diagrams of Bed Evolution for Vertically Averaged and Moment (VAM) Models

Mohamed Hassan Elgamal * and Mohd Aamir Mumtaz

Civil Engineering Department, College of Engineering, Imam Mohammad Ibn Saud Islamic University (IMSIU), Riyadh 11432, Saudi Arabia; mmaamir@imamu.edu.sa
* Correspondence: mhelgamal@imamu.edu.sa; Tel.: +966-545-859-725

Abstract: This study presents, for the first time, a detailed linear stability analysis (LSA) of bedform evolution under low-flow conditions using a one-dimensional vertically averaged and moment (1D-VAM) approach. The analysis focuses exclusively on bedload transport. The classical Saint-Venant shallow water equations are extended to incorporate non-hydrostatic pressure terms and a modified moment-based Chézy resistance formulation is adopted that links bed shear stress to both the depth-averaged velocity and its first moment (near-bed velocity). Applying a small-amplitude perturbation analysis to an initially flat bed, while neglecting suspended load and bed slope effects, reveals two distinct modes of morphological instability under low-Froude-number conditions. The first mode, associated with ripple formation, features short wavelengths independent of flow depth, following the relation $F^2 = 1/(kh)$, and varies systematically with both the Froude and Shields numbers. The second mode corresponds to dune formation, emerging within a dimensionless wavenumber range of 0.17 to 0.9 as roughness increases and the dimensionless Chézy coefficient C^* decreases from 20 to 10. The resulting predictions of the dominant wavenumbers agree well with recent experimental observations. Critically, the model naturally produces a phase lag between sediment transport and bedform geometry without empirical lag terms. The 1D-VAM framework with Exner equation offers a physically consistent and computationally efficient tool for predicting bedform instabilities in erodible channels. This study advances the capability of conventional depth-averaged models to simulate complex bedform evolution processes.

Keywords: stability analysis diagram; evolution of bedforms; low-regime bedforms; vertically averaged and moment models; velocity over varied topography; moment-based Chezy formula

MSC: 76-10; 00A69

1. Introduction

1.1. Background

One of the key characteristics of flows in alluvial channels is the dynamic interplay between the moving water and the deformable channel bed. This bidirectional interaction gives rise to distinctive morphological features on the bed surface, commonly referred to as bedforms. Of particular significance in hydraulic engineering is the inherent instability of sand waves. These migrating bedforms can modify flow patterns, potentially leading to adverse outcomes such as flooding and structural damage to hydraulic infrastructure, including dams and bridges [1,2].

Under low-flow regime conditions, initially, flat beds have been observed to develop small, triangular-shaped features known as ripples once the flow velocity surpasses a certain threshold. As the velocity continues to increase, these ripples evolve into larger, asymmetric bedforms referred to as dunes. At even higher velocities, dunes tend to disappear, leading to the re-establishment of a flat bed surface. These bedforms—ripples and dunes—significantly contribute to form resistance, a dominant component of total flow resistance in alluvial channels, often exceeding grain resistance by a considerable margin [3–6]. For this reason, it is imperative for hydro-morphological models not only to detect the presence of bedforms but also to accurately predict their geometrical characteristics. This capability is vital for mitigating potential navigation hazards and ensuring the robust design of flood control infrastructure [7].

The formation and evolution of bedforms have long attracted the attention of researchers and engineers. In 1925, Exner made a pioneering observation by identifying friction-induced phase lag between the bed profile and sediment transport rate as a key factor in bedform development [8]. This insight laid the foundation for the application of linear stability analysis (LSA) to study bedform evolution, which gained momentum approximately four decades later. Over the past 70 years, LSA has become a widely used tool to explore the physical mechanisms governing the transition from a flat bed to periodic bedforms. Small-amplitude stability analysis assumes bed perturbation heights to be small relative to the perturbation wavelength and flow depth, allowing for linearization of the governing equations of flow and sediment transport. Although such linearization excludes essential nonlinear dynamics, LSA remains a valuable method for elucidating the initial growth and decay behavior of bedforms and advancing our understanding of morphodynamic processes.

Previous LSA studies have generally adopted one of three classes of flow modeling approaches. The first class employs potential, irrotational, and quasi-steady or fully unsteady flow formulations. The second class incorporates more accurate two-dimensional (2D) rotational and viscous models, based on either vorticity transport equations or time-averaged Reynolds equations. The third class utilizes simplified, vertically averaged (VA), one-dimensional depth-averaged "Saint-Venant-type" equations, which are commonly adopted in practical hydrodynamic simulations, with or without the hydrostatic pressure assumption.

Kennedy was among the first researchers [9–12] to apply LSA using the potential flow framework, modeling dune formation as a two-dimensional problem. However, the inviscid nature of potential flow theory limited his model's ability to capture low-Froude-number instabilities unless an artificial, explicit phase lag was introduced between local flow velocity and sediment transport. Although Kennedy's lag parameter was intended to match observations, subsequent analyses revealed that it could approach the scale of the perturbation wavelength, raising questions about its physical realism [13]. Many researchers later contended that reliance on an imposed phase lag indicates a deficiency in the underlying model physics—missing key mechanisms such as sediment inertia, flow separation, or bedform coalescence. While Kennedy's original formulation interpreted the lag physically, it was ultimately deemed an artificial proxy, either unnecessary in models with improved physical realism or incompatible with the actual mechanisms responsible for dune initiation [14–16].

In a notable advancement, Coleman and Fenton [17] applied LSA to fully unsteady 2D potential flow and demonstrated that bedform development could be predicted without invoking Kennedy's explicit lag assumption. They attributed the implicit phase lag to a resonance mechanism between surface waves and bed perturbations. Nevertheless, based on comparisons with experimental data, they concluded that potential flow models are inadequate for capturing the evolution of bedforms [17].

To overcome the limitations of potential flow theory, researchers began incorporating more physically realistic models. Engelund employed a 2D vorticity-based model with a constant eddy diffusivity turbulence closure. Two modes of sediment transport were included: bedload and suspended load. His work highlighted the importance of non-hydrostatic pressure distributions and fluid friction for accurately simulating bedform growth [18]. Fredsøe used a quasi-steady, 2D rotational model and demonstrated that ripple modes could be captured when bedload transport was made sensitive to local bed slope [19]. Colombini utilized a 2D Reynolds-averaged model and showed that phase lag between sediment transport and bed elevation remains the primary driver of instability. He also demonstrated that dunes and antidunes can form without suspended load or sediment inertia, provided bed shear stress is evaluated at the interface between the flow and bedload layer [20]. Sumer and Bakioglu adopted a rotational model with bedload transport alone, assuming no flow separation [21]. While their analysis successfully captured ripple instabilities, it failed to predict dunes, prompting them to suggest that suspended load effects are essential for dune formation. However, McLean countered this view, arguing that dunes can be reproduced without suspended load if the flow structure is modeled with sufficient fidelity [22]. More recently, Ali and Dey employed a 2D Reynolds-averaged model with a one-equation turbulence closure and found that sand wave instability is sensitive to streamwise pressure gradient and Reynolds stress perturbations at the bed [23]. Ohata et al. explored the role of suspended sediment in suppressing dune formation and promoting plane beds, offering new insights into the structure of turbidite sequences [24].

The third group of studies employed one-dimensional, depth-averaged Saint-Venant equations for LSA. Gradowczyk was the first to apply LSA using hydrostatic, 1D Saint-Venant-Exner (SVE) equations but failed to capture any bedform instabilities [25]. This limitation was later confirmed by [26,27], who emphasized the importance of relaxing the hydrostatic assumption and improving the representation of bed shear stress (e.g., replacing the classical Chezy formula). Ref. [14] introduced a dynamic bedload transport model and analyzed both unsteady and quasi-steady flows. While their model could predict antidune instabilities, it remained unable to detect ripple or dune instabilities associated with low-flow conditions.

Ref. [28] enhanced the 1D Saint-Venant equations by incorporating a streamwise velocity profile derived from turbulence theory and applying the Boussinesq approximation to account for non-hydrostatic pressure variations. Their model included both bedload and suspended sediment transport and successfully identified instability regimes for both dunes (at low Froude numbers) and antidunes (at higher Froude numbers). Ref. [29] investigated ripple instabilities based on bedload transport alone, identifying a critical near-bed flow layer approximately 3.5 times the ripple height and showing a dependence of ripple wavelength on the Shields parameter. Most recently, Ref. [1] conducted both linear and weakly nonlinear analyses of sand wave formation using a depth-averaged model that included bedload and suspended load transport. Their work demonstrated the ability to predict both equilibrium wavelengths and amplitudes of sand waves and to assess their sensitivity to key flow and sediment parameters.

Although the depth-averaged Saint-Venant equations are widely applied in river engineering due to their computational efficiency and modest data requirements [30,31], their inherent inability to resolve vertical velocity structures often limits their predictive accuracy.

To overcome this shortcoming, the moment of momentum approach was introduced, giving rise to an advanced class of models known as vertically averaged and moment (VAM) models [32]. These models augment the classical depth-averaged framework by incorporating additional degrees of freedom that allow for the representation of non-uniform vertical velocity profiles, typically linear or parabolic in form, and, when required, by relaxing the hydrostatic pressure assumption to account for non-hydrostatic effects.

VAM models have demonstrated considerable success in broadening the applicability of traditional depth-averaged approaches across various hydraulic contexts. Their applications include the prediction of spatially variable bed shear stress under non-uniform flow conditions [27,33], the analysis of complex two-dimensional flow structures in channel bends [34–36], the estimation of transverse mixing in open channels driven by secondary current-induced shear dispersion [37], the quantification of turbulent kinetic energy distributions over bedforms [38], and the approximation of velocity fields across morphologically varying beds and bedforms [39].

The central objective of the present study is to investigate the capability of VAM models to predict the formation and evolution of bedforms originating from an initially flat bed, employing a linear stability analysis framework.

1.2. Study Objectives

The principal objectives of this study are threefold:

First, to conduct a rigorous linear stability analysis of sediment bedforms under low-flow conditions by introducing, for the first time, the vertically averaged and moment (VAM) approach into the theoretical framework.

Second, to evaluate the capability of the one-dimensional VAM model in predicting the distinct modes of bedform instabilities arising in the low-Froude-number regime. This analysis is carried out while focusing exclusively on bedload sediment transport mechanism and neglecting suspended load and bed slope effects.

Third, to compare the theoretical predictions derived from the VAM-based linear stability analysis with recent experimental observations in the labs.

To achieve these objectives, the analysis is systematically structured into four stages:

- Baseline Case—Classical SVE Framework: The traditional Saint-Venant–Exner (SVE) equations, formulated under the hydrostatic pressure assumption and incorporating the standard Chezy resistance relation, serve as the reference model for subsequent comparisons.
- Case 1—Incorporation of Non-Hydrostatic Effects: The baseline SVE equations are extended by integrating non-hydrostatic pressure terms derived from the moment of momentum approach, allowing assessment of their influence on instability predictions.
- Case 2—Hydrostatic VAM Model: The hydrostatic form of the VAM equations is employed, incorporating a modified Chezy-type resistance formulation tailored to moment-based velocity distributions for improved bed shear stress estimation.
- Case 3—Fully Extended VAM Model: This configuration combines both the moment-based velocity representation and non-hydrostatic pressure effects, providing the most comprehensive modeling framework for evaluating bedform evolution mechanisms.

1.3. Paper Organization

The remainder of this paper is structured as follows:

Section 2 presents the linear perturbation analysis of the conventional SVE equations.

Section 3 extends the analysis to revised formulations, exploring the effects of non-hydrostatic terms and VAM-based modeling.

Section 4 discusses the results obtained from the different LSA formulations.

Section 5 summarizes the key findings.

Section 6 outlines the study's challenges, limitations, and directions for future research.

2. Methodology

2.1. Perturbation Analysis

The response time of the flow to changes in bed topography is generally much shorter than the timescale associated with the morphological evolution of the bed itself. For this reason, it is common to treat the flow field as quasi-steady when analyzing the development of bedforms over a perturbed bed surface. This assumption was originally proposed and validated in the work of Richards [8] and has since been adopted in several related studies.

Based on the linear perturbation concept, the variables such as water depth h, flow velocity u or sediment flux q_s are decomposed into a base state (denoted by the superscript $^{(0)}$) and a small perturbation that is considered a deviation from the base state (denoted as superscript $^{(1)}$). Such decomposition allows us to study how small disturbances evolve over time and space. For instance, the water depth could be written as $h = h^{(0)} + h^{(1)}$

2.2. Linearization of Conventional Saint-Venant (SV) Equation (Reference Case)

Based on the schematic illustration provided in Figure 1, the depth-averaged continuity and momentum equations under steady-state conditions are formulated within the inclined coordinate system defined by the axes X and Z. By invoking the small perturbation hypothesis, these governing equations can be linearized. Accordingly, the first-order approximations of the depth-averaged continuity and streamwise momentum equations are expressed as follows:

$$\frac{\partial h^{*(1)}}{\partial x^*} + \frac{\partial U_o^{*(1)}}{\partial x^*} = 0 \tag{1}$$

$$\left(F^2 - 1\right)\frac{\partial U_o^{*(1)}}{\partial x^*} + \frac{\partial z_b^*}{\partial x^*} + \left(S_o + \frac{2F^2}{C^{*2}}\right)U_o^{*(1)} = 0 \tag{2}$$

where x is the coordinate parallel to the averaged bed slope, S_o; z_b is the local bed perturbation height measured from the averaged slope; h is the water depth; U_o is the depth-averaged velocity; F is the Froude number, $F = \frac{U_o^{(0)}}{\sqrt{gh^{(0)}}}$; and C^* is the dimensionless Chezy coefficient. $h^{*(1)} = \frac{h^{(1)}}{h^{(0)}}$; $x^* = \frac{x}{h^{(0)}}$; $z_b^* = \frac{z_b}{h^{(0)}}$; $U_o^{*(1)} = \frac{U_o^{(1)}}{U_o^{(0)}}$; $\bar{z} = z_b + \frac{h}{2}$. The superscript $^{(1)}$ indicates the order of the parameter, $^{(0)}$ means the base or the mean value, whereas $^{(1)}$ refers to the perturbation.

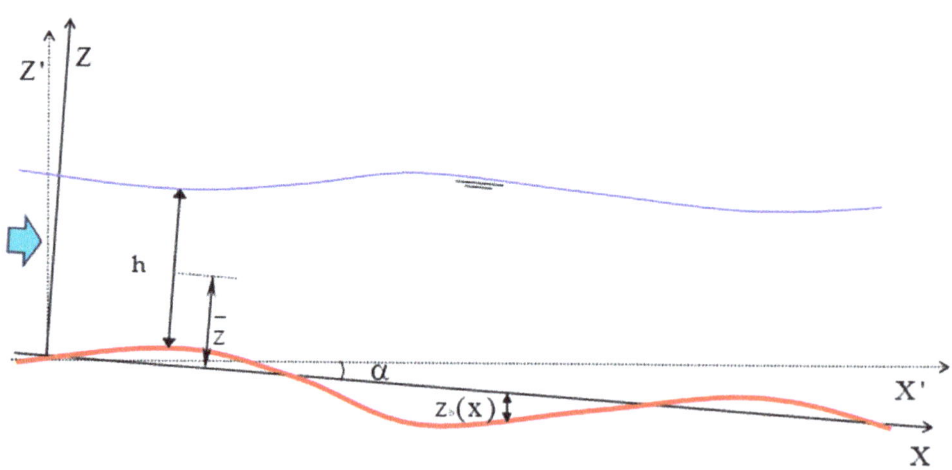

Figure 1. Coordinate definition.

In this study, the bed load transport was estimated using Chang's formulation, which is expressed as follows [40]:

$$q_s = \frac{k_t}{\gamma_s} U_o(\tau_b - \tau_c) \quad (3)$$

In this context, q_s denotes the volumetric bed load transport, while k_t is an empirical coefficient reflecting sediment properties; a higher k_t value implies that sediment particles are more readily for entrainment as bed load. For beds composed of medium to coarse sand, k_t typically approaches 0.1. γ_s represents the specific weight of sediment, τ_b is the applied bed shear stress, and τ_c is the critical shear stress threshold for sediment motion. For analytical simplicity, τ_c is assumed to be negligible, a simplification more appropriate for fine sediments than for coarser grains. By combining Equation (3) with the (Exner-like) sediment continuity condition, Equation (4) is obtained, which reveals that an accelerating flow (i.e., $\frac{\partial U_o^{*(1)}}{\partial x^*}$>0) induces a reduction in bedform amplitude, thereby promoting bed perturbation damping.

$$\frac{\partial z_b^*}{\partial t^*} = -\frac{\tilde{A}}{C^{*2}} F^2 \cdot \frac{\partial U_o^{*(1)}}{\partial x^*},\ \tilde{A} = \frac{3k_t \cdot \rho^*}{(1-n)} \quad (4)$$

Here, t is the time coordinate, t^* is the normalized time = $C \cdot t/h$, n represents the sediment porosity, while ρ^* denotes the ratio of water density to that of the sediment particles. From Equations (2) and (4), the momentum equation can be rewritten as:

$$\frac{\partial^2 z_b^*}{\partial x^{*2}} - \frac{C^{*2} \cdot (F^2 - 1)}{\tilde{A} \cdot F^2} \frac{h^{(0)}}{U_o^{(0)}} \frac{\partial^2 z_b^*}{\partial x^* \partial t} - \frac{3}{\tilde{A}} \frac{h^{(0)}}{U_o^{(0)}} \frac{\partial z_b^*}{\partial t} = 0 \quad (5)$$

Equation (5) constitutes an eigenvalue problem for determining the perturbation wave speed, C, under the assumption that the initially planar erodible bed undergoes a slight perturbation as described by Equation (6). Hereafter, $h^{(0)}$ will be denoted as h for simplicity.

$$z_b^* = \langle z_b \rangle \cdot exp[ikh(x^* - C \cdot t/h)] \quad (6)$$

The real and imaginary components of the bed wave speed can be determined as follows:

$$\frac{C_{real}}{U_o^{(0)}} = \frac{\tilde{A} \cdot (1 - F^2) F^2 \cdot \frac{k^2 h^2}{C^{*2}}}{\left(3 \cdot \frac{F^2}{C^{*2}}\right)^2 + (F^2 - 1)^2 \cdot k^2 h^2} \quad (7)$$

$$\frac{C_{im}}{U_o^{(0)}} = \frac{-3 \cdot \tilde{A} \cdot F^4 \cdot \frac{kh}{C^{*4}}}{\left(3 \cdot \frac{F^2}{C^{*2}}\right)^2 + (F^2 - 1)^2 \cdot k^2 h^2} \quad (8)$$

A positive imaginary component of the bed wave speed indicates that the perturbation will grow over time, whereas a negative value implies decay and stability of the initially planar bed. The normalized components of wave speed, given in Equations (7) and (8), depend on the Froude number (F), dimensionless wave number (kh), bed roughness parameter, and various sediment properties.

Equation (7) characterizes the migration behavior of bed perturbations; it demonstrates that bedforms propagate downstream when $F < 1$ and upstream when $F > 1$. Furthermore, Equation (8), which describes the normalized imaginary component of the wave speed, consistently yields negative values for all combinations of F and kh. This result implies that any imposed bed perturbation will diminish over time, ultimately restoring the bed to its original planar configuration. These findings suggest that the classical Saint-Venant equations do not predict the emergence of unstable bed modes under the considered conditions. This conclusion is in agreement with earlier studies conducted by several researchers [22,23,27].

3. Effect of SV Equation (SVE) Enhancements

3.1. Linearized Form of SVE with Non-Hydrostatic Terms (Case 1)

An important enhancement to the conventional Saint-Venant depth-averaged model involves accounting for non-hydrostatic effects in the pressure distribution. To incorporate these effects, a quadratic pressure distribution is assumed, as illustrated in Figure 2, a methodology previously adopted by a number of researchers, such as [32]. As a result, two additional degrees of freedom, denoted by h_1 and h_2, are introduced to the standard linear hydrostatic pressure profile.

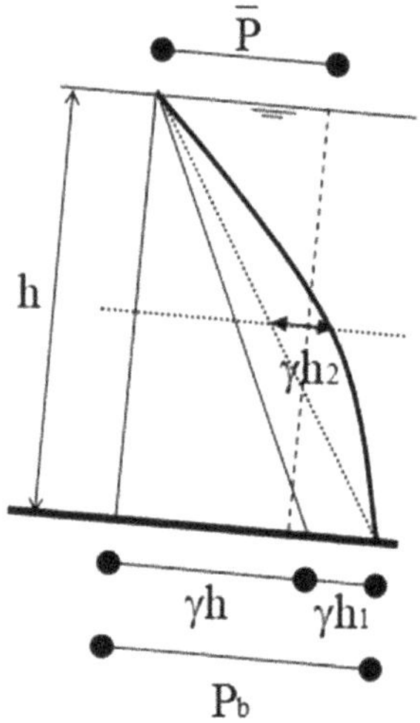

Figure 2. Pressure distribution including the non-hydrostatic effect.

To close the system of equations, two additional relations are required. Appropriate choices for these are the depth-averaged vertical momentum equation and the depth-averaged vertical moment of momentum equation. By assuming a uniform vertical profile for the downstream velocity, these equations can be considerably simplified and formulated as follows [32,34]:

$$g\cdot h_1^{(1)} \approx q\cdot U_o^{(0)}\cdot\left(\frac{\partial^2 \overline{z}^{(1)}}{\partial x^2}\right),\; g\cdot h_2^{(1)} \approx q\cdot\frac{U_o^{(0)}}{8}\cdot\left(\frac{\partial^2 h^{(1)}}{\partial x^2}\right),\; \overline{z} = z_b + \frac{h}{2} \tag{9}$$

Accordingly, the vertically averaged momentum equation in the streamwise (x) direction can be written as:

$$\frac{F^2}{2}\frac{\partial^4 z_b^*}{\partial x^{*4}} + \frac{C^{*2}}{4\cdot\widetilde{A}}\frac{h}{U_o^{(0)}}\frac{\partial^4 z_b^*}{\partial x^{*3}\partial t} + \frac{\partial^2 z_b^*}{\partial x^{*2}} - \frac{C^{*2}\cdot(F^2-1)}{\widetilde{A}\cdot F^2}\frac{h}{U_o^{(0)}}\frac{\partial^2 z_b^*}{\partial x^*\partial t} - \frac{3}{\widetilde{A}}\frac{h}{U_o^{(0)}}\frac{\partial z_b^*}{\partial t} = 0 \tag{10}$$

From Equations (6) and (10), the bed wave speed can be decomposed into its real and imaginary components, which are given as follows:

$$\frac{C_{real}}{U_o^{(0)}} = \frac{\widetilde{A}\cdot F^2\left(\left(1-F^2\right) - \frac{k^2h^2F^2}{3}\right)\cdot\frac{\left(k^2h^2 - \frac{k^4h^4F^2}{2}\right)}{C^{*2}}}{\left(3\cdot\frac{F^2}{C^{*2}}\right)^2 + \left(\left(F^2-1\right)\cdot kh + \frac{k^3h^3F^2}{3}\right)^2} \tag{11}$$

$$\frac{C_{im}}{U_o^{(0)}} = \frac{-3\cdot\widetilde{A}\cdot F^4\cdot kh\cdot\frac{\left(1-\frac{k^2h^2F^2}{2}\right)}{C^{*4}}}{\left(3\cdot\frac{F^2}{C^{*2}}\right)^2+\left((F^2-1)\cdot kh+\frac{k^3h^3F^2}{3}\right)^2} \tag{12}$$

The discussion and comments on Equations (11) and (12) are given in Section 4.

3.2. Linear Stability Formulation of the VAM-Hydrostatic Model (Case 2)

In 1993, Ref. [32] introduced the vertically averaged and moment (VAM) model, a one-dimensional formulation that combines depth-averaged and moment-based components. The moment equations are obtained by vertically integrating the continuity and momentum equations, each multiplied by the vertical coordinate prior to integration.

In this subsection, a linear stability analysis is conducted for the VAM equations under the assumption of hydrostatic pressure conditions, hereafter referred to as the VAM hydrostatic case. The effects of non-hydrostatic pressure will be examined in the following subsection (Case 3). In addition, this analysis adopts the recently developed moment-based Chezy formula for predicting bed shear stress, as proposed in [33]. The moment-based Chezy formula is expressed as:

$$u_*^2 = \frac{U_o}{C_2^2}(U_o - K_r u_1) \tag{13}$$

where C_2 is a dimensionless coefficient defined as $C_2 = C^*\sqrt{1-K_r\cdot\alpha}$; K_r is another dimensionless coefficient that varies linearly with the roughness ratio h/z_0; for more details about the significance of this coefficient, the reader is to refer to [33]; $\alpha \approx \frac{1.5}{C^*\cdot\kappa}$; and κ is the Von Karman constant.

The term u_1 denotes the surface velocity in excess to the depth-averaged velocity, assuming a linear velocity distribution, as illustrated in Figure 3. Notably, when $K_r = 0$, Equation (13) simplifies to the conventional Chezy formulation for shear velocity. The moment-based Chezy approach has demonstrated improved predictive capability for spatial variability in bed shear stress, particularly over non-uniform bed topographies [33].

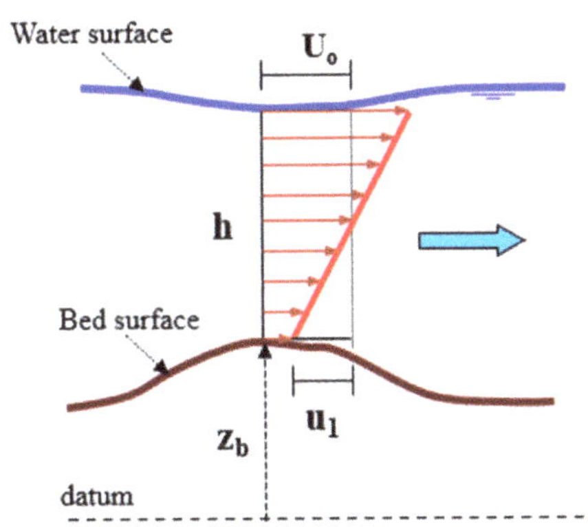

Figure 3. Definition of u_1.

The linearized form of the depth-averaged streamwise momentum equation, incorporating the shear stress representation given in Equation (13), yields Equation (14). Notably, when the calibration coefficient K_r is set to zero, Equation (14) simplifies to the classical form shown in Equation (2). The depth-averaged moment of momentum equation can further be expressed in a dimensionless form, as shown in Equation (15), where the eddy viscosity parameter F_e is defined by $F_e=\nu_t/(u^*\cdot h)$, with ν_t representing the eddy viscosity.

By combining Equations (1) and (13) and applying the sediment continuity relationship (Exner equation), Equation (16) is obtained. Collectively, Equations (1) and (14) through (16) can be consolidated into a coupled system of two equations with two unknowns. This system represents an eigenvalue problem used to solve for the complex wave speed C, as outlined in Equations (17) and (18).

$$\left(F^2-1\right)\frac{\partial U_o^{*(1)}}{\partial x^*}+\frac{\partial z_b^*}{\partial x^*}+\left(S_o+\frac{2F^2}{C_2^2}\right)U_o^{*(1)}-K_r\alpha\frac{F^2}{C_2^2}\left(U_o^{*(1)}+u_1^{*(1)}\right)=0 \tag{14}$$

If the calibration coefficient K_r is set to zero, Equation (14) reduces to Equation (2).

The depth-averaged x-moment of momentum equation can be written in a dimensionless form as:

$$\frac{\partial u_1^{*(1)}}{\partial x^*}+\frac{\partial U_o^{*(1)}}{\partial x^*}+3\left(\frac{K_r}{C_2^2}+\frac{4F_e}{C^*}\right)u_1^{*(1)}-\left(\frac{6}{\alpha C_2^2}-3\left(\frac{K_r}{C_2^2}+\frac{4F_e}{C^*}\right)\right)U_o^{*(1)}=0 \tag{15}$$

$$\frac{\partial z_b^*}{\partial t^*}=-\tilde{B}\frac{\tilde{A}}{C_2^2}F^2\cdot\frac{\partial U_o^{*(1)}}{\partial x^*}+\frac{\alpha\cdot K_r\tilde{A}}{3C_2^2}F^2\cdot\frac{\partial u_1^{*(1)}}{\partial x^*},\ \tilde{B}=\left(1-2\cdot\alpha\cdot\frac{K_r}{3}\right) \tag{16}$$

$$\frac{C_{real}}{U_o}=\frac{Cd_1k^2h^2\left(Cd_8-Cd_{11}k^2h^2\right)-Cd_3k^2h^2\left(Cd_7+Cd_{10}\right)}{\left(Cd_{11}k^2h^2-Cd_8\right)^2+\left(Cd_7+Cd_{10}\right)^2k^2h^2} \tag{17}$$

$$\frac{C_{im}}{U_o}=\frac{Cd_3kh\left(Cd_{11}k^2h^2-Cd_8\right)-Cd_1k^3h^3\left(Cd_7+Cd_{10}\right)}{\left(Cd_{11}k^2h^2-Cd_8\right)^2+\left(Cd_7+Cd_{10}\right)^2k^2h^2} \tag{18}$$

The coefficients Cd_1 through Cd_{11} generally depend on the Froude number, the dimensionless coefficient (K_r), the dimensionless Chezy coefficient, and sediment properties. Their explicit expressions are provided in Appendix A, while the complete derivation of Equations (17) and (18) is detailed in Appendix B.

3.3. Linear Stability Formulation of the Non-Hydrostatic VAM Model (Case 3)

As outlined earlier in Section 3.1, the influence of non-hydrostatic pressure components on the momentum equation is incorporated by assuming a quadratic pressure distribution, as illustrated in Figure 2. This assumption introduces two additional variables, h_1 and h_2, thereby necessitating two supplementary equations to close the system. These are provided by the depth-averaged vertical (z-direction) momentum equation and the depth-averaged vertical moment of momentum equation.

The depth-averaged z-momentum equation is given by Equation (19), where $u' = U(z) - U_o$; $w' = W(z) - W_o$; τ denotes shear stress; and the overbar indicates a depth-averaged quantity. Among the terms on the right-hand side of Equation (19), the first is the most dominant. The second term becomes more relevant in the case of fully developed bedforms but, due to its minimal effect in the context of small-amplitude perturbations, it is disregarded in the present linear analysis. Equation (19) establishes a relationship between the dynamic pressure term h1 and the spatial gradient of the depth-averaged vertical velocity Wo, which can be determined using the continuity moment equation, represented by Equation (20).

$$gh_1=q\frac{\partial W_o}{\partial x}+\frac{\partial h\cdot\overline{u'\cdot w'}}{\partial x}-\frac{1}{\rho}\frac{\partial h\cdot\overline{\tau}}{\partial x}-\frac{\tau_b}{\rho}\frac{\partial z_b}{\partial x}+g\cdot h\cdot(cos\cdot\alpha-1) \tag{19}$$

$$h\cdot W_o=\frac{\partial h\cdot\overline{z'\cdot u'}}{\partial x}+q\frac{\partial\overline{z}}{\partial x}=\frac{1}{6}\frac{\partial h^2\cdot u_1}{\partial x}+q\frac{\partial\overline{z}}{\partial x} \tag{20}$$

Here, $z' = z - \overline{z}$, where $\overline{z}=z_b+\frac{h}{2}$. denotes the centroid of the flow depth measured from the perturbed bed. Assuming a linear vertical profile for the streamwise velocity component, the vertical momentum equation (Equation (19)) can be simplified accordingly to Equation (21).

$$g \cdot h_1^{(1)} \approx q \cdot \left(\frac{u_1^{(0)}}{3} \frac{\partial^2 h^{(1)}}{\partial x^2} + \frac{h}{6} \frac{\partial^2 u_1^{(1)}}{\partial x^2} + U_o^{(0)} \cdot \left(\frac{\partial^2 \overline{z}^{(1)}}{\partial x^2} \right) \right) \tag{21}$$

The vertically averaged moment of momentum equation in the vertical (z) direction can be formulated as:

$$gh_2 = \frac{3}{2h} \begin{pmatrix} q \cdot W_o \frac{\partial \overline{z}}{\partial x} + h \cdot W_o \frac{\partial \overline{z' \cdot u'}}{\partial x} + \overline{z' \cdot u'} \frac{\partial h \cdot W_o}{\partial x} + h \cdot \overline{u' \cdot w'} \frac{\partial \overline{z}}{\partial x} + \\ q \frac{\partial \overline{z' \cdot w'}}{\partial x} + \frac{\partial h \cdot \overline{z' \cdot u' \cdot w'}}{\partial x} - h \cdot W_o^2 - h \cdot \overline{w'^2} - \frac{h \cdot \overline{\tau}}{\rho} \frac{\partial \overline{z}}{\partial x} - \\ \frac{1}{\rho} \frac{\partial h \cdot \overline{z' \cdot \tau'}}{\partial x} + \frac{h \cdot \tau_b}{2\rho} \frac{\partial z_b}{\partial x} \end{pmatrix} \tag{22}$$

By omitting the shear stress contributions along with other nonlinear and non-dominant terms, Equation (22) can be simplified, through the application of Equation (20), to yield Equation (23). This equation features the term $\overline{z' \cdot w'}$, which can be approximated by assuming a parabolic distribution for the vertical velocity component (refer to Appendix A for more details). Following further algebraic simplifications, Equation (23) leads to the reduced form presented in Equation (24).

$$\begin{aligned} gh_2^{(1)} &\approx \tfrac{3}{2h} \left(q \cdot W_o \tfrac{\partial \overline{z}}{\partial x} + h \cdot W_o \tfrac{\partial \overline{z' \cdot u'}}{\partial x} + \overline{z' \cdot u'} \tfrac{\partial h \cdot W_o}{\partial x} + q \tfrac{\partial \overline{z' \cdot w'}}{\partial x} - h \cdot W_o^2 \right) \\ gh_2^{(1)} &= \tfrac{3}{2h} \left(\overline{z' \cdot u'} \cdot h \tfrac{\partial W_o}{\partial x} + q \tfrac{\partial \overline{z' \cdot w'}}{\partial x} \right) \end{aligned} \tag{23}$$

$$g \cdot h_2^{(1)} \approx \frac{3}{2} \begin{pmatrix} \frac{u_1^{(0)} \cdot h}{6} \left(\frac{u_1^{(0)}}{3} \frac{\partial^2 h^{(1)}}{\partial x^2} + \frac{h}{6} \frac{\partial^2 u_1^{(1)}}{\partial x^2} + U_o^{(0)} \frac{\partial^2 \overline{z}^{(1)}}{\partial x^2} \right) + \\ q \frac{u_1^{(0)}}{6} \frac{\partial^2 \overline{z}^{(1)}}{\partial x^2} + q \cdot \frac{U_o^{(0)}}{12} \cdot \frac{\partial^2 h^{(1)}}{\partial x^2} \end{pmatrix} \tag{24}$$

Accordingly, the linearized streamwise momentum equation, now accounting for non-hydrostatic pressure effects, takes the form of Equation (25). This equation can be further simplified, resulting in Equation (26).

$$\begin{aligned} & q \cdot \tfrac{\partial U_o^{(1)}}{\partial x} + g \cdot h \cdot \tfrac{\partial h^{(1)}}{\partial x} + g \cdot h \cdot \tfrac{\partial z_b}{\partial x} + \tfrac{g \cdot h}{2} \tfrac{\partial h_1^{(1)}}{\partial x} + \tfrac{2}{3} g \cdot h \tfrac{\partial h_2^{(1)}}{\partial x} + \tfrac{2 \cdot U_o^{(0)} U_o^{(1)}}{C_2^2} \\ & - \tfrac{K_r}{C_2^2} \left(U_o^{(0)} u_1^{(1)} + u_1^{(0)} U_o^{(1)} \right) - g \cdot h^{(1)} \cdot S_o = 0 \end{aligned} \tag{25}$$

$$\begin{aligned} & \left(\tfrac{\alpha}{12} + \tfrac{\alpha^2}{36} \right) F^2 \tfrac{\partial^3 u_1^{*(1)}}{\partial x^{*3}} - \left(\tfrac{1}{3} + \tfrac{\alpha}{3} + \tfrac{\alpha^2}{18} \right) F^2 \tfrac{\partial^3 U_o^{*(1)}}{\partial x^{*3}} + \left(\tfrac{1}{2} + \tfrac{\alpha}{3} \right) F^2 \tfrac{\partial^3 z_b^*}{\partial x^{*3}} + \\ & \left(F^2 - 1 \right) \tfrac{\partial U_o^{*(1)}}{\partial x^*} + \tfrac{\partial z_b^*}{\partial x^*} + \left(S_o + \tfrac{2F^2}{C_2^2} \right) U_o^{*(1)} - K_r \alpha \tfrac{F^2}{C_2^2} \left(U_o^{*(1)} + u_1^{*(1)} \right) = 0 \end{aligned} \tag{26}$$

Additionally, the depth-averaged x-moment of momentum equation may be expressed in dimensionless form, as follows:

$$\begin{aligned} & \tfrac{\partial u_1^{*(1)}}{\partial x^*} + \tfrac{\partial U_o^{*(1)}}{\partial x^*} - \tfrac{1}{2\alpha F^2} \tfrac{\partial h_1^{(1)}}{\partial x} + 3 \left(\tfrac{K_r}{C_2^2} + \tfrac{4F_e}{C^*} \right) u_1^{*(1)} - \\ & \left(\tfrac{6}{\alpha C_2^2} - 3 \left(\tfrac{K_r}{C_2^2} + \tfrac{4F_e}{C^*} \right) \right) U_o^{*(1)} = 0 \end{aligned} \tag{27}$$

It is noteworthy that the influence of the h_2 term appears explicitly in the x-momentum equation (Equation (25)) but is absent from the x-moment of momentum equation (Equation (27)). This is attributed to the fact that h_2 represents the parabolic portion of the pressure distribution, which is symmetric about the flow's mid-depth, as illustrated in Figure 2, and produces no net moment within the linearized framework.

By combining Equations (1), (16), (19), (26), and (27), the governing system can be reduced to a pair of coupled equations involving two unknowns. This formulation constitutes an eigenvalue problem for the perturbation wave speed C, with the complete mathematical expressions detailed in Appendix A.

4. Results and Discussion

The analysis results are conveyed through the predicted directions of bedform migration during evolution and, more critically, the growth or decay rate of bedform amplitude. This rate is illustrated using stability diagrams, which display contour lines of the normalized growth rate (C_{im}/U_o) within the *kh*–*F* parameter space. Each diagram corresponds to specific values of the roughness parameter (K_r), the dimensionless coefficient (C^*), and sediment characteristics.

4.1. Migration Direction of Evolving Bedforms

Figure 4 illustrates the predicted bedform migration directions during their evolution, comparing outcomes derived from the conventional depth-averaged Saint-Venant (SV) model (Equation (7)) with those from the modified formulation that incorporates non-hydrostatic pressure terms (Equation (11)). The figure plots the bed wave propagation direction as a function of the dimensionless wave number and Froude number *kh* and *F*, respectively. Additionally, the results are benchmarked against Kennedy's established criterion delineating the maximum Froude number threshold for dune formation (that are known to propagate downstream), represented by the dotted line labeled *D-D* [9].

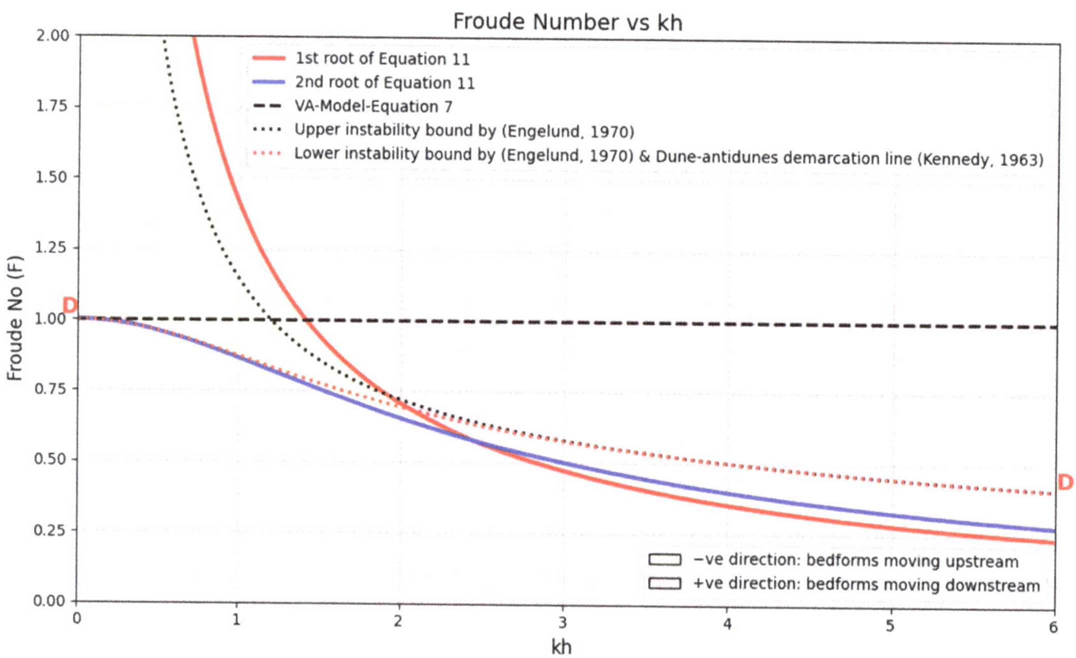

Figure 4. Estimated direction of bed wave perturbation. (for conventional SVE and SVE with non-hydrostatic terms).

The curves presented in the figure clearly indicate the transitions between downstream-moving and upstream-moving bedforms. These demarcation lines were calculated from their corresponding expressions for C_{real}/U_o (Equation (7) for the dashed line and Equation (11) for the solid lines) by enforcing the condition $C_{real}/U_o = 0$.

The importance of incorporating non-hydrostatic pressure effects becomes evident from the comparative analysis presented in Figure 4. These effects result in more physically realistic predictions of bed wave direction across the full range of wavenumbers considered. The revised model significantly improves predictive performance over the conventional hydrostatic Saint-Venant–Exner (SVE) model (Equation (7)), underscoring the critical role of non-hydrostatic terms in accurately representing bedform dynamics.

Figure 4 illustrates the demarcation line between dune and antidune regimes predicted by the conventional hydrostatic SVE model, shown as a horizontal dashed black line at $F = 1$. This line deviates notably from the empirically established boundaries proposed by Kennedy and Engelund, depicted as dotted brown and black lines, respectively. When non-hydrostatic effects are included, based on Equation (11), the resulting demarcation lines (shown in red and blue) more closely align with those of Kennedy and Engelund, demonstrating the improved physical realism of the non-hydrostatic depth-averaged formulation.

Figure 5 presents the normalized contour map of the real component of the perturbation wave speed, C_{real}/U_o, plotted within the kh–F parameter space using the VAM equations that account for non-hydrostatic effects. The results correspond to the case where $K_r = 2.0$, $C^* = 15$, and $F_e = 0.07$. The figure specifically highlights the behavior in the low-Froude-number regime ($F < 1$). Additionally, the diagram includes Kennedy's demarcation boundary (denoted as line *D–D*), which distinguishes between downstream-migrating dunes and upstream-migrating sand waves.

Figure 5a presents contour plots of the normalized real part of the wave perturbation velocity, C_{real}/U_o, across the kh–Froude number parameter space. These results are derived from the VAM equations that include non-hydrostatic pressure effects, using the parameter set, $K_r = 2.0$, $C^* = 15$, and $F_e = 0.07$. While the scope of the current analysis is confined to low-flow subcritical conditions, part of the supercritical regime is also depicted to facilitate direct comparison with Figure 4. The figure includes Kennedy's empirical demarcation line (labeled *D–D*), which delineates downstream-migrating dunes from upstream-migrating sand waves, along with Engelund's lower and upper instability limits (shown as red and blue dotted lines). The close agreement between the model-predicted transition boundaries and those proposed by Kennedy and Engelund highlights a substantial improvement over predictions from the Saint-Venant equations, even when enhanced with non-hydrostatic terms.

Although this study primarily focuses on bedforms within the low-flow regime, it is worthwhile to preliminarily evaluate the VAM model's predictive performance under high-flow conditions, particularly in capturing antidune migration direction. To this end, recent experimental data from [41] were employed for model validation. Table 1 summarizes the experimental runs where antidunes were observed to migrate either upstream or downstream.

(a)

(b)

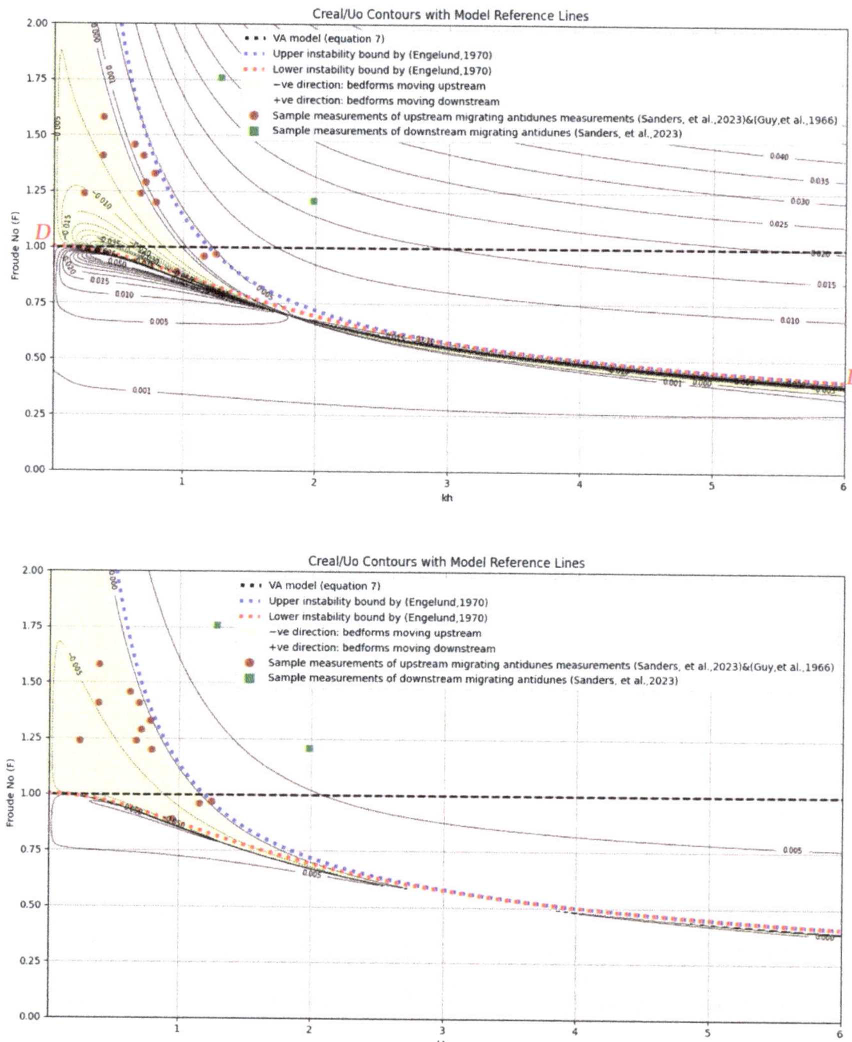

Figure 5. Normalized bed wave speed contour lines (C_{real}/U_o) for VAM equations considering the non-hydrostatic effects. (**a**) (K_r = 2.0, C^* = 15, F_e = 0.07), (**b**) (K_r = 1.3, C^* = 17, F_e = 0.15).

Table 1. Characteristics of sample measurements of antidunes traveling in both directions [41].

Run	Bed Slope (-)	h (cm)	Δ (cm)	λ (cm)	kh	C (cm/min)	U_o (m/s)	F	u^* (cm/s)	Bed Configuration
5-SS	0.013	4.98	4.5	80	0.391	−150	1.06	1.58	7.05	u/s antidune
6A-SS	0.015	5.52	5.5	90	0.385	–	0.95	1.41	7.06	u/s antidune
6B-SS	0.018	3.89	3	100	0.244	–	0.68	1.24	5.66	u/s antidune
7-SS	0.011	5.92	1	55	0.676	−18	0.89	1.24	6.67	u/s antidune
2-SJ	0.011	6.16	1.5	30	1.290	60	1.28	1.76	6.74	d/s antidune
6-SJ	0.0074	7.91	3.2	25	1.988	29	1	1.21	6.26	d/s antidune

The initial validation utilized the modern dataset of Sanders et al., which was generated using high-resolution techniques such as laser scanning, sonar, and acoustic Doppler profiling—offering enhanced spatial and temporal accuracy. By contrast, the classical dataset compiled by [42] relied on point gauge measurements, often taken after draining turbid flows, which may introduce notable uncertainties. Nevertheless, we acknowledge the foundational role of Guy's work and have incorporated all upstream-migrating antidune cases from his dataset into our analysis, along with their corresponding hydraulic parameters. These cases have now been added to the revised Figure 5a.

While some deviation between the model predictions and the experimental antidune data is observed under the default parameters ($K_r = 2.0$, $C^* = 15$, and $F_e = 0.07$), improved alignment is achieved in Figure 5b after adjusting the model parameters to ($K_r = 1.3$, $C^* = 17$, and $F_e = 0.15$). This observed sensitivity to parameter values underscores the importance of careful calibration, an issue that warrants focused attention in future investigations.

Remarkably, the VAM model accurately predicted the direction of antidune migration in both upstream- and downstream-moving cases.

Figure 5 illustrates that the dimensionless phase speed C_{real}/U_0 increases with increasing wavenumber kh, implying that shorter wavelength bedforms (i.e., those with smaller values of λ) migrate more rapidly than their longer-wavelength counterparts. This observation aligns with established findings in fluvial geomorphology, where smaller bedforms are generally observed to travel at higher rates compared to larger ones [43–47].

Supplementary Figures S1 and S2 present additional contour plots of C_{real}/U_0 across a range of Chezy roughness coefficients (C^*). The results show that increasing C^* expands the region in which antidunes migrate upstream. This behavior is consistent with hydraulic theory, as higher C^* values correspond to reduced bed resistance, which weakens flow–bedform interactions and lowers the energy required for upstream migration.

4.2. Bedform Evolution Analysis Based on the Hydrostatic VAM Model

Figure 6 and Supplementary Figures S3–S5 present stability diagrams (SDs) from the VAM-hydrostatic linear stability analysis (Equation (18)). These SDs show contours of normalized growth rate, C_{im}/U_0, across kh–Froude number space, with each diagram corresponding to parameter sets (K_r, C^*, F_e, and sediment properties). All SDs consistently reveal two distinct regions separated by a near-horizontal boundary: an upper decay zone (Zone C, negative growth) and a lower growth zone (Zone B, positive growth signaling bedform development).

Critically, while the non-hydrostatic Saint-Venant equations (SVE) model (Equation (12)) predicts no positive growth, confirming its inability to simulate bedform initiation, the VAM-hydrostatic model identifies growth within low-Froude regimes (Zone B). This demonstrates the superior physical fidelity of VAM's shear stress formulation (Equation (13)), which captures the phase lag between bed shear stress and topography evolution. By resolving this key mechanism, VAM enables depth-averaged frameworks to simulate bedform onset, advancing their utility in sediment transport and morphodynamic modeling.

Although the boundary between Zones B and C appears overly simplified compared to the curved demarcation lines given by Kennedy and Engelund (red dotted lines in Figure 6), the ability to predict positive growth marks a significant advancement for depth-averaged models in sediment transport and morphodynamics. Nonetheless, further refinement is needed, particularly for dynamic simulations involving full sediment–flow interactions, as discussed in the following subsection.

Within the region exhibiting positive growth rates, a distinct wavenumber emerges as the dominant mode responsible for the amplification of bedform disturbances. This most unstable wavelength is associated with Zone B of the stability diagrams. Figure 7a,b illustrate horizontal transects of the stability contours presented in Figure 6, extracted at a fixed Froude number of $F = 0.7$. The results indicate that the VAM-hydrostatic model predicts a single, well-defined instability mode corresponding to dune-type bedforms.

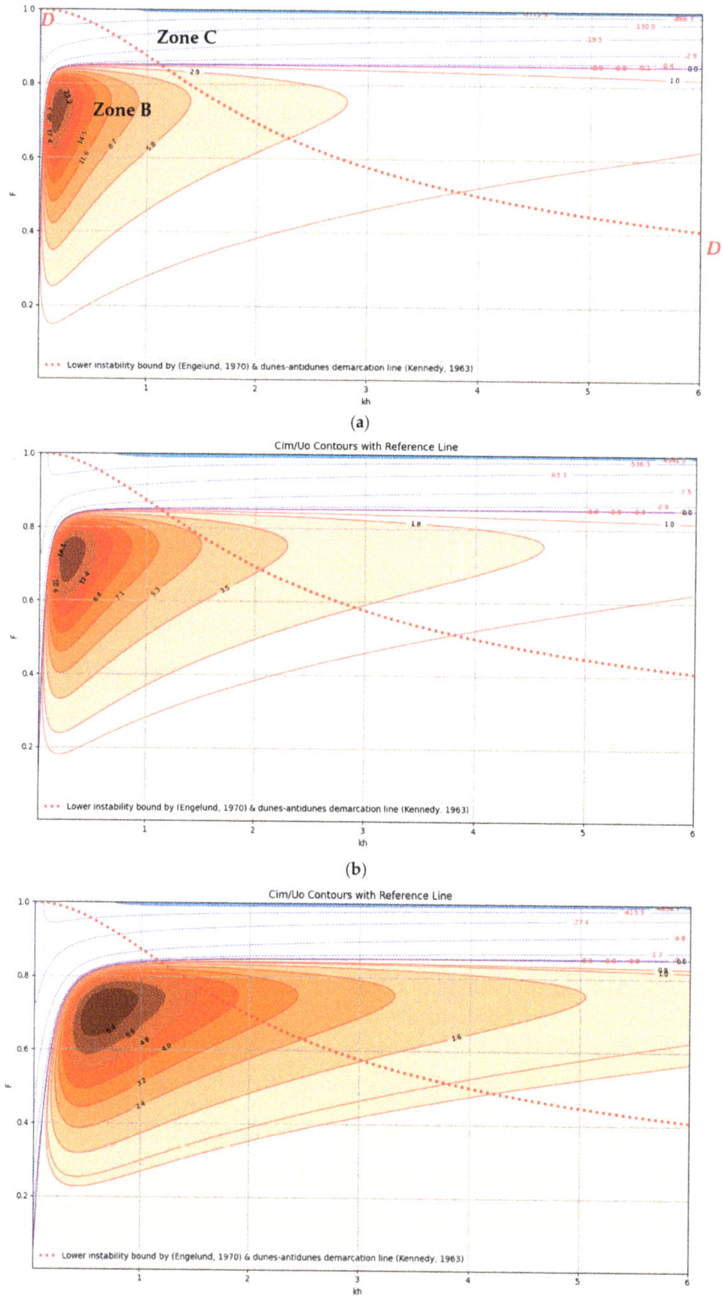

Figure 6. Stability diagram (contour lines of $10^5 \times C_{im}/U_o$) for VAM-hydrostatic equations, $K_r = 2.5$, $C^* = 15$, (**a**) $F_e = 0.07$, (**b**) $F_e = 0.15$, and (**c**) $F_e = 0.4$.

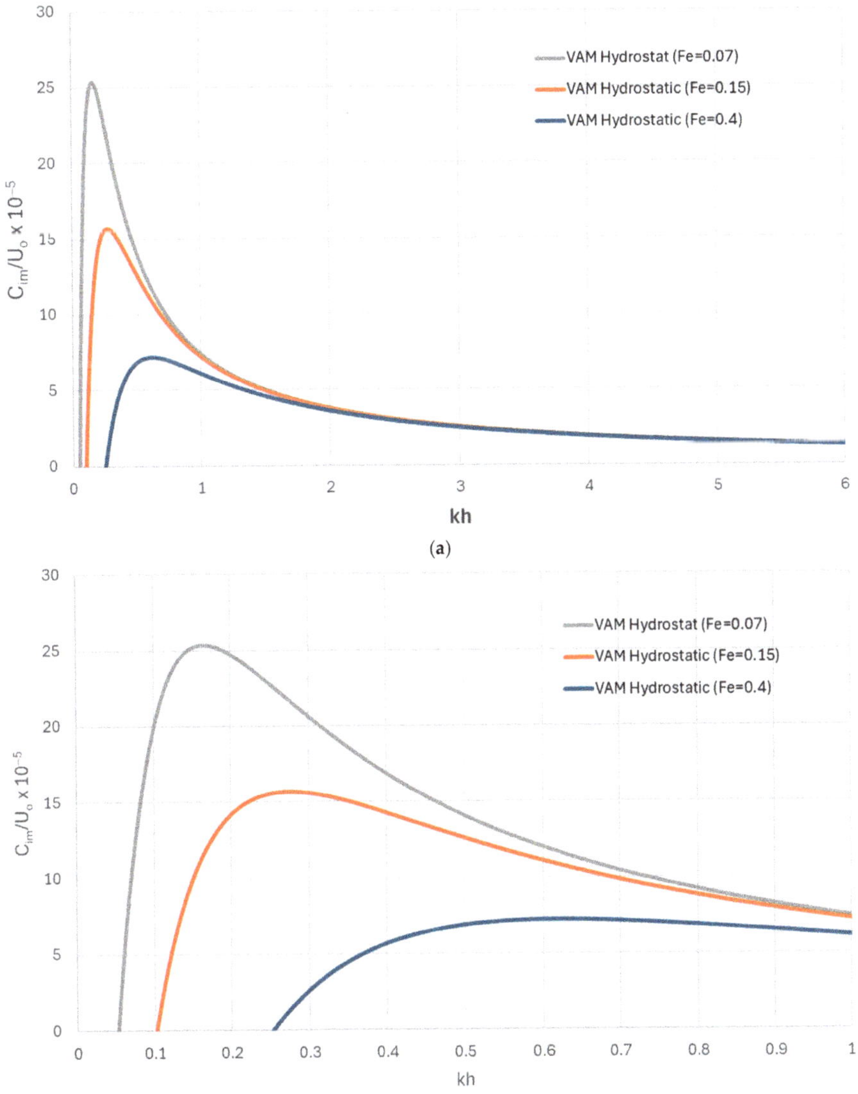

Figure 7. Horizontal transects of SD (shown in Figure 6) taken at $F = 0.7$. (**a**) kh ranges from 0 to 6. (**b**) kh ranges from 0 to 1.

Figure 7b provides a magnified view of Figure 7a, offering clearer insights into the influence of the turbulent eddy viscosity parameter (F_e). As F_e increases from 0.07 to 0.4, a systematic reduction in the maximum growth rate is observed—consistent with theoretical expectations. Concurrently, the corresponding dominant wavenumber increases from approximately $kh \approx 0.16$ to $kh \approx 0.61$, indicating a shift toward shorter bedform wavelengths with increasing turbulence intensity. The effect of F_e could be justified as the turbulent eddy viscosity coefficient controlling the intensity of momentum diffusion by turbulence. A higher eddy viscosity means stronger turbulent mixing of momentum, which smooths out velocity gradients and diminishes flow separation and inertia effects over bed undulations. Physically, turbulent diffusion transfers momentum more efficiently from faster to slower flow regions, so the flow becomes less perturbed by small-scale bed variations, which has a direct damping effect on the growth of bedforms. The influence of F_e on the dominant wavenumber is consistent with previous studies, which have emphasized the role of turbulence characteristics in determining the emergent wavelength of flow instabilities [43].

4.3. Bedform Evolution Analysis Based on Non-Hydrostatic VAM Formulation

The linear stability analysis results of the fully dynamic non-hydrostatic VAM formulation are presented through a series of stability diagrams (SDs) generated for various combinations of the roughness parameter (C^*), the momentum correction coefficient (K_r), and the eddy viscosity factor (F_e). Representative examples are shown in Figure 8a–c, while a broader set appears in the Supplementary Materials (Figures S6–S20). These diagrams are based on the imaginary component of the wave speed for the bed perturbation given in Equation (A45). To facilitate reproducibility, a Python 3 script was developed to generate SD plots for any user-defined combination of the governing parameters.

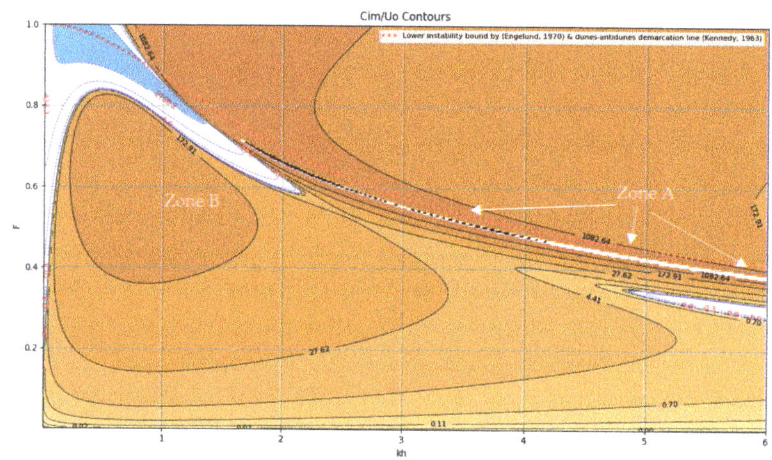

(a)

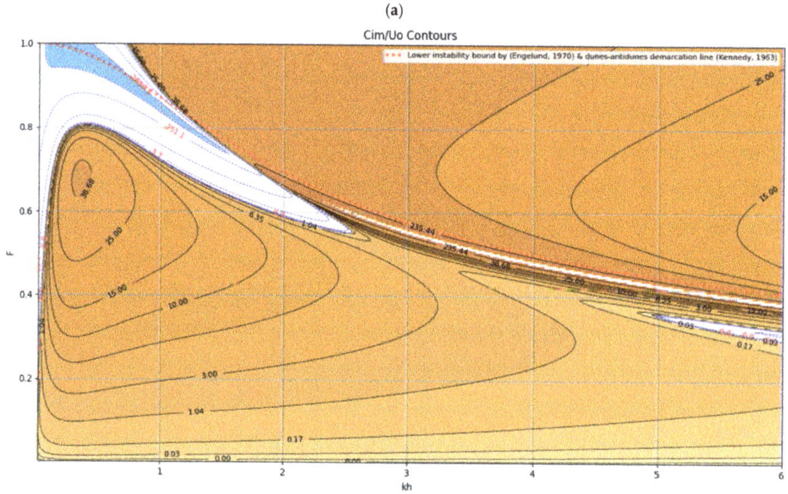

(b)

Figure 8. *Cont.*

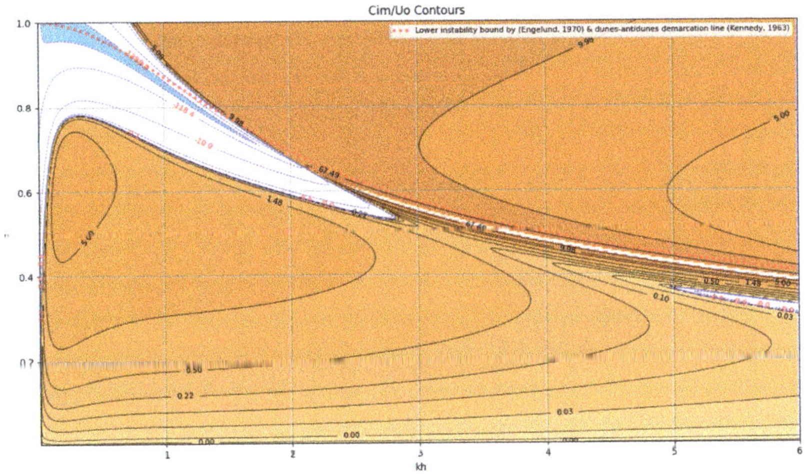

(c)

Figure 8. Stability diagram (contour lines of $10^5 \times C_{im}/U_o$) for VAM equations, K_r = 2.0, F_e = 0.2. (**a**) C^* = 10, (**b**) C^* = 15, and (**c**) C^* = 20.

Figure 8a–c display normalized growth rate contours (C_{im}/U_o) for the case K_r = 2.0 and F_e = 0.2 under three roughness scenarios (C^* = 10, 15, and 20). Regions with positive growth rates are indicated by brown-gradient contours, while areas of decay are shaded in blue. Two distinct instability zones are consistently observed below the Kennedy and Engelund demarcation curves (shown as dotted red and blue lines):

Zone A–A emerges just below the instability threshold identified by Kennedy and Engelund and is not predicted by the hydrostatic formulation (presented in Section 4.2). It corresponds to high wavenumbers (i.e., shorter wavelengths), which are indicative of ripple-like features.

Zone B represents the dune instability regime observed in previous hydrostatic cases and is associated with lower wavenumbers, corresponding to longer bedform wavelengths.

These zones identify preferential wavelengths where bedform disturbances are most likely to grow under low-Froude conditions. In contrast, the upper-left region of the diagrams consistently exhibits Zone C, a decay zone indicative of morphodynamic stability typically associated with plane bed configurations or washed-out dunes.

An important visible trend across Figure 8a–c is the inverse relationship between C^* and growth magnitude. As roughness decreases (i.e., higher C^*), interaction between the flow and the bed weakens, leading to a reduced tendency for bedforms to grow. This behavior emphasizes the role of bed resistance in modulating instability dynamics.

Figure 9a,b provide horizontal cross-sections of the growth rate contours at a fixed Froude number (F = 0.4) for the three C^* values. The plots use a logarithmic vertical scale to highlight the variations in growth rate across wavenumbers. The results confirm the presence of dual instability peaks, one associated with ripples (Zone A–A) and another with dunes (Zone B). As C^* decreases (from 20 to 10), both the growth rate and dominant wavenumber increase, with peak values shifting from $kh \approx 0.17$ to 0.9. These findings suggest that rougher beds promote the formation of shorter, faster-growing bedforms, while smoother beds promote longer, slower-growing dunes or stable flat beds, an observation that is consistent with previous experimental and theoretical studies [13,18,19].

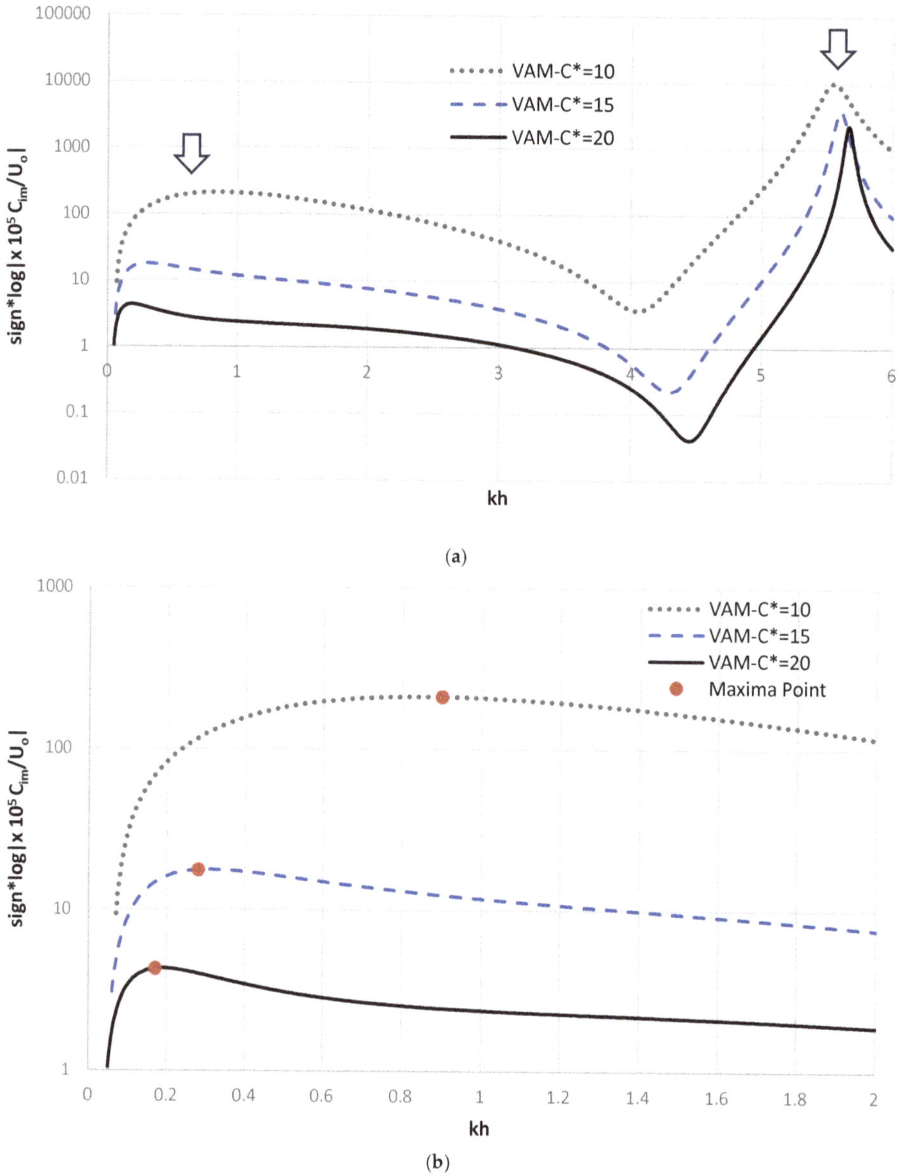

Figure 9. Horizontal transects taken at Froude No $F = 0.4$ for three VAM stability diagrams drawn for $K_r = 2.0$, $F_e = 0.2$ and different bed roughness C^*: (**a**) $kh = 0$ to 6, (**b**) $kh = 0$ to 2 (zoom in). (note: the arrows in (**a**) point to the locations of the dual peak values).

Furthermore, the critical (i.e., maximum) Froude number at which dune (of wavelength 6 times the water depth) growth ceases decreases with increasing C^*, approximately at a maximum $F = 0.75$ for coarse sand ($C^* = 10$), $F = 0.725$ for medium sand ($C^* = 15$), and $F = 0.70$ for fine sand ($C^* = 20$), as seen in Figure 8a–c. A similar trend was previously reported by Fredsøe [19] in his linear stability work.

It is also worth noting that the growth rate associated with Zone A is typically larger than that of Zone B. Given its association with shorter wavelengths, Zone A may represent the initial seed formations of ripples or sand wavelets that evolve into dunes.

As shown in Supplementary Figures S3–S5, the K_r coefficient plays a critical role in controlling instability characteristics. Reducing K_r lowers the maximum growth rate and shifts the instability boundary downward, effectively reducing the unstable region. At $K_r = 0$, the governing Equation (18) simplifies to Equation (8), and no bed instabilities are observed. For further discussion on the factors affecting K_r, readers are referred to references [33,37].

Although the VAM-hydrostatic model succeeds in identifying growth zones, it predicts an unrealistic horizontal boundary between stable and unstable regimes, deviating from the more physically consistent demarcations proposed by Kennedy and Engelund. In contrast, the inclusion of non-hydrostatic effects in the VAM framework aligns the model's predictions more closely with empirical evidence, providing a more accurate and physically grounded representation of bedform evolution.

It is also important to note that the wavelength of bed perturbations associated with instability Zone B exhibits a clear dependence on flow depth. In contrast, the wavelength characteristics of ripples, corresponding to Zone A–A, appear to be largely independent of water depth. Investigating the extent to which the ripple-scale bedform wavelengths in Zone A–A may still exhibit subtle sensitivity to flow depth remains an interesting direction for future research.

Zone A-A could be approximated by:

$$F^2 = \frac{1}{kh} \tag{28}$$

This relation could be reduced as follows to give an estimate for the wavelength of the ripples (λ_r):

$$\lambda_r = \frac{2\pi C_*^2}{g} u_*^2 \tag{29}$$

Finally,

$$\lambda_r = 2\pi(s \cdot g \cdot -1)\theta_{cr} C_*^2 \frac{\theta}{\theta_{cr}} d_{50} \tag{30}$$

$$\text{Where } \theta = \frac{u_*^2}{(s-1) g d_{50}} \tag{31}$$

The parameters θ_{cr} and s represent the dimensionless critical shear stress and the specific gravity of sediment particles, respectively. As expressed in Equation (30), the wavelength λ_r associated with bed perturbations in Zone A–A appears to be largely independent of flow depth and is primarily governed by bed roughness, which, in turn, is a function of the sediment grain size. For a range of $1 < \theta/\theta_{cr} < 10$ and a Chezy resistance coefficient $C^* = 15$, Equation (30) predicts λ_r values on the order of (100 to 1000) times d_{50}. These predictions are consistent with empirical observations of sand wavelets, where $\lambda_r \approx 175 d_{50}$ (with d_{50} in millimeters) as reported in [44], and sand ripples, where $\lambda_r \approx 1000 d_{50}$, as noted in [45].

4.4. Comparison with Bedform Measurements

4.4.1. Dominant Wavelengths for Ripples

To evaluate the accuracy of the LSA based on VAM model, experimental datasets for ripples from previous studies such as [46–48] were utilized. These experiments involved measurements of ripple geometry developed in fine sand beds.

Figure 10 shows the variations in the normalized dominant ripple wavelength with the Shields parameter θ. The figure compares the measurements with the results of Equation (30) that was approximately deducted from VAM LSA. Also, the proposed model previously developed by Boes and Dey [29] is added for comparison. The comparison shows that Equation (29) can reasonably predict the dominant wave lengths of the evolving ripples; however, the predictions are significantly affected by the value of C^*.

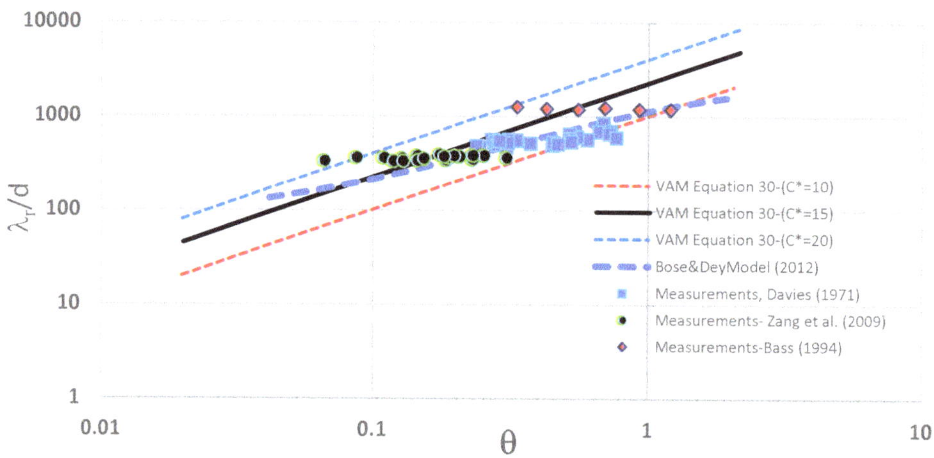

Figure 10. Variation in the normalized dominant ripple wavelength with the Shields parameter. (note, data comparison from: Boes and Dey [29], Davies [46], Bass [47], Zang et al. [48]).

4.4.2. Dominant Wavelength for Dunes and Low-Flow Regime Sand Waves

To facilitate a comparative evaluation of the LSA-VAM model predictions with observed low-flow regime sand waves and dunes, 10 experimental datasets were compiled from the literature. The key characteristics of these datasets are summarized in Table 2.

Table 2. Laboratory experiments for low-flow bedforms.

Data Type No.	Study (Author/Year)	No. of Runs	Water Depth (m)		Velocity (m/s)		Froude No.(F)		Bedform Height (Δ, mm)		Bedform Length (λ, mm)		Median Sediment Size (mm)	
			Min	Max	Min	Max	Min	Max	Min	Max	Min	Max	Min	Max
1	[49]	23	0.150	0.900	0.400	0.840	0.20	0.60	43.2	137	710.0	1500.0	0.430	0.810
2	[50]	8	0.154	0.389	0.590	0.830	0.35	0.52	17.0	122	790.0	1790.0	0.650	2.820
3	[51]	15	0.085	0.170	0.264	0.806	0.27	0.76	9.7	42.5	104.5	717.6	0.230	0.820
4	[52]	8	0.192	0.208	0.660	0.680	0.31	0.34	57.0	70.0	1350.0	1710.0	0.530	0.530
5	[53]	2	0.219	0.224	0.590	0.600	0.40	0.41	56.0	61.0	1130.0	1420.0	0.500	0.503
6	[54]	35	0.150	0.300	0.460	0.675	0.30	0.48	6.0	95.0	260.0	1640.0	0.800	0.800
7	[55]	5	0.186	0.212	0.354	0.717	0.26	0.50	20.0	40.0	290.0	1030.0	0.800	1.800
8	[56]	3	0.134	0.152	0.433	0.867	0.36	0.76	38.8	65.7	906.0	2060.0	0.550	0.550
9	[57]	5	0.195	0.250	0.350	0.550	0.22	0.35			140.0	620.0	0.328	0.617
10	[58]	21	0.055	0.186	0.382	0.686	0.36	0.74	22.8	140.	755.4	3486.2	0.830	0.830
Total/Extreme Value		125	0.085	0.9	0.167	0.867	0.10	0.76	6	137	104.5	2060	0.23	2.82

Figure 11 presents the stability diagram for the LSA-VAM model in the case of $C^* = 10$, $K_r = 1.0$, and $F_e = 0.2$. The diagram also shows the experimental data of all the laboratory experiments recently reported in the last two decades as per the characteristics given in Table 2. It is interesting to note that most of the data points lie in the positive-growth-rate area and outside the negative-growth-rate zones. It is also of interest to notice that the data seems to be arranged on and around the polyline tracing the ridges of the local positive growth rate (shown in dashed yellow color), which could be an indicator of the

LSA-VAM model despite its simplifications, but it generally captured correctly the modes of instabilities for the low-flow regime case quite well.

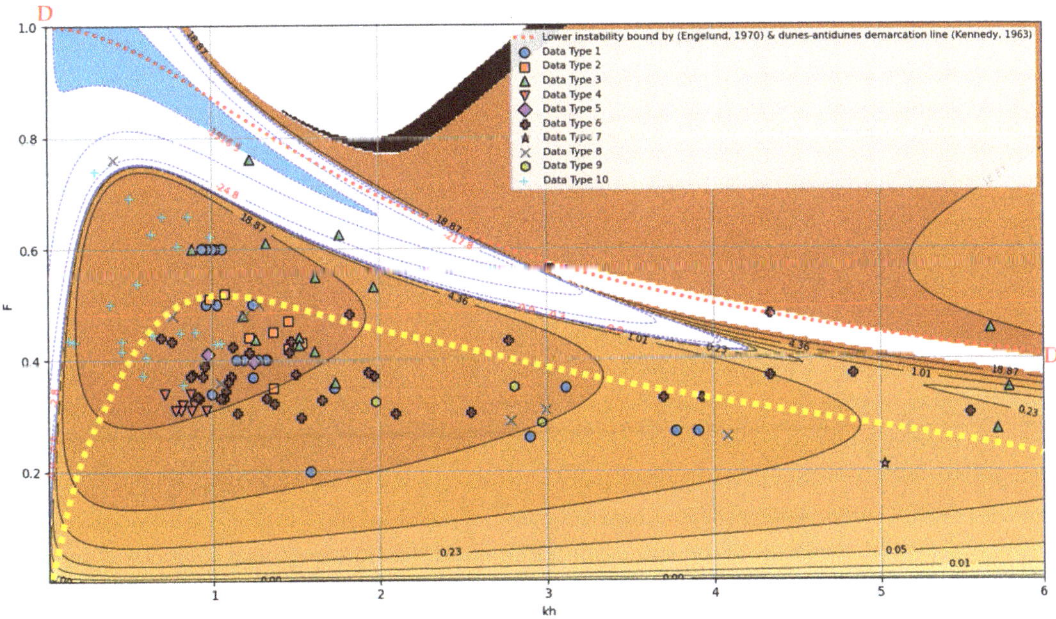

Figure 11. Stability diagram based on the non-hydrostatic VAM equations with parameters $C^* = 10$, $K_r = 1.0$, and $F_e = 0.2$. (presented contour lines of $10^5 \times C_{im}/U_o$) (note: the reference number for each data type shown in the legend corresponds to the same experimental number listed in Table 2) (dashed yellow line represents the maximum growth ridge line).

The results also highlight a noticeable sensitivity to the eddy viscosity parameter F_e. Under uniform flow conditions over a flat bed, F_e typically ranges between 0.06 and 0.08. However, in the presence of bedforms, particularly where flow separation is likely, this parameter tends to increase. For instance, spatial measurements from the fixed dune experiment T5 [59] revealed values of F_e varying between approximately 0.17 and 0.22. It was observed that higher values of F_e are associated with a reduction in the bedform growth rate and an increase in the dominant wavelength characterizing instability in Zone B.

4.5. Comparison with Colombini's Analysis

The linear stability analysis conducted in this study using the non-hydrostatic, depth-averaged VAM equations offers a distinct modeling perspective compared to the work of Colombini [20], who extended the classical theories of Engelund and Fredsøe [60] using a two-dimensional vertical Reynolds-averaged framework. Colombini's model evaluated bed shear stress at the top of the bedload layer, introducing an additional term associated with the longitudinal pressure gradient. This modification notably affects the imaginary component of the critical bed shear stress for determining instability, while having little influence on the real component. His formulation is grounded in Bagnold's sediment transport theory and emphasizes the delicate balance between stabilizing and destabilizing forces governing dune and antidune formation.

While both studies aim to predict the emergence and growth of bedforms under varying flow conditions, their modeling assumptions and target phenomena differ significantly. Colombini's analysis focused on dune and antidune regimes and did not address ripple-scale features. Consequently, his wavenumber range was limited to $kh \lesssim 1.5$, whereas the present VAM-based framework explores instabilities up to $kh \approx 6$ to capture ripple dynamics in the low-Froude regime. Notably, our analysis revealed the existence of dual instability modes, one associated with ripples (shorter wavelengths) and another with dunes (longer wavelengths), a feature not detected or discussed in Colombini's work.

Moreover, Colombini included a correction for gravitational effects in the bedload transport formula, which was not incorporated in the present model. His results also pointed out that suspended load and sediment inertia are not essential for antidune formation, which has been proved in our study too, although they may alter the growth rate surface. Importantly, Colombini identified that, under quasi-steady flow assumptions, resonance-like artifacts could appear in the growth-rate diagrams. By introducing time-dependent terms into the flow equations, these unrealistic resonances were shown to disappear, while the overall shape and location of the instability zones remained only moderately affected.

Another key distinction is the presentation of results. Colombini's stability diagrams do not include numerical growth rate contours, which limits direct quantitative comparison. Nonetheless, when adjusted for scale differences, the demarcation lines in Colombini's results are broadly consistent with those obtained in the present study, especially in identifying the boundary between dune and antidune regimes.

5. Conclusions

This study presented a novel linear stability analysis (LSA) framework for simulating bedform evolution under low-flow conditions using a vertically averaged and moment (VAM) approach. By comparing four modeling configurations—ranging from the classical Saint-Venant shallow-water equations to the fully extended VAM model—this research highlights how incorporating additional physics markedly improves predictive performance. In particular, the extended VAM model includes non-hydrostatic pressure effects and a moment-of-momentum-based velocity profile representation, which together enhance the depth-averaged formulation. The theoretical analysis and numerical results consistently show that these extensions lead to a more robust prediction of the initial bedform growth and dynamics.

The comparative findings demonstrate that the standard hydrostatic Saint-Venant model (with depth-uniform velocity assumptions) has limited capability in capturing the onset of bedforms under low-flow, bedload-dominated conditions. In contrast, the fully extended VAM model successfully predicts the emergence of both small-scale ripples and larger dune-like features while using only bedload sediment transport. This is a significant outcome, as it shows that, even without invoking suspended-load mechanisms, the VAM-based framework can reproduce the formation of ripples and dunes. The improved performance of the VAM approach underscores the value of including vertical flow structure and pressure dispersion in the analysis, features that prove essential for generating the instabilities associated with natural bedform development.

A key insight from the VAM formulation is the natural introduction of a phase-lag mechanism between the flow field and the bed evolution. Unlike simpler depth-averaged models that often assume an instantaneous adjustment of sediment transport to changes in flow, the VAM-based model inherently produces a delayed response. This physically relevant phase lag means that the peak bed shear stress and sediment transport do not occur exactly in phase with the bed elevation perturbations. Such a delay is crucial for realistic bedform behavior; it stabilizes the growth of finite-wavelength features and prevents the unbounded amplification of very short waves. In essence, the present model captures the timing offset between flow forcing and sediment movement that is known to govern ripple and dune formation, doing so as an emergent property of the governing equations rather than through ad hoc empirical tuning.

This study also illuminates how key model parameters influence bedform growth rates and migration patterns. The Chezy friction coefficient (C^*), the roughness parameter (K_r), and the eddy viscosity factor (F_e) each play distinct roles in modulating the instability characteristics. A higher friction (lower C^* or larger roughness) tends to dampen the growth of bedforms and can reduce their migration speed, as increased flow resistance curtails the intensity of sediment transport over evolving topography. Conversely, smoother flow conditions (higher C^* or lower roughness) promote more vigorous instability growth, leading to faster-developing and more rapidly migrating bedforms. The eddy viscosity factor, which represents the degree of turbulent momentum diffusion, affects the relative amplification of different wavelength perturbations; larger eddy viscosity values suppress short-wavelength variations (acting as a stabilizing influence on small ripples) and shift the dominance toward longer waves, while lower eddy viscosity allows finer-scale features to grow more readily.

Importantly, the VAM-based model's predictions show strong agreement with experimental observations for both ripples and dunes. The linear growth rates and most unstable wavelengths obtained from the analysis correspond closely with those observed in laboratory flume tests of ripple formation under low-flow conditions. Similarly, the model correctly predicts the trend toward longer wavelengths and slower growth rates, in line with measured dune datasets. The migration directions and relative celerities of the bedforms are also captured correctly (with downstream migration for these subcritical flow bedforms), matching qualitative observations. This level of agreement indicates that the model not only reproduces the expected behavior of bedform instability theory but also aligns quantitatively with real-world data, lending credence to its underlying assumptions and computational implementation.

The developed VAM-based LSA framework significantly advances the capabilities of depth-averaged morphodynamic modeling. By naturally integrating non-hydrostatic pressure distribution effects and a depth-varying velocity profile into a traditionally depth-averaged approach, the model bridges a critical gap between simple shallow-water equations and more complex three-dimensional simulations. The outcome is a more physically faithful yet computationally efficient tool for predicting initial bedform evolution under sediment transport by bedload.

6. Limitations and Outlook

This study has demonstrated the enhanced capability of the non-hydrostatic VAM framework over the conventional Saint-Venant (SV) depth-averaged model in analyzing bedform instabilities, particularly within low-flow regimes. Nevertheless, several limitations must be acknowledged when interpreting and applying these findings.

The current analysis focuses exclusively on bedforms occurring under low-Froude-number conditions ($F^2 \ll 1$), specifically ripples and dunes. As such, the conclusions drawn cannot be directly extended to high-flow regimes, such as those involving antidunes or other complex morphodynamical features. Future research should address the dynamics of bedforms under high-Froude conditions to broaden the scope of the model's applicability.

The model assumes a one-dimensional representation of bedforms with a constant channel width. Expanding the approach to two-dimensional bedforms, which introduces additional geometric and hydrodynamic complexities, would provide a more realistic framework for practical applications and warrants further investigation.

Only bed load transport was considered in this analysis. The exclusion of suspended sediment transport limits the comprehensiveness of the predictions, particularly in flows where suspension dominates the sediment transport regime. Future work should integrate both transport modes for a more holistic sediment dynamics model.

The current formulation assumes quasi-steady flow conditions based on the rationale that the flow adjusts much more rapidly than the bed morphology evolves. While this assumption is valid in many fluvial applications, it may be overly restrictive in dynamic environments such as estuaries, tidal inlets, dam-break scenarios, or situations involving rapidly evolving free-surface waves. In such cases, the coupling between flow and bedform development may require the use of fully unsteady flow equations. Future studies should consider applying the unsteady VAM framework to assess model performance under these more complex conditions.

The analysis relies on linear stability theory, which, while effective in capturing the initial emergence of bedforms from a flat bed, inherently assumes infinitesimal disturbances. In natural systems, initial perturbations are often of finite magnitude, thereby limiting the direct applicability of linear theory.

Moreover, linear stability analysis is not equipped to describe the nonlinear evolution of bedforms, including their coarsening, merging, and interactions over time. Such processes are critical for understanding the complete morphodynamical evolution in alluvial environments. To address this gap, future studies could incorporate weakly nonlinear analysis or fully dynamic numerical modeling of VAM equations to investigate the amplitude evolution and long-term behavior of bedforms.

Supplementary Materials: The following supporting information can be downloaded at: https://www.mdpi.com/article/10.3390/math13121997/s1, Figures S1–S20 present additional SD curves and transects corresponding to various parameter settings.

Author Contributions: Conceptualization, M.H.E.; Formal analysis, M.H.E.; Investigation, M.A.M.; Data curation, M.H.E.; Writing—original draft, M.H.E.; Writing—review & editing, M.A.M. All authors have read and agreed to the published version of the manuscript.

Funding: This research received no external funding.

Data Availability Statement: The original contributions presented in this study are included in the article. Further inquiries can be directed to the corresponding authors.

Conflicts of Interest: The authors declare no conflicts of interest.

Abbreviations

b	Channel/flume bed width
C	Wave speed of bed perturbation
C_{real}	Real part of wave speed of bed perturbation
C_{im}	Imaginary part of wave speed of bed perturbation
C^*	Dimensionless Chezy coefficient
C_2	Moment-based dimensionless Chezy coefficient
Cv_i	A set of dimensionless coefficients for VAM model, refer to Appendix A.2
Cd_i	A set of dimensionless coefficients for VAM-hydrostatic model, refer to Appendix A.1
F	Dimensionless Froude number
F_e	Eddy viscosity coefficient
g	Acceleration of gravity
h	Local water depth at distance x
i	$\sqrt{-1}$.
K_r	Dimensionless calibration coefficient with a value ranging from about 1.45 to 2.7
k	Turbulent kinetic energy per unit mass
k_t	Coefficient based on sediment properties (used in Chang's formula for bed load)
LSA	Linear stability analysis

n	Bed soil porosity
q	Specific discharge per unit width [m^2/s]
q^*	Dimensionless variable (refer to Equation (12))
u_1	Moment-based integral velocity scale along the flow x direction (refer to Figure 1)
U_o	Longitudinal depth-averaged velocity at location x
x	Horizontal coordinate in the flow direction
u_{1^*}	Normalized u_1 value (Equation (2))
x	Horizontal coordinate in the flow direction
z	Vertical distance from a given arbitrary horizontal datum up to an arbitrary point (refer to Figure 1)
z_{av}	Vertical distance from a given arbitrary horizontal datum up to the mid-water depth
z_b	Local bed level
MofM	Moment of momentum (refer to Figure 1)
SVE	Saint-Venant Equation
VA	Vertically averaged or depth averaged model
VAM	Vertically Averaged and Moment model
Δ	Bedform height
λ	Bedform wavelength
ν	Water kinematic viscosity
ν_t	Eddy viscosity
θ_{cr}	Dimensionless critical shear stress

Appendix A. Coefficients of VAM Model

Appendix A.1. VAM-Hydrostatic Equations

$$\frac{C_{real}}{U_o} = \frac{Cd_1k^2h^2(Cd_8 - Cd_{11}k^2h^2) - Cd_3k^2h^2(Cd_7 + Cd_{10})}{(Cd_{11}k^2h^2 - Cd_8)^2 + (Cd_7 + Cd_{10})^2k^2h^2} \tag{A1}$$

$$\frac{C_{im}}{U_o} = \frac{Cd_3kh(Cd_{11}k^2h^2 - Cd_8) - Cd_1k^3h^3(Cd_7 + Cd_{10})}{(Cd_{11}k^2h^2 - Cd_8)^2 + (Cd_7 + Cd_{10})^2k^2h^2} \tag{A2}$$

where

$$\mathrm{Cd_1 = 1{+}B_{u1}} \tag{A3}$$

$$\mathrm{Cd_2 = A_{u1}} \tag{A4}$$

$$\mathrm{Cd_3} = 3(1 + \mathrm{Bu_1})(K_r/\mathrm{C_2}^2 + 4F_e/C^*) - 6/\left(\alpha\cdot\mathrm{C_2}^2\right) \tag{A5}$$

$$\mathrm{Cd_4} = 3\mathrm{Au_1}(K_r/\mathrm{C_2}^2 + 4F_e/C^*\Big) \tag{A6}$$

$$\mathrm{Cd_5} = \Big(3/\mathrm{C_2}^2 - 2\cdot K_r\cdot\alpha/\mathrm{C_2}^2 - K_r\cdot\alpha\cdot\mathrm{B_{u1}}/\mathrm{C_2}^2 \tag{A7}$$

$$\mathrm{Cd_6} = K_r\cdot\alpha\cdot\mathrm{A_{u1}}/\mathrm{C_2}^2 \tag{A8}$$

$$\mathrm{Cd_7 = Cd_1{\cdot}Cd_6 + Cd_2{\cdot}Cd_5} \tag{A9}$$

$$\mathrm{Cd_8 = Cd_3{\cdot}Cd_6 + Cd_4{\cdot}Cd_5} \tag{A10}$$

$$\mathrm{Cd_{10}} = \mathrm{Cd_4}\cdot(1 - 1/F^2) \tag{A11}$$

$$\mathrm{Cd_{11}} = \mathrm{Cd_2}\cdot(1 - 1/F^2) \tag{A12}$$

$$\alpha = 1.5/(\kappa\cdot\mathrm{C}^*) \tag{A13}$$

$$\mathrm{Au_1} = 1/(\alpha\cdot K_r\cdot\mathrm{A}) \tag{A14}$$

$$\mathrm{A = k_{tt}\cdot(\rho_w/\rho_s)/C_2{}^2} \tag{A15}$$

$$\mathrm{k_{tt}} = \mathrm{k_t}/(1-\mathrm{n_s}) \tag{A16}$$

$$\mathrm{Bu_1} = (3-2\alpha\cdot K_r)/(\alpha\cdot K_r) \tag{A17}$$

$$\kappa = \text{von Karman constant} \approx 0.41 \tag{A18}$$

$$\mathrm{n_s} = \text{sediment porosity} \approx 0.4 \tag{A19}$$

$$\rho_w = \text{water density} \approx 1000\ \mathrm{kg/m^3} \tag{A20}$$

$$\rho_s = \text{sediment density} \approx 2600\ \mathrm{kg/m^3} \tag{A21}$$

Appendix A.2. VAM Equations

Constants depend on K_r and α:

$$\mathrm{Cv_1} = -\alpha/72.0; \tag{A22}$$

$$\mathrm{Cv_2} = (\alpha/3.0 + 0.5)/12.0; \tag{A23}$$

$$\mathrm{Cv_3} = -1/12; \tag{A24}$$

$$\mathrm{Cv_4} = \alpha/6; \tag{A25}$$

$$\mathrm{Cv_5} = \alpha/6; \tag{A26}$$

$$\mathrm{Cv_6} = 0.0; \tag{A27}$$

$$\mathrm{Cv_7} = \alpha\cdot(0.5K_r/\mathrm{C_2}^2 + 2F_e/C^*); \tag{A28}$$

$$\mathrm{Cv_8} = -(1/6)\cdot\alpha\cdot\left(6/\left(\alpha\cdot\mathrm{C_2}^2\right) - 3(K_r/\left(\mathrm{C_2}^2\right) + 4F_e/C^*)\right); \tag{A29}$$

$$\mathrm{Cv_{10}} = (\alpha^2/36.0 + \alpha/12.0)\cdot \mathrm{B_{u1}} - (1/3.0 + \alpha/3.0 + \alpha^2/18.0); \tag{A30}$$

$$\mathrm{Cv_{12}} = \alpha/3 + 0.5; \tag{A31}$$

$$\mathrm{Cv_{15}} = 3.0/\mathrm{C_2}^2 - (2+\mathrm{Bu_1})\cdot K_r\cdot\alpha/\mathrm{C_2}^2; \tag{A32}$$

$$\mathrm{Cv_{20}} = \mathrm{Cv_1}\cdot \mathrm{B_{u1}} + \mathrm{Cv_2}; \tag{A33}$$

$$\mathrm{Cv_{22}} = \mathrm{Cv_3}; \tag{A34}$$

$$\mathrm{Cv_{23}} = \mathrm{Cv_4}\cdot \mathrm{B_{u1}} + \mathrm{Cv_5}; \tag{A35}$$

$$\mathrm{Cv_{25}} = \mathrm{Cv_6}; \tag{A36}$$

$$\mathrm{Cv_{26}} = \mathrm{Cv_7}\cdot \mathrm{B_{u1}} + \mathrm{Cv_8}; \tag{A37}$$

Constants depend on F, K_r, and α:

$$\mathrm{Cv_{11}} = (\alpha^2/36 + \alpha/12)\cdot \mathrm{A_{u1}}/(F^2); \tag{A38}$$

$$\mathrm{Cv_{13}} = 1-1/F^2; \tag{A39}$$

$$\mathrm{Cv_{14}} = 1/F^2; \tag{A40}$$

$$\mathrm{Cv_{16}} = \mathrm{Au_1}\cdot K_r\cdot\alpha/\left(\mathrm{C_2}^2\cdot F^2\right); \tag{A41}$$

$$\mathrm{Cv_{21}} = \mathrm{Cv_1}\cdot \mathrm{A_{u1}}/F^2; \tag{A42}$$

$$\mathrm{Cv_{24}} = \mathrm{Cv_4}\cdot \mathrm{A_{u1}}/F^2; \tag{A43}$$

$$\mathrm{Cv_{27}} = \mathrm{Cv_7}\cdot \mathrm{A_{u1}}/F^2; \tag{A44}$$

Finally, the complex form of wave speed of a perturbation can be reduced to:

$$\frac{C}{U_o} = \frac{\begin{pmatrix} (Cv_{20}\cdot k^4h^4 - Cv_{23}\cdot k^2h^2)\cdot(Cv_{12}\cdot k^4h^4 - Cv_{14}\cdot k^2h^2) \\ -(Cv_{10}\cdot k^4h^4 - Cv_{13}\cdot k^2h^2)\cdot(Cv_{22}\cdot k^4h^4 - Cv_{25}\cdot k^2h^2) \end{pmatrix} + \begin{pmatrix} Cv_{26}\cdot kh\cdot(Cv_{12}\cdot k^4h^4 - Cv_{14}\cdot k^2h^2) \\ -Cv_{15}\cdot kh\cdot(Cv_{22}\cdot k^4h^4 - Cv_{25}\cdot k^2h^2) \end{pmatrix}\cdot i}{\begin{pmatrix} (Cv_{24}\cdot k^2h^2 - Cv_{21}\cdot k^4h^4)\cdot(Cv_{10}\cdot k^4h^4 - Cv_{13}\cdot k^2h^2) \\ +Cv_{11}\cdot k^4h^4\cdot(Cv_{20}\cdot k^4h^4 - Cv_{23}\cdot k^2h^2) \\ +Cv_{15}\cdot Cv_{27}\cdot k^2h^2 + Cv_{16}\cdot Cv_{26}\cdot k^2h^2 \end{pmatrix} + \begin{pmatrix} -Cv_{27}\cdot kh\cdot(Cv_{10}\cdot k^4h^4 - Cv_{13}\cdot k^2h^2) \\ +Cv_{15}\cdot kh\cdot(Cv_{24}\cdot k^2h^2 - Cv_{21}\cdot k^4h^4) \\ -Cv_{16}\cdot kh\cdot(Cv_{20}\cdot k^4h^4 - Cv_{23}\cdot k^2h^2) \\ +Cv_{11}\cdot Cv_{26}\cdot k^5h^5 \end{pmatrix}\cdot i} \tag{A45}$$

where I = $\sqrt{-1}$.

Appendix A.3. Coefficients of Velocity Profiles Approximations

$$q^{*} = 1/(C^{*} \cdot F_{vt}) \tag{A46}$$

$$a_1 = 0.0000998549 * q^{*2}; \tag{A47}$$

$$a_2 = (0.00354033 - 0.00019971 * K_r * q^{*}) * q^{*} \tag{A48}$$

$$a_3 = 0.457516 - 0.00354033 * K_r * q^{*} + 0.0000998549 * (K_r * q^{*})^2 \tag{A49}$$

$$b_1 = -0.114379 + 0.00258715 * K_r * q^{*} - 0.0000408497 * (K_r * q^{*})^2 \tag{A50}$$

$$b_2 = (-0.00258715 + 0.0000816995 * K_r * q^{*}) * q^{*} \tag{A51}$$

$$b_3 = -0.0000408497 * q^{*2} \tag{A52}$$

$$e_1 = 1 - 0.055555 * q^{*} \tag{A53}$$

$$e_2 = -1.16667 + 0.055555 * K_r * q^{*} \tag{A54}$$

$$f_1 = 1 - 1.9841142 * q^{*}/1000.0 \tag{A55}$$

$$f_2 = 10/21 + 1.9841142 * K_r * q^{*}/1000.0 \tag{A56}$$

$$\overline{u'^2} = a_1\cdot U_o^2 + a_2\cdot U_o\cdot u_1 + a_3\cdot u_1^2; \tag{A57}$$

$$\overline{z'u'^2} = h\cdot\left(b_1\cdot u_1^2 + b_2\cdot U_o\cdot u_1 + b_3\cdot U_0^2\right); \tag{A58}$$

$$W_b = (e_1\cdot U_o + e_2\cdot u_1)\cdot\frac{\partial z_b}{\partial x}; \tag{A59}$$

$$W_h = (f_1\cdot U_o + f_2\cdot u_1)\cdot\left(\frac{\partial z_b}{\partial x} + \frac{\partial h}{\partial x}\right); \tag{A60}$$

Appendix B. Derivation of Creal and Cim for VAM-Hydrostatic Model

The following basic equations are included in the model:

(a) The first order continuity equation reads:

$$\frac{\partial h^{*(1)}}{\partial x^{*}} + \frac{\partial U_o^{*(1)}}{\partial x^{*}} = 0 \tag{A61}$$

(b) The moment-based Chezy formula for bed shear stress reads:

$$u_*^2 = \frac{U_o}{C_2^2}(U_o - K_r u_1) \tag{A62}$$

(c) Considering (A62), the first-order x-momentum equation reads:

$$\left(F^2-1\right)\frac{\partial U_o^{*(1)}}{\partial x^*}+\frac{\partial z_b^*}{\partial x^*}+\left(S_o+\frac{2F^2}{C_2^2}\right)U_o^{*(1)}-K_r\alpha\frac{F^2}{C_2^2}\left(U_o^{*(1)}+u_1^{*(1)}\right)=0 \quad \text{(A63)}$$

(d) The first-order x-moment of momentum equation reads:

$$\frac{\partial u_1^{*(1)}}{\partial x^*}+\frac{\partial U_o^{*(1)}}{\partial x^*}+3\left(\frac{K_r}{C_2^2}+\frac{4F_e}{C_*}\right)u_1^{*(1)}-\left(\frac{6}{\alpha C_2^2}-3\left(\frac{K_r}{C_2^2}+\frac{4F_e}{C_*}\right)\right)U_o^{*(1)}=0 \quad \text{(A64)}$$

(e) The bed load sediment flux formula reads:

$$q_s\approx\frac{k_t}{\gamma_s}U_o(\tau_b)\approx\frac{\rho k_t}{\gamma_s}U_o\frac{U_o}{C_2^2}(U_o-K_r u_1) \quad \text{(A65)}$$

(f) Exner sediment mass balance formula reads:

$$\frac{\partial z_b}{\partial t}=-\frac{1}{1-n}\frac{\partial q_s}{\partial x} \quad \text{(A66)}$$

Differentiating (A65) w.r.t. x and substituting back in (A66) and consider the first-order values and neglect higher orders to get:

$$\frac{\partial z_b^*}{\partial t^*}=-\tilde{B}\frac{\tilde{A}}{C_2^2}F^2\cdot\frac{\partial U_o^{*(1)}}{\partial x^*}+\frac{\alpha\cdot K_r\tilde{A}}{3C_2^2}F^2\cdot\frac{\partial u_1^{*(1)}}{\partial x^*},\ \tilde{B}=\left(1-2\cdot\alpha\cdot\frac{K_r}{3}\right) \quad \text{(A67)}$$

Equation (A67) can be rearranged to get $\frac{\partial u_1^{*(1)}}{\partial x^*}$ term as a function of z_b^* and $U_o^{*(1)}$ as follows:

$$\frac{\partial u_1^{*(1)}}{\partial x^*}=\frac{A_{u1}}{F^2}\frac{\partial z_b^*}{\partial t^*}+B_{u1}\cdot\frac{\partial U_o^{*(1)}}{\partial x^*} \quad \text{(A68)}$$

Substitute (A68) in (A64) to get:

$$\frac{A_{u1}}{F^2}\frac{\partial z_b^*}{\partial t^*}+(1+B_{u1})\cdot\frac{\partial U_o^{*(1)}}{\partial x^*}-\left[\left(\frac{6}{\alpha C_2^2}-3\left(\frac{K_r}{C_2^2}+\frac{4F_e}{C_*}\right)\right)U_o^{*(1)}\right]+3\left(\frac{K_r}{C_2^2}+\frac{4F_e}{C_*}\right)u_1^{*(1)}=0 \quad \text{(A69)}$$

Differentiate (A69) w.r.t. x* then substitute (A68) in the resulting equation to get:

$$Cd_1\frac{\partial^2 U_o^{*(1)}}{\partial x^{*2}}+\frac{Cd_2}{F^2}\frac{\partial^2 z_b^*}{\partial x^*\partial t^*}+Cd_3\frac{\partial U_o^{*(1)}}{\partial x^*}+\frac{Cd_4}{F^2}\frac{\partial z_b^*}{\partial t^*}=0 \quad \text{(A70)}$$

Differentiate (A63) wrt x* then substitute (A68) in the resulting equation to get:

$$\left(1-\frac{1}{F^2}\right)\frac{\partial^2 U_o^{*(1)}}{\partial x^{*2}}+\frac{1}{F^2}\frac{\partial^2 z_b^*}{\partial x^{*2}}+Cd_5\frac{\partial U_o^{*(1)}}{\partial x^*}-\frac{Cd_6}{F^2}\frac{\partial z_b^*}{\partial t^*}=0 \quad \text{(A71)}$$

Equations (A70) and (A71) are two equations in two unknowns.

Consider a wave-like perturbations as follows:

$$z_b^*=\langle z_b\rangle\cdot exp[ikh(x^*-\frac{C}{U_o}\cdot t^*)] \quad \text{(A72)}$$

$$U_o^{*(1)}=\left\langle U_o^{*(1)}\right\rangle\cdot exp[ikh(x^*-\frac{C}{U_o}\cdot t^*)] \quad \text{(A73)}$$

For simplicity in the derivation, we define the complex exponential function as:

$$\text{cef} = exp[ikh(x^* - \frac{C}{U_o} \cdot t^*)]$$

With this definition, Equations (A72) and (A73) can be rewritten in abbreviated form as:

$$z_b^* = \langle z_b \rangle \cdot cef \tag{A74}$$

$$U_o^{*(1)} = \left\langle U_o^{*(1)} \right\rangle \cdot cef \tag{A75}$$

Based on (A74) and (A75), the following relations could be derived:

$$\frac{\partial z_b^*}{\partial t^*} = -\langle z_b \rangle \cdot \frac{C}{U_o} \cdot (khi) \cdot cef \tag{A76}$$

$$\frac{\partial z_b^*}{\partial x^*} = \langle z_b \rangle \cdot (khi) \cdot cef \tag{A77}$$

$$\frac{\partial^2 z_b^*}{\partial x^* \partial t^*} = \langle z_b \rangle \cdot \frac{C}{U_o} \cdot \left(k^2 h^2\right) \cdot cef \tag{A78}$$

$$\frac{\partial^2 z_b^*}{\partial x^{*2}} = -\langle z_b \rangle \cdot \left(k^2 h^2\right) \cdot cef \tag{A79}$$

$$\frac{\partial U_o^{*(1)}}{\partial x^*} = \left\langle U_o^{*(1)} \right\rangle \cdot (khi) \cdot cef \tag{A80}$$

$$\frac{\partial^2 U_o^{*(1)}}{\partial x^{*2}} = -\left\langle U_o^{*(1)} \right\rangle \cdot \left(k^2 h^2\right) \cdot cef \tag{A81}$$

Substitute (A72)–(A81) into (A70) and get:

$$\left(-Cd_1 k^2 h^2 + Cd_3 kh \cdot i\right) \left\langle U_o^{*(1)} \right\rangle + \left(\frac{Cd_2}{F^2} k^2 h^2 - \frac{Cd_4}{F^2} kh \cdot i\right) \frac{C}{U_o} \cdot \langle z_b \rangle = 0 \tag{A82}$$

Substitute (A72)–(A81) into (A71) and get:

$$\left(-\left(1 - \frac{1}{F^2}\right) k^2 h^2 + Cd_5 kh \cdot i\right) \left\langle U_o^{*(1)} \right\rangle - \left(\frac{k^2 h^2}{F^2} - \frac{Cd_6}{F^2} kh \cdot i\right) \frac{C}{U_o} \cdot \langle z_b \rangle = 0 \tag{A83}$$

Equations (A82) and (A83) can be expressed as a homogeneous linear system and reformulated in the standard matrix form as follows:

$$[A]\{amp\} = \{0\} \tag{A84}$$

where [A] represents the (2 × 2) coefficient matrix and {amp} is the vector of the perturbation amplitude. In the VAM-hydrostatic model, the system is reduced to:

$$\begin{bmatrix} \left(-Cd_1 k^2 h^2 + Cd_3 kh \cdot i\right) & \left(\frac{Cd_2}{F^2} k^2 h^2 - \frac{Cd_4}{F^2} kh \cdot i\right) \frac{C}{U_o} \\ \left(-\left(1 - \frac{1}{F^2}\right) k^2 h^2 + Cd_5 kh \cdot i\right) & -\left(\frac{k^2 h^2}{F^2} - \frac{Cd_6}{F^2} kh \cdot i\right) \frac{C}{U_o} \end{bmatrix} \begin{pmatrix} \left\langle U_o^{*(1)} \right\rangle \\ \langle z_b \rangle \end{pmatrix} = \begin{pmatrix} 0 \\ 0 \end{pmatrix} \tag{A85}$$

To obtain a non-trivial solution and avoid trivial values for the perturbation amplitudes, $\left\langle U_o^{*(1)} \right\rangle$ and $\langle z_b \rangle$, the determinant of the coefficient matrix must be set to zero, implying that:

$$\begin{vmatrix} \left(-Cd_1 k^2 h^2 + Cd_3 kh \cdot i\right) & \left(\frac{Cd_2}{F^2} k^2 h^2 - \frac{Cd_4}{F^2} kh \cdot i\right) \frac{C}{U_o} \\ \left(-\left(1 - \frac{1}{F^2}\right) k^2 h^2 + Cd_5 kh \cdot i\right) & -\left(\frac{k^2 h^2}{F^2} - \frac{Cd_6}{F^2} kh \cdot i\right) \frac{C}{U_o} \end{vmatrix} = 0 \tag{A86}$$

Decompose the bed wave speed into imaginary and real parts:

$$\frac{C}{U_o} = \frac{C_{real}}{U_o} + \frac{C_{im}}{U_o} \cdot i \tag{A87}$$

Substitute (A87) into (A86) to get the normalized real and imaginary parts of the bed wave perturbation as:

$$\frac{C_{real}}{U_o} = \frac{Cd_1 k^2 h^2 (Cd_8 - Cd_{11} k^2 h^2) - Cd_3 k^2 h^2 (Cd_7 + Cd_{10})}{(Cd_{11} k^2 h^2 - Cd_8)^2 + (Cd_7 + Cd_{10})^2 k^2 h^2} \tag{A88}$$

$$\frac{C_{im}}{U_o} = \frac{Cd_3 kh (Cd_{11} k^2 h^2 - Cd_8) - Cd_1 k^3 h^3 (Cd_7 + Cd_{10})}{(Cd_{11} k^2 h^2 - Cd_8)^2 + (Cd_7 + Cd_{10})^2 k^2 h^2} \tag{A89}$$

Equations (A88) and (A89) are identical to the equations previously presented in the main text as Equations (17) and (18).

References

1. Dey, S.; Mahato, R.K.; Ali, S.Z. Linear and Weakly Nonlinear Instabilities of Sand Waves Caused by a Turbulent Flow. *J. Hydraul. Eng.* **2024**, *150*, 04024005. [CrossRef]
2. Dey, S.; Ali, S.Z. Fluvial instabilities. *Phys. Fluids* **2020**, *32*, 061301. [CrossRef]
3. Julien, P.Y.; Klaassen, G.J. Sand-Dune Geometry of Large Rivers during Floods. *J. Hydraul. Eng.* **1995**, *121*, 657–663. [CrossRef]
4. Bradley, R.W.; Venditti, J.G. Reevaluating dune scaling relations. *Earth-Sci. Rev.* **2017**, *165*, 356–376. [CrossRef]
5. Schippa, L.; Cilli, S.; Ciavola, P.; Billi, P. Dune contribution to flow resistance in alluvial rivers. *Water* **2019**, *11*, 2094. [CrossRef]
6. Lefebvre, A.; Herrling, G.; Becker, M.; Zorndt, A.; Krämer, K.; Winter, C. Morphology of estuarine bedforms, Weser Estuary, Germany. *Earth Surf. Process Landf.* **2022**, *47*, 242–256. [CrossRef]
7. Karim, F. Bed-Form Geometry in Sand-Bed Flows. *J. Hydraul. Eng.* **1999**, *125*, 1253–1261. [CrossRef]
8. Richards, K.J. The formation of ripples and dunes on an erodible bed. *J. Fluid. Mech.* **1980**, *99*, 597–618. [CrossRef]
9. Kennedy, J.F. The mechanics of dunes and antidunes in erodible-bed channels. *J. Fluid. Mech.* **1963**, *16*, 521–544. [CrossRef]
10. Reynolds, A.J. Waves on the erodible bed of an open channel. *J. Fluid. Mech.* **1965**, *22*, 113–133. [CrossRef]
11. Hayashi, T. Formation of Dunes and Antidunes in Open Channels. *J. Hydraul. Div.* **1970**, *96*, 357–366. [CrossRef]
12. Hayashi, T. Erratum for 'Formation of Dunes and Antidunes in Open Channels'. *J. Hydraul. Div.* **1971**, *97*, 1135–1136. [CrossRef]
13. Chien, N.; Wan, Z. *Mechanics of Sediment Transport*; American Society of Civil Engineers: Reston, VA, USA, 1999.
14. Di Cristo, C.; Iervolino, M.; Vacca, A. Linear stability analysis of a 1-D model with dynamical description of bed-load transport. *J. Hydraul. Res.* **2006**, *44*, 480–487. [CrossRef]
15. Fourrière, A.; Claudin, P.; Andreotti, B. Bedforms in a Turbulent Stream. Part 2: Formation of Ripples by Primary Linear Instability and of Dunes by Non-Linear Pattern Coarsening. *arXiv* **2008**, arXiv:0805.3417.
16. Bradley, R.W.; Venditti, J.G. Mechanisms of Dune Growth and Decay in Rivers. *Geophys. Res. Lett.* **2021**, *48*, e2021GL094572. [CrossRef]
17. Coleman, S.E.; Fenton, J.D. Potential-flow instability theory and alluvial stream bed forms. *J. Fluid. Mech.* **2000**, *418*, 101–117. [CrossRef]
18. Engelund, F. Instability of erodible beds. *J. Fluid. Mech.* **1970**, *42*, 225–244. [CrossRef]
19. Fredsøe, J. On the development of dunes in erodible channels. *J. Fluid. Mech.* **1974**, *64*, 1–16. [CrossRef]
20. Colombini, M. Revisiting the linear theory of sand dune formation. *J. Fluid. Mech.* **2004**, *502*, 1–16. [CrossRef]
21. Sumer, B.M.; Bakioglu, M. On the formation of ripples on an erodible bed. *J. Fluid. Mech.* **1984**, *144*, 177–190. [CrossRef]
22. McLean, S. The stability of ripples and dunes. *Earth Sci. Rev.* **1990**, *29*, 131–144. [CrossRef]
23. Ali, S.Z.; Dey, S. Linear stability of dunes and antidunes. *Phys. Fluids* **2021**, *33*, 094109. [CrossRef]
24. Ohata, K.; Naruse, H.; Izumi, N. Linear-stability analysis of plane beds under flows with suspended loads. *Earth Surf. Dyn.* **2023**, *11*, 961–977. [CrossRef]
25. Gradowczyk, M.H. Wave propagation and boundary instability in erodible-bed channels. *J. Fluid. Mech.* **1968**, *33*, 93–112. [CrossRef]
26. Cui, Y.; Parker, G. Linear analysis of coupled equations for sediment transport. In Proceedings of the Congress of the International Association of Hydraulic Research, IAHR, San Francisco, CA, USA, 10–15 August 1997.

27. Elgamal, M.; Steffler, P. Stability Analysis of Dunes Using 1-D Depth Averaged...—Google Scholar. 2nd IAHR Symposium on Rivers, Coastal and Estuarine Morpho-Dynamics. Available online: https://scholar.google.com/scholar?hl=en&as_sdt=0,5&q=Stability+Analysis+of+Dunes+Using+1-D+Depth+Averaged+Flow+Models&btnG= (accessed on 27 April 2025).
28. Bose, S.K.; Dey, S. Reynolds averaged theory of turbulent shear flows over undulating beds and formation of sand waves. *Phys. Rev. E Stat. Nonlin Soft Matter Phys.* **2009**, *80*, 036304. [CrossRef]
29. Bose, S.K.; Dey, S. Instability Theory of Sand Ripples Formed by Turbulent Shear Flows. *J. Hydraul. Eng.* **2012**, *138*, 752–756. [CrossRef]
30. Yu, Q. Numerical Modeling of Fluvial Urban Floods: Implications for Flood Mitigation Strategies. Doctoral Dissertation, Université d'Ottawa | University of Ottawa, Ottawa, ON, Canada, 2025. Available online: https://ruor.uottawa.ca/items/4de5a89d-470b-484e-b400-e9d4b0c75f2b (accessed on 27 April 2025).
31. Koyuncu, B.; Akerkouch, L.; Le, T. On the depth-averaged models of ice-covered flows. *Environ. Fluid. Mech.* **2024**, *24*, 1263–1289. [CrossRef]
32. Steffler, P.M.; Yee-Chung, J. Depth averaged and moment equations for moderately shallow free surface flow. *J. Hydraul. Res.* **1993**, *31*, 5–17. [CrossRef]
33. Elgamal, M. A moment-based chezy formula for bed shear stress in varied flow. *Water* **2021**, *13*, 1254. [CrossRef]
34. Ghamry, H.K.; Steffler, P.M. Two dimensional vertically averaged and moment equations for rapidly varied flows. *J. Hydraul. Res.* **2002**, *40*, 579–587. [CrossRef]
35. Steldermann, I.; Torrilhon, M.; Kowalski, J. Shallow Moments to Capture Vertical Structure in Open Curved Shallow Flow. *J. Comput. Theor. Transp.* **2023**, *52*, 475–505. [CrossRef]
36. Ghamry, H.K.; Steffler, P.M.; Asce, A.M. Effect of Applying Different Distribution Shapes for Velocities and Pressure on Simulation of Curved Open Channels. *J. Hydraul. Eng.* **2002**, *128*, 969–982. [CrossRef]
37. Albers, C.; Steffler, P. Estimating Transverse Mixing in Open Channels due to Secondary Current-Induced Shear Dispersion. *J. Hydraul. Eng.* **2007**, *133*, 186–196. [CrossRef]
38. Elgamal, M. A Moment-Based Depth-Averaged K-ε Model for Predicting the True Turbulence Intensity over Bedforms. *Water* **2022**, *14*, 2196. [CrossRef]
39. Elgamal, M. Mapping Mean Velocity Field over Bed Forms Using Simplified Empirical-Moment Concept Approach. *Water* **2023**, *15*, 3351. [CrossRef]
40. Yang, C.T. *Sediment Transport: Theory and Practice*; McGraw-Hill: New York, NY, USA, 1996.
41. Sanders, S.; Jafarinik, S.; Hernandez Moreira, R.; Johnson, R.; Balkus, A.; Ahmadpoor, M.; Fryson, B.; McQueen, B.; Fedele, J.; Viparelli, E. Influence of Sand Supply and Grain Size on Equilibrium Upper Regime Bedforms. *J. Geophys. Res. Earth Surf.* **2023**, *128*, e2022JF006820. [CrossRef]
42. Guy, H.P.; Simons, D.B.; Richardson, E.V. *Summary of Alluvial Channel Data from Flume Experiments, 1956–1961*; Google Books; US Government Printing Office: Washington, DC, USA, 1966; Available online: https://books.google.com.eg/books?hl=en&lr=&id=3swyVPwkYFAC&oi=fnd&pg=PR1&dq=Summary+of+Alluvial+Channel+Data+From+Flume+Experiments&ots=N1c03CCA2Q&sig=43kU9nA6YFHKAw95b9yBD2Gg3jg&redir_esc=y#v=onepage&q=Summary%20of%20Alluvial%20Channel%20Data%20From%20Flume%20Experiments&f=false (accessed on 6 June 2025).
43. Coleman, S.E.; Melville, B.W. Initiation of Bed Forms on a Flat Sand Bed. *J. Hydraul. Eng.* **1996**, *122*, 301–310. [CrossRef]
44. Coleman, S.E.; Eling, B. Sand wavelets in laminar open-channel flows. *J. Hydraul. Res.* **2000**, *38*, 331–338. [CrossRef]
45. Yalin, M.S. *River Mechanics*; Elsevier: Amsterdam, The Netherlands, 2015.
46. Davies, T.R. *Summary of Experimental Data for Flume Tests over Fine Sand*; Rep. CE/3/71; Dept. of Civil Engineering, Univ. of Southampton: Southampton, UK, 1971.
47. Baas, J.H. A flume study on the development and equilibrium morphology of current ripples in very fine sand. *Sedimentology* **1994**, *41*, 185–209. [CrossRef]
48. Zhang, X.-D.; Tang, L.-M.; Xu, T.-Y. Experimental study of flow intensity influence on 2-D sand ripple geometry characteristics. *Water Sci. Eng.* **2009**, *2*, 52–59. [CrossRef]
49. Leclair, S.F. Preservation of cross-strata due to the migration of subaqueous dunes: An experimental investigation. *Sedimentology* **2002**, *49*, 1157–1180. [CrossRef]
50. Blom, A.; Ribberink, J.S.; De Vriend, H.J. Vertical sorting in bed forms: Flume experiments with a natural and a trimodal sediment mixture. *Water Resour. Res.* **2003**, *39*, 1–13. [CrossRef]
51. Coleman, S.E.; Zhang, M.H.; Clunie, T.M. Sediment-Wave Development in Subcritical Water Flow. *J. Hydraul. Eng.* **2005**, *131*, 106–111. [CrossRef]
52. Wren, D.G.; Kuhnle, R.A.; Wilson, C.G. Measurements of the relationship between turbulence and sediment in suspension over mobile sand dunes in a laboratory flume. *J. Geophys. Res. Earth Surf.* **2007**, *112*. [CrossRef]
53. Kuhnle, R.A.; Wren, D.G. Size of suspended sediment over dunes. *J. Geophys. Res. Earth Surf.* **2009**, *114*. [CrossRef]

54. Tuijnder, A. Sand in Short Supply: Modelling of Bedforms, Roughness and Sediment Tansport in Rivers Under Supply-Limited Conditions. Ph.D. Thesis, University of Twente, Enschede, The Netherlands, 2010. [CrossRef]
55. Guala, M.; Singh, A.; Badheartbull, N.; Foufoula-Georgiou, E. Spectral description of migrating bed forms and sediment transport. *J. Geophys. Res. Earth Surf.* **2014**, *119*, 123–137. [CrossRef]
56. Venditti, J.G.; Lin, C.Y.M.; Kazemi, M. Variability in bedform morphology and kinematics with transport stage. *Sedimentology* **2016**, *63*, 1017–1040. [CrossRef]
57. Vah, M.; Jarno, A.; Marin, F.; Le Bot, S. Experimental Study on Sediment Supply-Limited Bedforms in a Coastal Context. In *Estuaries and Coastal Zones in Times of Global Change: Proceedings of ICEC-2018*; Springer: Singapore, 2020; pp. 647–664. [CrossRef]
58. Geng, M.; Song, H.; Liu, S.; Zhang, Y.; Meng, L.; Yang, B.; Wang, L.; Gu, Y.; Rong, J.; Zhang, B. Characteristics and migration of subaqueous sand dunes influenced by internal solitary waves in the Dongsha Region, Northern South China Sea. *Geomorphology* **2024**, *461*, 109325. [CrossRef]
59. Van Mierlo, M.C.L.M.; De Ruiter, J.C.C. *Turbulence Measurements Above Artificial Dunes*; Deltares (WL): Delft, The Netherlands, 1988.
60. Englund, F.; Fredsoe, J. Sediment ripples and dunes. *Annu. Rev. Fluid. Mech.* **1982**, *14*, 13–37. [CrossRef]

mathematics

MDPI

Article

Numerical Comparisons of Heuristic Stress Topology Optimization Methods

Yongfeng Zheng, Jiale Qiu and Zhipeng Chen *

School of Mechanical and Electric Engineering, Guangzhou University, Guangzhou 510006, China; hnzyf08@gzhu.edu.cn (Y.Z.); 2112407086@e.gzhu.edu.cn (J.Q.)
* Correspondence: chenzhipeng@gzhu.edu.cn

Abstract

Mitigating excessive stress, a primary cause of structural failure, deformation, and premature fatigue, is critical in engineering design. Evolutionary (BESO) and proportional topology optimization (PTO) are standard heuristic approaches, yet their relative computational efficiency and accuracy for stress problems are not well understood. Addressing this gap, this paper conducts the first comprehensive comparisons of BESO and PTO for the stress minimization problem, also investigating the impact of the p-norm. Optimization results reveal PTO's significant advantage in computational speed. BESO sometimes produces designs with lower maximum stresses, though with higher structural compliance.

Keywords: heuristic algorithm; stress minimization; calculational efficiency; evolutionary optimization

MSC: 68U07

1. Introduction

Excessive stress will lead to early fracture, deformation, and fatigue damage, reducing the service life and security of the machinery. The traditional stiffness design is usually unable to meet the structural strength requirements, because there are significant differences between strength design and stiffness design [1]. Stress optimization is a complex research topic due to its computational singularity. Furthermore, how to improve the computational efficiency and accuracy of stress optimization methods is a difficult and important research topic [2,3].

The topology optimization technique possesses the characteristics of high design efficiency and large design freedom and is widely used in the conceptual design stage of engineering structures [4–6]. Some scholars have carried out relevant studies on stress-related topological optimization [7–10]. Duysinx and Bendsøe [8] first considered the continuum topology optimization under segmented stress constraints. The micro-continuous structure was proposed to interpolate the stiffness and allowable stress, and it was combined with the relaxation method to solve the singular phenomenon. Cheng and Guo [7] put forward an ε-relaxation method to eliminate the singular phenomenon. Le et al. [11] used density filters to control micro-structural size and used the density-based method with penalization to drive stress elements to generate 0–1 solutions. Allaire and Jouve [12] adopted the integration of global stress as the level set objective function. Van Miegroet and Duysinx [13] combined the extended finite element and level set methods to study the shape optimization problem, aiming to minimize the maximum stress. Xia et al. [14]

https://doi.org/10.3390/math13152353

first applied the bi-directional evolutionary structural optimization (BESO) method to stress optimization, which has some advantages. For example, optimization results usually possess clear boundaries, fundamentally avoiding the singular phenomena, which is attributed to the solid-void nature of BESO. Yaping Lai et al. [15] utilized BESO and multi-material BESO methods to propose a novel and unique pedestrian bridge design by applying topology optimization algorithms in the conceptual design and detailed structural design of bridges. In the work of Hélio Luiz Simonetti et al. [16], a qualitative comparison of the BESO and Smooth ESO (SESO) methods was conducted, revealing that both methods can effectively generate optimal topologies for three-dimensional structural systems when considering the effects of minimizing flexibility and structural self-weight. Biyikli and To [17] proposed a simple and efficient proportional topology optimization (PTO) method, which eliminates some numerical difficulties that emerged from analytical derivations and sensitivity calculations.

As classical heuristic algorithms, both the BESO and PTO methods have the merits of conceptual simplicity and calculational efficiency. However, their optimization efficiency and accuracy in the commonly concerned stress problem have always been a hot topic for many researchers. This paper first and in detail compares the optimization efficiency and accuracy of heuristic methods in stress optimization, through 3D bridge examples. Moreover, the influence of p-norm on the stress designs is also examined. This study is committed to providing good advice for designers to obtain more stable and reliable engineering structures.

2. Optimization Formulation and Sensitivity Analysis

The mathematical formulation to minimize the structural global stress, when subjected to material usage, is described as follows:

$$\begin{cases} \text{Minimize}: & \sigma_p \text{ in BESO}, \sigma_{vM} \text{ in PTO} \\ \text{Subject to}: & \mathbf{KU} = \mathbf{F} \\ & V_1(x) = \sum_{i=1}^{num} x_i v_i \leq V_{\text{req}} \\ & V_2(x) = \sum_{i=1}^{num} \rho_i v_i \leq V_{\text{req}} \\ & x_i = 0 \; or \; 1, i = 1, 2, \ldots, num, \text{in BESO} \\ & 0 \leq \rho_{min} \leq \rho_i \leq 1, i = 1, 2, \ldots, num, \text{in PTO} \end{cases} \tag{1}$$

where σ_p and σ_{vM} are the p-norm stress in BESO, and the von Mises stress in PTO. **K**, **U**, and **F** are the stiffness matrix, displacement, and external force imposed on the structure, respectively. V_1(x) is the material volume constraint in the BESO method, and V_2(x) is the material volume constraint in the PTO method during the optimization. x_i is the design variable in BESO, v_i is the elemental volume, V_{req} is the required material usage, and num is the total number of elements. ρ_i is the density variable in PTO and ρ_{min} is the minimal density value to prevent the calculational singularity.

Design variables in BESO are binary, while the PTO design variable is continuous. The objective function defined in Equation (1) is to minimize the maximum stress, which is nondifferentiable. Hence, it cannot be directly used with sensitivity methods. Instead, BESO uses the p-norm to measure von Mises stress during the optimization, whereas PTO does not require a sensitivity analysis. Therefore, the parameter p is not needed to evaluate structural stress. The p-norm stress can be calculated as

$$\sigma_p = \left(\sum_{i=1}^{num} \sigma_{vm,i}^p \right)^{\frac{1}{p}} \tag{2}$$

where $\sigma_{vm,i}$ is the von Mises stress of the elemental center, and p is the stress exponent. When p is equal to 1, the averaged stress can be obtained. Furthermore, if the p-value approaches infinity, the stress value can be maximized. In brief, the larger the p-value, the more accurate the calculation of the maximum von Mises stress. However, excessive p will lead to optimization problems, and the optimization program will experience severe oscillations. Hence, the p-value must be appropriately selected to ensure the smooth optimization. At the same time, the maximum von Mises stress can be well approximated. For more information about the selection of p, please check [8]. The von Mises stress is computed as

$$\sigma_{vM} = \left(\boldsymbol{\sigma}^T \mathbf{V} \boldsymbol{\sigma}\right)^{1/2} \tag{3}$$

$\boldsymbol{\sigma}$ signifies the stress in Voigt notation, and $\mathbf{V}$ means the stress coefficient matrix. In the 2D case, the von Mises stress can be calculated as

$$\sigma_{vM} = \sqrt{\sigma_x^2 + \sigma_y^2 - \sigma_x \sigma_y + 3\sigma_{xy}^2} \tag{4}$$

σ_x and σ_y are normal stresses along the horizontal and vertical directions, respectively. σ_{xy} is the coupling stress along two directions.

To approximately obtain 0/1 solutions, the elemental stiffness in PTO can be written as

$$E(\rho) = E_{min} + \rho^p E_0 \tag{5}$$

$E_{\min}$ is a small stiffness value (10^{-3} used in this study) related to void elements, so as to avoid the calculational singularity; E_0 is the solid stiffness matrix. p is the penalty factor, and p = 3 is used in this study.

Both the sensitivity analysis and filtering are needed in BESO. To successfully perform evolutionary optimization, the sensitivity information of the global stress with respect to the design variables needs to be primarily provided. According to the p-norm stress defined in Equation (2), the derivative of σ_p related to the design variable is written as

$$\frac{\partial \sigma_p}{\partial x_j} = \sigma_p^{1-p} \left(\sum_{i=1}^{num} \sigma_{vm,i}^{p-1} \frac{\partial \sigma_{vm,i}}{\partial x_j} \right), j = 1, 2, \ldots, num. \tag{6}$$

According to Equation (3), the derivative of elemental stress related to the stress vector is

$$\frac{\partial \sigma_{vm}}{\partial \boldsymbol{\sigma}} = \frac{1}{2} \left(\boldsymbol{\sigma}^T \mathbf{V} \boldsymbol{\sigma} \right)^{-1/2} 2\boldsymbol{\sigma}^T \mathbf{V} = \sigma_{vm}^{-1} \boldsymbol{\sigma}^T \mathbf{V} \tag{7}$$

so the derivative of the von Mises stress with respect to the design variable can be obtained as

$$\frac{\partial \sigma_{vm,i}}{\partial x_j} = \sigma_{vm,i}^{-1} \boldsymbol{\sigma}_i^T \mathbf{V} \frac{\partial \sigma_i}{\partial x_j} \tag{8}$$

where the effective stress vector can be expressed as $\sigma_i = \mathbf{D}_0 \mathbf{B}_i \boldsymbol{u}_i$, we can find that the stiffness matrix $\mathbf{D}_0$ and elemental strain–displacement matrix $\mathbf{B}$ are independent of design variables. The above derivative can be further written as

$$\frac{\partial \sigma_{vm,i}}{\partial x_j} = \sigma_{vm,i}^{-1} \boldsymbol{\sigma}_i^T \mathbf{V} \mathbf{D}_0 \mathbf{B}_i \mathbf{L}_i \frac{\partial \mathbf{U}}{\partial x_j} \tag{9}$$

where $\mathbf{L}_i$ is the nodal displacements related to the i-th element, which satisfies $\boldsymbol{u}_i = \mathbf{L}_i \mathbf{U}$. Differentiating both sides of the balance equation $\mathbf{KU} = \mathbf{F}$, we can obtain

$$\frac{\partial \mathbf{K}}{\partial x_j} \mathbf{U} + \mathbf{K} \frac{\partial \mathbf{U}}{\partial x_j} = \mathbf{0} \tag{10}$$

Substitute the above formula into Equation (9), and it can be rewritten as

$$\frac{\partial \sigma_{vm,i}}{\partial x_j} = -\sigma_{vm,i}^{-1} \sigma_i^T \boldsymbol{V} \boldsymbol{D}_0 \boldsymbol{B}_i \boldsymbol{L}_i \boldsymbol{K}^{-1} \frac{\partial \boldsymbol{K}}{\partial x_j} \boldsymbol{U} \tag{11}$$

Substitute Equation (11) into Equation (6), the derivative of the p-norm stress with respect to the design variable should be expressed as

$$\frac{\partial \sigma_p}{\partial x_j} = -\sigma_p^{1-p} \left(\sum_{i=1}^{num} \sigma_{vm,i}^{p-2} \boldsymbol{\sigma}_i^T \mathbf{V} \mathbf{D}_0 \mathbf{B}_i \mathbf{L}_i \right) \mathbf{K}^{-1} \frac{\partial \mathbf{K}}{\partial x_j} \mathbf{U} \tag{12}$$

Using the solution of the following adjoint problem:

$$\mathbf{K} \boldsymbol{\lambda} = \sum_{i=1}^{num} \sigma_{vm,i}^{p-2} (\mathbf{D}_0 \mathbf{B}_i \mathbf{L}_i)^T \mathbf{V} \sigma_i \tag{13}$$

The right side of the above formulation is assembled according to body forces, so Equation (12) can be further written as

$$\frac{\partial \sigma_p}{\partial x_j} = -\sigma_p^{1-p} \boldsymbol{\lambda}^T \frac{\partial \mathbf{K}}{\partial x_j} \mathbf{U} \tag{14}$$

the derivative of the stiffness matrix with respect to the design variable should be expressed as

$$\frac{\partial \mathbf{K}}{\partial x_j} = \sum_{i=1}^{num} \mathbf{L}_i^T \frac{\mathbf{k}_j}{\partial x_j} \mathbf{L}_i = \mathbf{L}_j^T \mathbf{k}_j^{(0)} \mathbf{L}_j \tag{15}$$

both $\boldsymbol{k}_j$ and $\boldsymbol{k}_j^{(0)}$ are elemental stiffness matrices, related to element j and the solid element, respectively. They can be respectively written as

$$\mathbf{k}_j = x_j \int \mathbf{B}_j^T \mathbf{D}_0 \mathbf{B}_j d\Omega_j \quad \text{and} \quad \mathbf{k}_j^{(0)} = \int \mathbf{B}_j^T \mathbf{D}_0 \mathbf{B}_j d\Omega_j \tag{16}$$

in which Ω_j is the j-th elemental domain. Substitute Equation (15) into Equation (14), and the sensitivity information of the p-norm stress with respect to the design variable should be finally expressed as

$$\frac{\partial \sigma_p}{\partial x_j} = -\sigma_p^{1-p} \boldsymbol{\lambda}_j^T \mathbf{k}_j^{(0)} \mathbf{u}_j \tag{17}$$

λ_j is the adjoint nodal vector with respect to element j.

3. Numerical Example

In this section, the computational accuracy and efficiency of PTO and BESO methods are compared through a 3D bridge structure, which is shown in Figure 1. The sizes of the design domain and non-designable domain are 160 × 10 × 37 and 160 × 10 × 3 elements, respectively. The non-designable domain refers to the side pavement. The four vertices at the bottom of the structure are fixed. According to European standards, the load for a pedestrian bridge is 5 kN/m^2. Since this design simplifies the model and employs a dimensionless design, a uniform force F = 0.01 N is applied to each unit on the bridge deck. The material used for optimization is an isotropic material. The material usage is taken as 0.3, and the filter radii are set to 2. To discuss the influence of p-norm on the 3D structural design, p takes three cases, such as 2, 3, and 4, in the BESO method. Figure 2 depicts the evolutionary topologies under four cases. Table 1 lists all the numerical results, and Figure 3 depicts the iteration curves under the PTO and BESO methods.

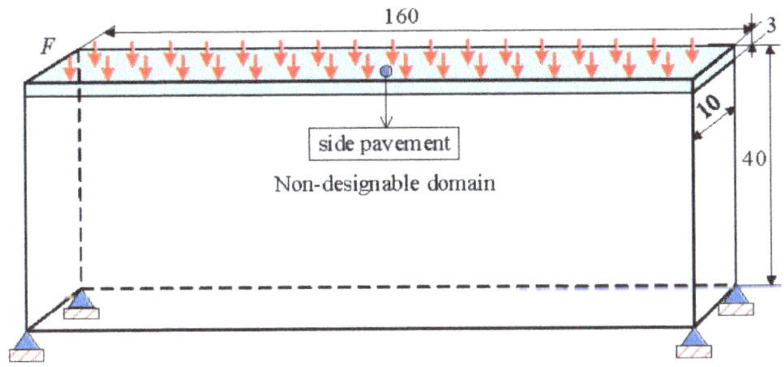

Figure 1. Load and boundary conditions for the 3D bridge structure.

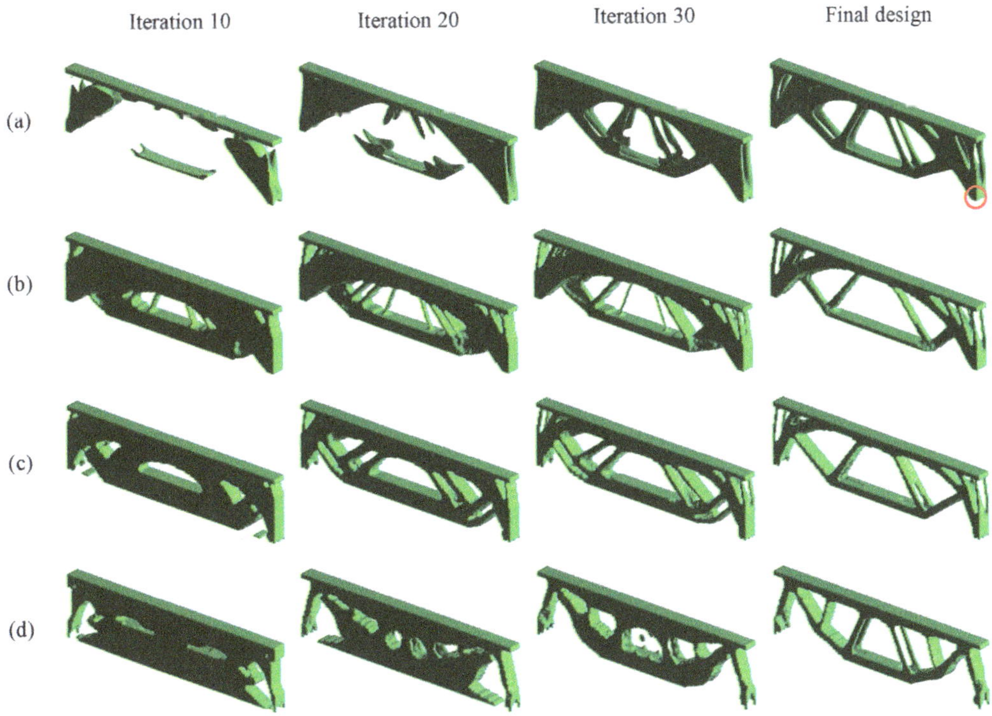

Figure 2. Topological results under PTO and BESO methods. (**a**) PTO method; (**b**) $p = 2$ in BESO; (**c**) $p = 3$ in BESO; and (**d**) $p = 4$ in BESO.

Table 1. Numerical results under the PTO and BESO methods.

Case	Method	The Maximum Stress (MPa)	Iteration Number	Total Optimization Time (s)	Compliance Values (N·mm)
Case 1	PTO	6.763	100	2975.5793	817.7253
Case 2	BESO_$p = 2$	6.792	100	5845.4522	797.5808
Case 3	BESO_$p = 3$	6.399	100	5538.1949	853.4656
Case 4	BESO_$p = 4$	6.336	100	5309.2488	1003.5918

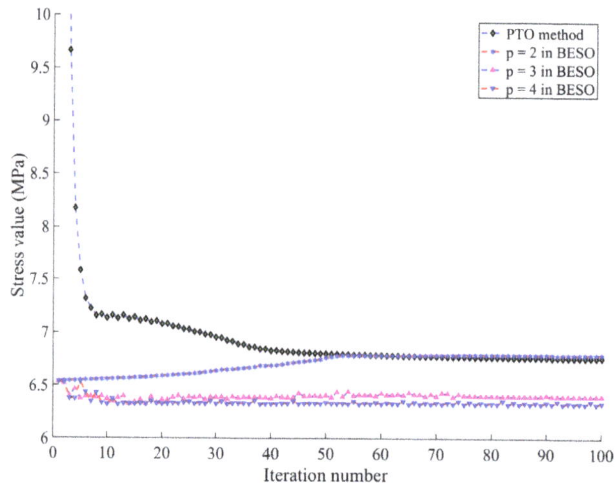

Figure 3. Iteration curves under the PTO and BESO methods.

As depicted in Figure 2, in all cases, the bridge structure converges to a clear and reasonable topological result. In Case 1, both the lateral supports and the longitudinal supports branch into four rods. In Case 2, neither the lateral supports nor the longitudinal supports branch; both are solid, continuous structures. In Case 3, the left and right supports are solid continuous structures, while the upper part of the longitudinal support is a continuous structure, and the lower part branches into four members. In Case 4, the left and right supports are solid continuous structures, while the longitudinal support branches into four members and is locally reinforced on both sides. Intuitively speaking, the final topology obtained by the PTO method is smoother than that obtained by the BESO method. Under four operating conditions, the maximum stress in the structure occurs at the same location, namely the fixed corner, indicated by the red circle. This also demonstrates the accuracy and effectiveness of the two heuristic algorithms in calculating structural stress.

As listed in Table 1, PTO has tremendous advantages over BESO methods in terms of total optimization and each iteration, which illustrates that PTO has obvious merit in terms of calculational efficiency. As the p-norm increases in BESO, the structural stress decreases, but the structural compliance gradually increases. For Case 2 with $p = 2$, the maximum stress in the PTO method is smaller than that in BESO, explaining that the PTO method has advantages in terms of trace amounts in the maximum stress, but the structural compliance in BESO is smaller than that in PTO. For Cases 3 and 4, the maximum stresses in BESO are smaller than those in PTO, but the structural compliances in PTO are smaller than those in BESO. The above analysis indicates that BESO has advantages in the maximum stress calculation, while sacrificing structural compliance.

As depicted in Figure 3, the four cases stably converge with the final designs. PTO optimizes from a uniform density of 0.3, and the stress value first decreases and then stabilizes at a certain value. The BESO method starts with full designs, and the iteration curves are more stable than those in PTO. Case 2 gradually increases to a certain value of 6.792, and Cases 3 and 4 are stable enough during the optimization, due to the increase in p-norm.

4. Conclusions

This paper first investigates the calculational efficiency and accuracy of heuristic algorithms in solving the stress minimization problem. The methods considered are BESO and

PTO methods; both of them are density-based optimization methods. BESO is sensitive, while PTO is insensitive. A numerical example explains that PTO has unparalleled advantages over BESO in calculation efficiency. For a 3D bridge structure with $p = 2$, the final stress values in PTO are smaller than those obtained in BESO. In BESO, the stress value gradually decreases with the increase in p, and the compliance obtained by $p = 3$ and $p = 4$ is greater than that obtained by PTO. This situation explains that the calculational accuracy in stress and compliance calculation is problem-dependent. Hence, if the engineering requirement in calculational accuracy is not high, we can fully use the PTO method to solve the stress-related optimization problem, due to its unparalleled efficiency.

Author Contributions: Conceptualization, Y.Z.; methodology, Y.Z.; writing—original draft preparation, J.Q.; writing—review and editing, Y.Z. and J.Q.; funding acquisition, Y.Z. and Z.C. All authors have read and agreed to the published version of the manuscript.

Funding: This research is funded by the National Natural Science Foundation of China (grant no. 52205265 and 52305458), and the Guangdong Basic and Applied Basic Research Foundation (grant no. 2025A1515011813).

Data Availability Statement: The data are available from the authors upon reasonable request.

Conflicts of Interest: The authors declare that they have no competing financial interests or personal relationships that could have appeared to influence the publication of this study.

References

1. Guo, X.; Zhang, W.S.; Wang, M.Y.; Wei, P. Stress-related topology optimization via level set approach. *Comput. Methods Appl. Mech. Eng.* **2011**, *200*, 3439–3452. [CrossRef]
2. Fan, Z.; Xia, L.; Lai, W.; Xia, Q.; Shi, T. Evolutionary topology optimization of continuum structures with stress constraints. *Struct. Multidiscip. Optim.* **2019**, *59*, 647–658. [CrossRef]
3. Xu, W.; Ning, J.; Lin, Z.; Qi, W.; Liu, H.; Wang, W. Multi-objective topology optimization of two-dimensional multi-phase microstructure phononic crystals. *Mater. Today Commun.* **2020**, *22*, 100801. [CrossRef]
4. Bendsøe, M.P.; Sigmund, O. *Topology Optimization: Theory, Methods, and Applications*; Springer Science & Business Media: New York, NY, USA, 2003.
5. Wang, Y.; Li, X.; Kai, L.; Long, K.; Wei, P. Open-source codes of topology optimization: A summary for beginners to start their research. *Comput. Model Eng. Sci.* **2023**, *137*, 1–34. [CrossRef]
6. Xiang, J.; Zhao, S.; Liu, B.; Zheng, Y.; Huang, J. Topology optimization of multi-material structures subjected to dynamic loads. *Appl. Math. Model.* **2025**, *138*, 115787. [CrossRef]
7. Cheng, G.D.; Guo, X. ε-relaxed approach in structural topology optimization. *Struct. Optim.* **1997**, *13*, 258–266. [CrossRef]
8. Duysinx, P.; Bendsøe, M.P. Topology optimization of continuum structures with local stress constraints. *Int. J. Numer. Methods Eng.* **1998**, *43*, 1453–1478. [CrossRef]
9. Xia, Q.; Shi, T.; Liu, S.; Wang, M.Y. A level set solution to the stress-based structural shape and topology optimization. *Comput. Struct.* **2012**, *90*, 55–64. [CrossRef]
10. Cai, S.; Zhang, W.; Zhu, J.; Gao, T. Stress constrained shape and topology optimization with fixed mesh: A B-spline finite cell method combined with level set function. *Comput. Methods Appl. Mech. Eng.* **2014**, *278*, 361–387. [CrossRef]
11. Le, C.; Norato, J.; Bruns, T.; Ha, C.; Tortorelli, D. Stress-based topology optimization for continua. *Struct. Multidiscip. Optim.* **2010**, *41*, 605–620. [CrossRef]
12. Allaire, G.; Jouve, F. Minimum stress optimal design with the level set method. *Eng. Anal. Bound. Elem.* **2008**, *32*, 909–918. [CrossRef]
13. Van Miegroet, L.; Duysinx, P. Stress concentration minimization of 2D filets using X-FEM and level set description. *Struct. Multidiscip. Optim.* **2007**, *33*, 425–438. [CrossRef]
14. Xia, L.; Zhang, L.; Xia, Q.; Shi, T. Stress-based topology optimization using bi-directional evolutionary structural optimization method. *Comput. Methods Appl. Mech. Eng.* **2018**, *333*, 356–370. [CrossRef]
15. Lai, Y.; Li, Y.; Liu, Y.; Chen, P.; Zhao, L.; Li, J.; Xie, Y.M. Application of bi-directional evolutionary structural optimization to the design of an innovative pedestrian bridge. *AI Civ. Eng.* **2024**, *3*, 9. [CrossRef]

16. Simonetti, H.L.; Almeida, V.S.; Neves, F.D.A.D.; Azar, S.Z.; Silva, M.M.D. BESO and SESO: Comparative Analysis of Spatial Structures Considering Self-Weight and Structural Reliability. *Appl. Sci.* **2024**, *14*, 6465. [CrossRef]
17. Biyikli, E.; To, A.C. Proportional topology optimization: A new non-sensitivity method for solving stress constrained and minimum compliance problems and its implementation in MATLAB. *PLoS ONE* **2015**, *10*, e0145041. [CrossRef] [PubMed]

MDPI AG
Grosspeteranlage 5
4052 Basel
Switzerland
Tel.: +41 61 683 77 34

Mathematics Editorial Office
E-mail: mathematics@mdpi.com
www.mdpi.com/journal/mathematics

www.ingramcontent.com/pod-product-compliance
Lightning Source LLC
Chambersburg PA
CBHW061556210926
51850CB00009B/2118